AP ENGLISH LITERATURE & COMPOSITION

PREMIUM PREP

26th Edition

The Staff of The Princeton Review

PrincetonReview.com

Penguin
Random
House

The Princeton Review
110 East 42nd Street, 7th Floor
New York, NY 10017
princetonreview.com
penguinrandomhouse.com

ISBN: 978-0-593-51845-8
eBook ISBN: 978-0-593-51846-5
ISSN: 2690-5388

The material in this book is up-to-date at the time of publication. However, changes may have been instituted by the testing body in the test after this book was published.

If there are any important late-breaking developments, changes, or corrections to the materials in this book, we will post that information online in the Student Tools. Register your book and check your Student Tools to see whether there are any updates posted there.

Editor: Patricia Murphy
Production Editors: Lyssa Mandel, Chris Stobart
Production Artist: Lisa Barham
Content Developer: Ali Landreau

Manufactured in the United States of America

10 9 8 7 6 5 4 3 2 1

26th Edition

EU Contact:
Penguin Random House Ireland
32 Nassau Street
Dublin D02 YH68
https://eu-contact.penguin.ie

The Princeton Review Publishing Team
Rob Franek, Editor-in-Chief
David Soto, Senior Director, Data Operations
Stephen Koch, Senior Manager, Data Operations
Deborah Weber, Director of Production
Jason Ullmeyer, Production Design Manager
Jennifer Chapman, Senior Production Artist
Selena Coppock, Director of Editorial
Aaron Riccio, Director, Editorial Admissions Content
Orion McBean, Senior Editor
Meave Shelton, Senior Editor
Chris Chimera, Editor
Patricia Murphy, Editor
Laura Rose, Editor
Isabelle Appleton, Editorial Assistant

Penguin Random House Publishing Team
Tom Russell, VP, Publisher
Alison Stoltzfus, Senior Director, Publishing
Emily Hoffman, Managing Editor
Mary Ellen Owens, Assistant Director of Production
Suzanne Lee, Senior Designer
Eugenia Lo, Publishing Assistant

For customer service, please contact **editorialsupport@review.com**, and be sure to include:

- full title of the book

- ISBN

- page number

Acknowledgments

The Princeton Review would like to thank Ali Landreau for her thorough review of this title and useful updates to the 26th Edition. The editor of this edition would like to thank Lisa Barham, Lyssa Mandel, and Chris Stobart for their hard work on this edition as well.

Permissions

Permission has been granted to reprint portions of the following:

–Excerpt(s) from *The Night Circus* by Erin Morgenstern, Copyright © 2011 by Night Circus, LLC. Used by permission of Doubleday, an imprint of the Knopf Doubleday Publishing Group, a division of Penguin Random House LLC. All rights reserved.

–"In My Craft or Sullen Art" By Dylan Thomas, from *The Poems of Dylan Thomas*. Copyright © 1946 by New Directions Publishing Corp. Reprinted by permission of New Directions Publishing Corp. and The Dylan Thomas Trust.

–Excerpt(s) from "This Is a Photograph of Me" from *The Circle Game* by Margaret Atwood. Copyright © 1966, 1998, 2012 Margaret Atwood. Reproduced by permission of House of Anansi Press, Toronto. www.houseofanansi.com

–"February" from *Morning In The Burned House* by Margaret Atwood. Copyright © 1995 by Margaret Atwood. Reprinted by permission of Houghton Mifflin Harcourt Publishing Company. All rights reserved.

–"Advice to a Prophet" from *Collected Poems 1943–2004* by Richard Wilbur. Copyright © 2004 by Richard Wilbur. Reprinted by permission of Houghton Mifflin Harcourt Publishing Company. All rights reserved.

–Except(s) from *The Poisonwood Bible* by Barbara Kingsolver. Copyright ©1998 by Barbara Kingsolver. Used by permission of HarperCollins Publishers.

–Excerpt(s) from *White Teeth: A Novel* by Zadie Smith, Copyright © 2000 by Zadie Smith. Used by permission of Random House, an imprint and division of Penguin Random House LLC. All rights reserved.

–From *Ultramarine* by Malcolm Lowry. Copyright © 2005 Estate of Malcolm Lowry. Used by permission of SLL/Sterling Lord Literistic, Inc. and The Overlook Press, an imprint of ABRAMS, New York. All rights reserved.

–"Paterson" by William Carlos Williams, from *Paterson*, Copyright © 1946, 1948,1949,1951,1958 by William Carlos Williams. Reprinted by permission of New Directions Publishing Corp.

–"The White Lilies" by Louise Gluck from *The Wild Iris* (1992, Ecco). Reprinted with kind permission of HarperCollins and Carcanet Press, Manchester, UK.

–Excerpt(s) from *There There: A Novel* by Tommy Orange, copyright © 2018 by Tommy Orange. Used by permission of Alfred A. Knopf, an imprint of the Knopf Doubleday Publishing Group, a division of Penguin Random House LLC. All rights reserved.

–Excerpt(s) from *The Water Dancer: A Novel* by Ta-Nehisi Coates, copyright © 2019 by BCP Literary, Inc.. Used by permission of One World, an imprint of Random House, a division of Penguin Random House LLC. All rights reserved.

–"Planetarium." Copyright © 2016 by the Adrienne Rich Literary Trust. Copyright © 1971 by W. W. Norton & Company, Inc, from *Collected Poems: 1950–2012* by Adrienne Rich. Used by permission of W. W. Norton & Company, Inc.

–"Cozy Apologia" from *American Smooth* by Rita Dove. Copyright © 2004 by Rita Dove. Used by permission of W. W. Norton & Company, Inc.

–"One Art" from *Poems* by Elizabeth Bishop. Copyright © 2011 by The Alice H. Methfessel Trust. Publisher's Note and compilation copyright © 2011 by Farrar, Straus and Giroux. Reprinted by permission of Farrar, Straus and Giroux. All Rights Reserved.

Contents

Get More
(Free) Content
at PrincetonReview.com/prep

As easy as 1·2·3

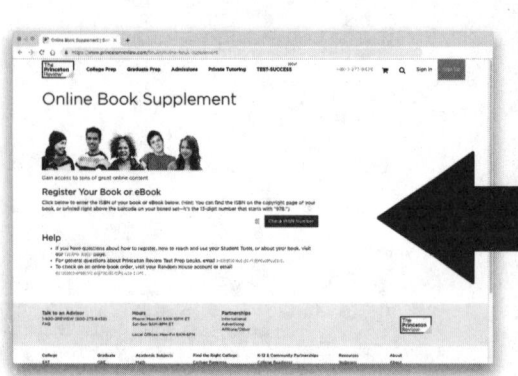

1 Go to PrincetonReview.com/prep or scan the **QR code** and enter the following ISBN to register your book:
9780593518458

2 Answer a few simple questions to set up an exclusive Princeton Review account. *(If you already have one, you can just log in.)*

3 Enjoy access to your **FREE** content!

Access Your Online Test Practice

Your AP Prep book comes with new interactive practice exams to help you prepare for digital test-taking! Find these tests in your online Student Tools, provided in two different formats:

- Fully digital versions with a timer option to simulate the exam experience
- Downloadable interactive PDF with digital features like clicking your answer and typing your free-responses

Check back often as we continue to update the included AP Student Tools.

PLUS, IN YOUR ACCOUNT YOU CAN:

- Get valuable advice about the college application process, tips for essay writing, and financial aid info
- Use our searchable rankings to learn more about your dream school

- Access comprehensive study guides, digital flashcards, and a vocab list
- Check whether there have been any updates or corrections to this edition

Need to report a potential **content** issue?

Contact **EditorialSupport@review.com** and include:

- full title of the book
- ISBN
- page number

Need to report a **technical** issue?

Contact **TPRStudentTech@review.com** and provide:

- your full name
- email address used to register the book
- full book title and ISBN
- Operating system (Mac/PC) and browser (Chrome, Firefox, Safari, etc.)

Look For These Icons Throughout The Book

 ONLINE ARTICLES

 GOING DEEPER

 PROVEN TECHNIQUES

 APPLIED STRATEGIES

 TIME-SAVING TIP

 STUDY BREAK

 OTHER REFERENCES

Learn From the Best

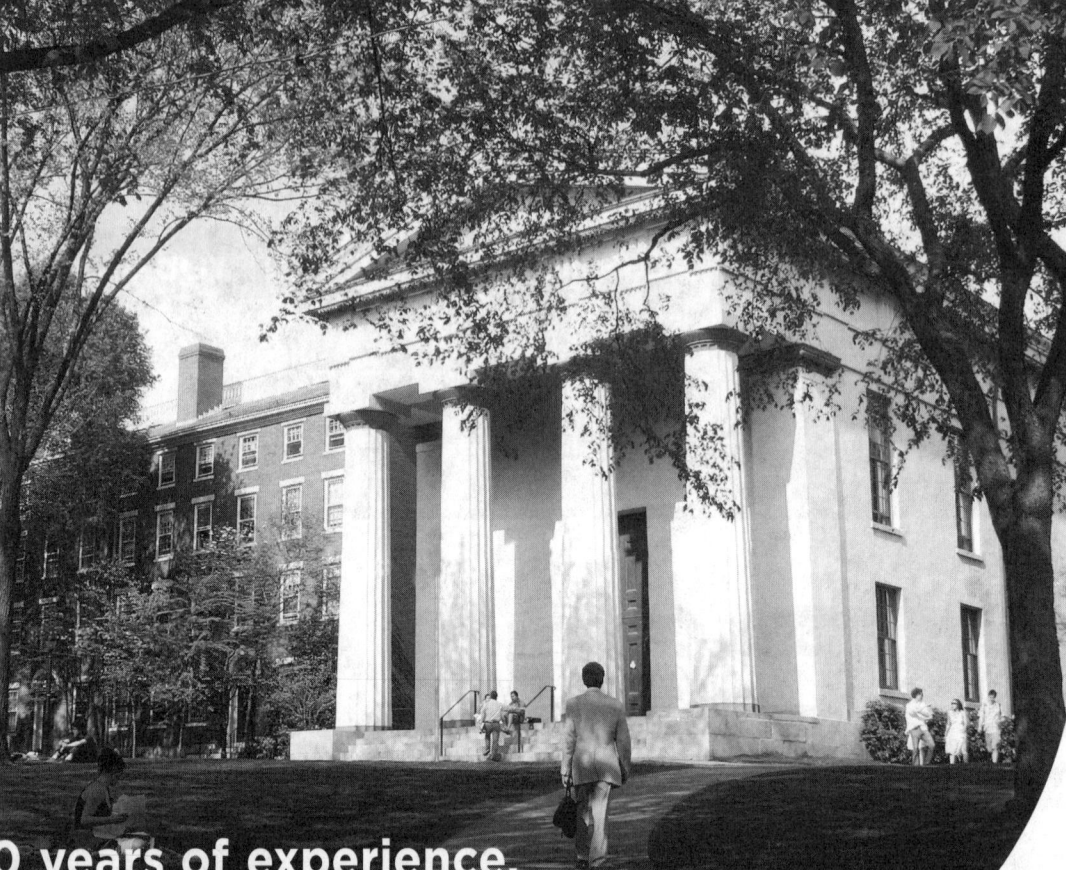

Part I
Using This Book to Improve Your AP Score

- Preview: Your Knowledge, Your Expectations
- Your Guide to Using This Book
- How to Begin

PREVIEW: YOUR KNOWLEDGE, YOUR EXPECTATIONS

Your route to a high score on the AP English Literature and Composition Exam depends a lot on how you plan to use this book. Respond to the following questions.

1. Rate your level of confidence about your knowledge of the content tested by the AP English Literature and Composition Exam:

   A. Very confident—I know it all
   B. I'm pretty confident, but there are topics for which I could use help
   C. Not confident—I need quite a bit of support
   D. I'm not sure

2. Circle your goal score for the Exam:

   5   4   3   2   1   I'm not sure yet

3. What do you expect to learn from this book? Circle all that apply to you.

   A. A general overview of the test and what to expect
   B. Strategies for how to approach the test
   C. The content tested by this exam
   D. I'm not sure yet

YOUR GUIDE TO USING THIS BOOK

This book is organized to provide as much—or as little—support as you need, so you can use this book in whatever way will be most helpful to improving your score on the AP English Literature and Composition Exam.

- The remainder of **Part I** will provide guidance on how to use this book and help you determine your strengths and weaknesses.

- **Part II** of this book contains Practice Test 1, along with its answers and explanations. We strongly recommend that you take this test before going any further, in order to realistically determine
  o your starting point right now
  o which question types you're ready for and which you might need to practice
  o which content topics you are familiar with and which you should carefully review
  Once you have nailed down your strengths and weaknesses with regard to this exam, you can focus your preparation, build a study plan, and be efficient with your time.

Need A Bubble Sheet?
Bubble sheets can be found on your online Student Tools.

- **Part III** of this book will
  - provide information about the structure, scoring, and content of the exam, including the latest updates that were recently announced by the College Board
  - help you to make a study plan
  - point you toward additional resources

- **Part IV** of this book will explore various strategies, such as
  - how to tackle multiple-choice questions
  - how to write effective essays
  - how to manage your time to maximize the number of points available to you

- **Part V** of this book covers the content you need to review and practice for the AP English Literature and Composition Exam.

- **Part VI** of this book contains Practice Tests 2 and 3 and their respective answers and explanations. We recommend that you take advantage of all 5 Practice Tests (one lives online). But don't take them all in a row—take them as you progress through your prep. Take Practice Test 1 (in the front of this book) first—before you even start any review—and see where you are and what areas you should focus on. Consider it a diagnostic. Then dive into prep and after a few weeks (or days, depending on your timeline), take Practice Test 2. See what subjects and test areas are still challenging for you. Take Practice Tests 3 and 4 in a similar way, after a few more weeks. Then close to your real test day, take Practice Test 5.

- The **Online Resources** contain two additional practice tests. Follow the study guide based on the amount of time you have to study for your exam. Use the digital flashcards to get familiar with key terms you might see on the test.

You may choose to use some parts of this book over others, or you may work through the entire book. Your approach will depend on your needs and how much time you have. Let's take a look at how you will make this determination.

AP Exams Go Digital
As of May 2025, some AP exams are fully digital and others are hybrid digital. For the latest info regarding specific AP subjects and testing accommodations, visit apcentral.collegeboard.org/exam-administrationordering-scores/digitalap-exams

HOW TO BEGIN

1. **Take Practice Test 1**

   Before you can decide how to use this book, you need to take a practice test. Doing so will give you insight into your strengths and weaknesses, and the test will also help you make an effective study plan. If you're feeling test-phobic, remind yourself that a practice test is a tool for diagnosing yourself—it's not how well you do that matters, but how you use the information gleaned from your performance to guide your preparation.

   So, before you read further, take Practice Test 1, which is found in Part II of this book. Be sure to do so in one sitting, following the instructions that appear before the test.

2. **Check Your Answers**

   Using the answer key on page 32 count the number of multiple-choice questions you got right and the number you missed. Don't worry about the explanations for now, and don't worry about why you missed questions. We'll get to that soon.

3. **Reflect on the Test**

   Now that you've taken your first test, respond to the following questions:

   - How much time did you spend on the multiple-choice questions?

   - How much time did you spend on each essay?

   - How many multiple-choice questions did you miss?

   - Do you feel you had the knowledge to address the subject matter of the essays?

   - Do you feel you wrote well-organized, thoughtful essays?

4. **Read Part III of this Book and Develop a Study Plan**

   Part III provides information on test content areas, structure, and scoring.

   As you read Part III, reevaluate your answers to the questions above. At the end of Part III, you will revisit and refine the questions. You will then be able to make a study plan, based on your needs and time available, that allows you to use this book most effectively.

5. **Engage with Parts IV and V as Needed**

   Notice the word *engage*. You'll get more out of this book if you use it intentionally than if you read it passively and hope for an improved score through osmosis.

The strategy chapters in Part IV will help you think about your approach to the question types on this exam. This part opens with a reminder to think about how you approach questions now and closes with a reflection section asking you to think about how/whether you will change your approach in the future.

The content chapters in Part V provide a review of the content tested on the AP English Literature and Composition Test, including the level of detail you need to know and how the content is tested.

6. **Take Practice Tests 2, 3, 4 and later, 5, and Assess Your Performance**
    Once you feel you have developed the strategies you need and gained the knowledge you lacked, you should take Practice Test 2, which is found in Part VI of this book. You should do so in one sitting, following the instructions at the beginning of the test.

    When you are done, check your answers to the multiple-choice questions. See whether a teacher will read your responses to the free-response questions and provide feedback.

    Once you have taken the test, reflect on what areas you still need to work on, and revisit the chapters in this book that address those deficiencies. Through this type of reflection and engagement, you will continue to improve.

    Repeat this for Practice Tests 3, 4, and 5.

7. **Keep Working**
    There are other resources available to you, including a wealth of information on APStudents.org. You can continue to explore areas that can stand to improve and engage in those areas right up to the day of the test. Visit the following page for exam practice and information: https://apstudents.collegeboard.org/courses/ap-english-literature-and-composition

Looking to Guarantee a 4 or 5?
We now offer one-on-one tutoring for a guaranteed 5 or an online course for a guaranteed 4 on the AP English Lit and Comp exam. For information on rates, availability, and to learn more about the guarantee, visit PrincetonReview.com/college/ap-test-prep

Part II
Practice Test 1

Practice Test 1

AP® English Literature and Composition Exam

At a Glance

Total Time
1 hour
Number of Questions
55
Percent of Total Grade
45%

DISCLAIMER: The official AP English Literature and Composition exam will be administered digitally. Instructions for the official exam may differ from this practice test.

Instructions

Section I has 55 multiple-choice questions and lasts 1 hour.

This section consists of selections from literary works and questions on their content, form, and style. After reading each passage or poem, select the best answer to each question.

You can go back and forth between questions in this section until time expires. The clock will turn red when 5 minutes remain—**the proctor will not give you any time updates or warnings**.

GO ON TO THE NEXT PAGE.

AP ENGLISH LITERATURE AND COMPOSITION

SECTION I

Questions 1 through 13 refer to the following. Read the following poem carefully before you choose your answers.

Phillis Wheatley's poem "On Imagination" was published in 1773. Wheatley was the first Black poet in America to publish a book, and in this poem she expresses her admiration for the power of imagination.

On Imagination

Thy various works, imperial queen, we see,
 How bright their forms! how deck'd with pomp by thee!
Thy wond'rous acts in beauteous order stand,
And all attest how potent is thine hand.

Line
 5   From Helicon's refulgent heights attend,
Ye sacred choir, and my attempts befriend:
To tell her glories with a faithful tongue,
Ye blooming graces, triumph in my song.

 Now here, now there, the roving Fancy flies,
10   Till some lov'd object strikes her wand'ring eyes,
Whose silken fetters all the senses bind,
And soft captivity involves the mind.

 Imagination! who can sing thy force?
Or who describe the swiftness of thy course?
15   Soaring through air to find the bright abode,
Th' empyreal palace of the thund'ring God,
We on thy pinions can surpass the wind,
And leave the rolling universe behind:
From star to star the mental optics rove,
20   Measure the skies, and range the realms above.
There in one view we grasp the mighty whole,
Or with new worlds amaze th' unbounded soul.

 Though Winter frowns to Fancy's raptur'd eyes
The fields may flourish, and gay scenes arise;
25   The frozen deeps may break their iron bands,
And bid their waters murmur o'er the sands.
Fair Flora may resume her fragrant reign,
And with her flow'ry riches deck the plain;
Sylvanus may diffuse his honours round,
30   And all the forest may with leaves be crown'd:
Show'rs may descend, and dews their gems disclose,
And nectar sparkle on the blooming rose.

Such is thy pow'r, nor are thine orders vain,
O thou the leader of the mental train:
35   In full perfection all thy works are wrought,
And thine the sceptre o'er the realms of thought.
Before thy throne the subject-passions bow,
Of subject-passions sov'reign ruler thou;
At thy command joy rushes on the heart,
40   And through the glowing veins the spirits dart.

 Fancy might now her silken pinions try
To rise from earth, and sweep th' expanse on high:
From Tithon's bed now might Aurora rise,
Her cheeks all glowing with celestial dies,
45   While a pure stream of light o'erflows the skies.
The monarch of the day I might behold,
And all the mountains tipt with radiant gold,
But I reluctant leave the pleasing views,
Which Fancy dresses to delight the Muse;
50   Winter austere forbids me to aspire,
And northern tempests damp the rising fire;
They chill the tides of Fancy's flowing sea,
Cease then, my song, cease the unequal lay.

---

1 ☐ Mark for Review

Who does "thy" refer to in line 1 ("Thy various works, imperial queen, we see,")?

(A) Imagination

(B) Winter

(C) Aurora

(D) the reader

GO ON TO THE NEXT PAGE.

2 ☐ Mark for Review

Line 13 ("Imagination! who can sing thy force?") is an example of

Ⓐ synecdoche

Ⓑ simile

Ⓒ personification

Ⓓ imagery

3 ☐ Mark for Review

What is the speaker trying to convey with lines 17–22 ("We on thy pinions…we grasp…th' unbounded soul.")?

Ⓐ Reality is more valuable than Imagination.

Ⓑ Imagination lets us leave unhappiness behind.

Ⓒ Imagination prevents us from being reasonable.

Ⓓ Imagination allows us to grasp possibilities outside the self.

4 ☐ Mark for Review

In line 26, "murmur" is an example of

Ⓐ onomatopoeia

Ⓑ euphemism

Ⓒ alliteration

Ⓓ anaphora

5 ☐ Mark for Review

What is the tone of the poem as a whole?

Ⓐ Curious then regretful

Ⓑ Whimsical then melancholy

Ⓒ Skeptical then frightened

Ⓓ Delighted then exasperated

6 ☐ Mark for Review

What change occurs from stanza 4 to stanza 7?

Ⓐ Imagination, yearning to grasp possibilities beyond the self, is set free.

Ⓑ Imagination, uncertain, retreats back to reality.

Ⓒ Imagination joins Winter to celebrate the rising sun and the golden mountains.

Ⓓ Imagination is grounded by reality, no longer free to wander.

7 ☐ Mark for Review

What can the reader infer from lines 53–54, ("They chill the tides of Fancy's flowing sea, Cease then, my song, cease the unequal lay.")?

Ⓐ Imagination is Fancy's most powerful tool.

Ⓑ Reality is ultimately more powerful than imagination.

Ⓒ The fight between imagination and reality is eternal.

Ⓓ Reality is unjust.

GO ON TO THE NEXT PAGE.

8 ☐ Mark for Review

What can the reader infer Winter is doing to the speaker?

(A) Setting her free

(B) Raising her to the mountain top

(C) Grounding her

(D) Punishing her

9 ☐ Mark for Review

In what style is *On Imagination* written?

(A) Free verse

(B) Rhyming couplets

(C) Haiku

(D) Elegy

10 ☐ Mark for Review

In lines 11–12, what does "Whose silken fetters…involves the mind" imply in context?

(A) Falling in love is painful

(B) Fancy is lost without love

(C) Without Imagination love is not possible

(D) Fancy is bound by love

11 ☐ Mark for Review

The speaker's primary purpose is most nearly to

(A) contemplate creativity

(B) declare love

(C) celebrate freedom

(D) question reality

12 ☐ Mark for Review

What can the reader infer from lines 34–36 ("O thou the leader…And thine the sceptre o'er the realms of thought.")?

(A) Imagination controls the mind.

(B) Imagination demands perfection.

(C) Imagination fosters creativity and free thought.

(D) Imagination hampers creativity.

13 ☐ Mark for Review

The poem as a whole can be understood as

(A) a pastoral about an artist

(B) a sonnet about the strength of the mind

(C) a ballad on the importance of creativity

(D) an allegory about enslaved people

GO ON TO THE NEXT PAGE.

Questions 14 through 25 refer to the following. Read the following passage carefully before you choose your answers.

The selection is an excerpt from the short story "Drenched in Light" by Zora Neale Hurston, published in 1924 in the monthly Opportunity: A Journal of Negro Life.

Par.

1   Isis saw no longer any reason to die. She came up out of the water, holding up the dripping fringe of the tablecloth.

2   "Naw indeedy. You go to Maitlan' by the shell road — it goes by mah house — an' turn off at Lake Sebelia to the clay road that takes you right to the do'."

3   "Well," went on the driver, smiling furtively, "Could you quit dying long enough to go with us?"

4   "Yessuh," she said thoughtfully, "Ah wanta go wid you."

5   The door of the car swung open. She was invited to a seat beside the driver. She had often dreamed of riding in one of these heavenly chariots but never thought she would, actually.

6   "Jump in then, Madame Tagedy, and show us. We lost ourselved after we left your barbecue."

7   During the drive Isis explained to the nice lady who smelt faintly of violets and to the indifferent men that she was really a princess. She told them about her trips to the horizon, about the trailing gowns, the gold shoes with blue bottoms — she insisted on the blue bottoms — the white charger, the time when she was Hercules and had slain numerous dragons and sundry giants. At last the car approached her gate over which stood the umbrella China-berry tree. The car was abreast of the gate and had all but passed when Grandma spied her glorious tablecloth lying back against the upholstery of the Packard.

8   "You Isie - e!" she bawled. "You lil' wretch you! come heah dis instant."

9   "That's me," the child confessed, mortified, to the lady on the rear seat.

10   "Oh, Sewell, stop the car. This is where the child lives. I hate to give her up though."

11   "Do you wanta keep me?" Isis brightened.

12   "Oh, I wish I could, you shining little morsel. Wait, I'll try to save you a whipping this time."

13   She dismounted with the gaudy lemon flavored culprit and advanced to the gate where Grandma stood glowering, switches in hand.

14   "You're gointuh ketchit f'um yo' haid to yo' heels m'lady. Jes' come in heah."

15   "Why, good afteroon," she accosted the furious grandparent. "You're not going to whip this poor little thing, are you?" the lady asked in conciliatory tones.

16   "Yes, Ma'am. She's de wustest lil' limb dat ever drawed bref. Jes' look at mah new table cloth, dat ain't never been washed. She done traipsed all over de woods, uh dancin' an' uh' prancin' in it. She done took a razor to me t'day an' Lawd knows whut mo'."

17   Isis clung to the white hand fearfully.

18   "Ah wuzn't gointer hurt Gran'ma, miss — Ah wuz jus' gointer shave her whiskers fuh huh 'cause she's old an' can't."

19   The white hand closed tightly over the little brown one that was quite soiled. She could understand a voluntary act of love even though it miscarried.

20   "Now, Mrs. er—er— I didn't get the name— how much did your tablecloth cost?"

21   "One whole big silvah dollar down at O'landah — ain't had it a week yit."

22   "Now here's five dollars to get another one. The little thing loves laughter. I want her to go on to the hotel and dance in that tablecloth for me. I can stand a little light today —"

23   "Oh, yessum, yessum," Grandma cut in, "Everything's alright, sho' she kin go, yessum."

24   The lady went on: "I want brightness and this Isis is joy itself, why she's drenched in light!"

25   Isis for the first time in her life, felt herself appreciated and danced up and down in an ecstasy of joy for a minute.

26   "Now, behave yo'seff, Isie, ovah at de hotel wid de folks," Grandma cautioned, pride in her voice, though she strove to hide it. "Lawd, ma'am, dat gal keeps me so frackshus, Ah doan know mah haid from mah feet. I orter comb huh haid, too, befo' she go wid you all."

27   "No, no, don't bother. I like her as she is. I don't think she'd like it either, being combed and scrubbed. Come on, Isis."

28   Feeling that Grandma had been somewhat squelched did not detract from Isis' spirit at all. She pranced over to the waiting motor and this time seated herself on the rear seat between the sweet, smiling lady and the rather aloof man in gray.

29   "Ah'm gointer stay wid you all," she said with a great deal of warmth, and snuggled up to her benefactress. "Want me tuh sing a song fuh you?"

30   "There, Hen, you've been adopted," said the man with a short, harsh laugh.

31   "Oh, I hope so, Harry." She put her arm about the red draped figure at her side and drew it closer until she felt the warm puffs of the child's breath against her side. She looked hungrily ahead of her and spoke into space rather than to anyone in the car. "I want a little of her sunshine to soak into my soul. I need it."

GO ON TO THE NEXT PAGE.

14 ☐ Mark for Review

How is the character of Helen, the white woman, portrayed?

Ⓐ Generous and caring

Ⓑ Self-centered and greedy

Ⓒ Underhanded and devious

Ⓓ Apathetic and unmoved

15 ☐ Mark for Review

How would you characterize the relationship between Isis and Helen, the white woman?

Ⓐ Parent and child

Ⓑ Teacher and student

Ⓒ Benefactor and artist

Ⓓ Savior and pauper

16 ☐ Mark for Review

The tone of the passage as a whole can best be described as

Ⓐ comedic

Ⓑ foreboding

Ⓒ hopeful

Ⓓ threatening

17 ☐ Mark for Review

What is the reader to infer the horizon represents from the sentence "She told them about her trips to the horizon, about the trailing gowns, the gold shoes with the blue bottoms. . . ." in paragraph 7?

Ⓐ The setting sun

Ⓑ Places Isis has traveled

Ⓒ Isis' desire to explore

Ⓓ Isis' future

18 ☐ Mark for Review

In paragraph 26, "Lawd, ma'am, dat gal keeps me so frackshus, Ah doan know mah haid from mah feet," what does "frackshus" most nearly mean in context?

Ⓐ Exhausted

Ⓑ Angry

Ⓒ Happy

Ⓓ Irritable

19 ☐ Mark for Review

What is the author trying to convey in paragraph 24 when she writes, "I want brightness and this Isis is joy itself, why she's drenched in light!"?

Ⓐ Wealthy people do not have happy lives

Ⓑ Happiness is not relative to wealth

Ⓒ Money buys happiness

Ⓓ Isis had supernatural powers

GO ON TO THE NEXT PAGE.

20 ☐ Mark for Review

"Isis is joy itself" is an example of

(A) simile

(B) synecdoche

(C) metaphor

(D) hyperbole

21 ☐ Mark for Review

What is the author most nearly trying to convey in paragraph 22 with the lines, "I want her to go on to the hotel and dance in that tablecloth for me. I can stand a little light today—" ?

(A) Wealth and social status are very important to artistic expression

(B) Artistic expression is dependent upon having an appreciative audience

(C) Black cultural expression is as valuable as more regimented forms of art practiced by white society

(D) The upper class decides what forms of artistic expression are most valuable

22 ☐ Mark for Review

How would you describe the change in Grandma's character after her encounter with Helen?

(A) Belligerent then placated

(B) Suspicious then fearful

(C) Frustrated then concerned

(D) Disgruntled then apathetic

23 ☐ Mark for Review

What is the author most nearly conveying by having Grandma and Isis speak in the Black vernacular?

(A) To illustrate the difference between written language and spoken language

(B) To highlight moments of excitement or enthusiasm

(C) That what Grandma and Isis say is of little value

(D) That the South has a rich and nuanced culture of its own

24 ☐ Mark for Review

Why does Helen give Grandma five dollars?

(A) So she can buy five tablecloths to replace her ruined tablecloth

(B) For giving her directions

(C) To mollify her rage so she would allow Isis accompany Helen to the hotel

(D) To impress her and gain her admiration

25 ☐ Mark for Review

The passage as a whole can best be understood as

(A) a commentary on race relations in the South

(B) an allegory about the Harlem renaissance

(C) a fable about friendship

(D) a story about self-confidence

GO ON TO THE NEXT PAGE.

Questions 26 through 33 refer to the following. Read the following poem carefully before you choose your answers.

Elizabeth Bishop's poem "One Art" was published in 1976. It comes from near the end of her career and life, and some think of the villanelle as autobiographical, since it was written during a time when she was separated from her partner.

One Art

The art of losing isn't hard to master;
so many things seem filled with the intent
to be lost that their loss is no disaster.

Line
5 Lose something every day. Accept the fluster
of lost door keys, the hour badly spent.
The art of losing isn't hard to master.

Then practice losing farther, losing faster:
places, and names, and where it was you meant
to travel. None of these will bring disaster.

10 I lost my mother's watch. And look! my last, or
next-to-last, of three loved houses went.
The art of losing isn't hard to master.

I lost two cities, lovely ones. And, vaster,
some realms I owned, two rivers, a continent.
15 I miss them, but it wasn't a disaster.

—Even losing you (the joking voice, a gesture
I love) I shan't have lied. It's evident
the art of losing's not too hard to master
though it may look like (Write it!) like disaster.

---

26   🔖 Mark for Review

The tone of the poem indicates that the speaker feels which of the following?

(A) Carelessness, anger, loneliness

(B) Panic, acceptance, relief

(C) Carelessness, heartbreak, acceptance

(D) Panic, carelessness, acceptance

27   🔖 Mark for Review

Which of the following is an example of personification used in the poem?

(A) Lines 2–3 ("so many things seem…their loss is no disaster.")

(B) Lines 4–5 ("Accept the fluster…the hour badly spent.")

(C) Lines 7–9 ("Then practice losing farther…you meant to travel.")

(D) Lines 13–14 ("I lost two cities…a continent.")

GO ON TO THE NEXT PAGE.

28 ☐ Mark for Review

In lines 13–14 ("And, vaster, / some realms I owned, two rivers, a continent"), the speaker uses which of the following to convey the depth of her losses and those she lists later in the poem?

(A) Personification

(B) Repetition

(C) Allusion

(D) Hyperbole

29 ☐ Mark for Review

Which of the following best describes the central contrast of the poem?

(A) The loss of small things versus important ones

(B) The pain of losing treasured things versus the relief of finding them again

(C) The relief of losing someone she didn't care for versus the pain of losing her home

(D) The intent to accept losses as "no disaster" versus the growing size and importance of the lost items

30 ☐ Mark for Review

How does the poet use the list of lost things to lend structure to the poem?

(A) The list of lost things distracts the listener from the tone of carelessness the speaker sets in line 3.

(B) The list of lost things distracts from the deeper heartbreak of the speaker's loss of her home in lines 13–15.

(C) The list of lost things builds in order of importance, highlighting the devastation she feels at the loss of her home in lines 13–15.

(D) The list of lost things builds in order of importance, helping emphasize the difficulty of losing the "you" addressed in line 16.

31 ☐ Mark for Review

The "lost door keys" in line 5 are a symbol of

(A) something the loss of which is not too painful to cope with

(B) the main loss the speaker experiences

(C) the first thing the speaker ever lost

(D) something important and painful for the speaker to lose

32 ☐ Mark for Review

All of the following contribute to the emotional effect of the poem EXCEPT

(A) the parenthetical statement in the last line

(B) the speaker's suggestion to practice losing things

(C) the contrast between things lost and things found again

(D) the structure of the list of lost things

33 ☐ Mark for Review

What is a possible meaning of the parenthetical statement "(Write it!)" in line 19?

(A) The speaker is suggesting that the listener write their own story of loss.

(B) The speaker is urging herself to remember the things she has lost by listing them.

(C) The speaker is insisting that the listener learn to not mourn lost things.

(D) The speaker is exhorting herself to admit the pain she is trying to accept.

GO ON TO THE NEXT PAGE.

Questions 34 through 45 refer to the following. Read the following passage carefully before you choose your answers.

This passage is excerpted from Edgar Allen Poe's "The Masque of the Red Death," a short story about a dangerous plague published in 1842.

Par.

1   The "Red Death" had long devastated the country. No pestilence had ever been so fatal, or so hideous. Blood was its Avatar and its seal—the redness and the horror of blood. There were sharp pains, and sudden dizziness, and then profuse bleeding at the pores, with dissolution. The scarlet stains upon the body and especially upon the face of the victim, were the pest ban which shut him out from the aid and from the sympathy of his fellow-men. And the whole seizure, progress and termination of the disease, were the incidents of half an hour.

2   But the Prince Prospero was happy and dauntless and sagacious. When his dominions were half depopulated, he summoned to his presence a thousand hale and light-hearted friends from among the knights and dames of his court, and with these retired to the deep seclusion of one of his castellated abbeys. This was an extensive and magnificent structure, the creation of the prince's own eccentric yet august taste. A strong and lofty wall girdled it in. This wall had gates of iron. The courtiers, having entered, brought furnaces and massy hammers and welded the bolts. They resolved to leave means neither of ingress or egress to the sudden impulses of despair or of frenzy from within. The abbey was amply provisioned. With such precautions the courtiers might bid defiance to contagion. The external world could take care of itself. In the meantime it was folly to grieve, or to think. The prince had provided all the appliances of pleasure. There were buffoons, there were improvisatori, there were ballet-dancers, there were musicians, there was Beauty, there was wine. All these and security were within. Without was the "Red Death."

3   It was toward the close of the fifth or sixth month of his seclusion, and while the pestilence raged most furiously abroad, that the Prince Prospero entertained his thousand friends at a masked ball of the most unusual magnificence.

4   It was a voluptuous scene, that masquerade. But first let me tell of the rooms in which it was held. There were seven—an imperial suite. In many palaces, however, such suites form a long and straight vista, while the folding doors slide back nearly to the walls on either hand, so that the view of the whole extent is scarcely impeded. Here the case was very different; as might have been expected from the duke's love of the bizarre. The apartments were so irregularly disposed that the vision embraced but little more than one at a time. There was a sharp turn at every twenty or thirty yards, and at each turn a novel effect. To the right and left, in the middle of each wall, a tall and narrow Gothic window looked out upon a closed corridor which pursued the windings of the suite. These windows were of stained glass whose colour varied in accordance with the prevailing hue of the decorations of the chamber into which it opened. That at the eastern extremity was hung, for example, in blue—and vividly blue were its windows. The second chamber was purple in its ornaments and tapestries, and here the panes were purple.

The third was green throughout, and so were the casements. The fourth was furnished and lighted with orange—the fifth with white—the sixth with violet. The seventh apartment was closely shrouded in black velvet tapestries that hung all over the ceiling and down the walls, falling in heavy folds upon a carpet of the same material and hue. But in this chamber only, the colour of the windows failed to correspond with the decorations. The panes here were scarlet—a deep blood colour. Now in no one of the seven apartments was there any lamp or candelabrum, amid the profusion of golden ornaments that lay scattered to and fro or depended from the roof. There was no light of any kind emanating from lamp or candle within the suite of chambers. But in the corridors that followed the suite, there stood, opposite to each window, a heavy tripod, bearing a brazier of fire that protected its rays through the tinted glass and so glaringly illumined the room. And thus were produced a multitude of gaudy and fantastic appearances. But in the western or black chamber the effect of the fire-light that streamed upon the dark hangings through the blood-tinted panes, was ghastly in the extreme, and produced so wild a look upon the countenances of those who entered, that there were few of the company bold enough to set foot within its precincts at all.

5   It was in this apartment, also, that there stood against the western wall, a gigantic clock of ebony.

GO ON TO THE NEXT PAGE.

34 ⬚ Mark for Review

In paragraph 3, "the pestilence raged most furiously abroad" is an example of

(A) hyperbole

(B) simile

(C) personification

(D) alliteration

35 ⬚ Mark for Review

What was the author trying to convey in paragraph 2 with the sentence, "When his dominions were half depopulated, . . . castellated abbeys"?

(A) The good health of the aristocracy

(B) The inequality inherent in social stratification

(C) The Prince's strong ties to his court

(D) The security of the castle

36 ⬚ Mark for Review

What can the reader infer from the sentence, "The external world can take care of itself," (paragraph 2) in context?

(A) That the Prince and his guests do not care about the rest of the country

(B) That the rest of the country has plenty of resources to care for themselves

(C) The outside world is welcome to join the party in the abbey

(D) Prospero is anxious to help the outside world

37 ⬚ Mark for Review

What is the tone of the passage as a whole?

(A) Hopeful

(B) Ironic

(C) Satirical

(D) Ominous

38 ⬚ Mark for Review

What is the author trying to convey by putting the clock on the western wall of the seventh chamber?

(A) The passage of time in life is inevitable

(B) The guests would not be concerned with the time during the party

(C) Time is precious

(D) Time is not important

39 ⬚ Mark for Review

What is the author's purpose in describing The Red Death in detail first, and introducing Prince Prospero second?

(A) To engender sympathy for the victims of The Red Death

(B) To instill fear in the audience

(C) To establish The Red Death as the driving force of the story

(D) To establish Prince Prospero as the driving force of the story

GO ON TO THE NEXT PAGE.

40 🔖 Mark for Review

"There were sharp pains . . . which shut him out from the aid and from the sympathy of his fellow men" (paragraph 1) is an example of

(A) simile

(B) imagery

(C) metaphor

(D) oxymoron

41 🔖 Mark for Review

How is the character of Prince Prospero portrayed?

(A) Self-centered and uncaring

(B) Regal and responsible

(C) Stalwart and stable

(D) Generous and charitable

42 🔖 Mark for Review

Why do guests avoid the seventh room?

(A) It is a stark reminder of the disease that rages on beyond the castle walls

(B) It is too dark to socialize with other guests

(C) The guests want to avoid seeing the clock

(D) It is too far removed from the rest of the party

43 🔖 Mark for Review

If the seventh room, draped in black, is a metaphor for death, what can the reader infer the author was trying to convey about the seven different colored rooms?

(A) They represented the seven days of the week

(B) They represented the seven colors of the rainbow

(C) They represented the seven deadly sins

(D) They represented the seven stages of life

44 🔖 Mark for Review

Why is the decor of the seven apartments paradoxical to the purpose of the party?

(A) The rooms were specifically ordered and decorated, while the party was wild and untamed

(B) The ebony clock kept strict time while the guests revel unconcerned

(C) The different color rooms are separated; the diverse guests are celebrating together

(D) The party is to forget mortality; the rooms remind guests of their mortality

45 🔖 Mark for Review

What is the author trying to convey in paragraph 4 with the phrases, "a deep blood colour. Now in no one of the seven apartments . . . "?

(A) That the room is very dark

(B) The Prince did not want guests in the seventh apartment

(C) Death is inevitable

(D) The Red Death is beyond the castle walls

GO ON TO THE NEXT PAGE.

Questions 46 through 55 refer to the following. Read the following passage carefully before you choose your answers.

This passage is excerpted from a speculative fiction novel by writer Erin Morgenstern, The Night Circus. *It was published in 2011 and has a nonlinear narrative written from multiple viewpoints.*

Par.

1   "Ha!" Hector exclaims, "Then you are willing to play."

2   The man in the gray suit hesitates only a moment before he nods. "Something a bit more complex than last time, and yes, I may be interested," he says. "Possibly."

3   "Of course it will be more complex," Hector says. "I have a natural talent to play with. I'm not wagering that for anything simple."

4   "Natural talent is a questionable phenomenon, inclination perhaps, but innate ability is extremely rare."

5   "She's my own child, of course she has innate ability."

6   "You admit she has had lessons," the man in the gray suit says. "How can you be certain?"

7   "Celia, when did you start your lessons?" Hector asks without looking at her.

8   "March," she answers.

9   "What year, dearest?" Hector adds.

10   "This year," she says, as though this is a particularly stupid question.

11   "Eight months of lessons," Hector clarifies. "At barely six years of age. If I recall correctly you sometimes start your own students a bit younger than that. Celia is clearly more advanced than she would be if she did not have natural ability. She could levitate that watch on her first try."

12   The man in the gray suit turns his attention to Celia.

13   "You broke that by accident, did you not?" He asks, nodding at the watch, sitting on the table. Celia frowns and gives him the tiniest of nods.

14   "She has remarkable control for one so young," he remarks to Hector. "But such a temper is always an unfortunate variable. It can lead to impulsive behavior."

15   "She'll either grow out of it or learn to control it. It's a minor issue."

16   The man in the gray suit keeps his eyes on the girl but addresses Hector when he speaks. To Celia's ears, the sounds no longer resolve into words, and she frowns as her father's responses take on the same muddled quality.

17   "You would wager your own child?"

18   "She won't lose," Hector says.

19   "I suggest you find a student you can tolerate parting with if you do not already have one to spare."

20   "I assumed her mother has no opinion on the matter."

21   "You assume correctly."

22   The man in the gray suit considers the girl for some time before he speaks again, and still, she does not comprehend the words.

23   "I understand your confidence in her ability though I encourage you to at least consider the possibility that she could be lost should the competition not play out in her favor. I will find a player to truly challenge her. Otherwise there is no reason for me to agree to participate. Her victory cannot be guaranteed."

24   "That is a risk I am willing to take," Hector says without even glancing at his daughter. "If you would like to make it official here, now go right ahead."

25   The man in the gray suit looks back at Celia, and when he speaks she understands the words once more. "Very well," he says with a nod.

26   "He made me not hear right," Celia whispers when her father turns to her.

27   "I know, dearest, and it wasn't very polite," Hector says as he guides her closer to the chair, where the man scrutinizes her with eyes that are almost as light and gray as his suit. "Have you always been able to do such things?" He asks her looking back at the watch again.

28   Celia nods.

29   "My, my mamma said I was the devil's child," she says quietly.

30   The man in the gray suit leans forward and whispers something in her ear too low for her father to overhear. A small smile brightens her face.

31   "Hold out your right hand," he says, leaning back in his chair. Celia immediately puts out her hand palm up unsure of what to expect. But the man in the gray suit does not place anything in her open palm. Instead he turns her hand over and removes a silver ring from his pinky. He slides it onto her ring finger. Though it is too loose for her slim fingers, keeping his other hand around her wrist. She is opening her mouth to state the obvious fact, that the ring, though very pretty, does not fit, when she realizes that it is shrinking on her hand. Her momentary glee at the adjustment is crushed by the pain that follows as the ring continues to close around her finger, the metal burning into her skin. She tries to pull away but the man in the gray suit keeps his hand firmly around her wrist. The ring thins and fades, leaving only a bright red scar around Celia's finger. The man in the gray suit releases her wrist and she steps back, retreating into a corner, and staring at her hand.

32   "Good girl," her father says.

GO ON TO THE NEXT PAGE.

46 ☐ Mark for Review

What can the reader infer from the line "'That is a risk I am willing to take,' Hector says without even glancing at his daughter" (paragraph 24)?

- (A) Hector has faith in Celia's abilities
- (B) Hector values Celia's skill more than he values her life
- (C) Hector is embarrassed to look Celia in the eye
- (D) Hector is trying to impress the man in the gray suit

47 ☐ Mark for Review

How can the relationship between Hector and the man in the gray suit be characterized?

- (A) Student and teacher
- (B) Old friends
- (C) Rivals
- (D) Colleagues

48 ☐ Mark for Review

What can the reader infer from the lines "She could levitate that watch . . . nodding at the watch, sitting on the table" (paragraphs 11–13)?

- (A) Hector was proud of his daughter for her natural ability
- (B) The man in the gray suit was concerned about Celia's lack of control
- (C) Celia's skills were still undeveloped
- (D) Time is a construct of man, and unimportant

49 ☐ Mark for Review

What is the author trying to convey in the sentences "He slides it onto her ring finger . . . the metal burning into her skin " (paragraph 31)?

- (A) Celia has just been permanently committed to the challenge
- (B) The man in the gray suit is now Celia's instructor
- (C) Celia was being punished for her lack of control
- (D) Celia's magic skills affect anything that touches her

50 ☐ Mark for Review

The tone of the passage as a whole can best be described as

- (A) whimsical
- (B) romantic
- (C) melancholy
- (D) foreboding

51 ☐ Mark for Review

How is the competition characterized based on paragraphs 14–15, "But such a temper is always an unfortunate variable. It can lead to impulsive behavior." "She'll either grow out of it or learn to control it. It's a minor issue"?

- (A) Order versus chaos
- (B) Power versus love
- (C) Anger versus indifference
- (D) Concern versus pride

GO ON TO THE NEXT PAGE.

52 🔖 Mark for Review

What can the reader infer from the contrasting references to the challenge in paragraph 14, "She has remarkable control for one so young" and "It can lead to impulsive behavior"?

(A) Hector and the man in the gray suit do not understand each other

(B) Hector and the man in the gray suit have a callous disregard for the lives of others

(C) Celia's welfare is of utmost concern to both Hector and the man in the gray suit

(D) The man in the gray suit is intimidated by Celia's skills

53 🔖 Mark for Review

In paragraph 16, "The man in the gray suit keeps his eyes on the girl but addresses Hector when he speaks" is an example of

(A) hyperbole

(B) synecdoche

(C) metonymy

(D) simile

54 🔖 Mark for Review

What is the author trying to convey in paragraph 16 with the lines "To Celia's ears, the sounds no longer resolve into words, and she frowns as her father's responses take on the same muddled quality"?

(A) Celia was too young to understand what her father and the man in the gray suit were saying

(B) Hector and the man in the gray suit did not want to scare Celia

(C) Celia is sad that she does not understand her father and the man in the gray suit

(D) Celia should not trust Hector and the man in the gray suit

55 🔖 Mark for Review

What is the narrator's attitude toward Hector?

(A) Pitying

(B) Admiring

(C) Duplicitous

(D) Condescending

STOP
END OF SECTION I

IF YOU FINISH BEFORE TIME IS CALLED, YOU MAY CHECK YOUR WORK ON THIS SECTION.
DO NOT GO ON TO SECTION II UNTIL YOU ARE TOLD TO DO SO.

The Exam

AP® English Literature and Composition Exam

At a Glance

Total Time
2 hours
Number of Questions
3
Percent of Total Grade
55%

DISCLAIMER: The official AP English Literature and Composition exam will be administered digitally. Instructions for the official exam may differ from this practice test.

Instructions

Section II has 3 free-response questions and lasts 2 hours.

This section of the exam requires answers in essay form. Each essay will be judged on its clarity and effectiveness in dealing with the assigned topic and on the quality of the writing. In responding to Question 3, select a work of fiction that will be appropriate to the question. Use a work that you are familiar with either from your AP English Literature and Composition class or from other literature you have previously read.

You may pace yourself as you answer the questions in this section, or you may use these optional timing recommendations:

It is suggested that you spend an equal amount of time, approximately 40 minutes, on each question.

You may use scratch paper for notes and planning, but credit will only be given for responses entered in this application. Text you enter as an annotation will not be included as part of your answer. You can go back and forth between questions in this section until time expires. The clock will turn red when 5 minutes remain—**the proctor will not give you any time updates or warnings.**

GO ON TO THE NEXT PAGE.

AP ENGLISH LITERATURE AND COMPOSITION

SECTION II

In Margaret Atwood's poem "This is a Photograph of Me," published in 2012, the speaker guides us, cryptically, through a mysterious photograph. Read the poem carefully. Then, in a well-written essay, analyze how Atwood uses poetic elements and techniques to convey its haunting and mysterious theme.

This Is A Photograph of Me

It was taken some time ago.
At first it seems to be
a smeared
Line print: blurred lines and grey flecks
5 blended with the paper;

then, as you scan
it, you see in the left-hand corner
a thing that is like a branch: part of a tree
(balsam or spruce) emerging
10 and, to the right, halfway up
what ought to be a gentle
slope, a small frame house.

In the background there is a lake,
and beyond that, some low hills.

15 (The photograph was taken
the day after I drowned.

I am in the lake, in the center
of the picture, just under the surface.

It is difficult to say where
20 precisely, or to say
how large or small I am:
the effect of water
on light is a distortion

but if you look long enough,
25 eventually
you will be able to see me.)

---

1 🔖 Mark for Review

In a well-written essay, analyze how Atwood uses poetic elements and techniques to convey the poem's haunting and mysterious theme.

In your response you should do the following:

- Respond to the prompt with a thesis that presents a defensible interpretation.
- Select and use evidence to support your line of reasoning.
- Explain how the evidence supports your line of reasoning.
- Use appropriate grammar and punctuation in communicating your argument.

GO ON TO THE NEXT PAGE.

The following excerpt is from the novel *The Poisonwood Bible* (1998) by Barbara Kingsolver. This passage is narrated by Orleanna Price, the matriarch of an American missionary family in the Belgian Congo during a politically turbulent era of the 1960s. Despite the family's best intentions, they suffer many tragedies during their ill-fated mission. Read the passage carefully. Then, in a well-written essay, analyze how Kingsolver uses literary elements and techniques such as imagery and point of view to convey guilt, pride, shame, and responsibility.

Par.

1 I know how people are, with their habits of mind. Most will sail through from cradle to grave with a conscience clean as snow. It's easy to point at other men, conveniently dead, starting with the ones who first scooped up mud from riverbanks to catch the scent of a source. Why, Dr. Livingston, I presume, wasn't he the rascal! He and all the profiteers who've since walked out on Africa as a husband quits a wife, leaving her with her naked body curled around the emptied-out mine of her womb. I know people. Most have no earthly notion of the price of a snow white conscience.

2 I would be no different from the next one, if I hadn't paid my own little part in blood. I trod on Africa without a thought, straight from our family's divinely inspired beginning to our terrible end. In between, in the midst of all those steaming nights and days darkly colored, smelling of earth, I believe there lay some marrow of honest instruction. Sometimes I can nearly say what it was. If I could, I would fling it at others, I'm afraid, at risk to their ease. I'd slide this awful story off my shoulders, flatten it, sketch out our crimes like a failed battle plan and shake it in the faces of my neighbors, who are wary of me already. But Africa shifts under my hands, refusing to be party to failed relations. Refusing to be any place at all, or anything but itself: the animal kingdom making hay in the kingdom of glory. So there it is, take your place. Leave nothing for a haunted old bat to use for disturbing the peace. Nothing, save for this life of her own.

3 We aimed for no more than to have dominion over every creature that moved upon the earth. And so it came to pass that we stepped down there on a place we believed unformed, where only darkness moved on the face of the waters. Now you laugh, day and night, while you gnaw on my bones. But what else could we have thought? Only that it began and ended with us. What do we know, even now? Ask the children. Look at what they grew up to be. We can only speak of the things we carried with us, and the things we took away.

2 🔖 Mark for Review

In a well-written essay, analyze how Kingsolver uses literary elements and techniques such as imagery and point of view to convey guilt, pride, shame, and responsibility.

In your response you should do the following:

- Respond to the prompt with a thesis that presents a defensible interpretation.
- Select and use evidence to support your line of reasoning.
- Explain how the evidence supports your line of reasoning.
- Use appropriate grammar and punctuation in communicating your argument.

GO ON TO THE NEXT PAGE.

Food, and eating, is often depicted in literature. Food can be symbolic of wealth, culture, family, tradition, and locale. It can be used as reward, punishment, community, and hope. Either from your own reading or from the list below, choose a work of fiction in which characters are affected by food. Then, in a well-written essay, analyze how the author's use of food contributes to an interpretation of the work as a whole. Do not merely summarize the plot.

Like Water for Chocolate
Babette's Feast
Heartburn
To the Lighthouse
Crazy Rich Asians
Fried Green Tomatoes
Middlesex
Gravity's Rainbow
The Lion, The Witch, and the Wardrobe
The Great Gatsby
Moby Dick
Oliver Twist
Charlie and the Chocolate Factory

3 ⬦ Mark for Review

In a well-written essay, analyze how the author's use of food contributes to an interpretation of the work as a whole. Do not merely summarize the plot.

In your response you should do the following:

- Respond to the prompt with a thesis that presents a defensible interpretation.
- Provide evidence to support your line of reasoning.
- Explain how the evidence supports your line of reasoning.
- Use appropriate grammar and punctuation in communicating your argument.

STOP
END OF EXAM
IF YOU FINISH BEFORE TIME IS CALLED, YOU MAY CHECK YOUR WORK ON THIS SECTION.

Practice Test 1: Answers and Explanations

PRACTICE TEST 1 ANSWER KEY

1.	A	21.	C	41.	A
2.	C	22.	A	42.	A
3.	D	23.	D	43.	D
4.	A	24.	C	44.	D
5.	B	25.	B	45.	C
6.	D	26.	C	46.	B
7.	B	27.	A	47.	C
8.	C	28.	D	48.	D
9.	B	29.	D	49.	A
10.	D	30.	D	50.	D
11.	C	31.	A	51.	A
12.	C	32.	C	52.	D
13.	D	33.	D	53.	B
14.	A	34.	C	54.	D
15.	C	35.	B	55.	C
16.	C	36.	A		
17.	C	37.	D		
18.	D	38.	A		
19.	B	39.	C		
20.	C	40.	B		

PRACTICE TEST 1 EXPLANATIONS

SECTION I : MULTIPLE CHOICE

Questions 1–13

Phillis Wheatley (1753–1784) spent much of her life enslaved. She was the first African American and second woman (after Anne Bradstreet) to publish a book of poems. Born around 1753 in Gambia, Africa, Wheatley was captured by slave traders and brought to America in 1761. This poem, "On Imagination," was published in *Poems on Various Subjects Religious and Moral* (1773).

1. **A**   "Thy" refers to the personified Imagination. The answer is (A) and not (D). Choices (B) and (C) are not introduced until later in the poem.

2. **C**   The answer is (C), personification. Presenting Imagination as a being who possesses force is a great example of personification. Choice (A) is not correct because synecdoche is a figure of speech where a part represents the whole, so synecdoche is not correct. Choice (B), simile, is a comparison, so that is not correct. Imagery is language that is visually descriptive.

3. **D**   The answer is (D), Imagination allows us to grasp possibilities outside the self. "We can surpass the mind" means Imagination allows us to go beyond ourselves. Do not be confused by (B) because it is not as accurate as (D). Always read all the options before making a choice! Choice (C) is not true because Imagination is not shown to prevent or hinder us, only to inspire, and facilitate aspiration. Choice (A) is the opposite of what is being conveyed.

4. **A**   The answer is (A), onomatopoeia, a word formed from a sound associated from what is being named. Be careful not to fall for (C), alliteration, because of the double "m" sound in murmur. Choice (D) is not correct because anaphora is the repetition of a word at the beginning of successive phrases. Choice (B) does not occur here.

5. **B**   The answer is (B) because the poem is fanciful and even playful, until the end when it takes on a sad tone, as Winter limits Imagination. Choice (A) is not correct because at the end the poem is more sad than regretful. Do not be tempted by (D) because the tone at the end of the poem is not exasperation, which is intense irritation. It is sad, or melancholy. Choice (C) is not evident here at all.

6. **D**   The answer is (D), "Winter grounds Imagination, limiting her ability to rise, to breathe, to soar." Choice (A) is not correct because Winter forbids Imagination to aspire. You can eliminate (B) because Imagination is not uncertain, and does not retreat, but is fettered by Winter. Choice (C) is not correct because Winter and Imagination are opposed to each other.

7. **B** The answer is Choice (B). "Cease the unequal lay" acknowledges the unequal relationship between imagination and reality because Winter imposes itself on Fancy, limiting her. That is why (A) is not correct. Choice (C) is not correct because reality imposes limits that even Imagination cannot surpass. Choice (D) is not correct—reality is not presented as unfair but more powerful than Imagination.

8. **C** Within the poem, the line "Winter forbids me to aspire" answers this question. The speaker seems unable to rise, to breathe, to imagine—Winter grounds her. Thus, the correct answer is (C), grounding her. Choice (D) is not correct—she is not being punished but returned to reality. Choices (A) and (B) are the opposite of what is happening.

9. **B** The answer is (B), rhyming couplets. The first three stanzas have four lines each, and the rhyme scheme for these stanzas is AABB. The final four stanzas have variable line lengths, mostly maintaining the rhyming couplets. In the final stanza, in lines 43–45, there is a rhyming triplet. Choice (A) is not correct because free verse poetry does not rhyme. Choice (C) is not correct because Haiku has a very specific structure of 3 lines of 5, 7, and 5 syllables per line. You can eliminate (D) because an elegy is usually a lament for the dead.

10. **D** The answer is (D), as "silken fetters" and "soft captivity" refer to the hold love has on Fancy. While love is likened to imprisonment, the descriptors "silken" fetters and "soft" captivity are meant to redeem the idea of love, so cross out (A). Choice (B) is not correct because Imagination provides inspiration for Fancy to reach beyond the self. The answer is not (C) because this does not answer the question as accurately as (D). Remember, the most precise option that completely, accurately answers the question is always a stronger pick than the choice that somewhat or vaguely answers the question. Choice (D) it is!

11. **C** Don't be fooled into picking (A) because the language of the poem is more celebratory than contemplative, with lines like "How bright their forms!" Choice (B) is not correct because the poem celebrates the freedom of the mind that makes love possible. Choice (D) is not correct because the poem does not question reality, as much as it acknowledges reality, which, in the poem, is Winter. The answer is (C) Celebrate freedom—the freedom of the mind—which is symbolic of personal freedom.

12. **C** The answer is (C) Imagination fosters creativity and free thought. Note that the quotation in the question stem ("O thou the leader . . . And thine the sceptre o'er the realms of thought") includes the word "thought" in particular. Because of that, (C) should jump out at you. Be careful about (A), as Imagination inspires free thought but does not have control of the mind. Choice (B) is not correct because Imagination does not demand perfection, but offers the opportunity for perfection. Finally, (D) is the opposite of what is being conveyed.

13. **D** Phillis Wheatley constructs a liberated world outside the confines of slavery. Imagination is ultimately topped by Winter's control. Phillis Wheatley lived much of her life as an enslaved person, and she uses the imagination as a vehicle to free the mind and soul, even when the body is fettered. Choice (A) is not correct because a pastoral is about land, (B) is not correct because it does not conform to the length of a sonnet. Choice (C) is not correct because a ballad tells a story. The poem is indeed an allegory about enslaved people, so (D) is the correct answer.

Questions 14–25

Zora Neale Hurston (1891–1960) was a writer, anthropologist, and ethnographer who wrote the classic novel *Their Eyes Were Watching God*. She was a folklorist who recorded cultural history, and was a fixture in New York City's Harlem Renaissance. This passage is an excerpt from Hurston's first published work, the short story *Drenched in Light*, set in 1920's Florida.

14. **A** Helen's concern for and interest in Isis was genuine, so the answer is (A), and not (C). Helen only wanted the company of Isis, so (B) is not correct. Choice (D) is the opposite, so it is not correct.

15. **C** Helen wants access to genuine cultural folk art, Isis's dancing. She pays Grandma five dollars to get permission to take Isis with her to the hotel. She provides the way and the means for Isis to engage in artistic expression. That is why (C) is more accurate than (A) or (B). Don't be confused by (D)—she is not providing salvation for Isis. She, in fact, is in awe of Isis's spirit.

16. **C** The tone of a piece is how it makes you feel. Hopeful means inspiring optimism about a future event. Choices (B) and (D) might be tempting because of Isis and Helen's confrontation with Grandma, but the passage overall is hopeful. And (A) does not apply here.

17. **C** The horizon represents Isis's desire to explore. Don't be confused by (D). While it is partially correct, it is not as specifically correct as (C) and remember, specificity wins the day! Isis has not been anywhere yet, so (B) is not correct. Choice (A) is not correct.

18. **D** Frackshus is Black vernacular for fractious, which means irritable. Don't be tempted by (A) or (B), either of which would describe Grandma's mood. Choice (C) is not accurate here.

19. **B** The wealthy woman seemed to lack joy in her life, a joy that she found in Isis, who lived in poverty. Choice (A) does not entirely capture the sentiment of the line. Always read all the options before making your choice. Choice (C) is the opposite of what the line is conveying, so it can be eliminated straight away.

20. **C** The answer is (C), metaphor. A metaphor is a direct comparison and "Isis is joy itself" is a perfect example of a solid metaphor. A simile is a comparison that uses "like" or "as," so (A) is not correct. Don't be confused by (D)—hyperbole is an exaggerated claim not meant to be taken seriously. When Helen says that Isis is joy itself, she does mean it literally—Isis brings her joy. Choice (B) does not apply here.

21. **C**   Isis's dancing is an example of Black folk art. That the wealthy white woman wants to facilitate Isis' artistic expression is Hurston's (a folklorist) way of equating it with forms of art usually enjoyed by white society. Don't be confused by (B), as the Helen admires Isis for her inner light, which is not dependent on appreciation. Choice (D) might seem tempting, but this option does not capture the sentiment of the cultural exchange between Helen and Isis. Finally, eliminate (A) as it is the opposite sentiment of the line.

22. **A**   When Helen and Isis first get to Grandma's, she's very quarrelsome. After Helen gives her five dollars and explains she would like Isis to come to the hotel with her, Grandma is mollified. That is why (A), belligerent then placated, is correct. Choice (B) is not correct because she does not exhibit signs of being suspicious of Helen, nor fearful of her. Don't be fooled by (C), as Grandma does express some frustration with Isis but that does not encapsulate Grandma's behavior entirely, nor does concerned. Choice (D) is not correct because Grandma is never apathetic (disinterested, indifferent).

23. **D**   Zora Neale Hurston was a folklorist from the South, and she used the Black vernacular to offer a compelling perspective on Black southern culture. Choices (A) and (B) are not as correct as (D). Hurston showcased Black southern culture as rich and nuanced. Choice (C) is not correct because Hurston used the Black vernacular to draw attention to her characters, not to hide them.

24. **C**   Helen told Isis she wanted to save her from getting a beating. One of the things Grandma was so angry about was her ruined tablecloth. So Helen gave her money to pay for the tablecloth and to mollify her and to get her to allow Isis to accompany Helen to the hotel. To mollify is to appease the anger or anxiety of someone—it's a great word to know. Choice (B) is not correct because Grandma did not give Helen directions—Isis did. Choice (A) is not correct because it's beyond the scope of this passage—it is never stated that Grandma wants or needs five tablecloths, or would use the extra money for more tablecloths. Choice (D) is not correct because Helen was not concerned with Grandma's admiration, her concern was saving Isis a beating.

25. **B**   The answer is (B). This requires a close reading of the text, as (A) and (B) both might seem like strong options. Hurston was a major figure in the Harlem Renaissance, and this story is representative of elements of the Harlem Renaissance, with Isis representing the artists, Helen representing wealthy white patrons who supported artists, and Grandma representing the older conservative establishment, like Booker T. Washington, who believed African-Americans should concentrate on vocational and agricultural training.

Questions 26–33

Elizabeth Bishop (1911 - 1979) was a lesbian American lyric poet and short story writer whose poems often featured themes of travel and a detailed and objective point of view. Bishop's poems are often praised for their precision and attention to balance and detail. "One Art" was published in *The New Yorker* in 1976.

26. **C** This question asks about tone. While the overt tone of *One Art* is somewhat careless, as the speaker claims that losing things *is no disaster*, the building size and importance of the lost things she lists shows that she grieves the loss of the person being addressed as *you* most of all. The spirit of the poem centers the speaker trying to find acceptance. Use Process of Elimination to whittle down your choices. *Panic* is not an emotion the speaker conveys, so eliminate (B) and (D). While *loneliness* and *heartbreak* might both describe her grief, *anger* is not conveyed, so eliminate (A). The correct answer is (C).

27. **A** The question asks for an example of personification in the poem: Look at the choices given and use Process of Elimination. Lines 2–3, *so many things seem filled with the intent / to be lost that their loss is no disaster*, gives human *intent* to inanimate objects, so keep (A). Eliminate (B) because lines 4–5, *Accept the fluster / of lost door keys, the hour badly spent*, give no human characteristics to the door keys: the fluster belongs to the listener. Similarly, in lines 7–9, *Then practice losing farther, losing faster: / places, and names, and where it was you meant / to travel*, there aren't any human characteristics given to objects, just a list of things lost and the suggestion to try losing things oneself: you can eliminate (C). In lines 13–14, *I lost two cities, lovely ones. And, vaster, / some realms I owned, two rivers, a continent*, the speaker uses exaggeration but no personification, so eliminate (D) as well. The correct answer is (A).

28. **D** The question asks which literary device the speaker uses in the line *And, vaster, / some realms owned, two rivers, a continent*. Eliminate (A) because there are no human characteristics given to the inanimate objects mentioned. Eliminate (C) for a similar reason: though exaggerated, the items she lists are just places and things, not symbols for anything else. Though the poem is full of repetition, it's not being used here: eliminate (B). The correct answer is (D), hyperbole: exaggeration or deliberate overstatement. It's unlikely that she owned and then lost whole realms, rivers, and continents, though the places she's lost may have felt that encompassing to her.

29. **D** This question asks for the central contrast of the poem. You should be able to recognize that it's something to do with the emotions she conveys: the overt tone is carelessness, but by the end the poem conveys a deep loss. Choice (D) is a good contender: the speaker repeats that each loss is *no disaster* but uses *the growing size and importance of the lost items* to convey her pain. You can eliminate (B) because it contains one part that isn't mentioned in the poem: the re*lief of finding them again*. Eliminate (C) because it contradicts the poem's message when it says that she felt *relief* when she lost someone. Compare (A) and (D): the contrast isn't between the different losses she experiences, but between her emotions about her loss. Eliminate (A). The correct answer is (D).

30. **D** This question asks about structure: specifically, how *the list of lost things* adds to that structure. You should notice that the list builds in order of importance, but even if you missed that you can use Process of Elimination here. Eliminate (A) and (B) because t*he list of lost things* is part of the structure of the poem, not a distraction. Since (C) and (D) both start with the same idea (*the list of lost things builds in order of importance*), compare the rest of each choice. Something is being *highlighted* or *emphasized*: is it *the loss of her home* or the loss of the person referred to as *"you"*? Logic dictates that if the lost items are being listed in order of importance, it should be the final one, *"you,"* that's the most important. Eliminate (C): the correct answer is (D).

31. **A** The question asks what *the lost door keys* are a symbol of. Since they are early in the poem (line 5), they are part of the poet's introduction to the idea that losing things isn't difficult. Eliminate (C) because there simply isn't any evidence that they are *the first thing the speaker ever lost*. Eliminate (B) and (D) because she doesn't bring up her more *painful* and *important* losses until later in the poem. The correct answer is (A), *something the loss of which is not too painful to cope with*.

32. **C** Since this question contains the word EXCEPT, strike it out and answer the question without it: which of the choices *contribute to the emotional effect of the poem*? Eliminate any choice that does contribute. Eliminate (A), as the parenthetical statement *(Write it!)* in line 19 is a command full of emotional turmoil, as the speaker forces herself to admit that she's a mess. Eliminate (B) as well, because *practice losing farther, losing faster* conveys the struggle the speaker faces when she tries to accept her greater losses. Eliminate (D) because *the structure of the list of lost things* builds up the emotion in the poem by increasing in importance and impact. The correct answer is (C), because *the contrast between things lost and things found again* is not present in the poem.

33. **D** The question asks for *a possible meaning of the parenthetical statement "(Write it!)"* from the last line of the poem. Since the speaker does *write it*, the command must be directed at herself, eliminating (A) and (C). Since what she tells herself to write is *disaster*, not the list of lost things, eliminate (B). Choice (D), *exhorting herself to admit the pain she is trying to accept*, fits with the tone of the poem.

Questions 34–45

Edgar Allan Poe (1809–1849), one of the best-known and most widely anthologized U.S. authors, wrote short stories, poetry, and criticism. His "The Murders in the Rue Morgue" is considered the first detective story. This passage is an excerpt from "The Masque of the Red Death," which exemplifies nineteenth-century horror and the macabre. It was published in 1842.

34. **C** This makes the disease seem like an angry person full of hatred, so the correct answer is (C), personification. Be careful of (A), hyperbole: exaggerated statements not meant to be taken literally. Make sure to read all options before making your choice as there may be an option that more accurately answers the question and as we have gone over, specificity and accuracy are the name of the game. Choices (B) simile and (D) alliteration do not occur here.

35. **B** The answer is (B). The Prince chose a thousand friends from the aristocracy to safely sequester in his castle, with no concern for anyone with lower status. The healthy members of the aristocracy were handpicked by the Prince and then protected in his castle. That is why the answer is not (A). Don't be tempted by (D) because while the castle was secure, that was not the point of the passage. Choice (C) is the opposite of what the passage is conveying.

36. **A** The answer is (A), the Prince and his guests do not care about the rest of the country because they decided that the rest of the world was not worth worrying about, literally. They were taking care of themselves—everyone else was on their own. The scene brings to mind the quotation attributed to Marie Antoinette during the French Revolution: "let them eat cake." That is like the Prince's attitude, selfish and tone-deaf. We already know that the country has lost half its population to the Red Death, so the answer is not (B). The gates around the castle are welded shut to keep the guests in and the Red Death and the rest of the world out. So the answer is not (C). The Prince had no concern for the world outside his castle, so the answer is not (D).

37. **D** The tone of a passage is the author's feelings about a subject. "Ominous" means giving the impression that something unfortunate is going to happen. Poe creates a feeling of uneasiness that something terrible is waiting ahead, so (D) is your best bet. The answer is not (B) or (C) because the tone of the story is gravely serious, not humorous, ironic, or satirical. The answer is not (A) because the author never relents from the feeling of uneasiness—we do not see any hope. Choice (D), ominous, it is.

38. **A** The answer is (A), The passage of time in life is inevitable. Time is a metaphor for mortality. The seven rooms represent the seven stages of life, with the seventh chamber—the one cloaked in black—representing death. The clock was on the western wall, symbolically where the sun sets. Choice (B) is not correct because the guests are very concerned about their mortality—that's why they are sequestered in the castle. Choice (C) might seem appealing, but don't fall for that one—it does not answer the question as accurately as (A). Choice (D) is not correct because time represents mortality, and is very important.

39.   **C**   The answer is (C) because this establishes the Red Death as the driving force of the story. When reading, be sure to notice the order in which elements are presented and the amount of text or space given to certain items—they can reveal clues about importance. Here, everything in the story happens because of the Red Death. The Prince is the main character, but the Red Death is the driving force behind the story. Do not be fooled by (A) or (B) because neither of them answers the question as accurately as (C) and accuracy and specificity are crucial. Choice (D) is not correct because Prince Prospero is the main character.

40.   **B**   The answer is (B): Imagery is language that invokes a visual or other kind of sense impression. A metaphor is when a word is applied to a subject to which it is not literally applicable—(C) is not correct. Simile is a comparison, so (A) is not correct. Choice (D) does not occur here.

41.   **A**   Each answer choice has 2 adjectives, and both must apply to this character (half wrong is all wrong, as we say). Choices (B) through (D) are all positive traits. But after reading the passage, we know that Prince Prospero was mostly concerned with his own well-being and that of very few of his court, so we don't think of him in a positive light. Choice (A), self-centered and uncaring, is the only choice that aligns with what we have read, so it's correct.

42.   **A**   The seventh room, draped in black, with scarlet windows that created "ghastly" effects on the guests who entered reminded guests of the Red Death, so (A) should call to you as the correct answer. It is not (C) because it does not answer the question as accurately and precisely as (A). Choices (B) and (D) are not implied in context.

43.   **D**   The answer is (D). Choice (A) is not correct because the party and the rooms are metaphors for mortality. Choice (B) is not correct because the seven colors of the rainbow (commonly referred to as ROYGBIV) are not all represented here. Choice (C) is not correct because the character traits such as greed, gluttony, and vanity are evident in the revelers, rather than in the rooms. The only answer it could be is (D). The seven stages of life with the colored rooms representing, going east to west, birth (blue), childhood (purple), adolescence (green), adulthood (orange), old-age (white), imminent death (violet), and death (black).

44.   **D**   The answer is (D). The purpose of the party is to forget the fatal disease raging beyond the castle walls. The clock was a constant reminder that time waits for no one. It was a constant reminder of mortality. Choice (A) is not correct because the guests at the party were carefully selected from a specific group of people by the Prince, much as the rooms were carefully ordered and decorated. Choice (B) is not correct because the guests were not unconcerned—the party is to distract them from the looming threat of death. Eliminate (C) because we don't know how the guests have ordered themselves within the rooms.

45. **C** The answer is (C): Death is inevitable. The last room is representative of the final stage of a person's life—death. And the scarlet windows in the room produce an effect on the face not unlike the Red Death itself, the very threat the party guests are sequestering themselves from. The message here is that all their efforts are futile; death is inevitable. Choices (A) and (B) do not answer the question as accurately as (C). Make sure to read all the options before making your choice. Choice (D) is not correct because the author is warning that death might be within the castle walls.

Questions 46–55

Erin Morgenstern (b. 1978) is an American multimedia artist and the author of two novels. This passage is an excerpt from *The Night Circus*, which was published in 2011 and won the Locus Award for Best First Novel.

46. **B** The answer is (B), Hector values Celia's skill more than he values her life. He exhibits a blatant disregard for her life, as he is willing to risk it. You may be tempted to choose (C) or (D), but those do not accurately encapsulate the sentiment of the line. Choice (A) does not apply here.

47. **C** The answer is (C), rivals. This entire encounter sets up a new challenge between them. Though (B) and (C) may also seem tempting, they are not as accurate. In this passage, there is no evidence that (A) is accurate.

48. **D** This requires an interpretive reading of the lines. The idea that Celia can so easily manipulate a timepiece, even shatter it, symbolizes the manipulation of time (D). While (B) and (C) are partially true, neither accurately sum up these lines. Choice (A) is not accurate.

49. **A** The answer is (A), Celia has now been permanently committed to the challenge. The metal burning into her skin is almost like a form of branding. You may have been tempted by (B) but that is not correct as it would be a few steps ahead of what is happening here—it's not what is happening in this moment. And (D) is also not correct because it was not Celia's magic that affected the ring. Finally, (C) does not apply here.

50. **D** The tone of this passage is (D), foreboding. The tone of a piece is the mood it evokes or the way it makes you feel. Foreboding means a strong sense of future misfortune. Melancholy (C) does not accurately describe this encounter as a whole. Choices (A) and (B) are not evident here—there is nothing light, fun, or romantic about this passage.

51. **A** The answer is (A), order versus chaos. This theme is evident in how concerned each of them is with the idea of impulsive behavior and then control. Don't be confused by (B) and (D) as neither pride nor love accurately describe Hector's feelings towards Celia. And (C) does not describe either man's attitude correctly.

52.   **D**   The man is impressed by Celia's control at her very young age but then expresses concern that her temper could result in impulsiveness; he is aware that with years and lessons, she will only get more powerful, and harder to control. Choice (A) is not correct because Hector and the man in the gray suit certainly do both understand the seriousness of what they are talking about. Choice (C) is not correct because neither man is concerned if harm comes to Celia. Choice (B) does not answer this question as accurately as (D) and we always go for accuracy. Read and consider all the options before making your choice.

53.   **B**   Synecdoche (B) means that a part is made to represent the whole, which is what we see here ("suit" stands for business executive). Metonymy is a lot like synecdoche but slightly different—it is the substitution of the name of the attribute for that of the thing meant (for example, referring to the President and their administration as "the White House") which isn't happening here, so (C) is not correct. Hyperbole is an exaggeration, not meant to be taken literally and that does not accurately describe this sentence, so (A) is out. Finally, (D) does not occur here.

54.   **D**   Hector and the man in the gray suit are concealing their words, and Celia should be wary (D). While Celia is very young, and not yet able to understand the ramifications of this challenge, that is not why she cannot understand them, so (A) is not correct. There may be some truth to (B) but that does not encapsulate the entire meaning of these lines. Though it says "Celia frowns," that is not to imply that she is sad but to illustrate her consternation at not being able to understand their words, so (C) is not correct.

55.   **C**   Hector is shown being solicitous towards Celia, while at the same time offering to risk her life to win the challenge. That is why (C), duplicitous (treacherous, deceitful) is correct. You may read some condescension in the passage with regards to Hector's parenting but (D) is not wholly accurate, nor is (A) pitying. Choice (B) is not accurate here.

SECTION II: FREE RESPONSE

Rubric—1 + 4 + 1 = 6 pts

A. Thesis (0–1 pts)
  - Responds to the prompt with a thesis that presents a defensible interpretation of the selected work.
B. Evidence and Commentary (0–4 pts)
  - Evidence: Provides specific evidence to support all claims in a line of reasoning.
  - Commentary: Consistently explains how the evidence supports a line of reasoning.
  - Explains how multiple literary elements or techniques in the poem contribute to its meaning.
C. Sophistication (0–1 pts)
  - Demonstrates sophistication of thought and/or develops a complex literary argument.

How to Score 6 points

Use The Idea Machine! The questions listed below will direct your reading to the material needed to write an essay.

The Idea Machine

1. What is the meaning of the work?
   a. What is the literal, face-value meaning of the work?
   b. What feeling (or feelings) does the work evoke?
2. How does the author get that meaning across?
   a. What are the important images in the work and what do those images suggest?
   b. What specific words or short phrases produce the strongest feelings?
   c. What do the characters, setting, structure, or narrators tell you about the passage?

Question 1—Poetry Analysis

- What is the meaning of the work?

  o Literal meaning: This is a picture of me right after I drowned. You'll have to look hard, but you can see me.

  o Feeling conveyed: A slow build-up to a horrifying revelation

- How does the author get that meaning across?

  o Images and phrases to underline:

    - "a smeared print: blurred lines and grey flecks"
    - "a thing that is like a branch"
    - "what ought to be a gentle slope"
    - "there is a lake"
    - "the effect of water on light is a distortion"

  o What do those words and phrases suggest?

    - At first these impart confusion. The reader expects a picture of a person: Why is it a blurry smear? Why is it a landscape with a house? Why does the speaker describe it so ambiguously?
    - The lake at first seems like a peaceful landscape. Once it is paired with "I drowned. I am in the lake," it becomes horrible.

  o What do the characters, setting, structure, or narrators tell you about the passage?

    - Speaker: The speaker of the poem is dead
    - Setting: Peaceful setting in opposition to the scene being described
    - Structure: The poem is neatly divided into two parts—the slightly strange description of a blurry landscape (we don't yet know the person is dead) versus the revelation that they are dead paired with a sort of desperation to be seen (in the parenthetical part).

Sample first paragraph

Margaret Atwood's "This Is a Photograph of Me" plays with the reader's expectations, slowly revealing that, rather than a photograph that centers a person, alive, this photograph is of the speaker shortly after they drowned in a lake. The way the poem begins with hesitant, ambiguous description; the confusion of what's being described—a landscape rather than a person; the matter-of-fact presentation; and the juxtaposition of the simple, peaceful scene with the raw truth of how the speaker died combine to give a chilling, desperate tone. The speaker seems to have no message other than the compulsion to have their death be recognized, which adds to the feeling of talking to a ghost.

Question 2—Prose Fiction Analysis

- What is the meaning of the work?
  - o Literal meaning:
    - Most people try to avoid blame by putting it on others or remaining ignorant. Specifically, she's talking about exploitation in Africa.
    - She would be no different, if she hadn't learned better during her time there.
    - That exploitation came about because of the attitude she and other people had: that the world revolved around them; that Africa was "unformed"; that they deserved to have "dominion over every creature that moved upon the earth."
  - o Feelings conveyed: guilt, pride, shame, and responsibility
- How does the author get that meaning across?
  - o Images and phrases to underline:
    - "walked out on Africa as a husband quits a wife, leaving her with her naked body curled around the emptied-out mine of her womb"
    - "I trod on Africa without a thought"
    - "I'd slide this awful story off my shoulders, flatten it, sketch out our crimes like a failed battle plan and shake it in the faces of my neighbors"
    - "Africa shifts under my hands, refusing to be party to failed relations"
    - "we stepped down there on a place we believed unformed, where only darkness moved on the face of the waters"
  - o What do those words and phrases suggest?
    - The simile is used to describe how profiteers exploited Africa, then left it behind.
    - "I" statements are used to introduce feelings of guilt and shame.
    - The metaphor suggests a desire to rid herself of blame.
    - The personification of Africa as an entity that forces the writer to take responsibility for her actions
    - The imagery shows how the writer and others like her saw Africa.
  - o What do the characters, setting, structure, or narrators tell you about the passage?
    - Narrator: The first-person point of view allows the author to take personal responsibility and explore her own emotions
    - Setting: The topic, Africa, is the only setting mentioned—this takes the reader out of a specific time and place, instead embedding you in the narrator's memories.
    - Structure: The passage is filled with opposition: profiteering and exploitation versus "a snow white conscience"; the internal conflict inherent in the desire to escape responsibility; who the author was and what she believed versus how she feels about it now.

Sample first paragraph

What happens when the carefree attitudes of youth become something to be ashamed of in maturity? Barbara Kingsolver's *The Poisonwood Bible* deals in heavy-hitting imagery that evokes strong emotions: The author's memories of her own ignorance and pride—her having "trod on Africa without a thought"—are juxtaposed against her later guilt and shame. She calls out the "habits of mind" that lead people to attempt to avoid responsibility for their actions, and admits that she would do so as well if she could: but her time in Africa has taught her better. She looks back with shame on the attitudes she and others had and their expectation that they would "have dominion over every creature that moved upon the earth." Although she asks "But what else could we have thought?" it is clear that she has learned enough to lament her earlier arrogance and ignorance.

Question 3—Literary Argument

(This example uses C.S. Lewis's *The Lion, the Witch, and the Wardrobe*.)

- What is the meaning of the work?
  - Literal meaning:
    - Four siblings find a fantasy land called Narnia in a wardrobe, travel there, and discover a terrible war taking place against an evil witch who turns creatures to stone when she is displeased and keeps the land in perpetual winter. One of the siblings betrays the others but, through faith and the sacrifice of the God-figure Aslan, he is redeemed and the children win a war against the Witch, freeing Narnia and restoring peace.

- How does the author get that meaning across?
  - Major themes in the work:
    - Christian allegory for the redemption of humankind by Jesus—Edmund "sins" by accepting forbidden food (Turkish delight) from the Witch and betraying his siblings. His life is forfeit until Aslan sacrifices himself for him. This act expunges Edmund's sin and rights the balance of the world in Narnia, ending the Witch's reign and the winter.
  - Theme related to the question: Food
    - Turkish delight as temptation/a parallel for original sin
    - Lucy eating with Mr. Tumnus and the meal prepared by the Beavers happen in an atmosphere of friendship, community, and faith
    - The tea tray that Father Christmas brings to the Pevensies and the Beavers represents a meal as a celebration, and the return of Christmas a return of faith and hope
    - The fact that the White Witch is never shown to eat anything marks her as different from the rest of the creatures and inherently untrustworthy
  - Important scenes/imagery:
    - Long descriptions of meals (both the food itself and the stories and companionship that accompany them), including the delightful tea with Mr. Tumnus, the enchanted Turkish delight accompanied by the Witch's interrogation of Edmund, and the meals with the Beavers and Father Christmas

Sample first paragraph

In C.S. Lewis's *The Lion, the Witch, and the Wardrobe*, food is both a symbol of faith and community and a symbol of temptation and sin. The author uses long and delightful descriptions of meals shared by Lucy and Mr. Tumnus, and later the Pevensie children and the Beavers, to introduce the faith and culture of Narnia and the inherent goodness in its creatures. He juxtaposes this with the temptation offered Edmund by the White Witch in the form of Turkish delight: an enchanted offering meant to ensnare and enslave. The fact that the Witch herself is never seen to eat marks her as untrustworthy and separate from the good Narnians. Aslan's later sacrifice, resulting in the freeing of Narnia from the Witch's perpetual winter, is prefigured by the arrival of Father Christmas, who brings gifts and food in a symbolic returning of the sustenance of faith to Narnia.

HOW TO SCORE PRACTICE TEST 1

Section I: Multiple Choice

$$\underline{\hspace{3cm}} \times 1.2273 = \underline{\hspace{3cm}}$$

Number Correct
(out of 55)

Weighted
Section I Score
(Do not round)

Section II: Free Response

(See whether you can find a teacher or classmate to score your essays using the guidelines in Chapter 5.)

Note: this score conversion chart should only be used as an estimate.

Question 1: $\underline{\hspace{2cm}} \times 4.5833 = \underline{\hspace{2cm}}$
(out of 6)   (Do not round)

Question 2: $\underline{\hspace{2cm}} \times 4.5833 = \underline{\hspace{2cm}}$
(out of 6)   (Do not round)

Question 3: $\underline{\hspace{2cm}} \times 4.5833 = \underline{\hspace{2cm}}$
(out of 6)   (Do not round)

AP Score Conversion Chart English Literature and Composition

Composite Score Range	AP Score
107–150	5
90–106	4
73–89	3
56–72	2
0–55	1

Sum = $\underline{\hspace{3cm}}$

Weighted Section II
Score (Do not round)

Composite Score

$$\underline{\hspace{2.5cm}} + \underline{\hspace{2.5cm}} = \underline{\hspace{2.5cm}}$$

Weighted
Section I Score

Weighted
Section II Score

Composite Score
(Round to nearest
whole number)

Part III
About the AP English Literature and Composition Exam

- The Structure of the AP English Literature and Composition Exam
- The AP English Literature and Composition Exam Is Fully Digital
- How the AP English Literature and Composition Exam Is Scored
- Overview of Content Topics
- How AP Exams Are Used
- Other Resources
- Designing Your Study Plan

THE STRUCTURE OF THE AP ENGLISH LITERATURE AND COMPOSITION EXAM

Test Date: Early May
Total Time: 3 hours (usually administered at 8:00 A.M.)

Section I: Multiple Choice (60 minutes)—45% of your grade
Total number of questions: 55
You will see 5 passages and/or poems and between 8–13 questions per passage/poem, for a total of 55 multiple-choice questions.

Section II: Free Response (120 minutes)—55% of your grade
Three Essays:
1. Poetry Analysis (40-minute essay on a single poem or comparison of two poems, which will be provided to you)
2. Prose Fiction Analysis (40-minute essay on a story, novel excerpt, or essay that is provided to you)
3. Literary Argument (40-minute essay on a given literary topic, supported by the reading)

Take Your Digital Tests Online
Register your book at princetonreview.com/prep to access your Digital Practice Tests 4 and 5 via your Student Tools.

THE AP ENGLISH LITERATURE AND COMPOSITION EXAM IS FULLY DIGITAL

College Board announced that beginning in May 2025 the AP English Literature and Composition exam will be conducted digitally. To take the exam, students must have access to College Board's Bluebook testing app, available for Windows, Apple, tablets, and Chromebooks. If your computer or tablet is owned or managed by your school, then a school official will likely have to install this app for you if it is not already on it. The test cannot be taken on a smartphone.

The testing app will allow you to annotate and highlight texts, eliminate answers, and flag questions for review later. You will also have access to scratch paper to plan responses to essay questions. Unlike other digital exams like the SAT, the digital AP exam will NOT be adaptive: this means that the difficulty of questions will not change depending on how well you do on earlier sections of the test.

With this change, it is important to note that the digital exam includes the same number of sections, number and types of questions, and timing as the paper exam. This means the strategies used for success on paper versions of the AP English Literature and Composition exam are just as applicable to the digital version. So don't worry, the practice tests in this book will still prepare you for test day.

For the latest information regarding the digital AP exams and testing accommodations, visit the College Board website at apcentral.collegeboard.org/exam-administration-ordering-scores/digital-ap-exams.

The Big Six and You

The AP English Literature and Composition course description content reflects content from the AP course, including the big ideas that undergird the questions you ask of all the literature you study. We're going to call the six big ideas the Big Six. The Big Six are concepts that enable you to study and understand literature—and to write about it. Five of the Big Six are elements of literature. The sixth is how you take the five elements and analyze literature yourself.

Let's review the Big Six. They are:

Character. Characters in literature show a wide range of values, beliefs, assumptions, biases, and cultural norms, and provide an opportunity to study and explore what the characters represent.

Setting. A setting and the details associated with it represent a time and place, but also convey values associated with the setting.

Structure. Structure refers to the arrangements of sections and parts of a text, the relationship of the parts to each other, and the sequence in which the text reveals information. These are all choices made by a writer that allow you to interpret a text.

Narration. Any narrator's or speaker's perspective controls the details and emphases that readers encounter; therefore, narration affects how readers experience and interpret a text.

Figurative language. Comparisons, representations, and associations shift meaning from the literal to the figurative. Figurative language can include word choice, imagery, and symbols. Simile, metaphor, personification, and allusions are all examples of figurative language.

Literary argumentation. How do you write about literature yourself? You develop your interpretation (using the first five of the Big Six!) and then communicate it. You need to develop a thesis—a defensible claim—and support it with textual evidence.

The multiple-choice section of the AP English Literature and Composition exam will be testing your knowledge of the Big Six. Each one is weighted a certain amount in the multiple-choice questions.

You are evaluated on your knowledge of the Big Six throughout the Exam. For the multiple-choice section, for example, you are evaluated on seven skill categories that map very closely to the Big Six. (Two of the skill categories, 5 and 6, are covered under Figurative Language, one of the Big Six.) The weighting is shown below.

Stay Up to Date!
For late-breaking information about test dates, exam formats, and any other changes pertaining to AP English Literature and Composition, make sure to check the College Board's website at apstudents. collegeboard.org/courses/ ap-english-literature-and-composition

Skill Category	Exam Weighting
1: Explain the function of character	16–20%
2: Explain the function of setting	3–6%
3: Explain the function of plot and structure	16–20%
4: Explain the function of the narrator or speaker	21–26%
5: Explain the function of word choice, imagery, and symbols	10–13%
6: Explain the function of comparison	10–13%
7: Develop textually substantiated arguments about interpretations of part or all of a text	10–13%

Who Writes the Exam?

The initial content for the exam is generally gathered by an AP Development Committee that is equally made up of high school and college teachers. This ensures that the material presented on the test falls within the range of topics associated with the course itself. Once those topics and questions have been written, however, they are often fine-tuned by professional test designers who work to keep the test, especially the multiple-choice section, similar to previous administrations. This is actually an asset to you, since that stability also adds a degree of predictability to the ways in which questions are shaped and wrong answers are selected. On multiple-choice tests, knowing how the wrong answers are written and how they can be eliminated is key. We'll discuss this topic in detail in Part IV, Chapter 4.

HOW THE AP ENGLISH LITERATURE AND COMPOSITION EXAM IS SCORED

What Your Final Score Means

After taking the test in early May, you will receive your scores sometime around the first week of July, which is right about when you've just started to forget about the whole experience. Your score will be, simply enough, a single number from 1 to 5. Here is what those numbers mean:

Score	2024 Percentage	Credit Recommendation	College Grade Equivalent
5	13.7%	Extremely Well Qualified	A
4	26.9%	Well qualified	A–, B+, B
3	31.8%	Qualified	B–, C+, C
2	16.5%	Possibly Qualified	N/A
1	11.1%	No Recommendation	N/A

Scores from May 2024 AP Exam administration. Data taken from the College Board website.

Your Multiple-Choice Score

In the multiple-choice section of the test, you receive one point for each question you answer correctly. You receive no points for a question you leave blank or answer incorrectly. That is, the famous "guessing penalty" on some standardized tests does not exist here. So, if you are completely unsure, guess. However, it is always best to use Process of Elimination (POE, as discussed in Chapter 4) to narrow down your choices and make an educated guess.

Your Essay Score

Each AP essay in the Free Response section is scored on a scale from 0 to 6, with 6 being the highest score. Each AP Reader (a high school or college-level English teacher) is given a precise rubric to guide their grading of the essay. Gone are the days of vague, "holistic" scoring—we're using scoring rubrics now!

The rubrics can be downloaded from the College Board's website, but here is a summary of how all 3 essay question types will be graded using this 6-point scale:

Thesis: 0–1 point

Evidence and Commentary: 0–4 points

Sophistication: 0–1 point

Essay Scoring Rubrics
You will see the scoring rubrics in Chapter 5, in the section **All About Essay Scoring**.

In essence, your essays must include a clear thesis, evidence to buttress your thesis (and commentary about that evidence). In addition, they must possess sophistication, which essentially means that you develop a complex literary argument. We will explore this in depth in Chapter 5.

Your Final Score

Your final 1 to 5 score is a combination of your section scores. Remember that the multiple-choice section counts for 45 percent of the total and the essays count for 55 percent. While this proportion makes them almost equal, they are not entirely equal. A somewhat convoluted mathematical formula is applied to arrive at your score.

Neither you nor the colleges you apply to will ever know your individual section scores on your AP Exam—the College Board doesn't share that information. You get a final AP exam score between 1 and 5, and that's it. In the immortal words of elementary school teachers everywhere, "you get what you get and you don't get upset." (Because you're going to crush this exam, dear reader!)

Does this mean you don't need to think about how your multiple-choice and essay scores combine? No. You should get a feel for how your multiple-choice score affects your final, total score.

Look at the overall test as two separate assessments:

> Multiple Choice: 55 questions; 45% of the overall score
>
> Free Response: 3 essays, each scored on a 0 to 6 scale; 55% of the overall score

The cutoff point for each grade varies from year to year and is set only after all the multiple-choice sections and essays have been scored. Regardless, a good bottom-line goal is to get at least 30 questions right on the multiple-choice sections and to earn at least 12 points on the essays. These two scores will net you a final passing grade of 3. Increases in either category can increase your final scores. The grading scale for the AP English Literature and Composition Exam looks something like this:

Essay Points	12	14	16	18
MC Points				
20	3	3	4	5
25	3	4	4	5
30	4	4	5	5
35	4	4	5	5
40	4	5	5	5
45	5	5	5	5
50	5	5	5	5
55	5	5	5	5

Conclusions

1. The bottom-line goal for a student aiming for a 4 is a 30 on the multiple-choice section, or a little more than half. The bottom-line goal on the essays is the minimum passing score on each essay, 4 ($3 \times 4 = 12$).
2. Set realistic goals for yourself. Look what happens if your multiple-choice score stays at 25 while you raise your essays one point each (from a 12 to a 14): You go from a 3 to a 4!

The average score is a 3, but earning a 5 is possible, even if you scored only within the 20 to 35 range on the multiple-choice section.

Now let's start practicing ways for you to get your best possible score.

Pacing Chart for AP English Literature and Composition Exam				
My Score on Practice	Shooting for Minimum of	Time Spent	Must Get Right	Guess
————	30 of 55	60 mins	30	25

The AP English Literature and Composition Exam is unlike other AP Exams in one other factor: time. The multiple-choice section is always one hour long. Be sure to visit your online Student Tools and/or the College Board's website for any additional or updated rubrics.

While you are getting the feel of the passages and the kinds of questions, take all the time you need. Your purpose, after all, is different at this stage, as you are familiarizing yourself with the process. Later, when you are practicing for the real experience, limit your time to precisely one hour.

Remember—you can guess. Look at it this way:

Time: 1 hour
Practice Test of 55 questions

This Is An Example
The chart right here is just an example of what you might see on test day. We know there will be 5 passages/poems and 8–13 questions per passage/poem.

Passage/Poem	Number of Questions	Number to Get Right	Number to Guess On
1	8	6	25 (from any section)
2	13	6	
3	10	6	
4	13	6	
5	13	6	

30 total (from any section)

Use a chart like this one to evaluate your performance when practicing:

The Time Factor			
Time Evenly Divided	Time I Spent	Time Shooting For	Number to Get Right
_____	_____	_____	_____

OVERVIEW OF CONTENT TOPICS

There is not a required reading list for the AP English Literature and Composition Exam, but the College Board provides a list of authors and poets with whom you should be familiar and whose work is of the caliber and density that you are expected to understand. They can be works written in, or translated into, English. Their list includes many of the following, plus we have included our recommended writers, as well.

Poetry

- John Ashbery
- W. H. Auden
- Amiri Baraka
- John Berryman
- Elizabeth Bishop
- William Blake
- Anne Bradstreet
- Edward Kamau Brathwaite
- Gwendolyn Brooks
- Robert Browning
- George Gordon, Lord Byron
- Lorna Dee Cervantes
- Geoffrey Chaucer
- Lucille Clifton
- Samuel Taylor Coleridge
- Billy Collins
- Gregory Corso
- Robert Creeley

Poetry (continued)

- Countee Cullen
- E.E. Cummings
- H. D. (Hilda Doolittle)
- Emily Dickinson
- John Donne
- Rita Dove
- John Dryden
- Paul Laurence Dunbar
- T. S. Eliot
- Lawrence Ferlinghetti
- Robert Frost
- Allen Ginsberg
- Barbara Guest
- Joy Harjo
- Seamus Heaney
- George Herbert
- Garrett Hongo
- Gerard Manley Hopkins
- Langston Hughes
- Ben Jonson
- John Keats
- Kenneth Koch
- Philip Larkin
- Denise Levertov
- Robert Lowell
- Andrew Marvell

- Claude McKay
- John Milton
- Marianne Moore
- Frank O'Hara
- Charles Olson
- Sylvia Plath
- Edgar Allan Poe
- Alexander Pope
- Ezra Pound
- Adrienne Rich
- Sonia Sanchez
- Anne Sexton
- William Shakespeare
- Ntozake Shange
- Percy Bysshe Shelley
- Leslie Marmon Silko
- Gary Snyder
- Cathy Song
- Wallace Stevens
- Alfred, Lord Tennyson
- Derek Walcott
- Walt Whitman
- Richard Wilbur
- William Carlos Williams
- William Wordsworth
- William Butler Yeats

Drama

- Aeschylus
- Edward Albee
- Amiri Baraka
- Samuel Beckett
- Anton Chekhov
- Caryl Churchill
- William Congreve
- Athol Fugard
- Lorraine Hansberry
- Lillian Hellman
- David Henry Hwang
- Henrik Ibsen
- Ben Jonson
- David Mamet
- Arthur Miller
- Molière

- Marsha Norman
- Sean O'Casey
- Eugene O'Neill
- Suzan-Lori Parks
- Harold Pinter
- Luigi Pirandello
- William Shakespeare
- George Bernard Shaw
- Sam Shepard
- Neil Simon
- Sophocles
- Tom Stoppard
- Luis Valdez
- Oscar Wilde
- Tennessee Williams
- August Wilson

Fiction (Novel and Short Story)

- Chinua Achebe
- Chimamanda Ngozi Adichie
- Sherman Alexie
- Isabel Allende
- Rudolfo Anaya
- Margaret Atwood
- Jane Austen
- James Baldwin
- Saul Bellow
- Charlotte Brontë
- Emily Brontë
- William S. Burroughs
- Octavia E. Butler
- Raymond Carver
- Willa Cather
- John Cheever
- Kate Chopin
- Sandra Cisneros
- Joseph Conrad
- Edwidge Danticat
- Daniel Defoe
- Anita Desai
- Charles Dickens
- Fyodor Dostoevsky
- George Eliot
- Ralph Ellison
- Louise Erdrich
- William Faulkner
- Henry Fielding
- F. Scott Fitzgerald
- E. M. Forster
- Charles Frazier
- John Gay
- Yaa Gyasi
- Mohsin Hamid
- Thomas Hardy
- Nathaniel Hawthorne
- Ernest Hemingway
- Oscar Hijuelos
- Brandon Hobson
- Khaled Hosseini
- Victor Hugo
- Zora Neale Hurston
- Kazuo Ishiguro
- Henry James
- Ha Jin
- Edward P. Jones
- James Joyce
- Jack Kerouac
- Porochista Khakpour
- Barbara Kingsolver
- Maxine Hong Kingston
- Joy Kogawa
- Jhumpa Lahiri
- Nella Larsen
- Margaret Laurence
- D. H. Lawrence
- Chang-rae Lee
- Bernard Malamud
- Gabriel García Márquez
- Cormac McCarthy
- Ian McEwan
- Herman Melville
- Toni Morrison
- Bharati Mukherjee
- Vladimir Nabokov
- Flannery O'Connor
- Orhan Pamuk
- Katherine Anne Porter
- Marilynne Robinson
- Sir Walter Scott
- Samuel Selvon
- Leslie Marmon Silko
- Jonathan Swift
- Amy Tan
- Mark Twain
- John Updike
- Luis Alberto Urrea
- Alice Walker
- Evelyn Waugh
- Eudora Welty
- Edith Wharton
- John Edgar Wideman
- Virginia Woolf
- Richard Wright

Expository Prose

- Joseph Addison
- Gloria Anzaldua
- Matthew Arnold
- James Baldwin
- James Boswell
- Jesús Colón
- Joan Didion
- Frederick Douglass
- W. E. B. Du Bois
- Ralph Waldo Emerson
- William Hazlitt
- bell hooks
- Samuel Johnson
- Charles Lamb
- Thomas Macaulay
- Mary McCarthy
- John Stuart Mill
- George Orwell
- Michael Pollan
- Richard Rodriguez
- Edward Said
- Lewis Thomas
- Henry David Thoreau
- E. B. White
- Virginia Woolf

HOW AP EXAMS ARE USED

Different colleges use AP Exam scores in different ways, so it is important that you go to a particular college's website to determine how it uses AP Exam scores. The three items below represent the main ways in which AP Exam scores can be used.

- **College Credit**. Some colleges will give you college credit if you score well on an AP Exam. These credits count toward your graduation requirements, meaning that you can take fewer courses while in college. Given the cost of college, this could be quite a benefit.
- **Satisfy Requirements**. Some colleges will allow you to "place out" of certain requirements if you do well on an AP Exam, even if they do not give you actual college credits. For example, you might not need to take an introductory-level course, or perhaps you might not need to take a class in a certain discipline at all.
- **Admissions Plus**. Even if your AP Exam will not result in college credit or even allow you to place out of certain courses, most colleges will respect your decision to push yourself by taking an AP course or even an AP Exam outside of a course. A high score on an AP Exam shows a proficiency in more difficult content than is taught in many high school courses, and colleges may take that into account during the admissions process.

More Great Books
For more information on colleges, you might want to check out some of our guide books, which include *The Best 390 Colleges, The Complete Book of Colleges, Paying for College,* and many more!

OTHER RESOURCES

There are many resources available to help you improve your score on the AP English Literature and Composition Exam, not the least of which are your **teachers**. If you are taking an AP class, you may be able to get extra attention from your teacher, such as obtaining feedback on your essays. If you are not in an AP course, reach out to a teacher who teaches AP English Literature and Composition and ask whether the teacher will review your essays or otherwise help you with content.

Go Online!

If you're looking for additional resources to prepare for the AP Exam, remember to visit the course home page on AP Students. Here you can find more information about the exam, including sample questions and scoring details.

Time Well Spent

If you're not sure how to best spend your time, register this book and log into your online Student Tools so that you can download our helpful, free study guide for this book.

Another wonderful resource is **AP Students**, the official site of the AP Exams. The scope of the information at this site is quite broad and includes the following:

- course descriptions, which include details on what content is covered and sample questions
- reading and writing study skills tips
- essay prompts from previous years
- information about exam fees and reductions
- tons of practice content: multiple choice, passages, and more

The AP Students home page address is http://apstudent.collegeboard.org.

The page where you can find gobs of information about AP English Literature and Composition is https://apstudent.collegeboard.org/apcourse/ap-english-literature-and-composition.

Finally, The Princeton Review offers tutoring for the AP English Literature and Composition Exam. Our expert instructors can help you refine your strategic approach and add to your content knowledge. For more information, call 1-800-2REVIEW.

DESIGNING YOUR STUDY PLAN

In Part I, you identified some areas of potential improvement. Let's now delve further into your performance on Practice Test 1, with the goal of developing a study plan appropriate to your needs and time commitment.

Read the answers and explanations associated with the multiple-choice questions (starting at page 33). After you have done so, respond to the following questions:

- How many days/weeks/months away is your AP English Literature and Composition Exam?

- What time of day is your best, most focused study time?

- How much time per day/week/month will you devote to preparing for your AP English Literature and Composition Exam?

- When will you do this preparation? (Be as specific as possible: Mondays and Wednesdays from 3:00 to 4:00 P.M., for example.)

- Based on the answers above, will you focus on strategy or content or both?

- What are your overall goals in using this book?

Part IV
Test-Taking Strategies for the AP English Literature and Composition Exam

PREVIEW

Review your responses to the questions in "Reflect on the Test" on page 4, and then respond to the following questions:

- How many multiple-choice questions did you miss even though you knew the answer?

- On how many multiple-choice questions did you guess blindly?

- How many multiple-choice questions did you miss after eliminating some answers and guessing based on the remaining answers?

- Did you find any of the essays easier/harder than the others—and if so, why?

HOW TO USE THE CHAPTERS IN THIS PART

For the following Strategy chapters, think about what you are doing now before you read the chapters. As you read and engage in the directed practice, be sure to appreciate the ways you can change your approach. At the end of Part IV, you will have the opportunity to reflect on how you will change your approach.

Chapter 1
Basic Principles of the Multiple-Choice Section

Books are a uniquely portable magic.

—Stephen King

WHAT ARE THE BASICS OF CRACKING THE EXAM?

As with any multiple-choice test, there will come a time when the studying is over, and you are as prepared as you are ever going to be. You will be sitting at your desk with your exam in front of you. The proctor, droning on at the front of the room, will finally finish reading the instructions and say, "You may begin the test."

At that moment, what you know isn't going to change. Your head will be crammed with knowledge, and you might wish you knew even more, but your score will depend on getting what you know onto that answer sheet.

Imagine your exact double sitting at the next desk. In terms of English literature, your double knows exactly what you know. Will you and your double's scores be the same? *Well, if you know how to beat the test, your score will be better.* You will squeeze every possible drop of what you know onto that answer sheet while your double will struggle to bring all their knowledge to the table. The scores will reflect the difference.

The multiple-choice section of the AP English Literature and Composition Exam is just like any other standardized test in that you should have three serious considerations:

1) Time management is crucial.
2) Process of Elimination is necessary for narrowing answers to more viable options.
3) You must answer EVERY question. Leave NOTHING blank.

Have a Plan

In order to do your best on the AP Exam, you need a plan. Stop worrying about doing things the "right way" and start concentrating on answering every question most efficiently. Unanswered questions have no chance, but even randomly answered questions have hope. Go into test day with a plan for answering questions you don't know and a plan for managing your time.

The Plan

Here's an outline of what you should do on the multiple-choice section:

1. Note the Time and Number of Passages or Poems

When the test begins, make note of the time. The proctor might put the start time on the board; most rooms have a clock, but don't count on either. Your best bet is to take a wrist watch and set it to 12:00. It's easy to read how much time you have left if you have everything in even increments. This is a good trick for taking any timed test.

Because you'll be faced with five passages or poems, you can bet on about 12 minutes per passage or poem, with questions. Keep track of time. Don't rush, but try not to dedicate too much time to any one passage or question.

2. Pick a Passage or Poem to Complete First

Some passages/poems may be a bit easier than others. There is no order of difficulty on the test, but you know yourself and your skills best. If you see 20th-century literature and 17th-century poetry, choose the one that makes you most comfortable. Reading the text that is easiest for you will help you to start the test confidently and efficiently. Then you reserve time for harder passages or poems to come.

No Order of Difficulty

Unlike some other exams, questions on the AP English Literature and Composition Exam are not arranged in order of difficulty. Passages deemed "easy" or "difficult" by the test-writers could appear earlier or later.

3. Pick a Passage or Poem to Complete Last

Scan the five texts for one that looks harder (to you) than the others. Save this one for the end so that you can use any extra time on it. If you complete all or any of the other passages in under 12 minutes apiece, you can dedicate the remaining time to the reading and questions that will be most difficult. Remember, this passage or poem is one on which you may have to guess because you don't know the answers or you're running out of time, but that's okay. If you answered the easier texts with more consideration, it won't hurt you as badly to miss a few here.

4. Work the Passage/Poem

Note our verb choice: *work*, not *read*. You'll see what we mean when we get to the next chapter.

5. Answer the Questions Using Planned-Ahead Strategies

All texts are not created equal. Because you can't count on easier texts first and more difficult texts later, you have to rely on your instinct and prior knowledge to assess the situation and go confidently in the direction of the test.

Letter of the Day (LOTD)

One such automatic strategy is to pick a "Letter of the Day" (LOTD) from A to D in advance. If you run into a situation in which you can't eliminate any answers or simply don't have time to look at the remaining questions, you can just bubble in that letter. (Remember, you are not penalized for wrong answers!)

This is a quick and easy way to make sure that you've answered every question. And theoretically, if the questions are evenly distributed across all four choices, being consistent in your guesses should help to pick up a couple of freebie points.

TIME MANAGEMENT

A key factor on standardized tests is time management. You have to answer 55 questions in 60 minutes, and that means there's no time to waste. The more questions you answer, the better chance you have of correct answers—LEAVE NOTHING BLANK.

Analyze yourself as a test-taker and determine how to tackle the test in the best way for you. We can present general guidelines to get you going, but you have to come up with your own personal plan for test day.

Do It Your Way

Don't listen to other kids say how "easy" that test was or how "it was so hard I didn't even get to everything!" If you worry about how others are testing, you won't be confident in your own abilities. Remember that the first thing you should do is look over the passages to determine your approach.

If you can get to all the passages and poems and answer all the questions with five minutes left over, great, but don't count on it. Plan ahead. There's no law that says you have to do the passages in order. Don't.

As we've already mentioned, the first thing you should do as soon as the multiple-choice section begins is look over the passages and poems—this is definitely allowed. Decide which text to tackle first but, much more important, decide which text to do last.

The object is to find the most difficult passage/poem and put off doing it until the end. There are a couple of reasons for doing this. First, if you're going to run out of time, why not run out of time on the passage/poem on which you might miss a lot of questions anyway? Second, a more difficult passage/poem is undoubtedly going to take the most time. You don't want to get into a situation in which you have to rush just to finish four out of the five texts. This is such a simple technique. All you have to do is remember to use it.

A Word of Advice
We recommend that you save the passage/poem (and questions) you find most challenging for last. This strategy ensures that you answer all of the questions you know before moving on to the ones you may not know and which, therefore, might cost you valuable time.

You Can Skip a Text and Still Get a Good Score

It's true. It is completely possible to get a final score of 5 without doing all the passages/poems. No, it isn't easy. It calls for excellent essays and accurate answers on the passages you do attempt. If you'd be satisfied with a final score of 4 (and you should be; it's an excellent score), and if you know that reading comprehension questions are tough for you, then you should definitely consider skipping one passage or poem. Of course, skipping one text does not mean leaving questions blank. When you get to questions that are too time-consuming or that you don't know the answers to (and you can't eliminate any options), use your Letter of the Day (LOTD).

ACTIVE READING

With five prose fiction and poetry analysis passages and 55 questions to do in an hour, you need a strategy to make the most of your reading time. It's called active reading, and it will help you wring information from the passage quickly.

Steps in active reading

1. Preview the questions—just the stems, not the answer choices. In this way, you'll have an idea of what information to watch for as you read the passage. This technique works well for some people and not for others. The passages in this book give you plenty of opportunity to try it a couple of times. If it works for you—if you can retain most or even some of the information you'll need to find in order to answer the questions—then you'll be one step ahead when you start reading the passage.

2. Identify the main point of each paragraph or stanza *before* you allow yourself to move on to the next one. This will force you to concentrate intensely and will avoid that lost, "what did I just read?" feeling that comes from skimming through a passage. It might help you to make a quick note of a key word or two for each part of the passage. Don't let this step slow you down, though. If a sentence or stanza really doesn't make sense to you, stop and close your eyes for a couple of seconds, look at it again, and, if necessary, just move on. It might make sense later in the context of one of the questions.

3. Ask questions constantly as you read. Why is the author talking so much about snowflakes? Why doesn't John want to go to the beach with his family? What is the red truck supposed to symbolize? Why does the author use "despondent" instead of "sad"? Why is this dream sequence here? Tear the prose fiction selection or poem apart instead of simply letting it flow into you as written. This step forces you to engage with the passage instead of letting it slip past you.

4. Identify the main point of the whole passage. There—you've got the theme and the author's purpose.

Once you learn active reading techniques, you'll probably find them useful far beyond the exam.

Spacing Out?

If you feel your eyes glazing over at any point during the test, stop, take a deep breath, and get yourself to refocus. We know it's easier said than done, but sharp concentration is a key to test success!

Types of Answer Choices

1. All True But One Word or Phrase

If part of the answer is wrong, then the whole thing is wrong. Read the entire answer choice to determine whether the answer is appropriate for what the question is asking.

2. Distractor/Absolute Wrong Answer

This is the answer that just cannot be the answer based on what you read in the passage. Through Process of Elimination (POE), you should be able to spot this answer pretty quickly.

3. Key/Right or Best Answer

This is the answer that is most suitable in response to the question. The Key may be similar to other answer choices; however, all parts of this answer fulfill the question and align with the passage.

4. Irrelevant Details/Information

Sometimes you'll see details and think, "ooh! I read that," but you have to be careful that this doesn't throw you from the true focus of the question. Some answer choices will include some relevant details but will also include speculative details or things that just aren't in the passage. Read the entire answer choice before making an incorrect choice based on one small detail.

Why Is This Wrong?
Half Wrong = All Wrong

The key is to take each answer a word at a time. Don't fixate on what's right about the answer; if any part of the answer is wrong, then eliminate the answer. **Half wrong equals all wrong**. In fact, one-tenth bad equals all bad. Read the following excerpt from Zadie Smith's *White Teeth* and the question that follows.

Par.

1   Early in the morning, late in the century, Cricklewood Broadway. At 0627 hours on January 1, 1975, Alfred Archibald Jones was dressed in corduroy and sat in a fume-filled Cavalier Musketeer Estate facedown on the steering wheel, hoping the judgment would not be too heavy upon him. He lay in a prostrate cross, jaw slack, arms splayed on either side like some fallen angel; scrunched up in each fist he held his army service medals (left) and his marriage license (right), for he had decided to take his mistakes with him. A little green light flashed in his eye, signaling a right turn he had resolved never to make. He was resigned to it. He was prepared for it. He had flipped a coin and stood staunchly by the results. This was a decided-upon suicide. In fact, it was a New Year's resolution.

....

2   While he slipped in and out of consciousness, the position of the planets, the music of the spheres, the flap of a tiger moth's diaphanous wings in Central Africa, and a whole bunch of other stuff that Makes Shit Happen had decided it was second-chance time for Archie. Somewhere, somehow, by somebody, it had been decided that he would live.

1   ☐ Mark for Review

Paragraph 1 of the passage best describes the author's portrayal of Alfred Archibald Jones as

(A) a sympathetic portrayal of a man who regrets his life

(B) a farcical portrayal of an attempted suicide

(C) a mock heroic portrait of a vintage car enthusiast

(D) a darkly ironic treatment of an overly sensitive man

(A) While the tone is somewhat arch, the description of him as "like some fallen angel" and lying "in a prostrate cross" indicates some sympathy for him. It is certainly not *un*sympathetic. Hold on to this one.

(B) We are told that he plans to commit suicide in the passage, so the last part of this answer is correct. But is the tone farcical? While there is some irony involved in saying that a "bunch of other stuff that Makes Shit Happen" decides his fate, "farcical" is too strong a word. Half wrong is all wrong, so eliminate this one.

(C) Is the passage mock heroic? Again, he "stood staunchly" by his decision and his "army service medals" indicate military service, which may lead you to associate him with heroism. But there's no indication he's particularly heroic in the passage. As for vintage car enthusiasm, you don't have an indication of whether his car—the "Cavalier Musketeer Estate" mentioned in the paragraph—is an old classic or not. Don't be distracted by a detail that may appear in the passage but does not provide the information needed to answer the question.

(D) There seems to be some irony in the passage, and an attempted suicide may lead you to conclude that it's dark. But you cannot be sure whether he's overly sensitive.

Eliminate the Obvious and Come Back

That leaves choices (A) and (D).

Ask yourself if the portrait is sympathetic. The author doesn't exactly seem to be shedding tears for him, so you're not sure. But neither is he condemned. You are also not clear about what the word "ironic" means. What should you do? Be brave.

POE = BFF

Process of Elimination (POE) is your friend when it comes to multiple-choice questions. Instead of trying to pinpoint the right answer, focus instead on getting rid of the ones that are wrong.

Process of Elimination (POE)

Pick (A). You couldn't find anything wrong with (A).

Don't be afraid to pick answers you aren't sure are right. Sometimes that's necessary. Just make sure you don't pick answers that you think are probably wrong. We know that sounds obvious, but students do pick weak answers and they know they're doing it. Why? Because one answer was kind-of-but-not-really-right while the other was totally unfamiliar. The student thinks the unfamiliar answer might be right but then again, it might be embarrassingly wrong. The student picks the kind-of-but-not-really-right answer and loses points but thinks that's okay because at least it wasn't the embarrassing answer. Relax! You can't embarrass yourself on this exam. The multiple-choice questions are scored by a machine. No one—not your AP teacher, not your classmates, not the AP Essay Readers—knows or cares which answer you pick. Be fearless. If POE leaves you with two or three answers you aren't sure about—*pick one*. In the example above, (A) was correct. Don't let uncertainty on the definition of "ironic" mislead you into thinking material is darkly ironic when another answer might be more appropriate for the passage. Often irony takes the form of a subtle kind of humor when what is said is different from what is meant. **Irony** is an important term, both for the test and for the study of literature in general. We give it a full treatment in the glossary on your Student Tools. But this is just one example, and irony comes in dozens of colors and flavors.

POE Summary

- When in doubt, narrow down the choices by looking for wrong answers.
- Eliminate what you can and then look more closely at what's left.
- Half wrong = all wrong.
- Don't leave any question blank, ever.

A PREVIEW OF COMING ATTRACTIONS

There's one more time management technique that you absolutely have to know. It's called the "Art of the Seven-Minute Passage." We'd like to tell you about it now, but unfortunately the full technique won't make sense until we've outlined the general principles of reading prose fiction or poetry analysis passages and shown you examples of the kinds of questions you'll see on the AP English Literature and Composition Exam. You'll find our explanation of the Art of the Seven-Minute Passage in Chapter 7.

Chapter 1 Summary

Have a Plan

- o Note the time and number of texts to read: there will always be a total of 55 items, and it will be a mix of poems and passages.

- o Pick a passage/poem to do first.

- o Pick a passage/poem to do last.

- o Work the text. Use active reading techniques.

- o Answer *all* the questions on the text, using our techniques.

Time Management

- o Guess aggressively.

- o Pick a text to do last based on what you consider your greatest weakness.

- o Skip a text, guess, or use your Letter of the Day (LOTD) on *all* the questions in that text, and still get a good score.

POE

- o Guess aggressively.

- o Use POE (Process of Elimination).

- o The best way to use POE is to look closely at the wording of each answer choice for what is wrong, and eliminate.

- o Bubble an answer for *all* questions, even if it's just your LOTD.

Chapter 2
Using Time Effectively to Maximize Points

My alma mater was books, a good library. . . . I could spend the rest of my life reading, just satisfying my curiosity.

—Malcolm X

BECOMING A BETTER TEST-TAKER

Very few students stop to think about how to improve their test-taking skills. Most assume that if they study hard, they will test well, and if they do not study, they will do poorly. Most students continue to believe this even after experience teaches them otherwise. Have you ever studied really hard for an exam and then blown it on test day? Have you ever aced an exam for which you thought you weren't well prepared? Most students have had one, if not both, of these experiences. The lesson should be clear: factors other than your level of preparation influence your final test score. This chapter will provide you with some insights that will help you perform better on the AP English Literature and Composition Exam and on other exams as well.

PACING AND TIMING

A big part of scoring well on an exam is working at a consistent pace. The worst mistake made by inexperienced or unsavvy test-takers is that they come to a question that stumps them and rather than just skip it, they panic and stall. Time stands still when you're working on a question you cannot answer, and it is not unusual for students to waste five minutes on a single question (especially a question involving the word *except*) because they are too stubborn to cut their losses. It is important to be aware of how much time you have spent on a given question and on the section you are working. There are several ways to improve your pacing and timing for the test:

- **Know your average pace.** While you prepare for your test, try to gauge how long you take on 5, 10, or 20 questions. Knowing how long you spend on average per question will help you identify how many questions you can answer effectively and how best to pace yourself for the test.

- **Keep an eye on the time.** There will be a clock on the screen to help you keep track of time. However, it's important to remember that constantly checking the clock is in itself a waste of time and can be distracting. Devise a plan. Try checking the clock every 15 or 30 questions to see whether you are keeping the correct pace or whether you need to speed up. This will ensure that you're cognizant of the time but will not permit you to fall into the trap of dwelling on it.

- **Know when to move on.** Since all questions are scored equally, investing appreciable amounts of time on a single question is inefficient and can potentially deprive you of the chance to answer easier ones later on. You should eliminate answer choices if you are able to, but don't worry about picking a random answer and moving on if you cannot find the correct answer. Remember, tests are like marathons; you do best when you work through them at a steady pace. You can always come back to a question you don't know. When you do, very often you will find that your previous mental block is gone, and you will wonder why the question perplexed you the first time around (as you gleefully move on to the next question). Even if you still don't know the answer, you will not have wasted valuable time you could have spent on questions that come easier to you.

- **Be selective.** You don't have to do any of the questions in a given section in order. If you are stumped by an essay or multiple-choice question, skip it or choose a different one and come back. Also, you probably do not have to answer every question correctly to achieve your desired score. Select the questions or essays that you can answer and work on them first. This will make you more efficient and give you the greatest chance of getting the most questions correct.

- **Use Process of Elimination (POE) on multiple-choice questions.** Many times, one or more answer choices can be eliminated. Every answer choice that can be eliminated increases the odds that you will answer the question correctly.

Go Online!
Check out us out on
YouTube for test taking
tips and techniques to help
you ace your next exam
at youtube.com/
ThePrincetonReview

Remember, when all the questions on a test are of equal value, no one question is that important and your overall goal for pacing is to get the most questions correct. Finally, you should set a realistic goal for your final score. In the next section, we will break down how to achieve your desired score and how to pace yourself to do so.

GETTING THE SCORE YOU WANT

Depending on the score you need, it may be in your best interest not to try to work through every question. Check with the schools to which you are applying to determine your needed score.

AP Exams in all subjects no longer include a "guessing penalty" of a quarter of a point for every incorrect answer. Instead, students are assessed only on the total number of correct answers. A lot of AP materials, even those you receive in your AP class, may not include this information. It's really important to remember that if you are running out of time, you should fill in all the bubbles before the time for the multiple-choice section is up. Even if you don't plan to spend a lot of time on every question or even if you have no idea what the correct answer is, you need to fill something in. Use your LOTD, as we discussed earlier.

TEST ANXIETY

Everybody experiences anxiety before and during an exam. To a certain extent, test anxiety can be helpful. Some people find that they perform more quickly and efficiently under stress. If you've ever pulled an all-nighter to write a paper and ended up doing good work, you know the feeling.

However, too much stress is definitely a bad thing. Hyperventilating during the test, for example, almost always leads to a lower score. If you find that you stress out during exams, here are a few preemptive actions you can take.

- **Take a reality check.** Evaluate your situation before the test begins. If you have studied hard, remind yourself that you are well prepared. Remember that many others taking the test are not as well prepared, and (in your classes, at least) you are being graded against them, so you have an advantage. If you didn't study, accept the fact that you will probably not ace the test. Make sure you get to every question you know something about. In either scenario, it's best to think of a test as if it were a game. How can you get the most points in the time allotted to you? Always begin with questions you can answer easily and quickly before tackling those that will take more time.

- **Focus on what you can control.** Don't stress out or fixate on what you don't know. Even if you've underprepared (which shouldn't be the case since you're using this book), you can still improve your score by maximizing the benefits of what you do know.

- **Try to relax.** Slow, deep breathing works for almost everyone. Close your eyes, take a few slow, deep breaths, and concentrate on nothing but your inhalation and exhalation for a few seconds. This is a basic form of meditation that should help you to clear your mind of stress and, as a result, concentrate better on the test. If you have ever taken yoga classes, you probably know some other good relaxation techniques. Use them when you can (obviously, anything that requires leaving your seat and, say, assuming a handstand position won't be allowed by any but the most free-spirited proctors).

- **Eliminate as many surprises as you can.** Make sure you know where the test will be given, when it starts, what type of questions are going to be asked, and how long the test will take. You don't want to be worrying about any of these things on test day or, even worse, after the test has already begun.

The best way to avoid stress is to study both the test material and the test itself. Congratulations! By using this book, you are taking a major step toward a stress-free AP English Literature and Composition Exam.

Looking for More Help with Your APs?
We now offer specialized AP tutoring and course packages that guarantee a 4 or 5 on the AP. To see which courses are offered and available, and to learn more about the guarantee, visit PrincetonReview.com/college/ap-test-prep

Chapter 3
Advanced Principles:
Reading the
Multiple-Choice
Passages

" That's the thing about books. They let
you travel without moving your feet.

—Jhumpa Lahiri "

READING THE PASSAGES IN THE MULTIPLE-CHOICE SECTION

Because of the time constraints, you should make sure that you go about reading the passages in the most efficient way possible. You might also want to use a slightly different approach depending on whether the passage is prose fiction or poetry analysis, but there are a few things you should keep in mind regarding both types of passages.

- You are reading in order to answer questions, not for enjoyment or appreciation. As you read, ask yourself, "Do I understand this well enough to answer a multiple-choice question about what it means?"
- You can come back to the passage anytime you want, and you *should* go back to the passage in order to answer the questions.

Both of these points address the same issue. The passages are on a test, but you don't do most of your reading on tests. Generally when you study for an English test, you read the works your teacher assigned and have to answer questions from memory; however, on the AP English Literature and Composition Exam, the passages will likely be unfamiliar, which can be a tad daunting. The test-writers deliberately select works that aren't typically taught in schools. The writers are great, familiar authors, but the works are more obscure.

The good news is that it's unlikely anyone else taking the test has seen the work before either; therefore, you're all starting with a similar level of knowledge. The best news is that this is an open-book test. You don't have to read the passage in the same way you read for English class. You're not looking to memorize information—you can use the passage to your advantage while answering the questions. Soak up the basic structure of the passage, but don't stress over remembering every little detail. Focus your attention only on what the questions are asking you, and find the parts of the passages that will help you answer appropriately.

Reading Prose Fiction Passages

The right way to read prose fiction passages in the multiple-choice section is simple. It's the method that works for YOU. Bear in mind that this is a timed test, so while we stand by the Active Reading tools provided in Chapter 1, you may want to modify or supplement those skills with the following. As you work through the practice drills and tests, make a point of trying different methods so that you can identify the one that's most efficient for you. It does you little good to fully understand a passage if that means you only have time to read and answer half the questions.

1. Preview the Questions

For some students, a quick reading of the questions provides *context*. For others, it's a total waste of time. When you're practicing on passages, try it each way and see what works best for you. Then, stick to that strategy. What you should do is read each question and only the question. Don't read the answer choices. Don't try to memorize the questions. Just get a sense of what they're asking you about— questions about literary devices or a certain character, for example. This can provide clues that will make your reading more active.

2a. Skim the Passage

There are two stances on active reading; one is to identify the main idea of each paragraph before moving on. The other expands upon the idea of previewing questions and suggests that you skim only the first and last sentences of the paragraphs to get an overall sense of what the passage is about. When you go back, either guided by questions or, time permitting, to read the passage (as outlined in the next step), you'll be less likely to trip up on context. The trade-off is the time you spend doing this.

2b. Read the Passage

Just read, without fixating on details, without getting stuck or going blank. When you hit a sentence you don't understand in a book, you don't panic, do you? You don't assume: "I might as well throw this book away . . . without that sentence it's just a useless collection of incomplete alphabetical symbols." When you read normally, you read for the *main idea*. You read to understand what's going on. When you hit a tricky sentence, you figure that you'll be able to make sense of it from what comes later, or that one missing piece of the puzzle isn't going to keep you from getting the outline of the overall picture. This is exactly how you want to read an AP English Literature and Composition Exam passage.

What Is the Main Idea?

For the AP English Literature and Composition Exam, main idea means the general point. It is the 10-words-or-fewer summary of the passage. The main idea is the gist, or the big picture. For example, suppose there's a passage about all the different ways a man is stingy, how he cheats his best friend out of an inheritance, and scrimps on food around the house so badly that his kids go to bed crying from hunger every night. The passage goes on for 50 or 60 lines describing this guy. The main idea is that this guy is an evil, greedy miser. If the passage gives a reason for the miser's obsession with money, you might include that in your mental picture of the main idea: This guy is an evil, greedy miser because he grew up poor. No doubt the passage tells you exactly how he grew up and where (in an orphanage, let's say), and exactly what kind of leftover beans he eats (lima) and exactly how many cold leftover lima beans he serves to his starving kids each night (three apiece), but those are details, not the big picture. Use the details to build up to the big picture.

The Magic Topic Sentence Has Vanished

We don't want you to think that the main idea can be found in some magic "topic sentence." The writers on the AP Exam are sophisticated; they often don't use any obvious clues like topic sentences. With poetry analysis passages especially, looking for topic sentences is a waste of time; however, use context clues to make inferences regarding theme and main idea.

Don't Be Afraid to Skim!
The idea of "skimming" might inspire panic in some students who want to read every single word. But when done correctly, skimming is a great way to get a sense of the passage before diving into the questions.

Summary—How Do You Read an AP Multiple-Choice Prose Fiction Passage?

- Preview the questions (optional).
- Skim the passage.
- Read for the main idea.

Reading Poetry Analysis Passages

Ideally, you read a poem several times, ponder, scratch your head, and read some more. Then again, ideally you have your favorite poem by your favorite poet, and all afternoon to read—not 12 minutes with some poem you couldn't care less about and between 8 and 13 multiple-choice questions staring you in the face.

It's a test, so you've got to read the poem efficiently, and the key to the process is keeping your mind open, especially the first time through.

It might help to be clear about the difference between a narrative and the kind of poetry you'll see on the AP Exam. A narrative unfolds and builds on itself. Although one's understanding of what came earlier in the narrative is deepened and changed by later developments, by and large the work makes sense as it flows; it is meant to be understood "on the run."

Verse is different. Yes, the way it unfolds is important, but one often doesn't even grasp that unfolding until the second or third (or ninetieth) read. A poem is like a sculpture; it is meant to be wandered around, looked at from all sides, and finally taken in as a whole. You wouldn't try to understand a sculpture until you'd seen the whole thing. In the same way, think of your first reading of a poem as a walk around an interesting sculpture. You aren't trying to interpret. You are just trying to look at the whole thing. Once you've seen it and taken in its dimensions, then you can go back and puzzle it out.

What we've just said applies to poetry in general. But how can you apply that to the AP Exam? Here's the answer: *when you approach a poem on the AP Exam, always read it at least twice before you go to the questions.*

Poem Preview

Leave analysis out of your first read of a poem. Instead, look at it as a whole and get a general feel for it.

Skim

The first read is to get all the words in your head. Go from top to bottom. Don't stop at individual lines to figure them out. If everything makes sense, great. If it doesn't, no problem. The main thing you want is a basic sense of what's going on. The main thing to avoid is getting a fixed impression of the poem before you've even finished it.

Then Focus

The second read should be phrase by phrase. Focus on understanding what you read in the simplest way possible. This is when you should look for the main idea.

Don't worry about symbols. Don't worry about deeper meanings. The questions will direct you toward those aspects of the poem. You will need to go back and read parts of it, perhaps the entire thing, several more times but only as is necessary to answer individual questions. To prepare yourself for the questions, all you need is a general sense of what the poem says and to get that understanding you need only the literal sense of the lines. We can't emphasize this point enough: *keep it simple.*

Panic and Obsession

Don't panic if you can't seem to grasp the meaning of a poem. Many people are probably struggling and completely baffled by the same poem. Don't skip the passage. Look for questions that take you to specific line item details ("In lines 56–60 . . . ") and attempt to answer those questions using the specific lines of poetry. POE is your friend here! Don't obsess over the poem or the answers. Do your best to provide an answer using POE but, if you really get stuck, don't dwell. Choose an answer (maybe your LOTD) and move on.

The Difficulties of Poetry Analysis

Good poetry makes conscious use of all language's resources. By pushing the limits of language, poetry creates a heightened awareness in the reader. Poets sometimes use uncommon vocabulary, odd figures of speech, and unusual combinations of words in strange orders; they play with time and stretch the connections we see between ideas. All of these essential resources can make poetry analysis seem difficult, but it can be done. One important thing to remember is that many poems are open to a myriad of valid interpretations. It's not your job to have a meaningful experience when reading poetry on a test; it's your job to read for language resources and main ideas that will help you to answer the questions correctly.

Reading Poetry Resourcefully

You can connect to a poem in many ways, but you aren't reading for a nice, meditative experience on the AP Exam: you're reading to answer the questions correctly. The following things are what you're looking to identify and analyze as you read:

- Punctuation use
- Diction (word choice)
- Imagery
- Theme/main idea
- Figurative language (metaphors, similes, synecdoche)
- Character
- Setting
- Structure
- Narrator

A Word by Any Other Name Would Still Smell As Neat
You won't necessarily have to define words like "synecdoche" or use them in a sentence, but you should be aware of the different varieties of figurative language, the better to be on the lookout for them. Be sure to read through the Glossary on your online Student Tools.

The Pros Read Poetry for Prose

The secret to understanding AP poetry analysis passages quickly and fully is to simply ignore the "poetry parts." Ignore the rhythm, ignore the music of the language, and above all, ignore the form. This means you should do the following:

- Ignore line breaks.
- Read in sentences, not in lines. Emphasize punctuation.
- Ignore rhyme and rhyme scheme.
- Be prepared for "long" thoughts—ideas that develop over several lines.

When approaching poetry, many students tend to do the opposite of what we suggest here: they emphasize lines and line breaks and totally ignore sentence punctuation.

True, sometimes there's no problem: when lines break at natural pauses and each line has a packet of meaning complete in itself (these are termed *end-stopped* lines), the poem becomes easier to read.

Challenging Poetry

Consider the next selection. It's the first 13 or so lines of "My Last Duchess" by Robert Browning. This is the kind of poetry you can expect to find on the AP Exam, but it is unlikely that you would see a poem that is this well known.

The poem is a monologue spoken by a nobleman, the Duke of Ferrara, to a representative of the Count of Tyrol. Ferrara seeks to take the wealthy count's daughter for his bride and is in the midst of discussing the arrangement with the count's representative. When Ferrara speaks of his "last duchess," he refers to his first wife, who has quite recently died at the age of 17 under mysterious circumstances. The implication is that Ferrara has had his first wife murdered, an implication the poem brings home with understated menace.

You won't be given this kind of information on the test but, with practice, you should be able to figure out many of the aspects of the poem by yourself. For example, the first two lines of the poem (which is printed below in sections) give a careful reader some important information. The speaker of the poem is a duke, who is talking about his "last duchess." He is standing in front of a painting of this woman who is no longer alive. All of this information, if assimilated readily and with an eye toward tone and the big picture, will help you answer questions, even if the questions don't ask specifically who the speaker is or whether the duchess is alive.

> That's my last duchess painted on the wall,
> Looking as if she were alive. I call
> That piece a wonder, now: Frà Pandolf's hands
> Worked busily a day, and there she stands.
> Will't please you sit and look at her? I said
> "Frà Pandolf" by design, for never read
> Strangers like you that pictured countenance,
> The depth and passion of its earnest glance,
> But to myself they turned (since none puts by
> The curtain I have drawn for you, but I)
> And seemed as they would ask me, if they durst,
> how such a glance came there; so, not the first
> Are you to turn and ask thus. . . .

Line
5

10

This poem is challenging, but it's not impossible with the right reading strategies. Remember: you're supposed to come into the test with a plan! The first few lines are relatively straightforward: the duke points to the painting, remarks on its life-like quality, mentions the artist (Frà Pandolf), and invites his listener to sit and contemplate the portrait for a moment. Although lines 3–4, "Frà Pandolf's hands/ Worked busily a day" consist of distinctly unmodern speech and might give some folks a moment's pause, there are signposts to help guide readers. Even if you don't know that "Frà" is used as a title of address to an Italian monk (and who does?), you can still figure out the big picture of this poem.

Then comes the remainder of the passage, beginning from line 5, "I said/'Frà Pandolf' by design, for never read," and the trouble begins. Now, the truth is that what is written there is easy enough that if you can break the habit of placing too much emphasis on line breaks, you can read it as prose. Browning has deliberately written his verse so that the lines break against the flow of the punctuation. If you expect little parcels of complete meaning at every break, you'll end up lost. Let's consider the troubling part written as prose:

"I said 'Frà Pandolf' by design, for never read strangers like you that pictured countenance, the depth and passion of its earnest glance, but to myself they turned (since none puts by the curtain I have drawn for you, but I) and seemed as they would ask me, if they durst, how such a glance came there."

Poem Woes
If the way lines break in a poem is completely confusing for you, read the poem as if it were prose. This strategy will help you crack even notoriously challenging poems by poets such as Robert Browning.

This is just one long sentence, broken by parenthetical asides, in which the duke says, "I said 'Frà Pandolf' on purpose because strangers never see that portrait (or its expression of depth and passion) without turning to me (because nobody sees the portrait unless I'm here to pull aside the curtain) and looking at me as though they want to ask, if they dare, 'How did that expression get there?'"

Read the poem as prose and you'll see it's pretty easy. If you have trouble doing this, try putting brackets around each sentence.

Now if you're really alert, you'll notice that the duke still hasn't exactly explained why he mentioned Frà Pandolf on purpose. He eventually does (in his sideways fashion), but if you read poetry without being ready for long thoughts that develop over several lines, you're going to read "I said, 'Frà Pandolf' by design, for never . . . " and expect the explanation—pronto. When it doesn't come you think you're lost, and once you think you're lost, you are. How is "that pictured countenance" an explanation of why he said "Frà Pandolf?" It isn't, and it never will be, but you can spend hours trying to come up with reasons why it is.

Don't get the wrong impression. Browning isn't easy reading. But you'll find that if you follow our suggestions for reading poetry, you can cut to the heart of what Browning and poets like him are saying. Ignore line breaks and instead pay close attention to punctuation and sentence structure. Be ready for "long" thoughts that develop over several lines or even stanzas. You'll still find the poems on the AP Exam challenging for a variety of reasons: because of their vocabulary, because of their compression of a great deal of information into just a few lines, and because of their often complicated and unusual sentence structure.

If you read poetry the way we suggest, however, you'll find that you can still use the context of what you do understand to answer questions.

Here's Browning's "My Last Duchess" in complete form. Read it according to our advice and see what you can get from it. (Many discussions of this famous poem exist online, and you can read a few in order to compare what you've figured out with what others have said about it.)

Prose Pros

Reading poetry effectively boils down to one simple concept: before you read a poem as poetry, read it as prose.

That's my last duchess painted on the wall,
Looking as if she were alive. I call
That piece a wonder, now: Frà Pandolf's hands
Line   Worked busily a day, and there she stands.
5   Will't please you sit and look at her? I said
"Frà Pandolf" by design, for never read
Strangers like you that pictured countenance,
The depth and passion of its earnest glance,
But to myself they turned (since none puts by
10   The curtain I have drawn for you, but I)
And seemed as they would ask me, if they durst,
how such a glance came there; so, not the first

Are you to turn and ask thus. Sir, 'twas not
Line   Her husband's presence only, called that spot
15   Of joy into the Duchess' cheek: perhaps
        Frà Pandolf chanced to say, "Her mantle laps
        "Over my lady's wrist too much," or "Paint
        "Must never hope to reproduce the faint
        "Half-flush that dies along her throat": such stuff
20   Was courtesy, she thought, and cause enough
        For calling up that spot of joy. She had
        A heart—how shall I say?—too soon made glad,
        Too easily impressed; she liked whate'er
        She looked on, and her looks went everywhere.
25   Sir, 'twas all one! My favor at her breast,
        The dropping of the daylight in the West,
        The bough of cherries some officious fool
        Broke in the orchard for her, the white mule
        She rode with round the terrace—all and each
30   Would draw from her alike the approving speech,
        Or blush, at least. She thanked men—good! but thanked
        Somehow—I know not how—as if she ranked
        My gift of a nine-hundred-years-old name
        With anybody's gift. Who'd stoop to blame
35   This sort of trifling? Even had you skill
        In speech—which I have not—to make your will
        Quite clear to such an one, and say, "Just this
        "Or that in you disgusts me; here you miss,
        "Or there exceed the mark"—and if she let
40   Herself be lessoned so, nor plainly set
        Her wits to yours, forsooth, and made excuse,
        —E'en then would be some stooping; and I choose
        Never to stoop. Oh sir, she smiled, no doubt,
        Whene'er I passed her; but who passed without
45   Much the same smile? This grew; I gave commands;
        Then all smiles stopped together. There she stands
        As if alive. Will't please you rise? We'll meet
        The company below, then. I repeat,
        The Count your master's known munificence
50   Is ample warrant that no just pretense
        Of mine for dowry will be disallowed;
        Though his fair daughter's self, as I avowed
        At starting, is my object. Nay, we'll go
        Together down, sir. Notice Neptune, though,
55   Taming a sea-horse, thought a rarity,
        Which Claus of Innsbrück cast in bronze for me!

Easier Poetry

Look at these lines from Thomas Gray's "Elegy Written in a Country Churchyard":

> Now fades the glimmering landscape on the sight,
> And all the air a solemn stillness holds,
> Save where the beetle wheels his droning flight,
> And drowsy tinklings lull the distant folds.

Read this passage aloud, and you can't help but stop on the line endings even if there were no commas. The lines build, one upon the next, shaping a picture as they combine to form a mildly complex sentence. The ease with which these lines can be read stems from the fact that each line contains only complete thoughts; there are no loose ends trailing from line to line. This is "nice" poetry; that is, it's nice to you. Each line ends on a natural pause that lets you gather your thoughts. Each line holds something like a complete thought with very little runover into the next line. Although the stanza is written in one sentence, it easily could have been written in four separate sentences:

> The landscape fades.
> The air is still.
> The beetle wheels and drones.
> The tinklings [of bells worn by livestock] lull the folds.*

*Folds are enclosures where sheep graze, or the flocks of sheep themselves.

This paraphrase is lousy poetry, but it gets the main idea across. If the poetry you see on the AP Exam reads like the example above, great. But if you think every poem should be like that stanza or if you try to make every poem read like that one, you're headed for trouble. The poetry on the AP Exam is likely to be more challenging.

Chapter 3 Summary

Basics of Reading Passages

o   You are reading in order to answer the questions—that's the whole point.

o   Reading for a test is different from normal reading. You have limited time, and you have to approach the passages in a way that takes that restriction into account.

o   You can reread the passage (or parts of it) anytime you want, and you should go back to the passage in order to answer the questions.

Reading Prose Fiction Passages

o   Preview the questions if it helps you.

o   Skim the passage.

o   Skimming should never take more than a minute.

o   Read for the main idea.

Reading Poetry Analysis Passages

o   Preview the questions if it helps you.

o   On the exam, read the poem twice before you answer the questions.

o   The first read is to get all the words in your head.
    •   The main thing you want is a basic sense of what's going on.
    •   Try not to get a fixed impression of the poem before you've even finished it.

o   The second read should be done phrase by phrase. Focus on understanding what you read in the simplest way possible. Don't worry about symbols. Don't worry about deeper meanings. Try to visualize what you're reading as you follow the narration of the poem. Also try reading the poem as you would read prose. (See "Poetry into Prose" below.)

o   You will need to go back and read parts of the poem—perhaps the entire poem—several more times, but only as necessary for your work on individual questions.

Poetry into Prose

o   Find the spine—the prose meaning—of the poem.
    •   Ignore line breaks.
    •   Emphasize punctuation. Read in sentences, not in lines.
    •   Be prepared for "long" thoughts: ideas that develop over several lines.

o   Before you read a poem as poetry, read it as prose.

Chapter 4
Cracking the System: Multiple-Choice Questions

> Education is not preparation for life; education is life itself.
>
> —John Dewey

QUESTION TYPES AND FORMATS

Once you've finished working a passage using active reading techniques, you need to answer the questions. If you've paid attention so far, you already know you're going to answer *all* of the questions, using your Letter of the Day to guess when you aren't sure of the answer. You should also know by now that you must approach the test efficiently, making the most of your time in order to get the best possible score.

In order to answer the questions efficiently, you'll need to be able to recognize two main types of questions:

- general comprehension questions that concern the prose fiction selection or poem as a whole
- detail questions that focus on one part of the passage

and two question formats:

- Standard
- EXCEPT/LEAST/NOT

Answer all of the questions. Use your Letter of the Day to guess if you don't know the answer.

General Comprehension Questions

General comprehension questions ask about the overall passage. These questions don't send you back to any specific line(s) or paragraph(s) in the passage.

Here are some examples of general comprehension questions.

- The passage is primarily concerned with . . .
- Which one of the following choices best describes the tone of the passage?
- Which one of the following choices best describes the narrator's relationship to her mother?
- How does the author's use of irony contribute to the effect of the poem?
- To whom does the speaker of the poem address his speech?
- It is evident in the passage that the author feels her home town is . . .

As these examples show, a general comprehension question can target either the passage as a whole, as the first question about theme (main point) does, or it can focus on one aspect of the entire passage, as the second question about tone does. In either case, the scope of the question covers the whole passage from beginning to end. If (in the third question) the narrator's relationship to her mother sounds harmonious in the first couple of lines but is revealed as adversarial throughout the rest of the passage, then "adversarial" is the answer that "best describes" the relationship. You need to consider the overall impression given by the whole passage.

General comprehension questions will often ask about the following:

- **The theme (main point) or author's purpose.** What is the author writing about? Why? What does the author intend for readers to think or feel or believe or do after they finish reading?

- **The tone.** What is the author's (or the narrator's) overall attitude toward the subject of the passage? Are they critical? Approving? Neutral? Is the author being humorous, satirical, ironic, or deadly serious? Are they skeptical or a believer? And—very important—how do you know what the author's attitude is?

- **The style.** Here you're looking for diction (word choice), syntax (sentence choice), and literary devices—in other words, how the author conveys the theme and purpose. Is the vocabulary sophisticated or something that almost all readers could understand? Are the sentence structures varied (a mix of simple and complex, loose and periodic)? Does the author rely on literary devices (such as allusions, repetition, and symbols) to convey the theme, or is the delivery straightforward?

- **The structure.** How does the narrative progress? Do events occur in chronological order? Is the progression interrupted by flashbacks or flashforwards or dream sequences? When are the main characters introduced? When do major points in the plot occur? Are two similar plots being developed in parallel? Is there a sudden change (perhaps in emphasis or tone) part of the way through? Why? How are the different pieces connected and—very important—why did the author choose to connect them in this way?

- **The narrator's point of view.** Does the author use a first-person narrator ("I") whose personality, background, and biases act as a filter through which events are described? Or is the narrator an objective, camera-type recorder of events? What impact does the type of narrator have on the passage? Is there more than one narrator?

- **The development.** How does the plot develop? What techniques does the author use in order to develop a character? How does the author develop the main point?

- **The character(s).** Who are the characters? How are they described? What qualities or attributes do they have? What do they indicate about the author's values, beliefs, or assumptions? Do they reveal any biases or assumptions of a time or place? Do the characters change? Stay the same?

- **The setting.** What, if anything, are you told about the setting? Where are the characters physically? What time period are they in? What do aspects of the setting reveal about the theme, the plot, or the characters? What effect do aspects of the setting have on the passage?

Detail Questions

Detail questions almost always send you back to specific places in the passage. They tell you where to look and ask something about a particular segment or even a specific word.

Always read at least one sentence or line before and after the place indicated in the question, so you'll have the correct context.

Here are some examples of detail questions.

- What significant change occurs in the speaker's attitude toward the countryside in lines 5–9?
- How do the final words of the third paragraph, "but then, I should have known better than to trust him," alter the remainder of the passage?
- In paragraph 1, the phrase "This loaf's big" is used as a metaphor for
- The poet's use of the word "sublime" (line 21) suggests that
- What does the pond in the first paragraph symbolize?
- Which of the following is the best paraphrase for the sentence that makes up paragraph 2?

If you're having trouble grasping the overall theme of a passage or the author's purpose, the specific questions are a good place to start. You'll learn more about the passage with each one you answer, and the whole passage just might fall into place.

QUESTION FORMATS

Standard

The most common question format on the exam, standard format questions have a straightforward question stem, followed by four answer choices. Here are some examples of standard format question stems:

- The metaphor "fountain of delight" in paragraph 2 has the effect of
- The dream described in lines 30–32 suggests that
- The author's attitude toward his subject could be characterized as

EXCEPT/LEAST/NOT

Even though the test-writers put EXCEPT, LEAST or NOT in capital letters, you could still miss those crucial words if you're just racing through the question stems instead of reading them carefully, word for word. In essence, these three qualifiers invert the answer you'd normally be looking for in a standard format question. Consider these examples:

- Ludwig seems to value all of the following characteristics in a business partner EXCEPT
- Which of the following characteristics does Ludwig consider the LEAST important in a business partner?
- Ludwig is NOT looking for which of these characteristics in a business partner?

Which three characteristics does the passage say Ludwig wants to see in a business partner? Those three will be in the answer choices. But those aren't what you're looking for. You want the one characteristic he does NOT consider important, or considers the LEAST important, or is the EXCEPTion to what he thinks is important.

To tackle these tricky questions, disregard the EXCEPT, LEAST or NOT; cross them out. You'll be left with a standard format question:

- Ludwig seems to value [which of] the following characteristics in a business partner ~~EXCEPT~~
- Which of the following characteristics does Ludwig consider ~~the LEAST~~ important in a business partner?
- Ludwig is ~~NOT~~ looking for which of these characteristics in a business partner?

Now eliminate any choice that would be a correct answer for your new, standard format question. The remaining choice will be the correct answer for the EXCEPT/LEAST/NOT version of the question.

How Much Grammar Do You Need to Know for the AP English Lit Exam?

There are usually three or four questions on basic grammar. That's one grammar question or fewer per passage, so grammar is not a big deal on the multiple-choice section. The samples we provide in Chapters 7 and 8 should give you a good idea of what the grammar questions are like. Because there are so few grammar questions, we don't recommend you spend a lot of time studying grammar. You'd be far better off working on writing timed essays or reading poetry.

Model Sentence I

Here's a great simple sentence to memorize for basic grammatical relations:

Sam threw the orange to Irene.

It isn't poetry, but this sentence clearly shows the basic grammatical relationships you need to concern yourself with on the AP Exam.

- *Sam* is the subject.
- *The orange* is the direct object.
- *Irene* is the indirect object.
- *Threw* is the verb.

Notice that in this sentence, the direct object is in fact an object (an orange). The orange is thrown to Irene, the indirect object. In other words, the indirect object receives the direct object. The concept is pretty simple.

Model Sentence II

There are two more sentence elements you should understand: the phrase and the clause. Here's a model sentence that should help you keep clear on their definitions.

Feeling generous, Sam threw the orange to Irene, who tried to catch it.

The heart of the sentence is still *Sam threw the orange to Irene*, as subject, verb, direct object, and indirect object all remain the same. But we've added a phrase to the beginning of the sentence and a dependent (also called *subordinate*) clause to the end. Both phrases and dependent clauses function as modifiers. *Feeling generous* (a phrase) modifies *Sam*; and *who tried to catch it* (a clause) modifies *Irene*.

The difference between clauses and phrases is simple:

> A **clause** has both a subject and a verb.
>
> A **phrase** does not have both a subject and a verb.

Because a clause has both a subject and verb, a clause is always close to being a sentence of its own. The dependent clause, *who tried to catch it,* could be turned into a complete sentence by replacing *who* with *Irene* or *she,* or adding a question mark at the end.

The hallmark of a phrase is its lack of a subject or verb (or both). Phrases obviously cannot stand alone. *Feeling generous* needs the addition of both a subject (*Sam*) and a verb (*was*) in order to become the sentence *Sam was feeling generous.*

Our model sentence contains another clause besides the dependent clause we've already mentioned. The other clause is *Sam threw the orange to Irene.* Because it has both a subject and a verb, it must be a clause. Notice that it doesn't need any changes in order to stand alone as a complete sentence: that makes it an *independent* clause.

Terms of Disservice

Grammar is one of those things that helps with just about everything else, from comprehension of a tricky sentence to linking up parallel ideas and identifying structure. But specific questions about grammar basically boil down to things like whether you know what an antecedent is. Because there are so few grammar questions on this test, it's better to focus on the active reading and POE skills that will help you get through the other questions.

ORDERING THE QUESTIONS

You can complete the questions in any order you like but that doesn't mean you should jump around and do them in any old order. After you finish reading a passage, but before you begin answering the questions, ask yourself, "Do I feel confident about this passage? Would I be able to explain this to a friend? Could I explain its main idea?"

The answer to this question determines the order in which you should tackle the test questions.

- If you feel confident about your comprehension of the passage, complete the questions in the order they are given to you. Don't worry about the order of the questions; you're in good shape.
- If you don't feel confident about the main idea, do the detail questions first.

The reasoning behind this ordering method is simple. The main idea is the crucial thing to get from a reading passage, whether prose fiction or poetry. When you have the main idea nailed down, you aren't likely to miss more than a few questions on the passage. Knowing the main idea will help you answer all of the other general questions and many of the specific questions as well.

When you don't feel confident about the main idea (which usually means the passage is pretty confusing), start with the specific questions because they tell you exactly where to go and also give you something on which to focus.

As you reread the highlighted portions of text toward which the specific questions point you, you should become more and more familiar with the passage. Often after doing a specific question or two, the meaning of the passage "clicks" for you, and you will get what's going on. Don't answer the general questions until you have a firm sense of the main idea. If, after answering all the specific questions, you still don't really know what the point of the passage is, give the general questions your best shot and move on.

Bonus Tips and Tricks . . .
Check us out on YouTube
for additional
test taking tips and must-
know strategies at
youtube.com/
ThePrincetonReview

CONSISTENCY OF ANSWERS #1

The main idea should be your guiding rule for most of the questions on any passage. We call this principle *Consistency of Answers*. As you work on a passage or poem, you will find that the best answer on several of the questions has to do with the main idea. Here's the rule: **when in doubt, pick an answer that agrees with the main idea.**

Consistency Is Key
When in doubt, choose an answer that agrees with the main idea of the passage.

CONSISTENCY OF ANSWERS #2

Pick answers that agree with each other. You'll also find that correct answers tend to be consistent. It's a simple idea that comes in very handy. For example, if you're sure the correct answer to question 9 is (B), and (B) says that Mr. Buffalo is extremely hairy, you can be sure that question 10's Mr. Buffalo isn't bald. Correct answers agree with each other.

The best way to understand how to use this very effective technique is to see it at work. You'll see plenty of examples in Chapters 7 and 8; we'll discuss this technique in detail when we work on actual questions.

GUESSING AGGRESSIVELY WITH POE

First things first: don't leave any questions blank! There is no guessing penalty: worst-case scenario, guess blindly. But guessing smartly is much better! POE is an acronym for Process of Elimination. You are probably already acquainted with POE in its simplest form: cross out the answers that you know are wrong.

There are always two ways to answer a multiple-choice question correctly. The first is to have the answer in mind right from the moment you read the question. If you understand the passage and the question, you'll often see the best answer among the choices. Far more often, however, you'll be slightly (or not-so-slightly) unsure. The test-writers are pretty good at spotting places in a text where students are likely to have trouble, and they tend to write questions about these spots. The test-writers are also pretty good at writing wrong answers that are quite appealing. Before you doubt yourself, however, make sure you have read the question carefully. It's possible to understand the passage but misread a question. The extra second or two you devote to reading the question may increase the number of questions you answer correctly. Still, no matter how strong a reader you are, some questions will cause you to have doubts about the answer. That's when you use The Princeton Review–style POE. What does that mean? It means: *Stop looking for the right answer—look for wrong answers and eliminate them.* Let's look at the same example we used on page 68, from Zadie Smith's *White Teeth:*

Par.

1   Early in the morning, late in the century, Cricklewood Broadway. At 0627 hours on January 1, 1975, Alfred Archibald Jones was dressed in corduroy and sat in a fume-filled Cavalier Musketeer Estate facedown on the steering wheel, hoping the judgment would not be too heavy upon him. He lay in a prostrate cross, jaw slack, arms splayed on either side like some fallen angel; scrunched up in each fist he held his army service medals (left) and his marriage license (right), for he had decided to take his mistakes with him. A little green light flashed in his eye, signaling a right turn he had resolved never to make. He was resigned to it. He was prepared for it. He had flipped a coin and stood staunchly by the results. This was a decided-upon suicide. In fact, it was a New Year's resolution.

    ....

2   While he slipped in and out of consciousness, the position of the planets, the music of the spheres, the flap of a tiger moth's diaphanous wings in Central Africa, and a whole bunch of other stuff that Makes Shit Happen had decided it was second-chance time for Archie. Somewhere, somehow, by somebody, it had been decided that he would live.

1   ☐ Mark for Review

Paragraph 1 of the passage best describes the author's portrayal of Alfred Archibald Jones as

Ⓐ a sympathetic portrayal of a man who regrets his life

Ⓑ a farcical portrayal of an attempted suicide

Ⓒ a mock heroic portrait of a vintage car enthusiast

Ⓓ a darkly ironic treatment of an overly sensitive man

This is a typical AP English Lit question. It asks for an evaluation of a passage for comprehension. The majority of the questions take this form. In the example above, you've been asked, essentially, "What's going on in paragraph 1?" The actual passage would have been longer (usually around 55 lines), and the rest of the passage would certainly help you understand this section by putting it in context, but nevertheless, there is enough here to answer the question.

If you don't immediately spot the best answer, use POE. Go to each choice and say, "Why is this wrong?" You can look back at the explanations on pages 69–70 to check your thinking.

Chapter 4 Summary

o   Recognize the basic categories of questions.
- General Comprehension
- Detail

o   Don't worry about grammar for the AP English Literature and Composition Exam. It isn't worth enough points to cause perspiration.

o   Do it your way.
- If you know the main idea, answer the questions in order.
- If you're uncomfortable with the main idea, answer detail and factual questions first.

o   Use Consistency of Answers.
- When in doubt, pick an answer that agrees with the main idea.
- Pick answers that agree with each other.

o   Guess aggressively as needed using POE.

Chapter 5
Basic Principles of
the Essay Section

"

Fill your paper with the breathings of
your heart.

—William Wadsworth

"

FORMAT AND CONTENT OF THE ESSAY SECTION

Section II of the AP English Literature and Composition Exam is the Free-Response, or essay, section. While the College Board officially refers to this section of the exam as "Free Response," in this book we will often refer to it as the "essay" section, and your responses as "essays," for the sake of brevity. The format of this section has been consistent for years. Here's what to expect.

- You will be asked to write a response, in essay form, to each of the following subjects:
    1. A passage of poetry or a comparison of two thematically related poems
    2. A passage of prose fiction
    3. A literary argument: an essay on a literary concept or idea supported by evidence from your own reading or a provided list
- You'll have two hours to complete this section, which works out to be 40 minutes per essay.

Remember the Big Six!

The AP exam expects you to make use of the Big Six during the essay section. Remember, that's character, setting, structure, narration, figurative language like metaphor and personification, plus using the skills of literary argumentation (developing a thesis supported by textual evidence). In fact, the essays are all exercises in literary argumentation! So while you may be reading a 20th-century novelist or an English Renaissance poet, don't forget the Big Six. As you read each passage for the essay, think about how character, setting, structure, and narration can help you develop what you want to say, and how any figurative language you see in the passage works.

What Will You Be Writing About?

When ETS considers the mix of literary periods and styles on the test, it includes the essay section in that mix. If you see two passages on 18th-century poetry in the multiple-choice section, you won't see any 18th-century poetry in the essay section. ETS also tries to give male and female authors (roughly) equal representation and aims to include at least one author who identifies as African American, Native American, Latino, or Asian.

What Are The Directions?

The College Board will give you a bit of text to orient you to the work (they will likely map out the work's themes and date of publication); then they will ask that you do four things, which they put in a handy bulleted list that we will print right here.

In your response you should do the following:

- Respond to the prompt with a thesis that presents an interpretation and may establish a line of reasoning.
- Select and use evidence to develop and support your line of reasoning.
- Explain the relationship between the evidence and your thesis.
- Use appropriate grammar and punctuation in communicating your argument.

If you have written essays for classes, you probably see that this is standard stuff that they want:

Thesis—Your take on exactly what they are asking. You're confident and eager to show them that you understand both the essay prompt and the work itself!

Evidence—You definitely get it and now we're diving into your reasoning. Here are your examples that back up your thesis.

More Evidence—Would they like some MORE examples with those examples? You're happy to oblige!

Finally, remember to use some solid vocabulary, correct punctuation, grammar, and spelling throughout. The word "throughout" makes us think about how much time you have to crank out this spectacular essay. It's time to talk pacing.

Pacing

On each individual essay, you can take as much or as little time as you like as long as you don't go over the two-hour limit for all three essays. Each essay is worth the same number of points, so it's a good idea to pace yourself and allot 40 minutes for each, give or take a few minutes. College Board recommends that, of those 40 minutes, students spend 15 minutes planning and 25 minutes writing for each essay. Doing that usually makes for a better essay than just writing without planning! Be mindful of your time. If you spend an hour and a half on your first essay, you're not going to finish the other two. Remember to take a watch so that you don't lose track of time.

The Importance of the Essay Section to Your Score

The essay section of the AP English Literature and Composition Exam counts for 55 percent of your total score. It is only slightly more important than the multiple-choice section of the test. It's obvious, but let's say it anyway: both sections are important to your score.

Which section *feels* more important is another issue. For most students, the essay section feels like the whole test. The multiple-choice section seems like a bunch of hoops you have to jump through before getting to the part that matters. Students tend to look at the essay section with quite a bit of anxiety. However, we're going to take the anxiety out of this process and replace it with knowledge and confidence.

Here's the interesting part: while it is true that the multiple-choice and essay sections are nearly equal in respect to determining your score, there is a world of difference between the two sections when it comes to score improvement.

More Great Titles from The Princeton Review

Are you also taking the AP English Language and Composition course? Check out *AP English Language & Composition Prep,* our comprehensive prep guide for the test.

When It Comes to Improving Your Score, the Essays Are King

If you're the kind of student who gets A's in class and then bombs on standardized tests, using our multiple-choice techniques will make a huge difference. If you are already a natural test-taker, that's great—our techniques will help you take your skills to the next level. You probably fall somewhere in between (the vast majority of students do), and so using our techniques for the multiple-choice section squeezes out a half-dozen or so extra points to ensure that you get your best possible score. Why settle for anything less? But when you work on improving your score (and your skills), the essays are different.

These Essays Are Different

Essay points add up fast. If we can show you a way to improve your essays by just 1 point—*bam*—then that means 3 extra essay points just like that, 1 for each essay. And there are only 18 total essay points available. And now that the College Board has made the essay grading "analytical" (no longer "holistic") and released detailed grading rubrics, you can know precisely how you can rack up points on the three essays.

Think about this: unlike the old, familiar multiple-choice questions, the essays are completely new. You've never done anything like them before, so you may as well learn to do them in a way that will get you the most points. "What!?" you're thinking, "It's the multiple-choice that's weird; I write essays *all the time* in school."

Sorry, but you're mistaken. You write essays, true—but not AP Exam essays.

Your Teacher Knows You

You usually write essays for teachers who know you and (we hope) care about you. They know what your writing looked like at the beginning of the semester, they know whether you do your homework, they know whether you spend most of class daydreaming, they know you occasionally make brilliant comments in class, and they know your real passion is for track or violin or painting or science or maybe even writing.

When your teachers see your name at the top of the page, they already know a thousand things about you, and all of it goes into their reading of what you write. The AP Reader, on the other hand, doesn't know you at all.

You Know Your Teacher

Second, and just as important, you don't know anything about the Reader of your AP essays. Who are they? In school, you know your teachers. You probably know what they want to hear. You may know that they detest misspellings, or that they love it when you use humor, or that they give extra credit for artistic originality. The AP essays are written to someone who is completely anonymous. When was the last time you wrote an essay to a total stranger for a grade?

Read It—Write It—Go!

AP essays are written under intense time restraints. You've probably never seen the excerpt or the prompt, but that's okay. You have the reading and writing strategies to tackle anything at this point. Your teachers have probably told you that good writing is rewriting; however, you don't have time to write and revise on the AP Exam. In a test setting, your draft is your final submission, and that means you have to be extra attentive to the structural and content quality of your writing. The type of writing you'll complete for the AP Exam is kind of the opposite of how you should approach a writing task. In short, the "ready, set, write" approach of the AP Exam feels a little unnatural, but you can do it.

Your AP teacher should be drilling you with this style of essay for the duration of the course because it is the closest thing to writing for the AP Exam that you'll experience before test day. Most in-class tests are administered over materials you've studied and know well, but AP Exam prompts are most likely unfamiliar to you and the rest of the test-takers. We call this a cold reading and writing—that just means this is a passage you're seeing and writing on for the first time. You will be graded on quality of writing and content, but remember that comprehension and originality are also important. Address the prompts directly; don't talk around the questions, and be sure to stay on top of the Conventions of Standard English (CSE). If you write clearly and on topic, you should be just fine.

It may be a little nerve wracking to write this way, but remember that everyone else is in the same boat. This chapter is designed to give you the tools you need to understand how the essays are scored so that you can tailor your writing to fit the rubrics. We aren't necessarily teaching you how to write well: we're trying to teach you how to write a high-scoring AP essay. AP essays are different beasts, but they can be tackled!

Need More Help on Essays?

We've got just the book for that! *How to Write Essays for Standardized Tests* contains advice and examples of best practices on an assortment of AP exams, plus ACT, and others!

Any Changes? Go Online
Download the detailed grading rubrics directly from the College Board's website for even more information.

ALL ABOUT AP ESSAY SCORING

The 0 to 6 Scale

Each of your three essays will be graded according to a 6-point scale. Zero is the worst you can get and 6 is the best. Students' scores are not spread out evenly over that range.

After the College Board released its revised AP English Literature and Composition Course and Exam Description in May 2019, it decided to change things again and released updates to that in September 2019. Never a dull moment in the world of AP test prep!

The September 2019 update included major updates to the Free-Response Section, as we mentioned earlier. These essays are now scored on a scale of 0–6 (no more 0–9) and holistic scoring has been replaced by analytical scoring.

"Analytic" Scoring

The essays are scored "analytically" now. They used to be scored "holistically" which was somewhat vague and subjective, so we are thrilled at the release of a clear scoring rubric and point-by-point guidelines. Let's look at the scoring rubrics by question type and remember that each question could earn 6 points maximum.

Question 1: Poetry Analysis

Thesis	0–1 point available	• You will get 1 point if the essay responds to the prompt with a thesis (can be a single sentence or more and anywhere within the response) that presents a defensible interpretation of the poem. If your thesis is more than one sentence, the sentences need to be in close proximity. • You will get 0 points if there is no defensible thesis, no coherent claims are made, or the thesis only restates the prompt and does not respond to it.
Evidence and Commentary	0–4 points available	• You will get 4 points if your essay provides specific evidence to support all claims in a line of reasoning, consistently explains how evidence supports that line of reasoning, and explains how multiple literary elements/techniques in a poem contribute to its meaning. Note that writing that suffers from grammatical and/or mechanical errors that interfere with communication cannot get 4 points total. • You will get 0 points if the essay is simply a repetition of provided information or offers information irrelevant to the prompt. • You will get 1 point if your essay provides evidence that is mostly general and summarizes without explaining evidence. • You will get 2 points if your essay provides some specific, relevant evidence, but no line of reasoning is established or your line of reasoning is faulty. • You will get 3 points if your essay provides specific evidence in support of all claims in your line of reasoning, explains how some of the evidence supports the line of reasoning, and explains how at least 1 literary element/technique contributes to the meaning of the poem.
Sophistication	0–1 point available	• You will get 1 point if your essay demonstrates sophistication of thought and/or develops a complex literary argument. • You will get 0 points if your essay oversimplifies the poem, uses ineffective language, only hints at interpretations of the poem, or makes sweeping generalizations about the content of the poem.

Question 2: Prose Fiction Analysis

Thesis	0–1 point available	• You will get 1 point if your essay responds to the prompt with a thesis (can be a single sentence or more and anywhere within the response) that presents a defensible interpretation of the passage. If your thesis is more than one sentence, the sentences need to be in close proximity.
		• You will get 0 points if there is no defensible thesis, no coherent claims are made, or the thesis only restates the prompt and does not respond to it.
Evidence and Commentary	0–4 points available	• You will get 4 points if your essay provides specific evidence to support all claims in a line of reasoning, consistently explains how evidence supports that line of reasoning, and explains how multiple literary elements/techniques in the passage contribute to its meaning. Note that writing that suffers from grammatical and/or mechanical errors that interfere with communication cannot get 4 points total.
		• You will get 0 points if the essay is simply a repetition of provided information or offers information irrelevant to the prompt.
		• You will get 1 point if your essay provides evidence that is mostly general and summarizes without explaining evidence.
		• You will get 2 points if your essay provides some specific, relevant evidence, but no line of reasoning is established or your line of reasoning is faulty.
		• You will get 3 points if your essay provides specific evidence in support of all claims in your line of reasoning and explains how some of the evidence supports that line of reasoning, and explains how at least 1 literary element/technique contributes to the meaning of the passage.
Sophistication	0–1 point available	• You will get 1 point if your essay demonstrates sophistication of thought and/or develops a complex literary argument.
		• You will get 0 points if your essay oversimplifies the passage, uses ineffective language, only hints at interpretations of the passage, or makes sweeping generalizations about the interpretation of the passage.

Question 3: Literary Argument

Thesis	0–1 point available	• You will get 1 point if your essay responds to the prompt with a thesis (can be a single sentence or more and anywhere within the response) that presents a defensible interpretation of the selected work. If your thesis is more than one sentence, the sentences need to be in close proximity. • You will get 0 points if there is no defensible thesis, no coherent claims are made, or the thesis only restates the prompt and does not respond to it.
Evidence and Commentary	0–4 points available	• You will get 4 points if your essay provides specific evidence to support all claims in a line of reasoning and consistently explains how evidence supports that line of reasoning. • You will get 0 points if the essay is simply a repetition of provided information or offers information irrelevant to the prompt. • You will get 1 point if your essay provides evidence that is mostly general and summarizes without explaining evidence. • You will get 2 points if your essay provides some specific, relevant evidence, but no line of reasoning is established or your line of reasoning is faulty. • You will get 3 points if your essay provides specific evidence in support of all claims in your line of reasoning and explains how some of the evidence supports that line of reasoning.
Sophistication	0–1 point available	• You will get 1 point if your essay demonstrates sophistication of thought and/or develops a complex literary argument. • You will get 0 points if your essay oversimplifies the prompt, uses ineffective language, only hints at interpretations of the selected work, or makes sweeping generalizations about the prompt.

Stay Up to Date!
For late-breaking information about test dates, exam formats, and any other changes pertaining to AP English Lit and Comp, make sure to check the College Board's website at apstudents.collegeboard. org/courses/ap-english-literature-and-composition

THE READER WANTS AN ESSAY THAT'S EASY TO SCORE

Readers are dedicated high school and university instructors who take a week out of their year to come to one site and grade essays. Of course, they are compensated for their time, but at times the grading can become monotonous. You need to make sure that your essay stands out from the hundreds of essays that each Reader scores.

Your job is to write an essay that's obviously better than average. You have to let the Reader feel confident about giving you at least a 5. Usually, the essays are generic and have no distinctive style to them. Often the essays are plot summaries that barely address the question. In many cases, the question is rewritten and the essay does not explore the topic adequately or with skill. Slogging through these mediocre essays, the Reader gives a score and turns to the next essay hoping for that outstanding paper. Readers want to reward the writers for what they do well, but the topic must be addressed. If an essay starts out dull and poorly written but makes one completely original point right at the very end, the writer can be rewarded. Sometimes, however, there are too many grammar and spelling errors that distract the Reader and the one important statement that the writer makes is lost among the myriad errors on the page. If you merely summarize the plot of the passage or do not adequately address the question, the Reader may have to give you a 2 or a 3, based on the grading rubric. You want to make it as easy as possible for the scorer to think your essay is good.

ANALYSIS OF THE SCORING RUBRIC

Look carefully over the Scoring Rubrics from earlier in this chapter. What do you see?

The College Board has shared an exact formula for how you can score a 6. You can rack up point by point following those scoring rubrics. The recurring theme is to go deeper, give more examples, flesh out those examples, and put things in context. But also, more than anything, be clear.

High-scoring essays aren't necessarily inspiring or life-changing, but they are very clear. They establish a clear thesis and bolster that point throughout. Note that in their scoring rubric, the College Board says that your thesis may appear anywhere within your essay, but we find it's easiest to share it up front. Lay down your thesis and then build on that, tallying points along the way as you layer on the evidence and commentary (again, from their rubric). Finally, dazzle them with your sophistication.

Here's a Tip!

It doesn't hurt to think like a reader as you practice the essays. In the free-response essays, you're going to see the following verbs. Be sure to understand what they mean to the people who will be scoring you.

Analyze: Examine methodically and in detail the structure of the topic of the question in order to interpret and explain the passage.

Choose: Select a literary work from among provided choices.

Read: Look at or view printed directions and provided passages.

If you understand what you read and can write in grammatical English, a 3 is your absolute low-end score. You will almost certainly do better than that with our help.

The Adequate Essay Formula

Almost every adequate essay is written by a student who doesn't know how to craft a real essay idea based on the question and thinks that the "essay formula" can somehow save him. Here's the thought process that invariably leads to a middle score: "Let's see . . . they want me to write about the language . . . well, what *else* would I write about? The whole *thing* is language. This is crazy. And 'how the author dramatized the story'—well, with *language* of course—great, that's about one sentence worth of essay. What am I going to say? I don't know what they want! Yikes! I can't sit here forever; *I've got to write something*. I know! I'll restate the question as a statement and then come up with three examples: one for diction, one for imagery, and one for point of view. Then I'll summarize it all for a conclusion. *That's the essay formula, right?* Okay, here goes."

Panic + No Idea of What Is Wanted = The Adequate Essay

This student is perfectly intelligent. The "formula" isn't crazy; in fact, it's taught all over the place. Restate the question as a statement. Support the statement with three examples from the passage. Summarize it for a conclusion.

It sounds good, but when a student tries to use it, he'll realize he still doesn't have one interesting thing to say. From beginning to end he'll feel lost, and writing the essay will feel like one big, meaningless exercise. He'll struggle and pick out bits of the passage that catch his eye and try to discuss them. He won't be exactly sure why they catch his eye, but he'll make up something. The discussion will be vague, overly generalized, and mechanical. (That's the description of adequate essays in the AP scoring guide, remember.) The adequate essay has to be vague, because if it were precise, the student would reveal that he has no precise understanding of what he's supposed to be writing about. The formula results in a weak, boring essay.

The formula, however, is actually a heroic effort on the student's part because no student is used to writing this way. When a student is writing from this place of panic and simply fulfilling a formulaic structure, a 3 is a success.

HOW TO MAKE IT EASY FOR THE READER TO GIVE YOU A HIGH SCORE

The most important part of your essay is the content. Your goal is to write meaty, content-filled essays that just blow the Reader away. But the Reader has to get to that content. There are a few vital things you must do to let your excellence come shining through with full impact. These basics have to do with the surface of your writing. That might seem cheap, but it's not. If the surface of your essay is clean and clear, the Reader can see through to the depths.

Indent

Keep It Clean
Don't underestimate the power of a tidy-looking essay. Write in paragraphs. No one wants to read a single paragraph that goes on for pages!

Your Reader's first impressions are crucial. Think about that character at the job interview with gum in his hair. If his battle isn't already lost, it's definitely an uphill fight the rest of the way. The overall look of your essay is a first impression. It's the smile on your face as you walk in the door. Your essay should look neat, organized, and clear. Make your paragraphs obvious. Indent twice as far as you normally would. When in doubt, make a paragraph. Ever look at a book, flip it open, and see nothing but one long paragraph? Your next thought is usually, "Oh please, don't make me have to read this!" That's exactly what Readers think when they see an essay without paragraphs. Neat presentation and indented paragraphs will show the Reader that you're super organized and you've got some great thoughts to share.

Write Perfectly . . . for the First Paragraph

Your "second first impression" (in case you were wondering, that's an **oxymoron**—see the glossary) is the first paragraph of the essay. Take extra care with your first paragraph. If you're unsure about the spelling of a word, don't use it. If you're unsure how to punctuate a sentence, rewrite it in a way that makes you feel confident. Don't make any mistakes in the first paragraph. Don't fret as much about the rest of the essay; the Readers expect mistakes. But the first paragraph needs to be strong because it sets the tone. If you try to write the whole essay perfectly, you'll write so slowly, or fill up your brain with so much worry, that you'll probably run out of time.

All you need is a few sentences to convince the Reader that you can write a good sentence when you want to. The glow of a good beginning carries over to the whole essay. Mistakes later on look like minor errors not even worth bothering with. After all, the Reader's already seen that you can write. Mistakes at the very beginning do just the opposite—they look like telling signs of inability and a weak grasp of fundamental English mechanics. Take extra care at the beginning of your essay; then relax and just write.

Show Off Your Literary Vocabulary

Readers do not give great grades to students who merely parrot the prompt. A good way to show that you understand what the question is asking is by paraphrasing the prompt in your response. If the prompt asks about diction, knowing that diction means "word choice" is great. Articulating how the author uses a particular form of diction is even better. Be sure that you know the meaning of key literary terms that frequently appear on the exam (see the glossary of literary terms), and have some good synonyms at hand so you can display varied word choice.

For poetry analysis, the big words are **diction**, **imagery**, **metaphor**, **rhyme**, and **form**. For prose fiction, substitute **point of view** and **characterization** for rhyme and form. Using the word "speaker" to refer to the poetry narrator and "narrator" when dealing with prose fiction is a convention worth employing because it will show that you are comfortable with the modes of writing that Readers will recognize from teaching students about literature. Remember, an entire point is dedicated to sophistication and that means both sophistication of thought and of language.

Use Snappy Verbs and Tasty Nouns

Spice up your writing. Try to write with some pizzazz. Don't let the test environment, the tension, or the anxiety caused by writing for a stranger take over your brain. Take risks. You may fall flat every so often, but the Reader will appreciate your effort and reward it. When you've gotten our essay techniques down, you'll understand that 90 percent of dull student writing on AP essays comes from confusion about what to write, which leads to inhibition. Don't be inhibited. Jazz it up a little. Show some stylistic flair.

Obviously, it's possible to go overboard here and if the Reader gets the impression you're just being silly, it won't help your score. It is important to write about the task at hand, not just your musings on life. But a dash of glitter is much better than none at all. By the way, big, important-sounding phrases are not your ticket to a high score. They're an obvious sign that you're full of it. So please don't try to write this kind of gibberish: "When Judy initially perceived Roger's rapid ambulatory movement along the pedestrian walkway bordering the automotive thoroughfare, she experienced tachycardia."

Vital Vocab
Key words to use in your essays include *diction, imagery, metaphor, rhyme, form, point of view,* and *characterization.*

Impressing Your Readers

If you write like someone who enjoys writing, the Readers will be impressed. Going back to the previous example, a student might write, "When Judy first sees Roger going down the street, she thinks he seems interesting." That's probably true, but what a bore! There are a thousand ways to liven up that sentence. It all depends on your personality and what is really happening in the story. How about, "When Judy first glimpses Roger dashing through the shadows of Sullivan Street, her heart flutters; she's already in love, she just doesn't know it yet." Or, "When Judy spots Roger flying down the sidewalk with the Sullivan Street gang nipping at his heels, she's dumbstruck by the wild vitality of his whirling limbs and blazing eyes." Cheesy? Over the top? Who cares? Nobody expects you to write like Marcel Proust. Actually, the Readers expect you to write like someone who's suffering through a tedious, nerve-wracking exercise because that's exactly how most of the essays are written.

We aren't saying you have to write tangled, complex sentences either; in fact, you should try to avoid them. Great, long, looping sentences usually just wander off into error and confusion. All you need to do is pay attention to your word choice. When you find yourself using a generic verb like *look*, *see*, *says*, *walk*, *go*, *take*, or *give*, or a generic noun like *street*, *house*, *car*, or *man*, ask yourself whether there isn't a more precise, more colorful word you can use. Why write *house* when you're referring to a *mansion*, or *car* when you're really writing about a *jalopy*? Just a little bit of this goes a long way. It shows you're not scared, and it might even look like you're having fun, which is very good.

The Questions

Each passage will be preceded by instructions to "Read the passage carefully. Then, in a well-written essay, analyze. . . ." These instructions may also contain some additional material orienting you to the passage, telling you things like who wrote it, the literary work it was drawn from, and any other special information the test-writers feel you need to know in order to understand the passage. Be sure to give the instructions a complete look in case there's any useful information there.

Answer the Question

If you write a great essay that the Reader doesn't think addresses the question, you'll get a lousy score. All three essays, even the literary argument, will be directed, and the questions will tell you exactly what the test-writers want—that's the theory, anyway. In reality, the questions can be infuriatingly vague but at the same time, not answering the question is the ultimate sin. Understanding and answering the question are crucial to writing a high-scoring essay.

Timing

Just like the passages in the multiple-choice section, the essay prompts should be answered in the order that works best for you. The one that appears easiest should be your first feat. Get your writing juices flowing, and soak up some of your confidence as you write. You want to write all three essays; therefore, you have to keep a handle on your time. Completing the easiest essay topic (for you) first will help you to save time for the harder responses. You're given 120 minutes (two hours) to complete all three essays. Ideally, you'll use only 40 minutes for each essay; however, how you choose to delegate your time between essays may mean more time for one writing task and less for another. Again, keep a watch close. Set it to 12:00. It's easy to see how much time has progressed and how much is left if you keep up with your time in this manner.

The Two Most Important Things to Ask Yourself When Tackling an AP Essay

1. What is the meaning?
2. How do I know it?

When you sit down to write an essay, you really can't write word one until you've deciphered what the prompt is asking you to do. Find the actual command and underline it, highlight it, or put a star by it. Remind yourself as you write exactly what you're working to accomplish with your essay.

Certain members of the Big Six are your friends when you're answering questions like "what is the meaning?" and "how do I know it?" Do the character, settings, structure, and narration inform your answers? They certainly can; give them a whirl.

Chapter 5 Summary

General Essay Information

o   There are three essays: one essay on a prose fiction passage, one essay on one or two poems, and one essay on a work that you select (the literary argument).

o   You have two hours to complete all three essays. Time yourself. Spend approximately 40 minutes on each essay.

o   The essays are a great place to improve your score.

Essay Scoring

o   Each essay is given a score from 0 to 6.

o   The essays are scored "analytically" according to a scoring rubric. Familiarize yourself with this rubric so you can learn how to tally up points, one by one, on exam day. The three categories of the rubric are thesis, evidence and commentary, and sophistication.

o   The Reader wants to read an essay that's easy to score.

o   High-scoring essays are interesting, clear essays. Middle-scoring essays are generic and boring. Low-scoring essays are plain old bad.

Presentation

o   Do everything in your power to make your essays readable.

o   Make your paragraph indentations easy to spot.

o   When in doubt, create a new paragraph.

o   Your first paragraph should be grammatically perfect. Your Reader will make a very quick judgment about your ability to write. Once the Reader has decided you can write a sentence, you'll get some slack later on (as long as you write neatly).

o   Have a solid literary vocabulary. You'll express yourself with greater clarity.

o   Try to use interesting, snappy verbs and nouns. It will impress the Reader and make them think you're comfortable, confident, and smart. Don't stress too much about overdoing the jazzy language, but don't go bananas.

o   Don't confuse interesting, snappy verbs and nouns with ten-dollar vocabulary words. Use the best, most precise word you can think of, not the one with the most syllables.

o   Understand the question. (Don't worry; there's much more on this subject in Part V.)

o   If you write a great essay that doesn't address the question, you won't get a great score.

o   Order the section. Do the essay you like best first, and save the worst one for last.

o   Manage your time—try to complete each essay in about 40 minutes.

Part V
Content Review and Practice for the AP English Literature and Composition Exam

Chapter 6
An Overview
of Literary
Movements

USING THIS OVERVIEW

If you have allotted yourself enough time before the test, this section gives you the opportunity to familiarize yourself with the potential content of the exam. If you are reading this book months before you are to take the test, you can use this section in a methodical, poem-by-poem manner. By reading the 200 representative poems listed in this chapter, you will gain a thorough sense of the kinds of poems that the College Board chooses from when writing its tests. If you are using this book during crunch time and the test is a few weeks away, our suggestion is to read a poem or two from each movement and to familiarize yourself more broadly with the ideas associated with each movement. If you are picking up this book for the first time when you have only a few days left to study for the exam, then skip this section and make sure you're familiar with the material in Part III and Part IV, which address cracking the test.

You may notice that this chapter is almost exclusively poetry-based. We have done it this way for two main reasons. First, students typically have more difficulty with poetry analysis than with prose friction. Reviewing this chapter will allow you to freshen up your knowledge on poets and poems, as well as the ideas associated with specific movements.

Second, if you are short on time, you can read more poems in a shorter amount of time than you can read full-length novels, plays, and short stories. Even reading a few poems from each movement will give you a sense of the notable characteristics of a specific period or genre.

Before getting into the overview, let's answer some questions you may have.

Does the AP English Exam Require Certain Readings?

A lot of students wonder if there's an AP English Lit and Comp reading list of specific books, poems, plays, and authors that they should be reading. While the College Board does not release an exact list of works or authors you should or must know, there are some books that crop up time and time again as classics, "the canon," and works expressing important themes that AP level students should be able to explore.

The test will choose texts from a variety of time periods and literary movements. While this chapter gives you a historical survey you should learn, the College Board will be including a greater number of 20th-century and contemporary works than those published before the 20th century.

For Further Exploration

It's not a list, but some specific works DO crop up in the College Board's AP English Literature and Composition Classroom Resources, which is posted on their website here: apcentral.collegeboard.org/courses/ap-english-literature-and-composition/classroom-resources?course=ap-english-literature-and-composition

Though the Advanced Placement English curriculum avoids requiring any specific list of authors or texts to be taught, there are certainly seminal works with which you should be familiar. Reading these works is important for the AP English Literature and Composition Exam, but also useful to become a well-read human who is aware of cultural references, certain popular metaphors and parables, characters, archetypes, and such. A list of these important authors to know is below, plus many additional works are tallied up later in this book in Chapter 11.

W. H. Auden

Elizabeth Bishop

William Blake

Anne Bradstreet

Edward Kamau Brathwaite

Gwendolyn Brooks

Samuel Taylor Coleridge

H. D. (Hilda Doolittle)

Emily Dickinson

John Donne

John Dryden

T. S. Eliot

Robert Frost

Seamus Heaney

George Herbert

Langston Hughes

John Keats

Robert Lowell

Andrew Marvel

Marianne Moore

Sylvia Plath

Alexander Pope

Adrienne Rich

Anne Sexton

Percy Bysshe Shelley

Walt Whitman

William Carlos Williams

William Wordsworth

William Butler Yeats

For a more complete list of authors
and poets, see pages 56–59.

How Can a List of Representative Authors Help Me Prepare for the Exam?

By itself, a list of authors or poets will not help you. To someone who doesn't know much about poetry, it will be more daunting than illustrative. However, when the list is reformatted to group writers by literary movement rather than list them alphabetically, you may find that the once intimidating list has become much more understandable and helpful. You will still need to do a good deal of reading in order to apply the concepts of each literary movement to this exam, as no shortcut exists for becoming well-read. This chapter, however, will give you an efficient and organized method to follow, and a good overview of each movement.

What Is a Literary Movement?

A literary movement (or school of literature or poetry) is a grouping of writers who share similar aims, years of publication, and bases of operation. Some writers acknowledge or even encourage the idea of being seen as members of a single group, such as William Wordsworth and Samuel Taylor Coleridge, who consciously published some of their earlier poems in a volume that also included essays about their shared aesthetic ideals. Other writers actively reject the notion of being grouped. One such person was John Ashbery, who often maintained a bemused wariness when the term "New York School" is applied to his work.

How Can Knowing the Literary Movement of a Poem Help Me?

Regardless of whether or not the poets acknowledge their participation in a movement, you can put the following information to good use. For example, if you recognize that a poem is in the metaphysical tradition, you will have some immediate, ready-made ideas about form, structure, narration, content, figurative language, and overall meaning. You will know to look for witty, surprising pairings of concrete and abstract ideas. You will expect irony and paradox to percolate beneath even the most religious content. And you will pay special attention to the ornate quality of the conceits. On the other hand, the moment you recognize that a poem is from the romantic tradition, you will be able to call up the phrases "sublime transcendence," "redemptive nature," and "imaginative power." If you have practiced using these phrases, you can use them appropriately for part of a meaningful and attentive analysis of the concrete particulars of a poem. Studying poems within the framework of their literary movements may also help you on the multiple-choice section. If you are familiar with the period of a poem provided in the multiple-choice section, you may more easily recognize the correct answer (or at least be able to eliminate answers that are obviously incorrect).

LITERARY MOVEMENT OVERVIEW

In the following overview, you will find some of the most important poets and poems of each movement as well as a list of what to look for in these poems. The best way to use these lists to help you crack the exam is to read some of the suggested poems and note where specific features of each movement show up. Practice writing an analytical essay on one poem from each movement, using at least two of the features from the list somewhere in your essay, and you'll be off to a great start. Or draft outlines of possible essays using different poems to familiarize yourself with the poems and relevant themes. The more familiar you are with some key phrases, the more likely you'll be to smoothly incorporate them into your analytical prose. Be warned: if you only adopt them without actually considering what they mean or without practicing using them, they are likely to seem artificial and may even hurt your score.

The following list concentrates on the schools of literature that are most commonly included on the AP English Literature and Composition Exam, and ignores other important movements that the College Board is less likely to emphasize. An excellent website for further study of the whole idea of literary movements is www.poets.org. It includes many links to brief poet biographies and sample poems from the movements listed in our overview. In fact, many of the representative poems in our overview were chosen because they are easily accessible through links from this website. Another great online resource is www.poetryfoundation.org.

Poetry Online

There are a bunch of great websites you can use to brush up on your knowledge of poems and poets. Check out poets.org and poetryfoundation.org

Metaphysical Poetry

Representative Metaphysical Poets and Poems
- John Donne (1572–1631)—"A Valediction: Forbidding Mourning"; "The Sun Rising"; "Death Be Not Proud—Holy Sonnet X"; "Woman's Constancy"; "Love's Alchemy"
- George Herbert (1593–1633)—"Easter Wings"; "The Collar"; "Jordan (I)"; "Love (III)"; "The Windows"
- Andrew Marvell (1621–1678)—"The Mower's Song"; "The Mower to the Glow-Worms"; "The Mower Against Gardens"; "The Garden"; "To His Coy Mistress"

A Quick Definition
Metaphysical poetry is a mostly 17th-century English poetic mode that breaks with earlier Renaissance ideas about romantic poetry. Instead of following in the footsteps of the troubadours, Petrarch and Shakespeare, who often wrote love poetry that placed the object of their poems on a pedestal, metaphysical poems often exhibit introspective meditations on love, death, God, and human frailty. The poems of John Donne, for example, are much more realistic about sexual relationships. Metaphysical poetry is famous for its obscurity (and therefore a favorite choice of the College Board).

What to Look for in Metaphysical Poetry
- Wit, irony, and paradox are paramount—wit is often seen in the pairing of dissimilar objects into the service of a clever, ironic analogy or paradoxical conceit. For example, see how Donne's speaker in "A Valediction: Forbidding Mourning" uses astronomy and math to illustrate his deep abiding love for his wife.
- Elaborate stylistic maneuvers (ornamental conceits, dazzling rhymes) are pulled off with aplomb. For example, look at how Herbert uses relative line length, stanza shape, rhyme, and repetition in "Easter Wings" to underscore the importance of human humility.
- Huge shifts in scale proliferate (for example, ants to planets). Consider how Marvell's speaker in "The Mower to the Glow-Worms" conflates glow-worms and comets, for example.
- These formal tendencies are used by metaphysical poets to talk about deep philosophical issues: the passage of time; the difficulty of ever being sure of any one thing; the uneasy relationships of human beings to one another and to God; the fearful, obsessive qualities that death often inspires in human consciousness. Sometimes, after all of the elaborate style is reduced and its content summarized, the truism that is left can seem clichéd. Most of the beauty of metaphysical poetry is in the dramatic unfolding of that truth through techniques like irony, conceits, and scale shifts.

Get It Donne
If metaphysical poetry comes up on the test (and it probably will), think John Donne. Review some of the poems listed here before test day if you need a refresher.

Augustans

Representative English Augustan Poets and Poems
- John Dryden (1631–1700)—"Mac Flecknoe"; "Marriage a-la-mode"; "Absalom and Achitophel"
- Alexander Pope (1688–1744)—"The Rape of the Lock"; "Windsor Forest"; "Epitaph on Sir Isaac Newton"

Related Prose Fiction and Plays
- *Gulliver's Travels* and "A Modest Proposal" by Jonathan Swift (1667–1745)
- *A Beggar's Opera* by John Gay (1685–1732)

A Quick Definition
Augustan poetry is best known for its rhymed, heroic-couplet satire. These pairs of lines in iambic pentameter often produce great forward propulsion, and most students report that reading them aloud helps with comprehension. Coming between the baroque metaphysical poets and the enthusiastically sincere romantic poets, the wickedly funny Augustan poets went back to antiquity for their inspiration. They translated Greek and Roman epics into English using heroic couplets and wrote their own original work based on classical forms.

What to Look for in Augustan Poetry
- Wit, irony, and paradox are still as important here as they were for the metaphysical poets, but one must also add brevity to the list when discussing the Augustans. Their poems can be quite long but because they employ the heroic couplet so pointedly, their observations are often quite pithy. As Pope put it in his poem "Essay on Criticism," "True wit is nature to advantage dress'd,/What oft was thought, but ne'er so well express'd."
- The ongoing subject of Augustan poetry is human frailty. Even when these poets used biblical subjects and allusions for their plots, as Dryden does in "Absalom and Achitophel," the tone taken often mocks human behavior: "What cannot praise effect in mighty minds, When flattery soothes, and when ambition blinds!"
- These poets were also likely to dress absurdly mundane plots (such as the secret cutting of a noble maiden's hair in "Rape of the Lock") in the outward appearance of heroic epic poetry for comic effect.
- Current events figure in these poems, either allegorically or directly. In his famous epitaph for Sir Isaac Newton, Pope wrote: "Nature and nature's laws lay hid in night; God said 'Let Newton be' and all was light," which addresses the ongoing controversies between the forces of religion and science in 18th century Europe. John Dryden's poem "Mac Flecknoe" satirizes another prominent poet of his day and takes sides in contemporary political debates, similar to how a present-day poet with Democratic leanings might make fun of Republican leaders.

Romantic Poetry

Representative English Romantic Poets and Poems
- William Wordsworth (1770–1850)—"I Wandered Lonely as a Cloud"; "Composed Upon Westminster Bridge Sept. 3, 1802"; "Lines Composed a Few Miles Above Tintern Abbey"; "My Heart Leaps Up When I Behold"; "Lucy"
- Percy Bysshe Shelley (1792–1822)—"Ozymandias"; "Ode to the West Wind"; "Adonais—An Elegy on the Death of John Keats"; "The Cloud"; "Hymn to Intellectual Beauty"
- John Keats (1795–1821)—"Ode on a Grecian Urn"; "When I Have Fears That I May Cease to Be"; "To Autumn"; "La Belle Dame Sans Merci"; "Ode to a Nightingale"
- William Blake (1757–1827)—"The Tiger"; "The Lamb"; "A Poison Tree"; "The Sick Rose"

Got a Question?
For answers to test-prep questions for all your tests and additional test taking tips, subscribe to our YouTube channel at youtube.com/ThePrincetonReview

Representative American Transcendental Poets and Poems
- Ralph Waldo Emerson (1803–1882)—"Ode to Beauty"; "The World-Soul"; "Song of Nature"
- Walt Whitman (1819–1892)—"When I Heard the Learn'd Astronomer"; "A Noiseless Patient Spider"; "Crossing Brooklyn Ferry"; "There Was a Child Went Forth"; "Song of the Open Road"

Related European Prose Fiction
- *Ivanhoe* by Sir Walter Scott (1771–1832)
- *Les Misérables* by Victor Hugo (1802–1885)

Related American Prose Fiction
- *The Scarlet Letter* by Nathaniel Hawthorne (1804–1864)
- "The Poet," an essay by Ralph Waldo Emerson that inspired Whitman to become a poet
- "Walking," an essay by Henry David Thoreau (1817–1862)

A Quick Definition
Romantic poetry written in English is a (mostly) 19th-century English and American poetic mode that breaks with earlier neoclassical ideas about poetry by specifically emphasizing that these poems were written in, as Wordsworth calls it, "the real language of men" and were about "common life." This poetry is emotional and often enthusiastic in its embracing of the large, impressive forces of nature and the infinite resources of the human imagination. Famous for having given us the image of tormented poets idly strolling over moors, looking through their wind-whipped hair at a tulip, these poems are often used on AP Exams because of their strong thematic content.

What to Look for in Romantic Poetry

- Natural imagery redeems the imagination of the individual stuck in the crowded, industrial torment of the city. See Wordsworth's "I Wandered Lonely as a Cloud," in which the speaker, on a couch, imagines himself floating above a "host of golden daffodils."

- The human imagination empowers the individual to escape from society's strictures, established authority, and even from fear of death. Think about how Whitman's speaker in "When I Heard the Learn'd Astronomer" needs to leave the room where the lecture is happening in order to better understand the perfect silence of the stars.
- The sublime (impressively big, obscure, or scary) is the main descriptive mode rather than the "merely beautiful." Look at how the speaker in Shelley's "Ozymandias" relies on words such as "vast," "colossal," and "boundless" to create a sense of how intimidating the statue must have been, and actually is.
- Transcendence is the ultimate goal of all the romantic poets. Wordsworth turns a city into a beating heart in "Composed Upon Westminster Bridge Sept. 3, 1802"; in "Ode to the West Wind," Shelley turns the west wind into poetic inspiration; Keats turns an old urn into a meditation on life and death in his "Ode on a Grecian Urn"; Whitman in his "Noiseless Patient Spider" turns a spider into a human soul surrounded by a vacant, vast expanse, yearning to be connected. What do all these poems have in common? Each finds transcendence in the ordinary.

The Symbolists

Representative French Symbolist Poets and Poems

- Charles Baudelaire (1821–1867)—"Spleen"; "*Harmonie du soir* (Harmonies of Evening)"; "*Correspondances* (Correspondences)"
- Stéphane Mallarmé (1842–1898)—"*L'Apres-midi d'un faune* (The Afternoon of a Faun)"; "*Soupir* (Sigh)"; "*Salut* (Salutation)"
- Paul Verlaine (1844–1896)—"*Il pleure dans mon couer* (It Rains in My Heart)"; "*Chanson d'automne* (Autumn Song)"; "*Langueur* (Languor)"
- Arthur Rimbaud (1854–1891)—"*Le bateau ivre* (The Drunken Boat)"; "*Voyelles* (Vowels)"

Symbolist-Influenced Poets Who Wrote in English

- Oscar Wilde (1854–1900)—"Chanson"; "Impression du Matin"; "Harmony"
- W. B. Yeats (1865–1939)—"The Lake Isle of Innisfree"; "Towards Break of Day"; "Broken Dreams"; "Leda and the Swan"; "Sailing to Byzantium"

- Arthur Symons (1865–1945)—"White Heliotrope"; "Colour Studies"; "Perfume"
- T. S. Eliot (1888–1965)—"The Love Song of J. Alfred Prufrock"; "Ash Wednesday"

Related Symbolist Prose Fiction

- *A Rebours* (Against the Grain) by Joris-Karl Huysmans (1848–1907)
- *The Picture of Dorian Gray* by Oscar Wilde (1854–1900)

A Quick Definition

The symbolists are often considered the link between the schools of romanticism and modernism. Full of the yearning for transcendence, which they inherited from the romantic poets, the symbolists took this yearning in a more decadent and sensual direction, foreshadowing the kind of sexual frankness one often finds in modernist work. Many of their poems will seem obscure on the first few readings, and College Board test makers are probably not going to use any of the French symbolists on the exam, but if you take the time to analyze the deep symbols and intuitive associations found in their work, you will be in a better place when you are asked to interpret a poem by Yeats or Eliot, whose work often does show up on the exam.

What to Look for in Symbolist Poetry

- Many symbolist poems deal with the crepuscular (dusk and dawn), and with the time between waking and sleep. Consider Wilde's "*Impression du Matin.*" Dreams or dream states figure prominently in many symbolist works of art, as dream experiences afford human beings one of the best opportunities to explore the relationship between states.
- *Synaesthesia*, the using of one sense to describe another, proved to be a favorite mode of the symbolists. For example, Rimbaud attributes colors and sounds to the different vowels in his poem "*Voyelles.*"
- The French symbolists proved particularly adept at using words with three or four simultaneous meanings, creating a resonance among groups of these words. For example, Mallarmé in "*Salut*" toasts younger poets gathered around a white tablecloth that can simultaneously be seen as a white sail for a boat and a white, blank page upon which these poets will eventually write. By carefully choosing his words, the speaker of this poem keeps all three meanings viable throughout this beautifully dense piece.
- Often associated with the "art for art's sake" movement that placed aesthetics and form above political relevance or reducible message, symbolist poetry finds its artistic counterparts in these kinds of paintings: Whistler's *Nocturne Blue and Gold—Old Battersea Bridge*, Turner's *Moonlight*, and Monet's *Waterloo Bridge in Grey Weather.*

Symbolists and Music

As you can tell from the items in this list, symbolists were drawn to the properties of music and attempted to create some of the same effects in their poetry by concentrating on simultaneous effects (similar to harmony) and by choosing mellifluous words meant to inspire a kind of languor in the reader.

Modernism

Representative Modernist Poets and Poems
- Wallace Stevens (1879–1955)—"Thirteen Ways of Looking at a Blackbird"; "The Snow Man"; "Peter Quince at the Clavier"; "Anecdote of the Jar"
- William Carlos Williams (1883–1963)—"Red Wheelbarrow"; "This Is Just To Say"; "Danse Russe"; "Spring and All"; "The Great Figure"; "The Yachts"; "Desert Music"; "The Descent"
- H. D. (Hilda Doolittle) (1886–1961)—"Star Wheels in Purple"; "Helen"; "Heat"
- Marianne Moore (1887–1972)—"Poetry"; "Baseball and Writing"; "To a Snail"
- T. S. Eliot (1888–1965)—"Love Song of J. Alfred Prufrock"; "Ash Wednesday"
- e. e. cummings (1894–1962)—"anyone lived in a pretty how town"; "next to of course god america i"; "spring is like a perhaps hand"; "i sing of Olaf glad and big"
- Ezra Pound (1885–1972)—"In Durance"; "In a Station of the Metro"; "Hugh Selwyn Mauberley"; "The Cantos"

Related Modernist Prose Fiction
- *A Portrait of the Artist as a Young Man* by James Joyce (1882–1941)
- *Mrs. Dalloway* by Virginia Woolf (1882–1941)
- *As I Lay Dying* by William Faulkner (1897–1962)
- *Heart of Darkness* by Joseph Conrad (1857–1924)
- *The Awakening* by Kate Chopin (1851–1904)

A Quick Definition

Modernism is often characterized as a revolutionary force. In the field of science, Einstein was reassessing time, space, and our relationship to these concepts. In global politics, two calamitous world wars bracketed decades of intense technological advances in the mass killing of soldiers and civilians. In the field of visual arts, surrealism, futurism, abstraction, and cubism overthrew most accepted traditional ideas about pictorial representation. Not surprisingly, literature in the 20th century also saw a thorough questioning of what had come before and a willingness to experiment with new forms, a goal shared with the symbolists but one with which the modernists were much more daring. Modern poets valued the idea of "make it new." Ezra Pound coined the phrase and encouraged writers to take old topics and revamp them with a modern twist. Modernists believed that poetry should be valuable and understandable. Some, like Marianne Moore, even argued that a poet who writes convoluted and frustrating verse just for the purpose of complexity is no poet at all. Modern poets and writers were often expatriates disillusioned with American life.

What to Look for in Modernist Poetry

- Chock full of allusions, these poems reduce human experience to fragments. For example, e.e. cummings breaks language down into its component parts, using pieces of overheard conversation alongside more grandiose pronouncements. In Hilda Doolittle's 18-line poem entitled "Helen," she assumes the reader has a working knowledge of the incident that prompts the Trojan War (chronicled in *The Iliad* by Homer) to make sense of why "All Greece hates/the still eyes in the white face."

- Some of these poems are influenced by cubism, and they try to see the world from as many points of view as possible at the same time. Wallace Stevens's "Thirteen Ways of Looking at a Blackbird" comes in thirteen sections, each of which refers explicitly or implicitly to a blackbird, and can be seen as a kind of analogue to Picasso's cubist presentation of a still life in *Guitar, Bottle, Bowl of Fruit and Glass on Table.*

- Romantic notions of the importance of individuality were overtaken by systematic representations of human consciousness in the emerging fields of psychology and sociology, so poems from this time are often concerned with how an individual relates to his environment (see Eliot's "The Love Song of J. Alfred Prufrock") or how the environment and setting help to create the individual (see Stevens's "The Snow Man").

- Romantic yearning for freedom (the bloody excesses of the French Revolution are an extreme example) was usurped by proponents of political systems, such as socialism or fascism, that saw human beings not as individuals but as servants of the state (see the Russian Revolution and the rise of the Third Reich). Modernist poems sometimes efface individuality, choosing to focus on machines or other inanimate objects rather than nature or human beings. For example, William Carlos Williams's "The Yachts" contains brutal imagery: "Arms with hands grasping seek to clutch at the prows/Bodies thrown recklessly in the way are cut aside./It is a sea of faces about them in agony, in despair/until the horror of the race dawns staggering the mind." But this use of imagery does not ever really feel personal; it feels more like a representation of mass death.

The Harlem Renaissance

Representative Poets and Poems of the Harlem Renaissance
- Paul Laurence Dunbar (1872–1906)—"Frederick Douglass"; "Sympathy"; "We Wear the Mask"
- Claude McKay (1889–1948)—"If We Must Die"; "The White House"; "The Tropics in New York"
- Langston Hughes (1902–1967)—"I, Too, Sing America"; "The Negro Speaks of Rivers"; "Theme for English B"; "Montage of a Dream Deferred"
- Countee Cullen (1903–1946)—"Incident"; "For A Lady I Know"; "Yet Do I Marvel"

Related Prose Fiction from the Harlem Renaissance
- *Their Eyes Were Watching God* by Zora Neale Hurston (1891–1960)
- *Passing* by Nella Larsen (1891–1964)
- *Black Boy* and *Native Son* by Richard Wright (1908–1960)
- *Invisible Man* by Ralph Ellison (1913–1994)

A Quick Definition

Art associated with the Harlem Renaissance was mostly created in the first half of the 20th century, after World War I, during the movement of African Americans to northern industrial cities (called the Great Migration). Harlem in New York City was one of the most famous African American neighborhoods during this time. Jazz, poetry, painting, novels, dance, electrified blues, and the study of folklore thrived in these neighborhoods and took on many of the same concerns as the modernists.

What to Look for in Harlem Renaissance Poetry
- Content is often directly related to African American concerns and issues of the time. Consider Dunbar's "Frederick Douglass," which elegizes the famous abolitionist in such a way as to draw attention to his continuing positive influence on the culture: "Oh, Douglass, thou hast passed beyond the shore,/But still thy voice is ringing o'er the gale!"
- Many Harlem Renaissance poems rely on repetitive structure similar to blues lyrics (see Dunbar's "Sympathy") or on fragmented structure similar to jazz improvisation (see Hughes's "Montage of a Dream Deferred").
- Several of these poets, especially Langston Hughes, consciously sought a new American idiom alongside other African American artists such as blues singer Bessie Smith. Other poets combined European forms like the sonnet with content and tone more related to African American concerns, such as McKay's "If We Must Die."

Postmodernism

A Quick Definition

Academic controversy continues as to whether works labeled postmodern are merely a later version of the modernist tendencies developed in the 20th century or whether they are actually part of a new and separate movement. Usually the most that academics can agree on regarding postmodernism is that the term "postmodern" is insufficient. Most postmodern works were created in the second half of the 20th century, and though they share some of the concerns and motivations of modernists, they often take these principles to a much different end. If Einstein's theory of relativity represents the modern era, Heisenberg's uncertainty principle is the emblem of the postmodern. In reductive terms, the uncertainty principle holds that one cannot know both the speed and the location of an object simultaneously, which introduces a note of chance or chaos into scientific inquiry.

Even more so than other literary labels, "postmodern" is a label that is rejected by the majority of artists who are labeled as such. Instead, smaller contingents of writers exist, often in conflict with other postmodern groups. These smaller groups include the **Beats**, the **confessional** poets, the **New York School of poets**, the **Black Arts movement**, and the **Black Mountain school**. Each of these groups is addressed separately below because each had such a different aesthetic program. A few statements can be applied to postmodern art in general, however, and will be discussed before going into the specific sub-movements.

What to Look for in Postmodern Poetry

- Parody, irony, and narrative instability often inform the tone.
- Allusions are just as likely to be made to popular culture as they are to classical learning.
- Strictly binary concepts (hot and cold; black and white) often collapse. Here, the predominant ideas are ones that spread across a spectrum rather than fit strictly into one box or the other.
- There is no real center. The Internet is a perfect example of a postmodern invention.
- The surface is often more interesting to postmodern artists than any ideas of depth. The following quote is attributed to Andy Warhol, a kind of patron saint of postmodernism and a notorious wig wearer: "Wear a wig and people notice the wig. Wear a silver wig and people notice the silver."

The Beats

Representative Beat Poets and Poems

- Lawrence Ferlinghetti (b. 1919–2021)—"A Coney Island of the Mind"; "The Changing Light"; "Vast Confusion"; "Wild Dreams of a New Beginning"
- Allen Ginsberg (1926–1997)—"Howl"; "America"; "A Supermarket in California"; "Kaddish"
- Gregory Corso (1930–2001)—"Marriage"; "Bomb"; "The Mad Yak"
- Gary Snyder (b. 1930)—"Four Poems for Robin"; "For All"; "Hay for the Horses"

Related Beat Prose Fiction

- *Naked Lunch* by William S. Burroughs (1914–1997)
- *On the Road* by Jack Kerouac (1922–1969)

A Quick Definition

A post–World War II phenomenon, the Beats used different settings over the years to practice their brand of hallucinogenic, visionary, and anti-establishment art: New York City (many of the original group were Columbia University students or dropouts), San Francisco, Tangiers, Prague, and Mexico City witnessed Beat events, as did many places in between.

Beat poets were quite good at mythologizing themselves, sharing a sense of personal frankness with the confessional poets and a sense of interdisciplinary energy (especially in its overlap with music) with the New York School. Buddhism was important to many members (especially Gary Snyder) as were many of the tenets of William Blake's version of romanticism, such as the importance of the individual, the imagination freed from society's constraints, and the yearning for transcendence. In Ferlinghetti's "The Changing Light," a reader can feel the deep connection Beats often felt to nature even as the speaker of this poem is describing a city scene. In Corso's "Marriage," the oppositional stance the Beats took toward the suburban bourgeoisie is in bold relief. Ginsberg's "America" shares much of the same satirical tone, but Ginsberg was also capable of writing angry, ranting, Whitmanesque masterpieces like "Howl" and a tender, meditative elegy for his mother in "Kaddish."

"First thought, best thought" describes the aesthetic ideal of the Beat poet. Moved by jazz improvisation and Buddhist ideas of impermanence, these poets considered themselves the chroniclers of their age. Politics directly informs many of their poems, either through specific references to members of the government or specific references to issues important to them, such as Gary Snyder's commitment to the environment.

Need More Help on Essays?

We've got just the book for that! *How to Write Essays for Standardized Tests* contains advice and examples of best practices on an assortment of AP exams, plus ACT, and others!

Confessional Poets

Representative Confessional Poets and Poems

- John Berryman (1914–1972)—"Dream Song 1"; "Dream Song 4"; "Dream Song 29"
- Robert Lowell (1917–1977)—"Skunk Hour"; "For the Union Dead"; "Memories of West Street and Lepke"; "Home After Three Months Away"
- Anne Sexton (1928–1967)—"Wanting to Die"; "The Truth the Dead Know"; "For My Lover, Returning to his Wife"
- Sylvia Plath (1932–1963)—"Daddy"; "Lady Lazarus"; "Balloons"; "Ariel"

Related Confessional Prose Fiction

- *The Bell Jar* by Sylvia Plath

A Quick Definition

As the name suggests, confessional poets took the personal pronouns (I, me, my) seriously and explored intimate content in their poetry. Love affairs, suicidal thoughts, fears of failure, ambivalent or downright violent opinions about family members, and other autobiographically sensitive material moved front and center in these poets' works. As Berryman wrote, using his alter ego "Henry" as a mask for his own feelings of distress in "Dream Song 1," "I don't see how Henry, pried/ open for all the world to see, survived." These poets "pried open" their innermost thoughts and opened them for all the world to see, even if it meant sharing one's troubled feelings about one's father, as Plath did in a poem full of Holocaust imagery entitled "Daddy," writing "Daddy, I have had to kill you./You died before I had time . . ."

In a cultural milieu much more discreet than that of the current era, these poets ripped the façade off an outwardly comfortable suburban life to reveal the doubts and anxieties that kept the occupants awake at night behind white picket fences. For example, Robert Lowell wrote in "Home After Three Months Away" how he felt when faced with the details of his life such as the recent birth of his child: "I keep no rank nor station./Cured, I am frizzled, stale and small." And Anne Sexton wrote with existential dread, "Since you ask, most days I cannot remember./I walk in my clothing, unmarked by that voyage./Then the almost unnameable lust returns." The "unnameable lust" is the speaker's desire for death, and she writes eloquently about it at a time when mental illness was much less understood or validated by society than it is today.

More than just poets who shared personal stories with their readers, these poets also invested a good deal of time and effort in their craft, constructing verse that paid careful attention to rewritten prosody.

New York School of Poets

Poetry and Art
Many of the New York School poets wrote art criticism, while Frank O'Hara even rose to the rank of assistant curator for the Museum of Modern Art.

Representative New York School Poets

- Barbara Guest (1920–2006)—"The Blue Stairs"; "Wild Gardens Overlooked by Night Lights"; "Sound and Structure"; "Echoes"
- Kenneth Koch (1925–2002)—"One Train May Hide Another"; "Talking to Petrizia"; "To Various Persons Talked to All at Once;" "Variations on a Theme by William Carlos Williams"
- Frank O'Hara (1926–1966)—"In Memory of My Feelings"; "The Day Lady Died"; "A Step Away from Them"; "Lines to a Depressed Friend"
- John Ashbery (b. 1927–2017)—"The Painter"; "The Instruction Manual"; "Daffy Duck in Hollywood"; "The New Higher"

A Quick Definition

New York School poets saw themselves as fellow travelers of the abstract expressionist school of painters. Their aesthetic mode overlapped with Beat spontaneity and confessional-poet frankness but was much more ironic and more interested in the surreal combination of high art and popular art allusions. Many of their poems, especially those called "Lunch Poems" by Frank O'Hara, seem to be catalogs of what one might see on a walk in midtown Manhattan. The urban environment, of course, allows for many spontaneous intersections. A taxi goes by a construction site. A billboard advertising tourism to a natural paradise hovers over a traffic jam, providing ironic contrast.

These poets often viewed themselves as artists who could help the reader see the world in new and different ways. For example, Guest writes "The Blue Stairs" in an ekphrastic mode (or a mode based on putting visual art into words), "Now I shall tell you/why it is beautiful/Design: extraordinary/color: cobalt blue" while O'Hara writes in "The Day Lady Died," an elegy for Billie Holiday, "and I am sweating a lot by now and thinking of/leaning on the john door in the 5 SPOT/ while she whispered a song along the keyboard/to Mal Waldron and everyone and I stopped breathing." Guest's speaker describes looking at a painting while O'Hara's speaker describes hearing a song at a jazz club, but both speakers are interested in inspiring us to look or listen again.

Surrealists wanted to jar their audience's senses by juxtaposing uncommon objects. John Ashbery mixes "Rumford's Baking Powder, a celluloid earring, Speedy Gonzales, the latest from Helen Topping Miller's fertile Escritoire" in his poem "Daffy Duck in Hollywood," and Kenneth Koch consciously mixes tones in his poem "To Various Persons Talked to All at Once," writing, "I suppose I wanted to impress you./It's snowing./The Revlon Man has come from across the sea./This racket is annoying./We didn't want the baby to come here because of the hawk./ What are you reading?/In what style would you like the humidity to explain?" These poets reveled in the combination of the serious and the silly, the profound and the absurd, the highly formal and the casual.

Black Arts Movement

Representative Black Arts Movement Poets and Poems

- Gwendolyn Brooks (1917–2000)—"The Bean Eaters"; "We Real Cool"; "The Lovers of the Poor"; "The Mother"
- Amiri Baraka (also known as LeRoi Jones) (1934–2014)—"Preface to a Twenty Volume Suicide Note"; "Black Art"; "Ka'Ba"; "In the Funk World"
- Sonia Sanchez (b. 1934)—"Ballad"; "Malcolm"; "I Have Walked a Long Time"; "For Sweet Honey in the Rock"
- Ntozake Shange (1948–2018)—"My Father Is a Retired Magician"; "For Colored Girls Who Have Considered Suicide When the Rainbow Is Enuf"

A Quick Definition

Poets of the Black Arts were often associated with members of the Black Power movement who grew frustrated with the pace of the changes enacted by the civil rights movement of the 1950s and 1960s. These poems are often politically charged, unrepentant challenges to the white establishment.

Black Mountain Poets

Representative Black Mountain Poets and Poems

- Charles Olson (1910–1970)—Excerpts from *The Maximus Poems*
- Denise Levertov (1923–1997)—"The Mutes"; "In California During the Gulf War"; "When We Look Up"
- Robert Creeley (1926–2005)—"Age"; "For Love"; "A Wicker Basket"; "America"

A Quick Definition

Besides teaching in the same place (Black Mountain College in Black Mountain, North Carolina) for some time and sharing an abiding interest in process over product, these poets seem quite different. Olson's poems spill across the page while Creeley's lines compress into tight corners. Levertov tackled political issues head-on, but Olson delved deeply into the archeology and history of Gloucester, Massachusetts.

Other Important Representative Poets and Poems

The poets and poems listed below are important but do not fit easily into the structure of literary movements.

Emily Dickinson (1830–1886). Writing in near absolute isolation during the transcendental period, this astonishingly prolific and powerful poet does not easily fit into the transcendental rubric, and shares many more attributes with the compressed wit and irony of the metaphysical poets. Poems: "Because I could not stop for death"; "I heard a fly buzz when I died"; "Tell all the truth but tell it slant"; "I measure every grief I meet."

Robert Frost (1874–1963). Frost was active during modernism's heyday, concerning himself with more traditionally minded verse forms and local color (the customs, manner of speech, dress, or any specificities of a place or period that contribute to its unique character) that cloaked a profound philosophical vein. Poems: "Out, Out"; "Birches"; "The Death of the Hired Man"; "Mending Wall"; "Design"; "Stopping by Woods on a Snowy Evening."

W. H. Auden (1907–1973). Auden, one of the giants of 20th-century literature, wrote the first half of his poems as an English citizen before World War II, and the second half as an American citizen after World War II. His work is more similar to the modernists than to any other school, but he really transcends labels. Poems: "As I Walked Out One Evening"; "In Memory of W. B. Yeats"; "The Unknown Citizen"; "Musée des Beaux Arts."

Elizabeth Bishop (1911–1979). Sometimes placed with the confessional poets because of her friendship with Robert Lowell, Bishop is more reticent than the confessional poets. Poems: "In the Waiting Room"; "Filling Station"; "At the Fishhouses"; "One Art"; "The Moose."

Adrienne Rich (1929–2012). An important feminist and political poet, Rich shared some background with the confessional poets but took the role of the poet in society so seriously that she transcended the personal and became an icon. Poems: "Diving into the Wreck"; "North American Time"; "Aunt Jennifer's Tigers"; "Miracle Ice Cream."

Seamus Heaney (1939–2013). Heaney uses rural imagery to take on issues of identity, from the post-colonial confusion of what it means to be Irish to the late 20th-century confusion of what it means to be a poet. Poems: "Digging"; "The Harvest Bow."

Chapter 6 Summary

o   There are many literary movements that you should be aware of. Be sure that you are familiar with:
- Metaphysical Poetry
- Augustan Poetry
- Romantic Poetry
- Symbolist Poetry
- Modernism
- Harlem Renaissance
- Postmodernism
- The Beats
- Confessional
- New York School
- Black Arts Movement
- Black Mountain

Chapter 7
Prose Fiction
Analysis Questions

USING THE SAMPLE PASSAGES AND QUESTIONS

There's no limit to the different kinds of questions that ETS can (and does) write for the AP English Literature and Composition Exam. As a result, we can't show you every type of question that may show up on the test. We can come pretty close, though, as questions are often reused from year to year. The best way to study these questions is by practicing on examples, but to understand and use the example questions, you need a passage.

There's no need to complete the questions immediately because we're going to take you through them one step at time, discussing the best approaches and specific techniques to use in answering them. Of course, if you want to see how you do on them before referring to our instructions, go right ahead.

After you've looked over the passages, read each question, try to answer it, and then follow our explanations. The correct answer to each question is given in the explanation, but don't just skim through the explanation looking for the answer to see whether you chose correctly. Read all of each explanation, regardless of whether you got the question right. Our explanations will point out details you overlooked and discuss how you might have approached the question differently.

At the end of this chapter, you'll have the opportunity to try a full passage and set of questions so that you can practice using the techniques and approaches discussed in this chapter.

TAKING CONTROL OF PROSE FICTION ANALYSIS PASSAGES

Expect anything from mystery to humor to fantasy (and a host of other literary genres, or categories) in the exam's prose fiction analysis passages, representing periods ranging from the 16th century to modern times. Moreover, each prose fiction analysis passage is just a piece of a larger work, sometimes with bits truncated (cut out) in order to fit the exam's roughly 500–700 word average length. So, you may feel that you've been dropped into the middle of something when you first start reading, and that you've been left hanging when you reach the end. As disorienting as that may seem, each passage is a self-contained selection that holds the answers you need.

You'll find two or three prose fiction analysis passages (interspersed with poetry analysis) in the multiple-choice section, with about 10 to 12 minutes to answer 8 to 13 questions about each one. That's around a minute or a bit more than a minute per question, and you need time to read the passage, too. How can you accomplish that?

First, *work* (don't *read*) the passage, using the active reading techniques described in Chapter 1. Your only objective is to answer the questions correctly, so use your active reading skills to take control and make the passage give you the information you need. Practice active reading until it becomes second nature.

Second, use the time management and pacing techniques explained in Chapter 2. Work at a steady pace, and don't waste time on questions you can't answer. Guess (using your Letter of the Day) and move on, quickly noting the question number in case you have a chance to go back to it.

Third, learn to recognize the question types, question formats, and the best way to approach each one. Review the information in Chapter 4, and practice with the passages in this book. That way, when you see a particular type of question on the exam, you'll be well prepared with a plan of action.

A Passage in 12–15 Minutes

1. Work—don't just read—the passage. Read actively.
2. Manage your time; pace yourself.
3. Learn the question types.

GETTING TO KNOW THE QUESTIONS

Typical prose fiction analysis passage questions are designed to test your critical reading skills. They give you an opportunity to show that you can grasp both the overall theme (the main point), and how various elements of the passage function to develop that theme. These questions assess your ability to analyze, interpret, and make inferences—to "read between the lines" and dissect *how* the author conveys their meaning. It also checks that you can do all of that quickly and accurately.

Prose fiction analysis passage questions tend to focus on elements that are likely familiar to you from previous literature studies, such as

- characters (their significance, perspectives, motives, complexities, and function in the passage, as well as the relationships among them)
- setting and its significance (including how characters relate to it)
- situation and its significance
- narration (who is telling the story, point of view, and reliability)
- plot
- theme(s)
- structure (how the passage progresses and why, including contrasts and conflict)
- perspectives (the narrator's and the author's) and the relationships of part to whole and parts to each other

Sound Familiar?
The items listed right here (well, left here, heh), are the Big Six, plus some guest stars.

Lines and Paragraphs
Note that with the changes for the 2025 exam, prose fiction analysis passages will now use paragraph numbers rather than line numbers (which are still given in poetry analysis passages). This means questions that tell you where to look will use paragraph references and the >> symbol paired with highlighting on the passage, rather than telling you specific line references.

- style (vocabulary and syntax, devices the author uses to convey their meaning)
- tone (the author's or narrator's attitude) and the elements that reveal it
- literary devices (figurative language such as allusions, metaphors, and symbols) and their functions in the passage

In the rest of this chapter, you can practice taking control of three prose fiction analysis passages and making them give you the correct answers. First are two sample passages. Try using active reading techniques and answering the questions. Then read the answer explanations that follow each one; they describe not only how to reach the correct answer but also how to approach each type of question when you encounter it in other passages. At the end of this chapter is a prose fiction analysis passage drill with questions and answer explanations to give you more practice.

SAMPLE PROSE FICTION ANALYSIS PASSAGE AND QUESTIONS

Edgar Allan Poe's "The Duc De L'Omelette"

Par.

1   Keats fell by a criticism. But who ever died of inept poetry? Ignoble souls!—De L'Omelette perished of an ortolan[1]. The story then, in brief:

2   That night the Duke was to sup alone. In the privacy of his bureau he reclined languidly on that ottoman for which he sacrificed his loyalty in outbidding his king—the notorious ottoman of Cadet.

3   He buries his face in the pillow. The clock strikes! Unable to restrain his feelings, his Grace swallows an olive. At this moment the door gently opens to the sound of soft music, and lo! the most delicate of birds is before the most enamored of men! But what inexpressible dismay now overshadows the countenance of the Duke? *"Horreur! Dog! Protestant! —the bird! Ah Good God! This modest bird you've quite unclothed and served without paper!"* It is superfluous to say more:—the Duke expired in a paroxysm of disgust. . . .

4   "Ha! ha! ha!" said his Grace on the third day after his decease.

5   "He! he! he!" replied the Devil faintly, drawing himself up with an air of hauteur.

6   "Why surely you are not serious," retorted De L'Omelette. "I have sinned—that's true—but, my good sir, consider!—you have no actual intention of putting such—such—barbarous threats into execution."

7   "No what?" said his Majesty—"come, sir, strip!"

8   "Strip, indeed! very pretty i' faith! no, sir, I shall not strip. Who are you, pray, that I, Duke De L'Omelette, Prince de Foie-Gras, just come of age, author of the 'Mazurkiad,' and member of the Academy, should divest myself at your bidding of the sweetest pantaloons ever made by Bourdon, the daintiest dressing gown ever put together by Rombert—take say nothing of undressing my hair—not to mention the trouble I should have in drawing off my gloves?"

9   "Who am I?—ah, true! I am Baal-Zebub, Prince of the Fly. I took thee, just now, from a rosewood coffin inlaid with ivory. Thou wast curiously scented, and labeled as per invoice. Belial sent thee—my Inspector of Cemeteries. The pantaloons, which thou sayest were made by Bourdon, are an excellent pair of linen drawers, and thy dressing gown is a shroud of no scanty dimensions."

10   "Sir!" replied the Duke, "I am not to be insulted with impunity!—Sir! you shall hear from me! In the meantime au revoir!"—and the Duke was bowing himself out of the Satanic presence, when he was interrupted and brought back by a gentleman in waiting. Hereupon his Grace rubbed his eyes, yawned, shrugged his shoulders, reflected. Having become satisfied of his identity, he took a bird's-eye view of his whereabouts.

11   The apartment was superb. Even De L'Omelette pronounced it "quite well done." It was not its length nor its breadth—but its height—ah, that was appalling!—there was no ceiling—certainly none—but a dense whirling mass of fiery-colored clouds. His Grace's brain reeled as he glanced upward. From above, hung a chain of an unknown blood-red metal—its upper end lost. From its nether extremity swung a large cresset. The Duke knew it to be a ruby; but from it there poured a light so intense, so still, so terrible. Persia never worshipped such, no great Sultan ever dreamed of such when, drugged with opium, he has tottered to a bed of poppies, his back to the flowers, and his face to the God Apollo. The Duke muttered a slight oath, decidedly approbatory.

12   The corners of the room were rounded into niches, and these were filled statues of gigantic proportions. But the paintings! The paintings! O luxury! O love!—who gazing on those forbidden beauties shall have eyes for others.

13   The Duke's heart is fainting within him. He is not, however, as you suppose, dizzy with magnificence, nor drunk with the ecstatic breath of the innumerable censers. (It's true that he thinks of these things to no small degree—but!) The Duke De L'Omelette is terror-stricken; for, through the lurid vista which a single uncurtained window is affording, lo! gleams the most ghastly of all fires!

14   The poor Duke! He could not help imagining that the glorious, the voluptuous, the never-dying melodies which pervaded that hall, as they passed filtered and transmuted through the alchemy of the enchanted window-panes, were the wailings and the howlings of the hopeless and the damned! And there, too!—there!—upon the ottoman!—who could he be?—he, the Deity—who sat as if carved in marble, and who smiled, with his pale countenance, bitterly?

15   A Frenchman never faints outright. Besides, his Grace hated a scene—De L'Omelette is himself again. Hadn't he read somewhere? wasn't it said "that the devil can't refuse a card game?"

16   But the chances—the chances! True—desperate; but scarcely more desperate than the Duke. Besides wasn't he the slyest player in the craftiest card-club in Paris?—the legendary "21 club."

17   "Should I lose," said his Grace "I will lose twice—that is I shall be doubly damned—should I win, I return to my ortolan—let the cards be prepared."

18   His Grace was all care, all attention, his Majesty all confidence. His Grace thought of the game. His majesty did not think; he shuffled. The Duke cut.

19   The cards are dealt. The trump is turned—it is—it is—the king! No—it was the queen. His Majesty cursed her masculine habiliments. De L'Omelette placed his hand upon his heart.

20   They play. The Duke counts. The hand is out. His majesty counts heavily, smiles and is taking wine. The Duke palms a card.

---

[1] An ortolan is a small dove-like bird considered a supreme delicacy by nineteenth-century gourmets.

21   "It's your deal," said his Majesty, cutting. His Grace bowed, dealt, and arose from the table—turning the King.
22   His Majesty looked chagrined.
23   Had Alexander not been Alexander, he would have been Diogenes; and the Duke assured his antagonist in taking his leave, "Were one not already the Duke De L'Omelette one could have no objection to being the Devil."

---

1   ☐ Mark for Review

The primary purpose of the passage is to portray

(A) the characteristics of an exaggerated type through the figure of De L'Omelette

(B) a reassuringly humorous vision of hell through a narrative in which the Devil himself is bested

(C) the evil consequences of excessive pride

(D) the pivotal change that occurs in De L'Omelette through his encounter with the Devil

---

2   ☐ Mark for Review

Which of the following best describes the Duke De L'Omelette?

(A) He is a typical eighteenth-century nobleman.

(B) He is a caricature of a snob.

(C) He is a man more wicked than the Devil.

(D) He is a man transformed by his encounter with a power greater than his own.

---

3   ☐ Mark for Review

In context, "Strip, indeed! very pretty i' faith! . . . not to mention the trouble I should have in drawing off my gloves?" (paragraph 8) serves to reinforce the reader's impression of the Duke's

(A) quick temper

(B) exquisite taste

(C) sense of self-importance

(D) misunderstanding of his situation

---

4   ☐ Mark for Review

The author's portrayal of the Duke De L'Omelette is best described as

(A) a sympathetic portrait of a man with overly delicate sensibilities

(B) a comically ironic treatment of an effete snob

(C) a harshly condemnatory portrait of a bon vivant

(D) an admiring portrait of a great artist

---

5   ☐ Mark for Review

Which of the following descriptions is an example of the narrator's irony?

(A) "Unable to restrain his feelings, his Grace swallows an olive." (paragraph 3)

(B) "I took thee, just now, from a rosewood coffin inlaid with ivory." (paragraph 9)

(C) "The Duke knew it to be a ruby; but from it there poured a light so intense, so still, so terrible." (paragraph 11)

(D) "And there, too!—there!—upon the ottoman!—who could he be?—he, the Deity—who sat as if carved in marble, and who smiled, with his pale countenance, bitterly?" (paragraph 14)

6 🔖 Mark for Review

In paragraph 11, the word "appalling" suggests the Duke

- (A) has found the room's decor unacceptable
- (B) has approbation for clouds
- (C) finds the apartment extraordinary
- (D) suffers from a paroxysm

7 🔖 Mark for Review

Which of the following best implies the contextual meaning of the phrase "sacrificed his loyalty" (paragraph 2) within the context of the story?

- (A) The Duke has fallen into disfavor with the King by outbidding him.
- (B) The Duke has betrayed his country.
- (C) The Duke has allowed his desire for the ottoman to override his deference to the King.
- (D) The Duke values the ottoman more greatly than his prestige.

8 🔖 Mark for Review

In which of the following is the narrator most clearly articulating the Duke's thoughts?

- (A) "Ignoble souls!" (paragraph 1)
- (B) "It is superfluous to say more:—" (paragraph 3)
- (C) "Having become satisfied of his identity, he took a bird's-eye view of his whereabouts." (paragraph 10)
- (D) "But the chances—the chances! True—desperate;" (paragraph 16)

9 🔖 Mark for Review

Which of the following implies a speaker other than the narrator?

- (A) "But who ever died of inept poetry?" (paragraph 1)
- (B) "That night the Duke was to sup alone." (paragraph 2)
- (C) "The apartment was superb." (paragraph 11)
- (D) "His majesty did not think, he shuffled." (paragraph 18)

10 🔖 Mark for Review

Which of the following best describes the situation in paragraph 6 and the events that came immediately *before* it?

- (A) The Duke has just noticed the Devil and laughs at him. The Devil returns the laugh, but quietly because he feels insulted.
- (B) The Duke has just heard the Devil explain the tortures that lie in store for him. He believes the Devil is joking and laughs. The Devil mocks his laughter, implying that it is no joke.
- (C) The Duke and the Devil have been talking, but the exact topic has purposefully been left vague.
- (D) The Duke has just heard the Devil's plans for him and laughs defiantly at the Devil. The Devil puns on the Duke's use of the word "Ha!" by saying "He!" indicating that "He," the Duke, will be punished for his sins.

11 ☐ Mark for Review

Which of the following reinforces the effect of the passage most strongly?

Ⓐ Lighthearted situations narrated with deep seriousness

Ⓑ Calculated objectivity offset by occasional interjections of subjective emotion

Ⓒ Underlying contempt partially concealed by objectivity

Ⓓ First-person outbursts of effusive emotion in an otherwise third-person narration

12 ☐ Mark for Review

The narrator's attitude toward the Duke can be best described as

Ⓐ complete objectivity

Ⓑ slight distaste

Ⓒ bemused confusion

Ⓓ satiric glee

13 ☐ Mark for Review

The phrase "as if carved in marble" (paragraph 14) is an example of

Ⓐ irony

Ⓑ lyricism

Ⓒ a metaphor

Ⓓ a simile

About Poe's "The Duc De L'Omelette"

This passage was adapted from a short story called "The Duc De L'Omelette." You'll sometimes see adapted passages on the AP English Literature and Composition Exam. All it means is the passage was edited to make it appropriate for all high school students and to meet the test's length requirements. The actual Poe story uses a great deal of French, but keeping the French parts would give an unfair advantage to those who studied or speak French.

The passage demonstrates the kind of language and stylistic devices you'll see on prose fiction analysis passages on the AP English Literature and Composition Exam, but they aren't all this weird. If it seemed long, don't panic—it is about one-third longer than the usual AP passage. (We wanted to use a long passage in this example to give you plenty to work with and to provide abundant fodder for our sample questions. Keep in mind that with a total of 55 questions, some of the passages will have fewer than 13 questions.) If you see a passage of this length on the test, there will then be a shorter passage somewhere to compensate.

Answers and Explanations to the Questions

We give detailed explanations to the 13 questions that followed the passage. The passages and questions on our practice test are designed to imitate the actual exam. Here, we've chosen the questions with an eye toward teaching you our techniques, but even so, the mix of the types of questions is fairly representative of the questions you'll see on an AP passage.

We've broken the questions down into small groups in order to illustrate specific types of questions you're likely to see. We don't want you to memorize the names of these types or spend a lot of time practicing identifying these types. There are no points for doing that. If you do remember them, great, but all we want is for you to become familiar with the most common types of questions on the test and to see how the same techniques, applied in slightly different ways, work on question after question.

GENERAL COMPREHENSION QUESTIONS

The first question is a general question and as you know, general questions ask about the whole passage, not just some detail of the passage.

The question sets will often (but not always) start out with general questions. We've placed the questions on this passage in the order that lets us best explain them to you. Remember that when you actually take the test, you should attempt the questions in the order given if you feel comfortable with your comprehension of the passage. If you feel pretty lost, then you should put any general questions off until last, in the hope that working with the specific questions will give you more confidence about your comprehension of the passage and its main idea.

Primary Purpose

The classic general question is the primary purpose question:

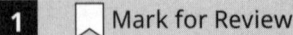

| **1** | 🔖 Mark for Review |

The primary purpose of the passage is to portray

(A) the characteristics of an exaggerated type through the figure of De L'Omelette

(B) a reassuringly humorous vision of hell through a narrative in which the Devil himself is bested

(C) the evil consequences of excessive pride

(D) the pivotal change that occurs in De L'Omelette through his encounter with the Devil

Here's How to Crack It

Understand the question by understanding the answer choices. What does "primary purpose" mean?

When you see a primary purpose question, it means you must look for an answer that covers the broad outline of the story. This advice goes for all general questions; it is what makes them general. Remember that you are looking for a choice that accurately describes some facet of the entire passage.

Now use the answer choices themselves to focus on exactly what primary purpose the test-writers are looking for.

The question itself indicates that the primary purpose of the passage is to portray something. What is it portraying? Use POE.

Take (A). Does the whole passage deal with an exaggerated type? Well, the Duke is an exaggeration of something. This is a guy who takes time to approve of the decor in hell. Choice (A) seems to be a reasonable summation of the whole passage. Leave it. Now take each of the remaining choices in turn.

Look at (B). The whole passage is not all about a "reassuringly humorous vision of hell." Each paragraph does not point out how harmless hell is. The humorous part is the Duke's taking it all more or less in stride. Eliminate (B).

POE In Action

Here's how you might approach a question using the POE strategy. Look for the *wrong* answers first.

Choice (C) talks about "the evil consequences of excessive pride." The passage is all about the Duke's excessive pride, but what are the consequences? There are none. The end of the story finds the Duke returning to his ill-prepared ortolan, which is right where he started, so you have to wonder whether it's going to kill him all over again. Remember, *half wrong equals all wrong*. Eliminate (C).

Eliminate (D) because the Duke doesn't change at all. When the point of a passage is to show a dramatic change, you'll know it. The whole passage will build to that change.

You're left with (A), the correct answer.

What phrase have we kept repeating? "The whole passage." General questions call for you to consider the whole passage, not one small piece of it.

This answer turned out to mainly be about a character, but that wasn't obvious until we chose it. The next question will specifically ask about character.

Another thing we did was focus on key phrases in the answer choices. "What consequences?" we asked when we looked at (C). We didn't get taken in by the phrase "excessive pride." Learning how to focus on an answer choice is a skill that comes with practice. As you follow our explanations, your skill will improve. In fact, after that discussion, the next question should be a breeze.

―――――――――○―――――――――

Overall Character

AP passages tend to be focused on one thing. Here the focus is on the Duke. A passage might focus on the description of an event or a place, but the most common focus is on a character. Yes, here's where the first of the Big Six comes in handy.

―――――――――○―――――――――

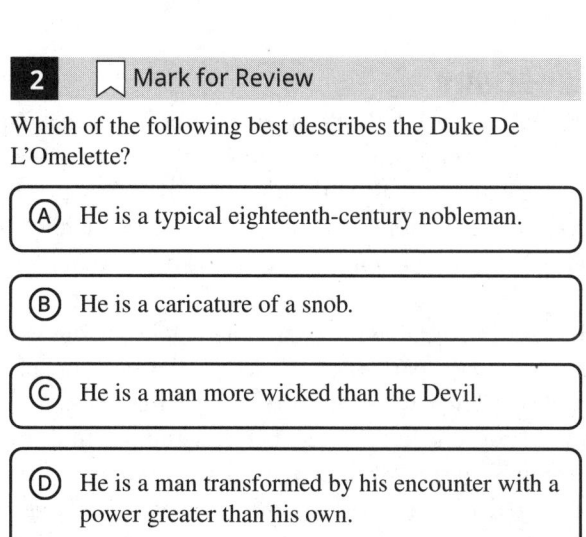

2   ⬚ Mark for Review

Which of the following best describes the Duke De L'Omelette?

Ⓐ He is a typical eighteenth-century nobleman.

Ⓑ He is a caricature of a snob.

Ⓒ He is a man more wicked than the Devil.

Ⓓ He is a man transformed by his encounter with a power greater than his own.

Here's How to Crack It

The question asks you to describe the main character: the Duke De L'Omelette. The correct answer is (B) and finding it probably didn't cause you much trouble. The only problem might have been the term *caricature*, which means "exaggerated portrait." It is a term you should know (it's in our glossary). Do you notice any similarities between the correct answer to question 1 and the correct answer here? You should. One speaks of an exaggerated portrayal of a type, and one speaks of a caricature of a snob. These are almost the same answer. The only difference is that the second question's answer spells out what "type" is being caricatured: the snob. This is an example of Consistency of Answers. Both answers are consistent with the main idea, and when answers are consistent with the main idea, they are consistent with each other. In this case the answers are extremely similar. If you thought the Duke was an exaggerated portrayal in question 1, why would he suddenly become a "typical eighteenth-century nobleman" in question 2? That would be inconsistent, so eliminate (A). The Duke is either exaggerated or he's typical, but he can't be both. Choice (C) is for students who read into things too much. The Duke wins the card game at the end. Does that mean he's more wicked than the Devil? No. Choice (D) isn't supported by the passage. You'd think the Duke would be transformed by his encounter with the Devil, but he isn't. At the end of the story you should have gotten the feeling that De L'Omelette is going to go right back to his old ways.

Consistency of Answers doesn't just apply to general questions. It is just as helpful with detail questions.

DETAIL QUESTIONS

Detail questions (aka specific questions) make up the majority of questions on the multiple-choice section of the test. These are questions (or answer choices) that direct you to a specific place in the passage and ask about your comprehension of the details.

Highlight Questions

Most of the time (but not always), the detail questions give you a paragraph number, or a range of paragraphs, along with a >> symbol that leads to a highlighted section of the passage with which to work. (On the poetry analysis passages, the test will give you line references and highlighting instead.) We call these highlight questions. For these questions there are just two things you need to keep in mind:

- Go back to the passage and reread the paragraph(s) in question. Don't rely on your memory, particularly under the time pressure of the exam. Your memory will likely lead you astray. If the highlighted section is short, read at least one full sentence before it and one full sentence after it to get enough context. Keep in mind that a word or phrase you are being asked to define may not have the meaning you would infer from the wording of the question. It is important that you refer to the word in the context of the paragraph.

- Keep the main idea in mind, and use Consistency of Answers whenever possible.

Try This One

---

3 ☐ Mark for Review

In context, "Strip, indeed! very pretty i' faith! . . . not to mention the trouble I should have in drawing off my gloves?" (paragraph 8) serves to reinforce the reader's impression of the Duke's

Ⓐ quick temper

Ⓑ exquisite taste

Ⓒ sense of self-importance

Ⓓ misunderstanding of his situation

Here's How to Crack It

This question asks about the main character again, specifically what impression the reader gets of him. But more importantly, it calls for you to go back and read a whole paragraph. Go back and read it. Because the whole paragraph is referred to here (highlighted, on a screen) reading a full sentence before and after the highlighted portion doesn't make a big difference in getting the question right, but it doesn't hurt, either, and takes just an extra two or three seconds. Make it a habit to read a little above and below the highlighted lines: it'll be worth a couple of points in the long run.

Essentially, the paragraph in question discusses the Duke's outrage at the Devil's command to disrobe.

If you misunderstand the question, you have a good chance of getting the answer wrong. The passage shows aspects of all the answer choices. The Duke shows a quick temper, mentions his tastes (which are not so much exquisite as they are ostentatious), mentions his accomplishments, and misunderstands his situation. But the correct answer is (C).

All the answer choices seem right, so what gives? The solution lies in understanding the question and how the question relates to the main idea. The question asks: What does the passage serve to reinforce? Nearly everything in this very compact story serves to reinforce the central impression of the story—the Duke's outrageous sense of self-importance. He isn't merely a snob; he's completely besotted with his own fabulous self. The Duke thinks he's the apex of human intellectual and social development. In fact, (A), (B), and (D) are all facets of the Duke's vanity. His anger is angered vanity. His tastes are flawless; they must be, thinks the Duke, because they're his. Even his misunderstanding is an aspect of his vanity. The Duke doesn't quite comprehend his surroundings because he can't imagine being in a position to take orders from anyone. All these things revolve like planets around the Duke's sense that he's the center of the universe.

If you had a solid grasp on the central theme of the story, the Duke's self-love, you might have found this question easy. Choices (A), (B), and (D) are details. Choice (C) is the main thing. If you had trouble, all you had to do to get this question correct was muse, "Hmm, they all look possible, but which one is most consistent with the main idea?" Well, a snob thinks he's better than everyone and is very important. Choice (C), sense of self-importance, is most in agreement with that.

Question 3 is an example of using Consistency of Answers. Here's another:

---

4   ▢ Mark for Review

The author's portrayal of the Duke De L'Omelette is best described as

(A) a sympathetic portrait of a man with overly delicate sensibilities

(B) a comically ironic treatment of an effete snob

(C) a harshly condemnatory portrait of a bon vivant

(D) an admiring portrait of a great artist

Here's How to Crack It

This question asks about how the author portrays the Duke (our main character). Think about how the Duke acts and what he says, and what those things reveal about him.

Look at the answer choices next. Take each answer a word at a time and remember: half wrong equals all wrong. If any part of the answer is wrong, don't hesitate to eliminate it. Yes, it's true that the portrait is of a man with delicate sensibilities (A), but is it sympathetic? Hardly. Get rid of it. You might not understand "effete" in (B), so hold on to it. However, "harshly condemnatory" in (C) should sound wrong to you. The Duke is harshly condemnatory of the servant who brings in his meal, but the passage itself does not disapprove of either of them. Half bad equals all bad, so eliminate it. Now look at (D): John Keats was a great artist, but the Duke? From this passage you sure can't say that, so cross this one off too. This leaves you with (B) even if you're not quite sure what it means. But here's a pop quiz: What technique tells you the answer must be (B)? Consistency of Answers.

Now we aren't saying every single question uses Consistency of Answers. It should be one of the first things you think about when you approach a question, but there are definitely questions that focus on a detail in such a way that Consistency of Answers doesn't come into play.

Here's an example:

---

5   ☐ Mark for Review

Which of the following descriptions is an example of the narrator's irony?

(A) "Unable to restrain his feelings, his Grace swallows an olive."(paragraph 3)

(B) "I took thee, just now, from a rosewood coffin inlaid with ivory." (paragraph 9)

(C) "The Duke knew it to be a ruby; but from it there poured a light so intense, so still, so terrible." (paragraph 11)

(D) "And there, too!—there!—upon the ottoman!—who could he be?—he, the Deity—who sat as if carved in marble, and who smiled, with his pale countenance, bitterly?" (paragraph 14)

Count on This
You can count on only a
very few specific things
showing up on the exam.
One of them is irony.

Here's How to Crack It

Notice that in this question the paragraph references come in the answer choices. That's not uncommon. Properly speaking, this isn't a specific question or a general question or a literary-term question. The answer choices send you back to the passage to find a specific example of something that occurs throughout the whole passage: irony, which is a literary term. But, you don't get points for putting questions in categories anyway; the important thing is to get the question right, efficiently.

The way to get this question right is to know what irony is. Learn to recognize its many forms. We discuss irony in our glossary of literary terms for the AP English Literature and Composition Exam. (Yep, we're going to say that every time we mention irony.)

The correct answer is (A). You should have noticed the entire tone of the piece is somewhat ironic. Most of the passage is written with a deliberate undercurrent of meaning that changes the effect of the literal meaning of the lines. This, above all, is the hallmark of irony; there's more than meets the eye. But let's get back to (A). Why is it ironic? Let's take the statement "Unable to restrain his feelings, his Grace swallows an olive." At face value, the Duke's feelings became so strong that he had to swallow an olive. Now, in no way can swallowing an olive be the outcome of unrestrained feelings unless one has pretty unusual feelings, which is precisely the point. The Duke's anticipation of dinner having reached a fevered pitch, he buries his face in a pillow. The clock bangs out the long-awaited hour and, unable to restrain himself, the Duke . . . swallows an olive. One thing this shows is how fanatically the Duke takes his meals. At the same time, the juxtaposition (to *juxtapose* means to place things side by side) of the Duke's unrestrained feelings and his act of swallowing an olive show something else: the Duke's biggest feelings are actually puny; the Duke's crescendo of passion is capped by swallowing an olive. That's the ironic part. The author in effect says, "In the Duke's opinion this is something big, but we can all see that it's rather small." When the literal meaning of a word or phrase implies its opposite, you're dealing with irony.

Hey, didn't we say that the whole piece was ironic? If that's true, what makes the other choices wrong? Well, okay, the whole piece *is* ironic. In effect, the passage tells us that the Duke thinks he's absolutely first-rate, but we can see that he's really quite laughable. However, for this question you must consider the answer choices in isolation. None of the others alone carry the double meaning that is so crucial to irony. Choice (B) is a description of a coffin. Choice (C) describes the ruby that illuminates the Devil's chamber in hell. Choice (D) describes the moment the Duke realizes, at last, that the creature he's dealing with is truly the Devil himself.

Okay, enough about irony, on to the next kind of question.

Single Phrase or Word Questions

AP questions will often ask you to look at a single word or phrase:

---

6 ☐ Mark for Review

In paragraph 11, the word "appalling" suggests the Duke

Ⓐ has found the room's decor unacceptable

Ⓑ has approbation for clouds

Ⓒ finds the apartment extraordinary

Ⓓ suffers from a paroxysm

Here's How to Crack It

It's true that for the AP English Literature and Composition Exam, a strong vocabulary helps a lot. If you did not know the meaning of *decor* in (A), *approbation* in (B), or *paroxysm* in (D), you may have been at a loss. You could eliminate (A) because you know that the Duke found the apartment *superb*. Then you would be left with (B), (C), and (D).

Keep in mind that you are only to answer the question being asked—to examine the contextual meaning of one word. To do that, you must go back and read the context in which the word appears: the first part of paragraph 11. Read the couple of sentences before and the sentence containing the word *appalling*. Notice that this part of the passage is describing the setting, and the Duke's reaction to it. You can safely eliminate (D) from the list because in the sentence that contains the word *appalling*, a reference to the Duke's suffering or discomfort is not implied. Even if you don't know what *paroxysm* means (a convulsion), you can use POE to get rid of this answer choice. Now look carefully at (B). In the sentence, *appalling* refers to the room, not the clouds. So you can eliminate this choice too, even if you don't know that *approbation* is approval. You're left with the correct answer, (C), in which the word *extraordinary*, which may seem very different from *appalling*, actually shows a commonality: both words describe something shocking.

Questions 5 and 6 are two questions in a row that don't use Consistency of Answers. The streak's over. Here's a question that asks about a single phrase, yet you can still use Consistency of Answers to assist your POE.

7 ☐ Mark for Review

Which of the following best implies the contextual meaning of the phrase "sacrificed his loyalty" (paragraph 2) within the context of the story?

(A) The Duke has fallen into disfavor with the King by outbidding him.

(B) The Duke has betrayed his country.

(C) The Duke has allowed his desire for the ottoman to override his deference to the King.

(D) The Duke values the ottoman more greatly than his prestige.

Here's How to Crack It

When approaching this question, you should first go back and read around the highlighted portion. Because the highlight may only cover a sentence, or even a fragment of a sentence, you should read at least a full sentence before and after the highlight. (If you want to read more, by all means, do. The full sentence before and after is just a guideline. If it takes you a little more reading to get your bearings in the passage, that's fine.)

Now, use POE to get rid of what is obviously wrong. If you stay focused on what the phrase in question means it should be easy to eliminate at least one of the answers. Does "sacrificed his loyalty" mean the Duke has betrayed his country? That should sound a little too intense: We're talking about buying a couch here (an ottoman is a kind of couch). Eliminate (B).

Can you eliminate two more answer choices? The best way is to ask yourself which answer choice is most in keeping with the Duke's character. Do you think the Duke cares about his prestige more than his couch? Of course he does. He would never sacrifice his prestige. L'Omelette thinks of appearances above all else. Eliminate (D). What about (A)? It is certainly reasonable that the Duke fell into disfavor with the King for outbidding him. But is this what "sacrificed his loyalty" means? No. And if you have any doubts, ask yourself what that interpretation has to do with the rest of the passage. Is the rest of the passage about the Duke's loss of favor with the King? No. That leaves (C), the correct answer. It is perfectly in keeping with the other answers and the rest of the passage: the Duke shows little deference to the Devil; why would he defer to the King?

The next two questions ask for your comprehension of specific details, but the questions center less on the meaning of the words than on what they indicate about the narrator.

Question-Comprehension Questions

Some questions are straightforward, some are vague, and a few are downright tricky. You need to pay close attention to the wording of questions and when you see an unusual phrase, it's a good idea to ask yourself why the phrase is worded that way. For many questions, just understanding what the question is asking is half the battle.

---

8 ▢ Mark for Review

In which of the following is the narrator most clearly articulating the Duke's thoughts?

Ⓐ "Ignoble souls!" (paragraph 1)

Ⓑ "It is superfluous to say more:—" (paragraph 3)

Ⓒ "Having become satisfied of his identity, he took a bird's-eye view of his whereabouts." (paragraph 10)

Ⓓ "But the chances—the chances! True— desperate:" (paragraph 16)

Here's How to Crack It

This question has little to do with the main idea. Your first task is to understand the question. What is meant by "articulating the Duke's thoughts"? Well, try to put it in your own words. The question could be rewritten as "When is the narrator speaking for the Duke?" There's nothing wrong with putting a question in your own words so as to understand it better. In fact it's a good idea, as long as you're careful and don't just drop off the parts of a question that confuse you. Reading the questions accurately is just as important as reading the passages. The passage isn't worth any points; the questions are.

Now that you know that the question is asking when the narrator is speaking for the Duke, look at the answer choices with an eye to perspective. Who is speaking in each one? How do you know? Use POE. Eliminate what you can right away. When is the narrator clearly speaking as himself? Choices (B) and (C) both seem like examples of straightforward narration, so eliminate them. That leaves just (A) and (D). In (A), the narrator responds to a question. He exclaims in a very Duke-like way, but the Duke hasn't even been introduced yet. How could the reader know it was the Duke speaking? The reader couldn't. All that's left is (D), the correct answer. In (D), the narrator steps into the Duke's mind for a moment to record his thoughts, and then just as quickly steps out with the words "but no more desperate than the Duke."

Question 9 picks up where question 8 left off; a variation on the same theme.

9   ☐ Mark for Review

Which of the following implies a speaker other than the narrator?

(A) "But who ever died of inept poetry?" (paragraph 1)

(B) "That night the Duke was to sup alone." (paragraph 2)

(C) "The apartment was superb." (paragraph 11)

(D) "His majesty did not think, he shuffled." (paragraph 18)

Here's How to Crack It

Read the questions carefully. The difference between question 8 and question 9 is that question 8 asks which answer choice shows the Duke's speech (or thoughts), whereas question 9 wants to know which implies a speaker other than the narrator. Question 9 is tougher. If your approach to question 9 got stuck somewhere back on question 8 and you were still looking for the narrator to speak the Duke's thoughts (or perhaps the Devil's), you might have easily gotten this question wrong.

As always, use POE. Clearly, (B), (C), and (D) are spoken by the narrator. What about (A)? Well, (A) is spoken by the narrator as well but *implies* another speaker, someone who asks the question, "Who ever died of poor poetry?" The narrator, speaking as himself, responds to that question: "Ignoble souls!" If the structure of this interchange wasn't clear to you, here's an explanation: "Who ever died of poor poetry?" is a rhetorical question (a question to which the answer is obvious—of course, most people would say, no one has ever been killed by a bad poem). That's where the narrator jumps in and says, "Oh ho, you think the answer to that question is so very obvious but that's because your souls have no finer qualities; it may seem unbelievable to you, but some very delicate spirits have died of immaterial things like bad poetry. De L'Omelette, for example, died of a badly prepared meal." All that (and a little more) is contained in the first paragraph of the passage. This paragraph is a good example of how gifted writers make every word count.

--------○--------

Ready for one more detail question? It's a good example of how weird things can get on the AP Exam, as it asks about the meaning of a piece of the passage that isn't there.

Weirdness

--------○--------

10   🔖 Mark for Review

Which of the following best describes the situation in paragraph 6 and the events that came immediately *before* it?

Ⓐ The Duke has just noticed the Devil and laughs at him. The Devil returns the laugh, but quietly because he feels insulted.

Ⓑ The Duke has just heard the Devil explain the tortures that lie in store for him. He believes the Devil is joking and laughs. The Devil mocks his laughter, implying that it is no joke.

Ⓒ The Duke and the Devil have been talking, but the exact topic has purposefully been left vague.

Ⓓ The Duke has heard the Devil's plans for him and laughs defiantly at the Devil. The Devil puns on the Duke's use of the word "Ha!" by saying "He!" indicating that "He," the Duke, will be punished for his sins.

Here's How to Crack It
You may sometimes run across a weird or unexpected question on the test. In this case, you're being asked to make sense of an abrupt shift in the story, from the Duke's death to his meeting the Devil, and essentially to fill in the blanks. In other words, you are asked to describe this particular piece of the plot, which involves a contrast between the perspectives of two characters: the Duke and the Devil.

Use POE and remember to read at least one sentence before and one sentence after, so as to piece things together. Choice (A) can be eliminated outright, as there is no indication in the text that the Devil feels insulted. (The "hauteur" in paragraph 5 hints that the opposite may be true.) Choice (C) is vague, but what the Duke and Devil have been discussing is not—the Duke refers to a specific topic, "barbarous threats," and elaborates in the paragraph after next. Finally, (D) suggests that "He!" is being used as a bizarre pun, but there's nothing to support that in the text. Choice (B) is correct, and is the best (and simplest) explanation of the Devil's mocking reply.

Staying simple doesn't just apply to poetry analysis. Many students get into trouble when reading the answer choices and think about the wrong answers so much that they get led into outer space. This comes from looking at every answer choice as though it could be correct. Three out of four answer choices are wrong. At least one answer choice is usually wildly wrong. If something looks nuts, don't spend five minutes trying to figure it out. If it looks nuts, it is.

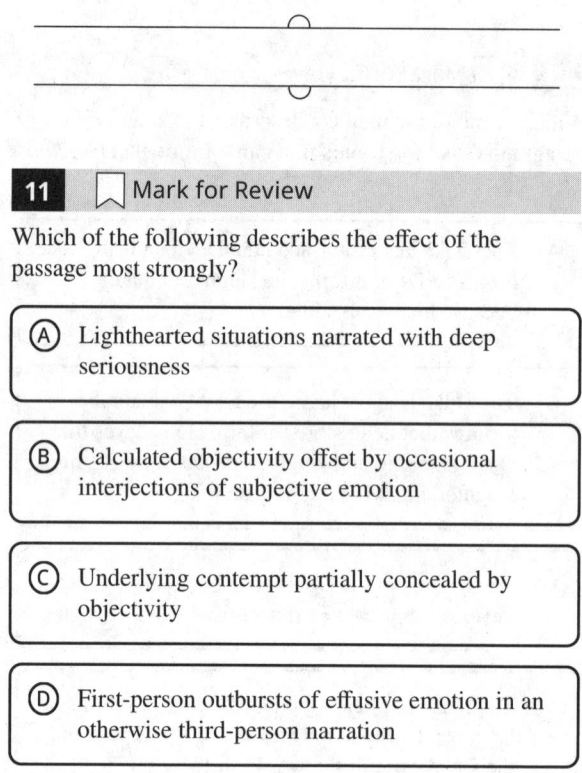

11 🔖 Mark for Review

Which of the following describes the effect of the passage most strongly?

- (A) Lighthearted situations narrated with deep seriousness
- (B) Calculated objectivity offset by occasional interjections of subjective emotion
- (C) Underlying contempt partially concealed by objectivity
- (D) First-person outbursts of effusive emotion in an otherwise third-person narration

The Complexity of the Test

It's unlikely that you'll see an AP question this complex and multi-layered, but it's better to expect the unexpected and over-prepare than to be caught off guard. Think of it this way: if you can parse a question like this, you're ready for the AP Exam.

Here's How to Crack It

Again, from the question alone you can't know exactly what the question asks. That's fine. Look over the answer choices. You can see that they refer to the tone, style, and structure of the passage. The test-writers like to throw these mixtures at you. The way to work on this kind of question is to break the answer choices into bite-size parts, and then check the passage to see whether you can find an example of that part. For example, are there lighthearted situations, (A)? Well, going to hell isn't exactly lighthearted. (So the choice is already wrong, but let's keep going.) Are the situations narrated with deep seriousness? No, not exactly. Narrated with a straight face perhaps, but not deeply serious. The idea is to break the choices into pieces you can use. Remember, half wrong equals all wrong.

The correct answer is (D). As always, use POE and look at the whole passage. Make your initial eliminations. Choice (A) is wrong because the situations are not so much lighthearted as absurd and the narrator is not deeply serious, but nearly as bizarre and out of control as the Duke. Choice (C) should be unappealing as well. What "contempt"? What "objectivity"? Eliminate it. Although the Duke shows contempt for his situation, this isn't the overall effect of the passage that the question asks for.

This leaves (B) and (D). Take each answer choice and go back to the passage. Do you see any "calculated objectivity"? Not really; almost every sentence is loaded with one of the Duke's preposterous emotions. Almost everything comes to us through a filter of the Duke's impressions, especially in the longer sentences. It isn't accurate to call the subjective (first-person element) "occasional." That is enough to eliminate (B), leaving you with just one remaining choice, (D). For safety's sake you should now examine it. "Outbursts of effusive emotion"? Well, there are all those exclamation points all over the place. As a matter of fact, half of the time the author seems to be shouting. The story is told in the third person, yet much of the time the Duke's persona, his voice, or the attitude behind his voice seems to be speaking. Choice (D) is correct.

Use the Glossary

If any of the terms we've used in this explanation— *first person, third person, subjectivity*—gave you trouble, you should refer to their definitions in the glossary, which is located on your online Student Tools.

Attitude questions are just tone questions; they ask about the underlying emotional content of the passage:

> **12** 🔖 Mark for Review
>
> The narrator's attitude toward the Duke can be best described as
>
> (A) complete objectivity
>
> (B) slight distaste
>
> (C) bemused confusion
>
> (D) satiric glee

Here's How to Crack It

This is a tone question: specifically, it asks about the narrator's perspective on the main character. The correct answer is (D). POE, as usual, helps a great deal. On tone questions, there are usually a couple of answer choices that you can dismiss without a second glance. There's no way you could call the passage an example of (A), complete objectivity; it's much too weird. Doesn't the whole passage feel high-strung, as though old Edgar A. Poe had a few too many cups of coffee on top of whatever else he was drinking that day? That feeling never goes with objectivity. Choice (B) might have been appealing because it didn't sound too extreme. In general, mild is better than extreme on tone questions but unfortunately, "slight distaste" is wrong; there's no evidence that the narrator feels a slight distaste for the Duke. Remember, you wanted to pick what the *narrator* feels. You might have felt slight distaste, but the question didn't ask how you felt. Speaking of how you felt, (C) is a type of answer choice that occasionally appears on the exam. When students are struggling, they're drawn to answers that suggest their own mental state, such as *confused, depressed, anxious,* and *fearful,* even when such words are plain wrong. The answer feels right, not because it's correct, but because it's how the student feels taking a test. There's no evidence in the story that the narrator is confused or doesn't understand the Duke; in fact, he seems to understand the Duke a little too perfectly.

This leads to (D), the correct answer. "Glee" may seem a bit strong, but in this case it fits. The narrator tells the story with energy, enthusiasm, and a completely unabashed use of exclamation points—that's a tip-off right there. Good writers don't overuse exclamation points. (The great Irish novelist James Joyce called them, derisively, "shriek marks.") Poe doesn't overuse them here, but it could easily seem like it. Poe uses exclamation points because, if for the Duke a badly prepared bird is upsetting enough to kill him, the Duke's life must be filled with exclamation points. This is one of the elements (and there are many) which make the passage satiric. *Satire* (see the glossary) is an important concept for the AP Exam. When a passage pokes fun at an exaggeratedly foolish type (in this case, the type of arrogant man who considers himself supreme in all things), you can be sure it's satire. The gleefulness stems from the evident enjoyment Poe takes in describing the Duke's peculiar foolishness. Of course, Poe has the Duke win in the end, which makes sense because Poe himself had a lot of the Duke in him.

Literary Term Questions

○

13 ☐ Mark for Review

The phrase "as if carved in marble" (paragraph 14) is an example of

(A) irony

(B) lyricism

(C) a metaphor

(D) a simile

Here's How to Crack It

This is an absolutely straightforward literary term question. You are sure to see a few questions like it on the test. Of course you should use POE, but the best solution for literary term questions is to know the terms. That's why we've included our glossary (in your Student Tools). As we mentioned earlier, there are just a few things you can be sure will make an appearance somewhere on the test. Among those things are the terms *simile* and *metaphor*.

The correct answer here is (D). The phrase is a simile. A comparison that uses *like* or *as* is a simile. Even if these terms don't show up on your test as the best answers to a question (and chances are that's exactly how they will show up), at the very least they'll show up as answers you'll be able to eliminate. If you aren't aware that the phrase in question is a simile, eliminate what you can and take your best guess. Believe it or not, all the terms in the question are defined in our glossary.

○

Excerpt from Ta-Nehisi Coates's *The Water Dancer*

Par.

1   And I could only have seen her there on the stone bridge, a dancer wreathed in ghostly blue, because that was the way they would have taken her back when I was young, back when the Virginia earth was still red as brick and red with life, and though there were other bridges spanning the river Goose, they would have bound her and brought her across this one, because this was the bridge that fed into the turnpike that twisted its way through the green hills and down the valley before bending in one direction, and that direction was south.

2   I had always avoided that bridge, for it was stained with the remembrance of the mothers, uncles, and cousins gone Natchez-way. But knowing now the awesome power of memory, how it can open a blue door from one world to another, how it can move us from mountains to meadows, from green woods to fields caked in snow, knowing now that memory can fold the land like cloth, and knowing, too, how I had pushed my memory of her into the "down there" of my mind, how I forgot, but did not forget, I know now that this story, this Conduction, had to begin there on that fantastic bridge between the land of the living and the land of the lost.

3   And she was patting juba on the bridge, an earthen jar on her head, a great mist rising from the river below nipping at her bare heels, which pounded the cobblestones, causing her necklace of shells to shake. The earthen jar did not move; it seemed almost a part of her, so that no matter her high knees, no matter her dips and bends, her splaying arms, the jar stayed fixed on her head like a crown. And seeing this incredible feat, I knew that the woman patting juba, wreathed in ghostly blue, was my mother.

4   No one else saw her—not Maynard, who was then in the back of the new Millennium chaise, not the fancy girl who held him rapt with her wiles, and, most strange, not the horse, though I had been told that horses had a nose for things that stray out from other worlds and stumble into ours. No, only I saw her from the driver's seat of the chaise, and she was just as they'd described her, just as they'd said she'd been in the olden days when she would leap into a circle of all my people—Aunt Emma, Young P, Honas, and Uncle John—and they would clap, pound their chests, and slap their knees, urging her on in double time, and she would stomp the dirt floor hard, as if crushing a crawling thing under her heel, and bend at the hips and bow, then twist and wind her bent knees in union with her hands, the earthen jar still on her head. My mother was the best dancer at Lockless, that is what they told me, and I remembered this because she'd gifted me with none of it, but more I remembered because it was dancing that brought her to the attention of my father, and thus had brought me to be. And more than that, I remembered because I remembered everything—everything, it seemed, except her.

1   Mark for Review

The narrator's development from childhood until the present includes

(A) remembering the setting of his mother's abduction in vivid detail

(B) forgetting, and then later reasoning out, which way his mother must have been taken

(C) seeing visions of his mother dancing in a blue mist

(D) becoming as talented a dancer as his mother was

2   Mark for Review

What does the fact the neither Maynard, nor the fancy girl, nor the horse can see what the narrator is seeing contribute to the meaning of the story?

(A) It means that the vision is a symptom of madness in the narrator.

(B) It illustrates the differences in personality between the narrator, Maynard, the fancy girl, and the horse.

(C) It shows that Maynard and the fancy girl are not paying attention to the scenery.

(D) It allows the narrator to examine an image of his mother that includes the traits he has learned she had.

3 ☐ Mark for Review

Each of the following details helps reveal the narrator's cultural and historical setting EXCEPT

Ⓐ "though there were other bridges spanning the river Goose, they would have bound her and brought her across this one" (paragraph 1)

Ⓑ "I had always avoided that bridge, for it was stained with the remembrance of the mothers, uncles, and cousins gone Natchez-way" (paragraph 2)

Ⓒ "from mountains to meadows, from green woods to fields caked in snow" (paragraph 2)

Ⓓ "And she was patting juba on the bridge, an earthen jar on her head, a great mist rising from the river below" (paragraph 3)

4 ☐ Mark for Review

Which of the following best describes the narrator's attitude toward the stone bridge?

Ⓐ He finds the bridge too painful to face until he realizes that it can unlock his memories of his mother.

Ⓑ He avoids the bridge because it reminds him of relatives he dislikes.

Ⓒ He is indifferent to the bridge until he sees the dancing woman outlined in blue there.

Ⓓ He has no interest in the bridge, since there are several others which span the same river.

5 ☐ Mark for Review

The primary conflict in the passage can be described as

Ⓐ driving versus dancing

Ⓑ trauma versus longing

Ⓒ technology versus nature

Ⓓ memory versus experience

6 ☐ Mark for Review

The fact that the passage is narrated in first person allows the reader access to all of the following EXCEPT

Ⓐ the thoughts of the main character

Ⓑ the personal history of the main character

Ⓒ the name of the main character

Ⓓ the names of people the main character knows

7 ☐ Mark for Review

Which information might a third-person narrator have been able to provide that the narrator of this passage could not?

Ⓐ An accurate physical description of the narrator's mother

Ⓑ A colorful description of the power of memory

Ⓒ A definite answer to the question of which bridge the narrator's mother was taken over

Ⓓ The feelings the narrator has upon seeing the vision of his mother dancing

8 ⬜ Mark for Review

The stone bridge is a symbol of which two concepts for the narrator?

(A) The memory of people lost and the way to a new life

(B) An idyllic past and a difficult future

(C) The difficulty he has remembering and the key to unlocking his memories

(D) The pain of losing loved ones and a door to memory

9 ⬜ Mark for Review

In paragraph 2, "how it can open a blue door from one world to another, how it can move us from mountains to meadows, . . . that memory can fold the land like cloth," the author uses which literary device to convey the power of memory?

(A) Irony

(B) Allusion

(C) Paradox

(D) Personification

10 ⬜ Mark for Review

In the passage, what does the color blue represent?

(A) Images that are memories or constructs

(B) The way the Virginia earth represents life

(C) The dance called patting juba

(D) The narrator's mother

About Coates's The Water Dancer

This passage was taken from a novel, *The Water Dancer*, by Ta-Nehisi Coates. This one is on the shorter side for a prose passage. It demonstrates plenty of the language and stylistic devices you'll see on prose fiction analysis passages: imagery, symbols, poetic language, and contrasts between characters, settings, and even realities. Don't worry! The same techniques you used on "The Duc De L'Omelette" will work here: work the passage using your active reading skills; manage your time wisely; and know the types and formats of questions and how to approach each one.

Answers and Explanations to the Questions

Here, once again, you'll find detailed explanations to the questions that followed the passage. We've tried to cover a few more skills here, but these are still representative of the questions you'll see on the test.

These questions begin with some twists on detail questions that require a bit of question comprehension.

---

1 🔖 Mark for Review

The narrator's development from childhood until the present includes

- (A) remembering the setting of his mother's abduction in vivid detail

- (B) forgetting, and then later reasoning out, which way his mother must have been taken

- (C) seeing visions of his mother dancing in a blue mist

- (D) becoming as talented a dancer as his mother was

Here's How to Crack It

What's going on here? This question is asking about a character's development since his childhood—in other words, how he has changed over time.

You know from reading the passage that the narrator has some trouble remembering his mother, and you can use that to do some POE here: Eliminate (A), since remembering details about his mother is exactly what he struggles to do.

Now look at (D). The narrator mentions that one reason he remembered that his mother was a good dancer was *because she'd gifted him with none of it*. He's not a good dancer, so eliminate (D). Now take a look at (B) and (C). Both have some support from the passage, but *seeing visions of his mother dancing* is something that is happening in the present moment in the story, so it's not part of this character's development from his childhood. Remember that a good answer must answer the question given—you can eliminate (C).

Choice (B) is a good paraphrase of the first two paragraphs—the narrator reasons that this bridge is the one upon which she must have been taken, even though he had *pushed his memory of her into the "down there" of his mind*. The correct answer is (B).

The next one is slightly weirder: it asks how a specific detail contributes to the overall meaning of the passage. Think about what the detail is, and choose an answer that fits the general theme of the passage.

---

2 ☐ Mark for Review

What does the fact the neither Maynard, nor the fancy girl, nor the horse can see what the narrator is seeing contribute to the meaning of the story?

(A) It means that the vision is a symptom of madness in the narrator.

(B) It illustrates the differences in personality between the narrator, Maynard, the fancy girl, and the horse.

(C) It shows that Maynard and the fancy girl are not paying attention to the scenery.

(D) It allows the narrator to examine an image of his mother that includes the traits he has learned she had.

Here's How to Crack It

This question is asking about a contrast between characters: only one of them can see the dancing woman. What does that mean to the story? You can bet the answer will focus on the narrator, as most of the passage is about him and his memories.

Eliminate (C), as Maynard and the fancy girl only take up 3 lines—you can't say whether or not they are paying attention with so little to go on. You can also eliminate (B); while we are dealing with a contrast between these other characters and the narrator, the passage doesn't have enough on Maynard, the fancy girl, and the horse to indicate their personalities.

Choice (A) focuses on the narrator, but makes a claim that isn't supported by the passage—that the vision *is a symptom of madness*. What does happen is that the narrator fills in the image of the dancing woman with all the details he knows about his mother, so the correct answer is (D).

———————○———————

You've seen questions asking what specific details reveal about characters, tone, and plot: the test-writers can also include questions about setting. Try the next two to see a couple of variations on how they might do that.

———————○———————

| 3 | 🔖 Mark for Review |

Each of the following details helps reveal the narrator's cultural and historical setting EXCEPT

- (A) "though there were other bridges spanning the river Goose, they would have bound her and brought her across this one" (paragraph 1)

- (B) I had always avoided that bridge, for it was stained with the remembrance of the mothers, uncles, and cousins gone Natchez-way" (paragraph 2)

- (C) "from mountains to meadows, from green woods to fields caked in snow" (paragraph 2)

- (D) "And she was patting juba on the bridge, an earthen jar on her head, a great mist rising from the river below" (paragraph 3)

Here's How to Crack It

This question is asking about the details that *reveal the cultural and historical setting of the passage.* The paragraph references in the answer choices remind you to go back and read those portions of the text in context.

Notice, also, that it's an EXCEPT question: Cross out EXCEPT and eliminate answers that satisfy the remaining statement.

They would have bound her and brought her and *the mothers, uncles, and cousins gone Natchez-way* both give clues to the reader that the passage takes place during the era of slavery in the United States, so eliminate (A) and (B).

Now look at (C) and (D). Though *from mountains to meadows, from green woods to fields caked in snow* looks at first glance like straightforward setting description, the narrator is actually describing the power of memory, not a real place, when he uses these phrases. Keep (C) for now.

Though it's a bit more subtle than the clues given in (A) and (B), *patting juba on the bridge, an earthen jar on her head* is an image that conveys an earlier time, both because *juba* is a historical dance, and because carrying water in earthen jars is no longer common in this part of the world. Eliminate (D). The correct answer is (C).

In the previous passage, you saw a tone question that asked about the author's attitude toward the main character. You will also see tone questions that address a specific detail, rather than the passage or a character as a whole.

4	🔖 Mark for Review

Which of the following best describes the narrator's attitude toward the stone bridge?

(A) He finds the bridge too painful to face until he realizes that it can unlock his memories of his mother.

(B) He avoids the bridge because it reminds him of relatives he dislikes.

(C) He is indifferent to the bridge until he sees the dancing woman outlined in blue there.

(D) He has no interest in the bridge, since there are several others which span the same river.

Here's How to Crack It

This question is asking about the attitude of the narrator toward *the stone bridge*. The test-writers often employ questions about relationships—between elements of the plot, between characters, and between the characters and their setting, as happens here.

Look for ways in which the passage tells you the narrator's feelings when it comes to the stone bridge. The narrator *had always avoided that bridge, for it was stained with the remembrance of the mothers, uncles, and cousins gone Natchez-way* and yet also *know[s] now that this story . . . had to begin there on that fantastic bridge*, so you can see that the narrator's attitude toward the bridge has changed. Look for an answer that covers that change.

You can eliminate (B), since there's no indication in it of his change in attitude, and it misinterprets his negative feelings as simple dislike.

Now look at (C) and (D): both *is indifferent* and *has no interest* mean that the narrator has no strong feelings about the bridge, which is contradicted by both parts of the attitude shift the passage illustrates. Eliminate those as well.

Choice (A) is the only one that covers both his previous avoidance (because the bridge was *too painful to face*) and his new interest in the bridge once he realizes *the awesome power of memory*. The correct answer is (A).

The next three questions fall roughly into the category of general questions, though they represent some less common skills. Use what you know about the passage as a whole to answer these.

---

5 Mark for Review

The primary conflict in the passage can be described as

(A) driving versus dancing

(B) trauma versus longing

(C) technology versus nature

(D) memory versus experience

Here's How to Crack It

Rather than the primary purpose, theme, or even character, this question is asking about the primary *conflict* in the passage. Remember, conflict can also be thought of as opposition, or any kind of sharp contrast. You're looking for the *primary* one.

Remember when we said that AP passages tend to be focused on one thing, and that the most common focus is on a character? This passage is mainly about the narrator, who is also the main character. He spends most of the passage trying to reminisce about his mother, though he's stymied by his lack of memories of her.

Use Consistency of Answers: in Question 4 you chose *He finds the bridge too painful to face until he realizes that it can unlock his memories of his mother.* Though that is the main character's perspective on a single symbol, it conveys the general sense that his trip down memory lane is both painful and enticing.

You can eliminate (C), since the passage contains plenty of *nature* but little to no *technology*. Both *driving* and *dancing* are happening in the passage, but they aren't even close to being the primary conflict, so eliminate (A).

While *memory* is certainly central to the conflict in the passage, it seems to be two different feelings about memory that give rise to the conflict. Even the main *experience* the narrator has, the vision of his mother, is just another kind of memory; eliminate (D). The real conflict is that he finds those memories painful (*trauma*) but is driven to explore them anyway (*longing*). The correct answer is (B).

The question below and the one that follows it concentrate on the point of view of the narrator. Use what you know about point of view, keeping in mind the themes of the passage you've seen so far.

---

6 ▢ Mark for Review

The fact that the passage is narrated in the first person allows the reader access to all of the following EXCEPT

(A) the thoughts of the main character

(B) the personal history of the main character

(C) the name of the main character

(D) the names of people the main character knows

Here's How to Crack It

This question is asking about what information the reader has access to because of the point of view of the narrative. Since it's an EXCEPT question, cross out EXCEPT and eliminate answers that satisfy the remaining statement.

The most obvious thing that a first-person narrative allows for is the thoughts of the narrator, so eliminate (A). The personal history of the narrator, especially concerning his mother, is also a major theme: eliminate (B). What about names? The passage gives you the name of *Maynard*, who is riding in the chaise with the narrator, and lists several more names as examples of *my people*. However, it never gives you the name of the narrator himself. Eliminate (D); the correct answer is (C).

Here's a slightly more complex question covering the same idea (point of view). Keep the same ideas about what point of view means and the general themes of the passage in mind as you approach it.

---

7   🔖 Mark for Review

Which information might a third-person narrator have been able to provide that the narrator of this passage could not?

- (A) An accurate physical description of the narrator's mother

- (B) A colorful description of the power of memory

- (C) A definite answer to the question of which bridge the narrator's mother was taken over

- (D) The feelings the narrator has upon seeing the vision of his mother dancing

Here's How to Crack It

This question is asking what information a third-person narrator would have been able to include in the passage that the first-person narrator doesn't. You can eliminate those things that are definitely included in the passage: eliminate (B) and (C).

Whereas *the feelings the narrator has upon seeing the vision of his mother dancing* are not explicitly stated in the passage (though some are implied), this kind of information is something that first-person narrators are perfectly able to provide, so eliminate (D) as well.

The narrator has trouble remembering his mother: his vision is conjured from the things he knows about her. His own mind is unable to give the reader details about exactly what she looked like, but it's possible that a third-person narrator could provide that. The correct answer is (A).

Remember that some of the themes you'd expect to see in poetry passages also show up in prose: symbols, imagery, literary devices. Try these last three questions for another look at how those can appear in prose questions.

---

8   ☐ Mark for Review

The stone bridge is a symbol of which two concepts for the narrator?

(A) The memory of people lost and the way to a new life

(B) An idyllic past and a difficult future

(C) The difficulty he has remembering and the key to unlocking his memories

(D) The pain of losing loved ones and a door to memory

Here's How to Crack It

This question is asking about the use of the stone bridge as a *symbol*. It's used as a symbol for two different things in the passage, so the correct answer has two parts.

First, the narrator tells us that this is the bridge his mother was taken across when she was taken away from him, and also that he *had always avoided that bridge, for it was stained with the remembrance* of her and other lost relatives. Eliminate those answers that don't contain this painful remembrance as one of the meanings: (B) and (C).

Then the narrator uses *that fantastic bridge between the land of the living and the land of the lost* to represent a way for him to remember his mother. *The way to a new life* is unrelated to memory, so eliminate (A). The correct answer is (D).

Here's a literary term question, just as you saw in the previous passage. Remember that both good POE and *knowing your literary terms* are key to good performance on these questions. Look through the glossary in your Student Tools, especially if you have trouble remembering the definitions any of these terms.

---

9 ☐ Mark for Review

In paragraph 2, "how it can open a blue door from one world to another, how it can move us from mountains to meadows, . . . that memory can fold the land like cloth," the author uses which literary device to convey the power of memory?

Ⓐ Irony

Ⓑ Allusion

Ⓒ Paradox

Ⓓ Personification

Here's How to Crack It

This question is asking what literary device is used *to convey the power of memory* in the given lines. Since memory is given some human attributes, such as the ability to perform actions (opening doors, folding cloth), *personification* is the best answer. The correct answer is (D).

Try one more question. It's a variation on the task in question 8—here you need to find mention of a specific color among the imagery used in the passage, and determine what it represents.

10 ☐ Mark for Review

In the passage, what does the color blue represent?

Ⓐ Images that are memories or constructs

Ⓑ The way the Virginia earth represents life

Ⓒ The dance called patting juba

Ⓓ The narrator's mother

Here's How to Crack It

This question is asking what *the color blue* represents in the passage. The author uses the color blue twice to describe the narrator's vision of the dancing woman, and once to describe a *door from one world to another* that memory has the power to open.

Eliminate (B) because the only color *the Virginia earth* is connected to in the passage is red.

Both *the dance* and *the narrator's mother* are close, as he sees her dancing and *wreathed in ghostly blue*, but neither of these answers includes the *blue door* between worlds, so eliminate (C) and (D).

Blue represents the images the narrator sees or imagines that have to do with memory: the correct answer is (A).

A FEW FINAL WORDS

If you worked through the passages as we instructed, you just learned a great deal about how to take the multiple-choice questions on the AP English Literature and Composition Exam. It probably took close to five times longer here than working on a real passage would, but that's to be expected—you're learning. This does bring up an important point though: time. We've taken you through the passages and familiarized you with some typical questions so that when you're on your own, you can work efficiently and accurately, answering all the questions in about 12–15 minutes.

But what if it doesn't work that way? Let's say you had reasoned that a passage was the most difficult on the test and decided to do it last. By the time you got to it, you had only seven minutes left. Seven minutes to do that passage! You would use up most of that time just reading it. Should you give up?—No! This is where all the study you've put into the questions can really pay off. Check out the Art of the Seven-Minute Passage—and enjoy!

The Art of the Seven-Minute Passage

When you hit the last passage on the test, check your time. If you have seven minutes or fewer left, you have to change your strategy. You don't have enough time to do the passage the normal way. It's time for emergency measures. What is the worst thing to do in an emergency? Panic. Don't. The best defense against panic is preparation. Know exactly what you're going to do. Here it is:

- Don't read the passage. Just *don't* do it.

- Go straight to the questions.

- Answer the questions in the following order:

  1. **Answer any literary term or grammar questions.** You barely need the passage at all for these questions. If you know the point at issue, you'll just snap up a point. Otherwise apply as much POE as you can and guess.

  2. **Go to any question that asks for the meaning of a single word or phrase.** These questions always highlight the word in the passage. Go to the passage and read a sentence before and after the highlighting. Answer the question.

  3. **Go to any other question that gives you a highlighted area in the passage.** (Not answer choices that include highlights, but questions.) Read the highlighted portion and answer the question.

  4. **Go to any question on tone or attitude.** By this time, you've read quite a bit of the passage just by answering questions. You've read enough to be able to make a good guess about where the author's coming from.

  5. **Go to any questions that have highlighted sections of the passage in the answer choices.** Answer them all.

  6. **Do whatever is left over**—character questions, primary purpose questions, weird questions, and so on. If you need to, read some of the passage to get them. Go ahead and read. Keep working until the proctor tells you to stop.

That's the Art of the Seven-Minute Passage. It works in six, five, four, three, two, or one minute(s) too; with less time, you don't get as far down the list, that's all.

7 Minutes to Go!
If you find yourself in a situation in which you have only 7 minutes left but several questions still unanswered, don't panic. Instead, follow this simple six-step system.

What If I Have Seven Minutes and Fifteen Seconds Left?

Seven minutes or fewer is a good rough guideline for when to use the Don't Read the Passage technique. Your pace on multiple-choice passages should be about 12 minutes a passage. If you have an awkward amount of time left for the last passage—that is, somewhere between 7 and 15 minutes—you'll have to decide which approach to use. You have two choices. The first is to just read and work faster, to step on the gas big-time. The other choice is to go straight to the questions, that is, to use the Art of the Seven-Minute Passage technique. It's your call. At the seven-minute mark (or 7 minutes and 3 seconds, whatever), you should go straight to the questions. With 10 minutes left you should probably try to read the passage fast but then attempt the questions in the seven-minute order. At, say, 14 minutes, you should just work normally, but keep in mind that you don't have any time to waste worrying about those silly things students worry about, like whether you've guessed too many (C)s.

Prose Fiction Analysis Passage Drill

Suggested time: 12 minutes

Questions 1 through 14 refer to the following. Read the following passage carefully before you choose your answers.

The passage, an excerpt from Anna Karenina *by Leo Tolstoy (published in 1878), describes one of the central characters and his dog.*

1   Getting on his boots and stockings, taking his gun, and carefully opening the creaking door of the barn, Levin went out into the road. It was still gray out-of-doors.

2   "Why are you up so early, my dear?" the old woman, their hostess, said, coming out of the hut and addressing him affectionately as an old friend.

3   "Going shooting, granny."

4   Laska ran eagerly forward along the little path. Levin followed her with a light, rapid step, continually looking at the sky. He hoped the sun would not be up before he reached the marsh. But the sun did not delay. In the transparent stillness of morning the smallest sounds were audible. A bee flew by Levin's ear with the whizzing sound of a bullet. He looked carefully, and saw a second and a third. The marsh could be recognized by the mist which rose from it, thicker in one place and thinner in another, so that the reeds and willow bushes swayed like islands in this mist. Laska walked beside her master, pressing a little forward and looking round. . . .Levin examined his pistols and let his dog off. Levin patted Laska, and whistled as a sign that she might begin.

5   Laska ran joyfully and anxiously through the slush that swayed under her.

6   Running into the marsh among the familiar scents, Laska detected at once a smell that pervaded the whole marsh, the scent of that strong-smelling bird that always excited her more than any other. Sniffing in the air with dilated nostrils, she felt at once that not their tracks only but they themselves were here before her, and not one, but many. They were here, but where precisely she could not yet determine. To find the very spot, she began to make a circle, when suddenly her master's voice drew her off. "Laska! here?" he asked, pointing her to a different direction. She stopped, asking him if she had better not go on doing as she had begun. But he repeated his command in an angry voice, pointing to a spot covered with water, where there could not be anything. She obeyed him, pretending she was looking, so as to please him, went round it, and went back to her former position, and was at once aware of the scent again. Now when he was not hindering her, she knew what to do, and without looking at what was under her feet, and to her vexation stumbling over a high stump into the water, but righting herself with her strong, supple legs, she began making the circle which was to make all clear to her. The scent of them reached her, stronger and stronger, and more and more defined, and all at once it became perfectly clear to her that one of them was here, behind this tuft of reeds, five paces in front of her; she

stopped, and her whole body was still and rigid. Her tail was stretched straight and tense, and only wagging at the extreme end. Her mouth was slightly open, her ears raised. One ear had been turned wrong side out as she ran up, and she breathed heavily but warily, and still more warily looked round, but more with her eyes than her head, to her master. He was coming along with the face she knew so well, though the eyes were always terrible to her. He stumbled over the stump as he came, and moved, as she thought, extraordinarily slowly. She thought he came slowly, but he was running.

7   Noticing Laska's special attitude as she crouched on the ground, as it were, scratching big prints with her hind paws, and with her mouth slightly open, Levin knew she was pointing at grouse, and with an inward prayer for luck, especially with the first bird, he ran up to her. Coming quite close up to her, he could from his height look beyond her, and he saw with his eyes what she was seeing with her nose. In a space between two little thickets, to a couple of yards' distance, he could see a grouse. Turning its head, it was listening. Then lightly preening and folding its wings, it disappeared round a corner with a clumsy wag of its tail.

8   "Fetch it, fetch it!" shouted Levin, giving Laska a shove from behind.

9   She darted forward as fast as her legs would carry her between the thick bushes.

10   Ten paces from her former place a grouse rose with a guttural cry and the peculiar round sound of its wings. And immediately after the shot it splashed heavily with its white breast on the wet mire. Another bird did not linger, but rose behind Levin without the dog. When Levin turned towards it, it was already some way off. But his shot caught it. Flying twenty paces further, the second grouse rose upwards, and whirling round like a ball, dropped heavily on a dry place.

11   When Levin, after loading his gun, moved on, the sun had fully risen, though unseen behind the storm-clouds. The moon had lost all of its luster, and was like a white cloud in the sky. Not a single star could be seen. Crows were flying about the field, and a bare-legged boy was driving the horses to an old man. The smoke from the gun was white as milk over the green of the grass.

12   One of the boys ran up to Levin.

13   "Uncle, there were ducks here yesterday!" he shouted to him, and he walked a little way off behind him.

14   And Levin was doubly pleased, in sight of the boy, who expressed his approval, at killing three snipe, one after another, straight off.

1 ☐ Mark for Review

One effect of paragraph 11 is to emphasize

(A) the author's ability to create a sense of foreboding

(B) the passage of time explicitly

(C) the use of specific details to frame the passage

(D) the impact of the weather on the events

2 ☐ Mark for Review

How is the word "vexation" used in the sentence "Now when he was not hindering her, . . . which was to make all clear to her" (paragraph 6)?

(A) To demonstrate Levin's confusion about Laska's clumsiness

(B) To underscore the danger of Laska's mission

(C) To reveal Laska's bewilderment as to why she stumbled

(D) To emphasize Laska's single-mindedness

3 ☐ Mark for Review

The passage suggests that Levin

(A) is visiting with family

(B) is anxious about his ability to provide for his family

(C) has a strained relationship with Laska

(D) is on familiar terms with those whom he encounters

4 ☐ Mark for Review

What is the function of the following sentence from paragraph 7: "Coming quite close up to her . . . seeing with her nose" in relation to the description from paragraph 6: "They were here, . . . she began to make a circle"?

(A) Levin's hunting skills are superior to Laska's.

(B) Laska requires Levin's supervision when hunting.

(C) The author highlights the synergistic relationship between Laska and Levin.

(D) The author underscores Levin's dependence on Laska.

5 ☐ Mark for Review

Which sentence demonstrates Laska's relationship to Levin?

(A) "Levin patted Laska, and whistled as a sign that she might begin." (paragraph 4)

(B) "She obeyed him, pretending she was looking, so as to please him, went round it, and went back to her former position, and was at once aware of the scent again." (paragraph 6)

(C) "He was coming along with the face she knew so well, though the eyes were always terrible to her." (paragraph 6)

(D) "Then lightly preening and folding its wings, it disappeared round a corner with a clumsy wag of its tail." (paragraph 7)

6 ☐ Mark for Review

The author views Levin

(A) with impartial objectivity

(B) with wry optimism

(C) as a domineering master

(D) through a critical lens

7 ☐ Mark for Review

The passage as a whole is most indebted to which literary tradition?

(A) Romanticism

(B) Realism

(C) Modernism

(D) Naturalism

8 ☐ Mark for Review

In context of the passage as a whole, paragraphs 4 and 5 serve to

(A) provide a description of the setting

(B) foreshadow later events

(C) build anticipation

(D) establish perspective

9 ☐ Mark for Review

In paragraph 14, the author characterizes Levin as

(A) proud and content

(B) pleased and exhausted

(C) powerful and victorious

(D) astonished and boastful

10 ☐ Mark for Review

The narrator suggests that the individuals Levin encounters are characterized by

(A) envious curiosity about Levin's excursion

(B) exuberant pleasure for Levin's skill

(C) pious respect for Levin's hunting prowess

(D) warm regard for Levin

11 ☐ Mark for Review

What dominant technique is the author using in the sentences "To find the very spot, she began to make a circle, . . . and was at once aware of the scent again" (paragraph 6)?

(A) Personification

(B) Irony

(C) Anthropomorphism

(D) Dialogue

12 ☐ Mark for Review

The sentence "Now when he was not hindering her, . . . which was to make all clear to her" in paragraph 6 contains all of the following EXCEPT

(A) a character flaw

(B) alliteration

(C) suspense

(D) juxtaposition

13 ☐ Mark for Review

The sentences "'Laska! here?'. . . where there could not be anything" in paragraph 6 suggest

(A) Levin's temperamental nature

(B) Laska's submissive nature toward Levin

(C) Laska's ability to speak to Levin

(D) Laska's inexperience with hunting

PROSE FICTION ANALYSIS PASSAGE DRILL: ANSWERS AND EXPLANATIONS

Considered one of the greatest writers of all time, Leo Tolstoy was a Russian author, and *Anna Karenina* was his second novel. This novel, along with *War and Peace*, are hallmark examples of realism in literature.

1. **C** Coming at the end of the passage, this description of the sun bookends the passage nicely (paragraph 11). Therefore, the correct answer is (C). The passage ends on a pleasant note, so the author is not creating a sense of foreboding, so eliminate (A). The effect of these lines is not to highlight the passage of time explicitly or implicitly, so (B) is incorrect. Rather, these lines offer further description of the setting and are written in such a way that they parallel the description provided at the beginning of the passage. The weather is not impacting Levin's hunting—he's done quite well so far—so (D) is also incorrect.

2. **D** *Vexation* means annoyance or irritation, not confusion, so eliminate (A) and (C). This word highlights Laska's desire to find the source of the smell, and she's irritated that the stump got in her way. However, she does not let it or her stumble impede her forward progress for very long. She is focused on the task at hand and does not let this event distract her, making (D) the correct answer. There is no evidence in the passage that she's in danger, (B).

3. **D** Although Levin refers to the old lady as "granny" (note the lowercase g), and the boy calls Levin "Uncle," Levin is not related to either of them. The old woman is the hostess of the place at which he is staying, and he comes across the boy while he is hunting, so eliminate (A) and (B). There is no evidence in the text to support (C). Since he does speak with the old woman in a friendly way, and the boy addresses him in a casual way, we can infer that Levin treats those whom he encounters in an informal and warm way. Therefore, (D) is the answer.

4. **C** The first highlighted portion illustrates the advantage Levin's height gives him. From his vantage point, Levin can see what Laska's nose has tracked. The second portion highlighted demonstrates Laska's ability to put the pair in close proximity to the bird—a tracking skill she has but Levin does not. Therefore, these lines emphasize how the combined efforts of the pair allow them to pinpoint the bird's exact location. The correct answer is (C). In (A), the cooperative interaction is minimized. The fact that Levin, not Laska, can actually see the bird makes (D) wrong. Finally, (B) does not reflect the purpose of these lines, nor is it supported by the text.

5. **B** Laska is obedient to her master. She follows his commands and seeks to please him. The correct answer is (B). Choice (D) is referring to the grouse, not Laska, and is incorrect. Choice (A) does not answer the question—it asks for Laska's relationship to Levin. This choice is from Levin's perspective. In the context of the whole passage, there is no evidence to support (C). She does obey Levin, she moves "eagerly" and "joyfully," and she does want to please him. She is not afraid of him or threatened by him.

6. **A** The author shows Levin's friendly exchanges with the people he encounters, his manner toward Laska, and his thoughts as he hunts. The reader is given a wide range of information from which to draw their own conclusions about Levin. Therefore, the author provides a neutral view, and (A) is the best answer. Choice (C) could be inferred at certain parts, but there are moments that undermine it. We see a softer side of Levin, for example, when he pats Laska on the head and allows her to run off leash, both of which would discount (C). There's a moment when he prays for luck on his bird, which undermines (D). The author is not sarcastic, (B), nor is he critical toward Levin, (D), overall.

7. **B**   Tolstoy is classified as a writer of realism, so the correct answer is (B). Note that the naturalism movement did not occur until well after Tolstoy wrote *Anna Karenina*. Literature from the realism movement is notable for its use of detail, transparent language, truthfulness, and omniscient narrators. Writers of realism sought to reflect the true, daily reality of life—this passage is a prime example of realism.

8. **A**   The last question helps with this question: this passage is representative of the realism movement, so thorough descriptions of the setting and characters will be present in the work. The purpose of this section of the text is to give the reader a vivid description of what the characters are experiencing and doing, so the correct answer is (A). There is no foreshadowing, (B), or rising anticipation, (C). The perspective changes in this passage, thereby eliminating (D).

9. **A**   Levin is quite pleased with himself and satisfied with his haul, at what appears to be just the start of his day of hunting. Therefore, the correct answer is (A). There is no evidence in the text that he feels exhausted, (B), powerful, (C), astonished, or boastful, (D).

10. **D**   Use the answer to question 3 to help you on this question. His interactions with the old woman and boy are both friendly and cordial. Everyone is getting along nicely, and both seem to enjoy Levin's presence, so the correct answer is (D). There is no evidence of envy, (A). The old woman makes no comment regarding Levin's skill, so eliminate (B) and (C).

11. **C**   This is a pure definition question, and you need to know the difference between personification and anthropomorphism. When an animal is given human characteristics, behavior, or motivation, anthropomorphism is at work. Personification requires that the nonhuman quality or thing take on a human shape. In this case, Laska seems to have human thoughts (asking him if she had better not go on doing as she had begun) and motivations (pretending she was looking, so as to please him) but never takes on human form. The correct answer is (C). Note that in order for there to be dialogue, both characters would have to be speaking. Since only Levin is actually speaking, (D) cannot be correct.

12. **A**   There is evidence of alliteration, (B), since the initial s sound is repeated in *stumbling, stump, strong, supple, she,* and *circle.* She has an intense desire to find the bird, and each event presented in this sentence adds a layer of light suspense, (C). The idea of Levin hindering her (sending her off in the wrong direction) and the stump acting as an impediment, presented with her desire to reach the source of the scent, is an example of juxtaposition, (D). Laska stumbling is not a character flaw, nor is Levin hindering her a flaw in his character, so the correct answer is (A).

13. **B**   Use the earlier questions to help you here, especially question 5. Laska obeys her master despite not feeling his command is correct, which makes her obedient and submissive, so keep (B). She cannot actually speak to Levin—remember, this is realism—so eliminate (C). There is no evidence that Laska is inexperienced, (D). If anything, there is evidence to the contrary, since she knows she needs to *go on doing as she had begun.* Choice (A) might be tempting, but this answer has been wrong before—the rest of the passage does not indicate that Levin has an erratic or volatile disposition. The answer that is best supported by the text is (B).

Chapter 7 Summary

- When a question seems unclear, the answer choices can help you make sense of it.

- On general questions, you are looking for a choice that accurately describes some facet of the entire passage.

- Learn to focus on key phrases in the answer choices in order to eliminate using the "half wrong equals all wrong" technique.

- Use Consistency of Answers.

- For highlight questions, keep the main idea in mind and use Consistency of Answers whenever possible. Also, go back to the passage and reread the highlighted portions, as well as one full sentence before and after the highlighting.

- Pay close attention to the wording of questions. Put questions in your own words if that makes things easier for you. Be careful not to just ignore confusing parts, though.

- Expect a weird question or two. The test-writers like to get creative on the AP English Literature and Composition Exam. We can't prepare you for everything, just almost everything.

- Our glossary of terms has many valuable definitions and will get you some points; head to your Student Tools to brush up on important key terms!

- Use the Seven-Minute Passage technique for the last passage if you have seven minutes or fewer left: don't read the passage, and answer the questions starting with those that require no knowledge of the passage or those that can be answered by referring to specific highlighted portions.

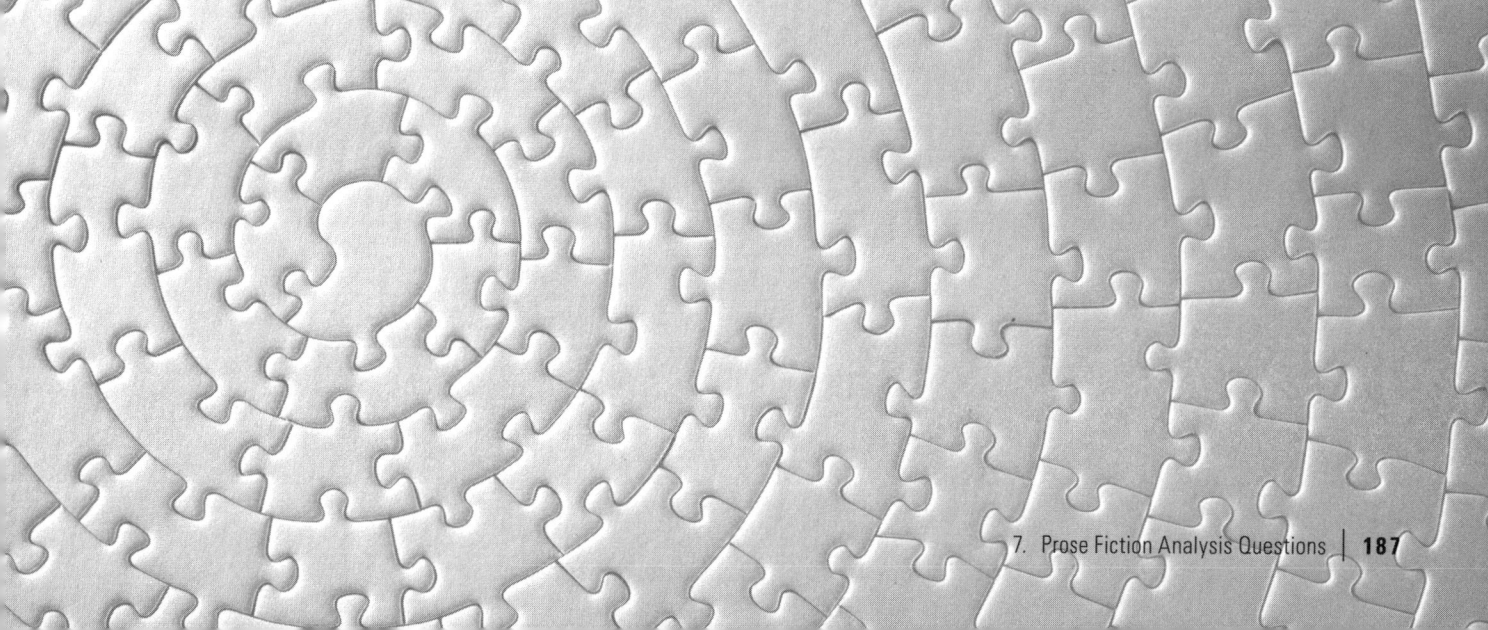

Chapter 8
Poetry Analysis
Questions

READING POETRY LIKE A PRO

Answering multiple-choice questions about poetry analysis passages involves many of the same principles as does answering questions about prose fiction. There are some differences, however.

First, the poetry analysis passages tend to contain more questions that rely on knowledge than the prose fiction passages. You will certainly see a question or two on the literary devices (for example, personification or metaphor) in the poem. You might see a question about the way a line scans or what the rhyme scheme is called, but these are nothing to worry about. Recent tests have not included a single question on scansion or the names of classical poetic forms. The test-writers do, however, like to use poetry for questions about grammar because poets use the kind of tangled syntax that makes for challenging grammar questions.

Second, the poetry you'll see on the AP Exam tends to make for harder reading than the prose fiction passages. Hard, but possible. There's a certain style of poetry that tends to appear on the AP English Literature and Composition Exam. In order to write questions properly, the test-writers are limited in the kind of material they can use. As a result, you won't see poems that stretch language and meaning to its limits, or poems that are open to such a variety of interpretations that asking meaningful multiple-choice questions about them is too difficult. Nor will you see beautiful and elegant but direct and simple poems. Also, you won't see any especially "out there" or experimental postmodern poetry on the exam. The AP Exam generally features poems of 100 to 300 words that use difficult language to make a precise point. The poem below and the questions that follow should give you a good idea of what to expect on the test. This is an excellent place to practice what you've learned in previous chapters. For even more practice, work through the two poetry analysis drills and the bonus questions at the end of this chapter.

Use all of the techniques we've taught you.

- Read the poem as prose.
- Focus on the main idea.
- When answering the questions, use POE and Consistency of Answers.
- Be sure to read before and after highlighted portions.

SAMPLE POETRY ANALYSIS PASSAGE AND QUESTIONS

Andrew Marvell's "On a Drop of Dew"

See how the orient[1] dew,
Shed from the bosom of the morn
   Into the blowing[2] roses,
Line Yet careless of its mansion new,
5 For the clear region where 'twas born
    Round in itself incloses:
    And in its little globe's extent,
Frames as it can its native element.
    How it the purple flow'r does slight,
10   Scarce touching where it lies,
But gazing back upon the skies,
    Shines with a mournful light,
      Like its own tear,
Because so long divided from the sphere.
15   Restless it rolls and unsecure,
     Trembling lest it grow impure,
Till the warm sun pity its pain,
And to the skies exhale it back again.
    So the soul, that drop, that ray
20 Of the clear fountain of eternal day,
Could it within the human flow'r be seen,
    Remembering still its former height,
    Shuns the sweet leaves and blossoms green,
25   And recollecting its own light,
Does, in its pure and circling thoughts, express
The greater heaven in an heaven less.
    In how coy[3] a figure wound,
30   Every way it turns away:
So the world excluding round,
    Yet receiving in the day,
    Dark beneath, but bright above,
    Here disdaining, there in love.
35   How loose and easy hence to go,
How girt and ready to ascend,
Moving but on a point below,
It all about does upwards bend.
Such did the manna's sacred dew distill,
40 White and entire, though congealed and chill,
Congealed on earth: but does, dissolving, run
Into the glories of th' almighty sun.

[1] pearly, sparkling
[2] blooming
[3] modest

---

1 ☐ Mark for Review

The overall content of the poem can best be described by which statement?

- (A) The characteristics of a drop of dew are related to those of the human soul.

- (B) The life cycle of a drop of dew is contemplated.

- (C) The human soul is shown to be a drop of dew.

- (D) The physical characteristics of a drop of dew are analyzed.

2 ☐ Mark for Review

In context, "careless of its mansion new" (line 4) most nearly means

- (A) the dew drop does not understand the value of its beautiful surroundings

- (B) the dew drop does not assist the flower in any way

- (C) the dew drop is unconcerned with its beautiful surroundings

- (D) the human soul does not value the body

3 ☐ Mark for Review

The speaker's metaphor for the human body is

(A) "the orient dew" (line 1)

(B) "the clear fountain" (line 20)

(C) "the sweet leaves and blossoms green" (lines 23–24)

(D) "th' almighty sun" (line 42)

4 ☐ Mark for Review

Which of the following is the antecedent of "its" in "Does, in its pure and circling thoughts,/ express" (lines 26–27)?

(A) "soul" (line 19)

(B) "day" (line 20)

(C) "flow'r" (line 21)

(D) "height" (line 22)

5 ☐ Mark for Review

All of the following aspects of the dew drop are emphasized in the poem EXCEPT

(A) its disregard for the physical world

(B) its desire to regain the heavens

(C) its purity

(D) its will to live

6 ☐ Mark for Review

The contrast in lines 29–34 serves to

(A) illustrate the inherent modesty of flowers

(B) indicate that the human soul prefers heaven to earth

(C) show the dew drop's readiness to evaporate

(D) explain that the world is dark while the sky is bright

7 ☐ Mark for Review

Lines 19–28 make explicit

(A) the analogy between the drop of dew and the soul

(B) the actual differences between the drop of dew and the soul

(C) the soul's need for the body

(D) the soul's thoughts

8 ☐ Mark for Review

Each of the following pairs of phrases refers to the same action, object, or concept EXCEPT

(A) "mansion new" (line 4) . . ."purple flow'r" (line 9)

(B) "globe's extent" (line 7) . . ."the sphere" (line 14)

(C) "that drop" (line 19) . . ."that ray" (line 19)

(D) "exhale" (line 18) . . ."dissolving" (line 41)

9 ☐ Mark for Review

Which of the following best paraphrases the meaning in context of "So the world excluding round,/ yet receiving in the day" (lines 31–32)?

(A) Although the dew drop evaporates in the sun, it arrives anew each day.

(B) The world evaporates the drop of dew when it receives the light of the sun.

(C) The dew drop is impervious to everything but time.

(D) Although the dew drop and the soul shut out the material world, they let in the light of heaven.

10 ☐ Mark for Review

In line 42, the sun is symbolic of

(A) fire

(B) rebirth

(C) the soul

(D) God

11 ☐ Mark for Review

Which of the following sets of adjectives is best suited to describing the poem's tone?

(A) Mysterious, moody, and spiritual

(B) Pious, proper, and academic

(C) Intricate, delicate, and worshipful

(D) Witty, clever, and ironic

12 ☐ Mark for Review

In the final four lines of the poem, the poet suggests that

(A) the dew drop will ultimately be destroyed by the sun

(B) the cycle of life and death is continual

(C) the dew drop will return to earth in the form of "manna"

(D) death brings spiritual unity with God

13 ☐ Mark for Review

Which of the following adjectives is LEAST important to the poem's theme?

(A) "blowing" (line 3)

(B) "clear" (line 20)

(C) "pure" (line 26)

(D) "loose" (line 35)

About Andrew Marvell's "On a Drop of Dew"

This poem is challenging but absolutely typical of what you will find on the AP Exam. Marvell (1621–1678) was one of the metaphysical poets (check your overview of literary movements), and the previous poem is an excellent example of this school of poetry's verse. The metaphysical poets were a loosely connected group of 17th-century poets who fashioned a type of elaborately clever, often witty verse with a decidedly intellectual twist. The metaphysical poets are noted for taking a comparison—for example, "a drop of dew is like the soul"—and developing it over dozens of lines. Lots of metaphysical poetry appears on the multiple-choice section, not because metaphysical poetry is necessarily great but because unlike most poetry, it lends itself well to multiple-choice questions. So, reading any of the metaphysicals' poetry is great practice for the AP Exam.

Answers and Explanations to the Questions

1 | Mark for Review

The overall content of the poem can best be described by which statement?

(A) The characteristics of a drop of dew are related to those of the human soul.

(B) The life cycle of a drop of dew is contemplated.

(C) The human soul is shown to be a drop of dew.

(D) The physical characteristics of a drop of dew are analyzed.

Here's How to Crack It

This is a main-idea question. Remember, you could have left it alone and come back to it if you hadn't found the main idea yet, but chances are you didn't have too much trouble. If you had any trouble eliminating choices, it was probably with (C). Does the poet really show that the human soul is a drop of dew? No. Marvell uses a drop of dew to speak about the human soul, but he isn't suggesting that a person's inner spirit is actually composed of condensed water. In fact, in the poem the drop of dew isn't so much a water droplet as it is a receptacle for light. This point becomes important in later questions. You should have eliminated (B) on the premise that it is much too literal to be correct; you're looking for the deeper main idea of the poem. If (D) threw you, then you weren't paying attention to the word *physical*. You should have asked yourself, "Wait a minute, this dew drop trembles with fear at the thought of becoming impure: Can I call that a physical analysis?" Marvell's drop of dew is a being with a personality and desires; all of these things are studied, not just its physical characteristics. Choice (A) is similar in concept but without any added stuff to throw you off, so it's the best answer.

---

2 ☐ Mark for Review

In context, "careless of its mansion new" (line 4) most nearly means

(A) the dew drop does not understand the value of its beautiful surroundings

(B) the dew drop does not assist the flower in any way

(C) the dew drop is unconcerned with its beautiful surroundings

(D) the human soul does not value the body

Here's How to Crack It

Question 2 is a straightforward highlight question, which asks for the meaning of a specific phrase. The test writers like to test you on your ability to interpret words in context, especially in poems that contain imagery and comparisons, such as this one. After reading around the line reference, you can easily eliminate (D). The line in question discusses only the dew drop upon a rose petal. It does not refer to the human soul. Of the remaining choices, (A) and (B) both imply that in context, "careless" means that the dew drop does not take care of the rose, which is simply a misreading. Chances are you didn't have much trouble on this question. The poet says that the drop of dew reflects the sky (its home), rather than its actual surroundings (the rose). The correct answer is (C).

3   🔖 Mark for Review

The speaker's metaphor for the human body is

Ⓐ "the orient dew" (line 1)

Ⓑ "the clear fountain" (line 20)

Ⓒ "the sweet leaves and blossoms green" (lines 23–24)

Ⓓ "th' almighty sun" (line 42)

Here's How to Crack It

The question asks what metaphor the poem uses for the human body. To answer this question you must either trace Marvell's involved metaphor, noting that in lines 19–21 he describes the soul as being housed within the "human flow'r," or use POE. All three incorrect answers refer to either a spiritual entity (the dew) or its source (the fountain and sun) and so can be eliminated. The correct answer is (C).

4   🔖 Mark for Review

Which of the following is the antecedent of "its" in "Does, in its pure and circling thoughts,/ express" (lines 26–27)?

Ⓐ "soul" (line 19)

Ⓑ "day" (line 20)

Ⓒ "flow'r" (line 21)

Ⓓ "height" (line 22)

Here's How to Crack It

Question 4 is a typical grammar question and hinges on your knowing the term **antecedent**. That term, and other grammatical terms you need for the test, can be found in the glossary on your Student Tools. By asking for the antecedent, the question is simply asking what the word *its* stands for in the given phrase. Analyzed grammatically, the only correct usage (and you'll only be asked about correct usage) is the soul. You might also have reasoned, "For which of the choices would it make sense to have 'pure and circling thoughts'?" Only (A) makes sense.

Practice, Practice, Practice
On the College Board's website they share real AP questions for you to practice with. Check out apstudents.college-board.org/

---

5   🔖 Mark for Review

All of the following aspects of the dew drop are emphasized in the poem EXCEPT

- (A) its disregard for the physical world

- (B) its desire to regain the heavens

- (C) its purity

- (D) its will to live

Here's How to Crack It

Question 5 is an EXCEPT question. An excellent way to proceed is to disregard the EXCEPT; cross EXCEPT out.

Eliminate any choice that fits the remaining question, which now reads: *All* [Which] *of the following aspects of the drop of dew are emphasized in the poem.*

To do this you *must* refer back to the passage. Remember: Never work from memory! "Careless of its mansion new" lets you eliminate (A). "Like its own tear/ Because so long divided from the sphere" takes care of (B). "Trembling lest it grows impure" lets you eliminate (C). This leaves only (D), which is the correct answer.

---

6 ☐ Mark for Review

The contrast in lines 29–34 serves to

(A) illustrate the inherent modesty of flowers

(B) indicate that the human soul prefers heaven to earth

(C) show the dew drop's readiness to evaporate

(D) explain that the world is dark while the sky is bright

Here's How to Crack It

Question 6 is a highlight question that asks for the purpose of a contrast in a particular part of the poem. The *it* referenced on line 30 has the same antecedent as *its* in question 4: the *soul* (line 19). So in this part of the poem Marvell is comparing the soul *turn[ing] away* from the world to its longing for heaven. You can eliminate (A) and (C) because they imply that the subject here is *flowers* and *the dew drop*, respectively. Eliminate (D) because the contrast in the poem is not between the literal world and sky but between the soul's feelings for earth and heaven. The correct answer is (B).

7 ☐ Mark for Review

Lines 19–28 make explicit

(A) the analogy between the drop of dew and the soul

(B) the actual differences between the drop of dew and the soul

(C) the soul's need for the body

(D) the soul's thoughts

Here's How to Crack It

The key here is to understand the question. When something is made explicit, it is stated or spelled out. *Explicit* is the opposite of *implicit*. Your task is to see what lines 19–28 show clearly. Using POE, you should eliminate (C) immediately; it talks only about the drop of dew, whereas the lines in question refer primarily to the human soul. Choice (D) is a trap answer. The lines in question do refer to the soul's thoughts, but they do not spell them out; the thoughts are not made explicit. Choice (B) talks about differences between the soul and the drop of dew. This answer choice is the exact opposite of the lines' intent. They discuss the similarities of the drop and the soul. In fact, they make the analogy between the drop of dew and the soul explicit—therefore, (A) is the correct answer.

Go Online!
Check out us out on YouTube for test taking tips and techniques to help you ace your next exam at youtube.com/ThePrincetonReview

---

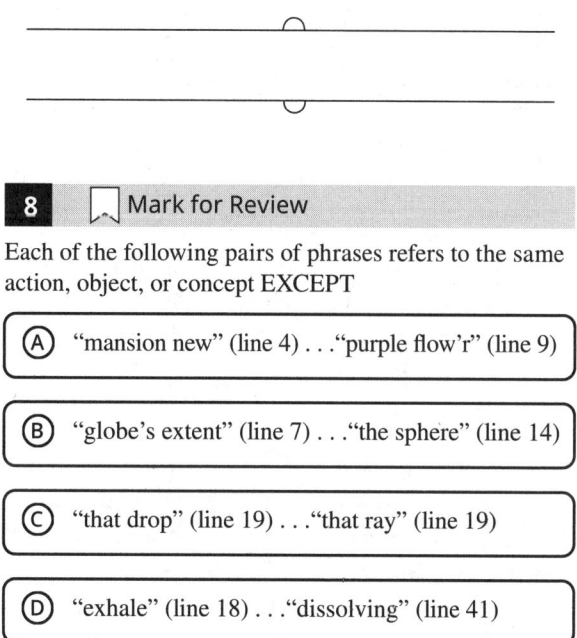

8 ☐ Mark for Review

Each of the following pairs of phrases refers to the same action, object, or concept EXCEPT

(A) "mansion new" (line 4) . . ."purple flow'r" (line 9)

(B) "globe's extent" (line 7) . . ."the sphere" (line 14)

(C) "that drop" (line 19) . . ."that ray" (line 19)

(D) "exhale" (line 18) . . ."dissolving" (line 41)

Here's How to Crack It

This is another EXCEPT question, a common type on the exam. Cross out EXCEPT and eliminate answers that satisfy the remaining statement: *Each of the following pairs of phrases refers to the same action, object, or concept.* Use POE. In (A), "mansion new" and "purple flow'r" both refer to the rose the drop of dew perches on. Eliminate it. In (C), "that drop" and "that ray" seem to refer to different things but both in fact refer to the soul—so eliminate (C). In (D), "exhale" and "dissolving" both refer to the process by which the drop of dew vanishes (evaporation, if you want to be scientific about it). In (B), "globe's extent" and "sphere" seem to both refer to the dew drop, but in fact, the sphere refers to the skies above—the "heavenly sphere." Thus, (B) is the correct answer.

Nitpicky? Maybe, but this question is an excellent example of the kind of careful reading you'll be called upon to do on the actual test.

---

9   ⬚ Mark for Review

Which of the following best paraphrases the meaning in context of "So the world excluding round,/ yet receiving in the day" (lines 31–32)?

(A)   Although the dew drop evaporates in the sun, it arrives anew each day.

(B)   The world evaporates the drop of dew when it receives the light of the sun.

(C)   The dew drop is impervious to everything but time.

(D)   Although the dew drop and the soul shut out the material world, they let in the light of heaven.

Here's How to Crack It

This kind of comprehension question is probably the most common type of poetry analysis question on the AP Exam. In essence, you'll be given a line and asked to answer the question, "So, what does it mean?" As always, read around the line and then use POE. Paraphrase "the world excluding round" as "the drop that turns away from the world" and you can eliminate (A) and (B). None of those choices include that idea. Choice (C) mentions that the drop of dew is impervious. That isn't a good paraphrase of "world excluding round," and you can eliminate it with confidence by reasoning that *time* is not mentioned in the lines in question at all. That leaves only the correct answer, (D).

10 ☐ Mark for Review

In line 42, the sun is symbolic of

- Ⓐ fire
- Ⓑ rebirth
- Ⓒ the soul
- Ⓓ God

Here's How to Crack It

On this question, we hope you saw that the sun symbolized God. The word *almighty* should have been a big clue. Additionally, metaphysical poets are often concerned with spiritual issues. If you've used your overview of literary movements to prepare for this exam, the answer may be even more obvious. The correct answer is (D).

Different Levels of Difficulty

Get used to the range of difficulty on the AP Exam. Some of the questions are subtle and challenge even the most experienced readers, while others are a piece of cake. Don't freak out and think you must have missed something when a question seems easy: just collect the point. Don't miss the easy questions by over-thinking. And don't worry about missing difficult questions. If those are all you miss, you're on your way to earning a score of 5.

11 ☐ Mark for Review

Which of the following sets of adjectives is best suited to describing the poem's tone?

- Ⓐ Mysterious, moody, and spiritual
- Ⓑ Pious, proper, and academic
- Ⓒ Intricate, delicate, and worshipful
- Ⓓ Witty, clever, and ironic

Here's How to Crack It

This is a tone question. On tone questions, always use POE, and remember that "half wrong equals all wrong." Every answer choice has something right in it but only the correct answer choice has *nothing* wrong in it. In (A), yes, the poem's tone is spiritual, but is it mysterious and moody? Not really. Eliminate it. Choice (B) has one promising word—*pious*, as the poem discusses God—but *proper* and *academic* do not fit. That isn't right. Eliminate it. In (D), well, it's true that the poem is witty and clever, but is it also ironic? Metaphysical poets typically are ironic—that is, hidden messages and contradictions often lurk below the surface of a metaphysical poem's text, but "On a Drop of Dew" is an exception. Marvell says what he means in a clever way but not ironically. That leaves (C), which sums things up fairly well: intricate, delicate, and worshipful.

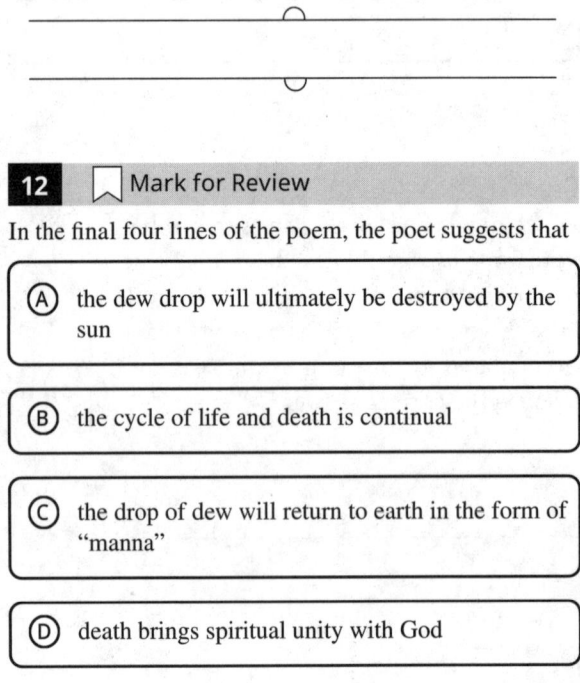

12   ⎗ Mark for Review

In the final four lines of the poem, the poet suggests that

(A) the dew drop will ultimately be destroyed by the sun

(B) the cycle of life and death is continual

(C) the drop of dew will return to earth in the form of "manna"

(D) death brings spiritual unity with God

Here's How to Crack It

If you answered question 10 correctly, this one shouldn't be much tougher. If you understand that the sun symbolizes God, then you should also understand that the dew's dissolving into the sun is a metaphor for the soul's ascent to heaven. The incorrect answer choices all add extraneous points or misconstrue the emphasis of this essentially simple idea. Choice (A) suggests that the dew would be destroyed. That misses the point. The dew's evaporation is not a destruction but a reunion with the divine. Choice (B) is extraneous: the cycle of life is not a thematic point of the poem. Choice (C) tries to trap you by confusing the manna with the dew drop. The poem suggests that the dew drop is like manna in that both are distilled from the spiritual realm. The poem does not suggest that the dew will somehow become manna. The correct answer is (D).

---

13 🔖 Mark for Review

Which of the following adjectives is LEAST important to the poem's theme?

(A) "blowing" (line 3)

(B) "clear" (line 20)

(C) "pure" (line 26)

(D) "loose" (line 35)

Here's How to Crack It

The test-writers are fond of asking questions about theme, despite the fact that pinning down the themes of many poems is problematic. When you're asked about the theme, don't try to come up with an exact definition. Just think about the main point, the important stuff. Again, POE is the way to work. Cross out LEAST and work with the remaining question, eliminating choices that are important to the theme. An important aspect of the poem is the metaphor of the dew drop and the soul. A good way to start would be to eliminate those choices that describe any aspect of that relationship. In this way you could eliminate (B) and (C), because all are qualities of the dew drop that relate to qualities of the soul. A moment of study should tell you that (D) is also important. The dew drop is "loose," or ready to ascend; it grips this world only lightly. That is a thematic point. And (A)? Well, *blowing* means blooming. Is it important that the rose is in bloom? Does Marvell return to the fact of the rose being in bloom later in the poem? Does blooming somehow relate to the soul? No. Choice (A) is least thematically important, and thus (A) is the correct answer.

A Few More Examples

Try these for strenuous, but excellent, practice. A couple of these are harder than real AP questions, but not by much. The following is an excerpt from Percy Bysshe Shelley's "Alastor; or, The Spirit of Solitude."

Nature's most secret steps
He like her shadow has pursued, wher'er
The red volcano overcanopies
Its fields of snow and pinnacles of ice
Line
5   With burning smoke, or where bitumen lakes
On black bare pointed islets ever beat
With sluggish surge, or where the secret caves
Rugged and dark, winding among the springs

Of fire and poison, inaccessible
10 To avarice or pride, their starry domes
Of diamond and of gold expand above
Numberless and immeasurable halls,

Frequent with crystal column, and clear shrines
Of pearl, and thrones radiant with chrysolite.

First, try a grammar question.

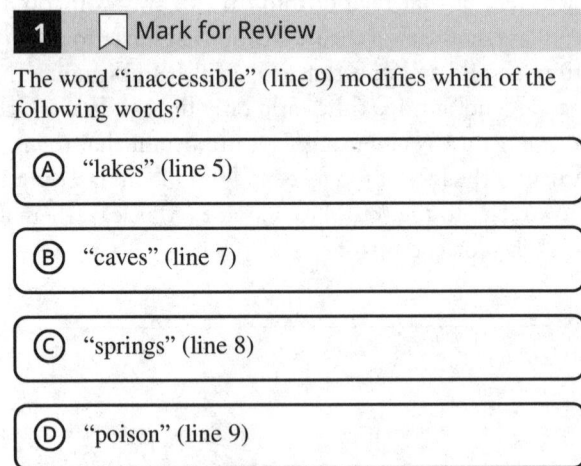

1   ☐ Mark for Review

The word "inaccessible" (line 9) modifies which of the following words?

(A) "lakes" (line 5)

(B) "caves" (line 7)

(C) "springs" (line 8)

(D) "poison" (line 9)

Here's How to Crack It

You should recognize that *inaccessible* is an adjective (the ending *-ible* gives it away). That observation means that you need to decide which noun or pronoun it modifies. Unfortunately, all of the choices are nouns. If you look carefully, you will see that *or* (in line 7) introduces an independent clause. Because of the use of commas, the participial phrase *winding among the springs* modifies *caves*. *Of fire and poison* is a prepositional phrase modifying *springs*. The correct answer, then, is (B), *caves*. Tough, isn't it?

Now, try thinking about the structure of the poem.

---

2 ☐ Mark for Review

In relation to the first two lines, the remainder of the poem serves primarily to

(A) describe the relationship between "He" and "her shadow" (line 2)

(B) list all the possible places to which "wher'er" (line 2) might refer

(C) intricately describe examples of "secret steps" (line 1)

(D) give a reason for "her shadow" (line 2) to pursue particular places in nature

---

Here's How to Crack It

Question 2 is a structure question: it asks how the bulk of the poem relates to the first two lines. This poem consists mostly of description: from line 3 (*The red volcano . . .*) to the end, it describes places in nature with detailed and flowery language. In contrast, the first two lines are somewhat cryptic: put it in everyday language and it says something like "He pursues nature's most secret places (just like her shadow does)." You don't need to know who *he* is (or whose shadow is being mentioned) to understand that the descriptions of nature are the places *he pursues* (travels to).

Since the relationship between the two "characters" mentioned is not spelled out in the poem—in fact, we don't even know who they are—you can eliminate (A). Eliminate (D) because the reason that they travel to these places is not given. You're left with (B) and (C): does the poem *list all the possible places* or *intricately describe examples*? You should be able to see that *all* the possible locations in nature wouldn't fit in this small poem, so eliminate (B). Instead, there are three *examples*: the *volcano*, the *bitumen lakes*, and the *secret caves*. Each one is described in detail, so (C) is correct.

Try this poem by Emily Dickinson.

> There's a certain Slant of light,
> Winter Afternoons—
> That oppresses, like the Heft
> Of Cathedral Tunes—
>
> *Line*
> 5 Heavenly Hurt, it gives us—
> We can find no scar,
> But internal difference,
> Where the meanings, are—
>
> None may teach it—Any—
> 10 'Tis the Seal Despair—
> An imperial affliction
> Sent us of the Air—
>
> When it comes, the Landscape listens—
> Shadows—hold their breath—
> 15 When it goes, 'tis like the Distance
> On the look of Death—

3 🔖 Mark for Review

In line 5, "it" refers to

- (A) "Cathedral Tunes" (line 4)

- (B) "Heavenly Hurt" (line 5)

- (C) "Slant of light" (line 1)

- (D) "look of Death" (line 16)

Asking what a pronoun refers to is a favorite of the AP Exam writers. Do you see that this isn't so much a question of grammatical analysis as it is of comprehension? The correct answer is (C). The *slant of light* is the antecedent.

───────────── ○ ─────────────

Prose Fiction Analysis Passage Drill 1

Suggested time: 12 minutes
Questions 1 through 11 refer to the following. Read the following poem carefully before you choose your answers.

The poem is "On the Death of J.C. an Infant," written by Phillis Wheatley and published in 1773.

NO more the flow'ry scenes of pleasure rise,
Nor charming prospects greet the mental eyes,
No more with joy we view that lovely face
Smiling, disportive, flush'd with ev'ry grace.

Line
5   The tear of sorrow flows from ev'ry eye,
Groans answer groans, and signs to sighs reply;
When sudden pangs shot thro' each aching heart,
When, Death, thy messenger dispatch'd his dart?
Thy dread attendants, all-destroying Pow'r,
10   Hurried the infant to his mortal hour.
Could'st thou unpitying close those radiant eyes?
Or fail'd his artless beauties to surprize?
Could not his innocence thy stroke controul,
Thy purpose shake, and soften all thy soul?

15   The blooming babe, with shades of Death o'er-spread,
No more shall smile, no more shall raise its head,
But, like a branch that from the tree is torn,
Falls prostrate, wither'd, languid, and forlorn.
"Where flies my James?" 'tis thus I seem to hear
20   The parent ask, "Some angel tell me where
"He wings his passage thro' the yielding air?"
Methinks a cherub bending from the skies
Observes the question, and serene replies,
In heav'ns high palaces your babe appears:
25   Prepare to meet him, and dismiss your tears."
Shall not th' intelligence your grief restrain,
And turn the mournful to the chearful strain?
Cease your complaints, suspend each rising sigh,
Cease to accuse the Ruler of the sky.
30   Parents, no more indulge the falling tear:
Let Faith to heav'n's refulgent domes repair,
There see your infant, like a seraph glow:
What charms celestial in his numbers flow
Melodious, while the foul-enchanting strain
35   Dwells on his tongue, and fills th' ethereal plain?

Enough—for ever cease your murm'ring breath;
Not as a foe, but friend converse with Death,
Since to the port of happiness unknown
He brought that treasure which you call your own.
40   The gift of heav'n intrusted to your hand
Cheerful resign at the divine command:
Not at your bar must sov'reign Wisdom stand.

1   Mark for Review

Taken as a whole, the poem is best understood to be

(A) an epitaph

(B) an elegy

(C) a parable

(D) a dirge

2   Mark for Review

The poet's use of syncope throughout the poem serves

(A) to save copying time, since this poet wrote in longhand

(B) to form alliteration with the surrounding words

(C) to make the line fit the poem's meter

(D) to make it evident that a new subject is being addressed

3   Mark for Review

Line 29 contains an example of

(A) an apostrophe

(B) an allusion

(C) free verse

(D) a metaphor

4 ☐ Mark for Review

The poet makes use of all of the following literary devices in lines 1–4 EXCEPT

(A) metaphor

(B) consonance

(C) iambic pentameter

(D) enjambment

5 ☐ Mark for Review

Grammatically, the word "wings" (line 21) is a

(A) noun

(B) direct object

(C) adjective

(D) verb

6 ☐ Mark for Review

The tone in lines 1–21 is best characterized as

(A) disdainful

(B) nostalgic

(C) reverential

(D) woeful

7 ☐ Mark for Review

Lines 30–31 can best be paraphrased as

(A) "Dismiss your tears and return your faith to heaven"

(B) "Your tears are important: know that heaven will heal you"

(C) "The angels of heaven will mend the tears in your heart"

(D) "Your faith, not your tears, will replace the repugnant structures of heaven"

8 ☐ Mark for Review

Each clause in lines 28–29 is best described as a

(A) question

(B) command

(C) concession

(D) declaration

9 ☐ Mark for Review

The primary purpose of lines 22–25 is to

(A) engage the listeners by offering a peaceful anecdote

(B) remind the parents they will see their infant in heaven

(C) recount the infant's words to those left on earth

(D) console the grieving parents

10 ☐ Mark for Review

In lines 13–14, "thy" refers to

(A) each aching heart

(B) the poet

(C) Death

(D) the attendants

11 ☐ Mark for Review

Which course of action would the speaker most wish the audience to take?

(A) Be resigned to the harsh realities of life

(B) Stop indulging in misery

(C) Accept that the loss of a child is inevitable

(D) Entrust the infant to a higher power

POETRY ANALYSIS PASSAGE DRILL 1: ANSWERS AND EXPLANATIONS

Sold into slavery at age seven, Phillis Wheatley was educated by her Boston slave owner and in 1773 became the first published African American poet. Her preferred poetic form was the couplet, and elegies comprised more than one-third of her published works.

1. **B**   This is a definition question. An elegy is a poem that mourns the death of someone, which makes the correct answer (B). None of the remaining answers would work. An epitaph is the inscription on a tombstone, so eliminate (A). A parable is a story that instructs, so (C) is also incorrect. A dirge is a song lamenting the dead, so (D) can be eliminated.

2. **C**   This question is tricky if you don't know the definition of syncope. *Syncope* involves the shortening of a word by removing internal letters and inserting an apostrophe. Poets often employ this technique, and Wheatley uses it frequently in this poem. By modifying the sound of certain words, the poet ensures that the line's metrical rhythm is kept intact. The correct answer is (C).

3. **B**   This is another definition question. The use of the word *Ruler* makes this line an example of an allusion, specifically a biblical allusion as "Ruler" refers to God. Wheatley often wrote about her Christian faith in her poems, so it would not be surprising to find such allusions in her poems. The correct answer is (B).

4. **A**   One example of consonance, (B), in lines 1–4, is the repetition of the s sound (scenes, rise, prospects, smiling, grace). The poem is written in iambic pentameter, (C). The end of line 3 contains an example of enjambment, (D). The device not appearing in these four lines is metaphor. The correct answer is (A).

5. **D**   Make sure to read the entire sentence, not just line 21. Start with line 20 at the beginning of the quotation: "Some angel tell me where He wings his passage thro' the yielding air?" The word *wings* is not being used as a noun, as it is normally used. Eliminate (A) and (B). The parent is asking where the infant wings (or flies) through the air (i.e., where did he go?). Thus, the word *wings* is being used as a verb. The correct answer is (D).

6. **D**   Remember that this poem is an elegy. Elegies are written about someone who has died, so the tone is likely sorrowful. Lines 1–12, for example, confirm this. The poet expresses great sadness through the use of phrases like *no more joy, tear of sorrow, Death,* and *Hurried the infant to his mortal hour.* The tone is indeed sorrowful, which makes the best answer (D).

7. **A**   The meaning of the word *repair* in this context is to return to or to go to a place, not to fix something. Knowing that, eliminate (B) and (C). If you know what *repugnant* means (repulsive), then eliminate (D), since there is nothing in these lines that suggests the "heav'n's refulgent domes" are repulsive or offensive. (By the way, *refulgent* means "shining brightly.") This leaves the correct answer, which is (A).

8. **B**   The three clauses begin with cease, suspend, and cease, which are all verbs in the imperative mood. The imperative mood is used when a speaker makes a command. In this poem, the speaker is requesting that the parents stop complaining about, sighing/crying for, and implicating God in the loss of their infant. There are no questions asked in these lines, so eliminate (A). The speaker doesn't ask them to give up something—the parents have already lost something—in order to reach an agreement, so (C) is also incorrect. A declaration would fall under the indicative mood, and declaratives usually express statements and contain a subject, which is not the case in these lines; (D) is incorrect. The speaker is clearly telling the parents to do something, so the best answer is (B).

9. **D**   With purpose questions, ask yourself why are these lines here, not what did the writer say. If you do the latter, you will likely pick (B), which is not the purpose of these lines. The speaker is offering the mourning parents solace and, to do so, offers them a peaceful thought: a cherub telling the parents their child is safe in heaven. Therefore, the speaker's purpose is to comfort them. The correct answer is (D). These lines are not an example of anecdote, (A), and the words are that of the cherub, not the infant, (C).

10. **C**   The word *thy* is a possessive pronoun. When dealing with pronouns, you want to locate the antecedent. Whose stroke controlled? Whose purpose should be shaken? Whose soul should be softened? You will need to go back to line 8 to find the antecedent, which is Death. It is Death who hurried the infant to his mortal hour and with whom the speaker is pleading. The correct answer is (C).

11. **D**   The speaker, in an effort to comfort the grieving parents, is reminding them that the child is in heaven and urging them to put their faith in God. Choices (A), (B), and (C) are all too negative and do not align with the message of the speaker. While the speaker does acknowledge the sacrifice, the takeaway message is more than their sacrifice—it is to hold fast to their faith in God.

Prose Fiction Analysis Passage Drill 2

Suggested time: 12 minutes

Questions 1 through 9 refer to the following. Read the following poem carefully before you choose your answers.

This poem is "Skyscraper," by Carl Sandburg, published in 1916.

By day the skyscraper looms in the smoke and sun and
has a soul.
Prairie and valley, streets of the city, pour people into
Line it and they mingle among its twenty floors and are
5   poured out again back to the streets, prairies and
valleys.
It is the men and women, boys and girls so poured in and
out all day that give the building a soul of dreams and
thoughts and memories.
10   (Dumped in the sea or fixed in a desert, who would care
for the building or speak its name or ask a policeman
the way to it?)

Elevators slide on their cables and tubes catch letters
and parcels and iron pipes carry gas and water in and
15   sewage out.
Wires climb with secrets, carry light and carry words,
and tell terrors and profits and loves—curses of men
grappling plans of business and questions of women in
plots of love.

20   Hour by hour the caissons reach down to the rock of the
earth and hold the building to a turning planet.
Hour by hour the girders play as ribs and reach out and
hold together the stone walls and floors.
Hour by hour the hand of the mason and the stuff of the
25   mortar clinch the pieces and parts to the shape an
architect voted.
Hour by hour the sun and the rain, the air and the rust, and
the press of time running into centuries, play on the
building inside and out and use it.

30   Men who sunk the pilings and mixed the mortar are laid
in graves where the wind whistles a wild song without
words
And so are men who strung the wires and fixed the pipes
and tubes and those who saw it rise floor by floor.
35   Souls of them all are here, even the hod carrier begging at
back doors hundreds of miles away and the bricklayer
who went to state's prison for shooting another man
while drunk.
(One man fell from a girder and broke his neck at the end
40   of a straight plunge—he is here—his soul has gone
into the stones of the building.)

On the office doors from tier to tier—hundreds of names
and each name standing for a face written across with a
dead child, a passionate lover, a driving ambition for a
45   million dollar business or a lobster's ease of life.
Behind the signs on the doors they work and the walls tell
nothing from room to room.
Ten-dollar-a-week stenographers take letters from corporation officers, lawyers, efficiency engineers, and tons of
50   letters go bundled from the building to all ends of the
earth.
Smiles and tears of each office girl go into the soul of the
building just the same as the master-men who rule the
building.

55   Hands of clocks turn to noon hours and each floor empties
its men and women who go away and eat and come
back to work.
Toward the end of the afternoon all work slackens and all
jobs go slower as the people feel day closing on them.
60   One by one the floors are emptied . . .The uniformed
elevator men are gone. Pails clang . . . Scrubbers work,
talking in foreign tongues. Broom and water and mop
clean from the floors human dust and spit, and machine
grime of the day.
65   Spelled in electric fire on the roof are words telling miles
of houses and people where to buy a thing for money.
The sign speaks till midnight.
Darkness on the hallways. Voices echo. Silence holds . . .
Watchmen walk slow from floor to floor and try the
70   doors. Revolvers bulge from their hip pockets . . . Steel
safes stand in corners. Money is stacked in them.
A young watchman leans at a window and sees the lights
of barges butting their way across a harbor, nets of
red and white lanterns in a railroad yard, and a span
75   of glooms splashed with lines of white and blurs of
crosses and clusters over the sleeping city.
By night the skyscraper looms in the smoke and the stars
and has a soul.

1 ☐ Mark for Review

What is implied by lines 10–12 ("Dumped . . . to it")?

(A) The building depends on people.

(B) It would be just as easy to tear down the skyscraper and dump its bricks and mortar and steel girders as it is to let it stand.

(C) The skyscraper is important only because of the city in which it is located.

(D) The speaker doesn't think the building has any value.

2 ☐ Mark for Review

It can be inferred that the speaker

(A) would prefer it if the skyscraper were gone

(B) works in the skyscraper or in a building much like it

(C) venerates the skyscraper

(D) is critical of the contemporary social order

3 ☐ Mark for Review

The image in line 28, "the press of time running into centuries," suggests

(A) the speaker's attitude of awe for the building

(B) one of the poem's themes

(C) the central metaphor of the poem

(D) an allusion to the city itself

4 ☐ Mark for Review

According to the poem, which of the following is NOT true of the skyscraper?

(A) It has outlasted its original creators.

(B) It carries advertising messages to surrounding residents.

(C) It is permanent but not eternal.

(D) It is empty at night.

5 ☐ Mark for Review

How do the first and last lines contribute to the structure of the poem?

(A) They reinforce the fact that the skyscraper has a soul.

(B) They give the poem a formal, "bookended" quality, stating and then restating an image.

(C) They reinforce the theme of time passing while the skyscraper endures.

(D) They present the skyscraper's connection to major objects in the universe.

6 ☐ Mark for Review

What can you infer from the poet's diction?

(A) The poet's intended audience was ordinary people, like the blue-collar construction workers, the watchmen and the "Ten-dollar-a-week stenographers" (line 48) in the poem.

(B) The poet was writing primarily for men.

(C) The poet was accustomed to writing novels and short stories, not poetry.

(D) The poet wanted his writing to appeal to "the master-men who rule the building" (lines 53–54) and the "corporation officers, lawyers, efficiency engineers" (lines 48–49).

7 ⬛ Mark for Review

In line 22, the statement that "the girders play as ribs" is an example of which literary device?

Ⓐ An allusion

Ⓑ A double entendre

Ⓒ A simile

Ⓓ Pathos

8 ⬛ Mark for Review

The watchmen, the office girls, the night cleaners, and the construction workers have all of the following characteristics in common EXCEPT

Ⓐ They are enablers.

Ⓑ They won't end up in an office with their name on the door.

Ⓒ They give the building its soul.

Ⓓ They are proud of their association with the building.

9 ⬛ Mark for Review

Which of the following best summarizes the significance to the poem of lines 16–19 ("Wires . . . love")?

Ⓐ Just as the skyscraper gives people a place to work, so the telephone lines give them a way to make plans to achieve what they want.

Ⓑ It reinforces the poet's assertion that it is the people using the skyscraper who give it life and soul.

Ⓒ The telephone wires in the skyscraper may be inanimate, but they carry dramatic conversations and plans for action.

Ⓓ Although the stenographers are faceless and the executives are behind identical doors on identical floors, these people are not bland and ordinary. Their lives are filled with secrets and intrigue and ambition.

POETRY ANALYSIS PASSAGE DRILL 2: ANSWERS AND EXPLANATIONS

About "Skyscraper"

Skyscrapers—a solution to the shrinking amount of land in big city downtown areas—were still a relatively new phenomenon when American poet Carl Sandburg wrote this in 1916. They were called "skyscrapers" because, in comparison to the surrounding buildings, they appeared tall enough to scrape the sky.

1. **A**   Remember, when a question stem sends you to a specific line in a poem, always read at least a line before and a line after in order to understand the context. If you looked only at lines 10–12, you might think the correct answer is (C). In this case, you only need to read one line before—"It is the men and women, boys and girls so poured in and out all day that give the building a soul of dreams and thoughts and memories"—to see that the correct answer is (A). The skyscraper has value, permanence, and a sense of life by virtue of the people who work in it, maintain it, and consider it important, not because of the city in which it stands. Choices (B) and (D) aren't implied: the speaker doesn't suggest that dumping the skyscraper in the sea would be easy, and doesn't give his own opinion of the building's value.

2. **D**   This question calls for two things: an understanding of the poem as a whole, and an ability to distinguish the poet from the narrator. The first requirement eliminates (B)—there is much more to the descriptions in the poem than an obvious familiarity with the day-to-day routine of working in a downtown office building. The poet's tone is too neutral to suggest either hostility, (A), or veneration, (C), for the building, so eliminate those two choices. That leaves (D). He juxtaposes the "Ten-dollar-a-week stenographers" (line 48) and "the master-men who rule the building" (lines 53–54). He states that, at night, "Scrubbers work, talking in foreign tongues" (lines 61–62) and refers to the blue-collar workers who erected the building so white-collar "corporation officers, lawyers, efficiency engineers" (lines 48–49) could work there. The poet is suggesting a criticism of the class system and gender inequality of his time. Although the narrator's tone is relatively neutral when he refers to these groups, it is the author who chose to include them in the poem.

3. **B**   POE works well on this question. The quoted phrase is neither a metaphor nor an allusion, so (C) and (D) can be eliminated. When you read the line before and after, there is no mention of the speaker's opinion, which eliminates (A). That leaves (B) and indeed, when you consider the poem as a whole, one of the themes running through it is time. For example, the builders ended their short lives long ago, but the skyscraper they constructed still stands. "Hands of clocks turn" (line 55); day turns into night turns into day. The skyscraper "has a soul" (lines 1–2), which is eternal.

4. **D** In this EXCEPT/LEAST/NOT format question, first eliminate the "NOT," leaving the standard format question, "which of the following is true of the skyscraper?" Then eliminate the four choices that would be correct answers to that question. Choice (A) (lines 30–32) and (B) (lines 65–65) are both true of the building. So is (C)—the skyscraper may be anchored to the planet (lines 20–21), but time and weather are wearing it down (lines 27–29). It is "permanent" compared to the long-gone men who built it but not "eternal" as the sun and stars are. That leaves (D) as the correct answer. Scrubbers (line 61) and watchmen (line 69) work in the building at night, so it is not empty. This is the only statement that is NOT true of the building.

5. **B** The key words in the question stem are "contribute to the *structure*." This is an example of how reading the question stem carefully, word for word, pays off. All of the answer choices are true of the first and last lines but only one concerns the poem's structure. That's (B). The first line presents the skyscraper and its soul, looming "in the smoke and sun." The poem then goes on to develop the building's relationship to people, past and present, and its own life-like qualities. Then the last line returns to recap the first line; the building and its soul now loom "in the smoke and the stars."

6. **A** This question asks you to assess the poet's vocabulary and choice of words throughout the entire poem and then make an inference from your assessment. What do you see in the language he chooses? Is it dominated by sophisticated words that only well-educated people would understand? No, so you can eliminate (D). Is it filled with lyrical references to dewdrops and cherubs? Is it over-flowing with symbols and imagery and obscure references to ancient Greek gods? No, Sandburg uses concrete, down-to-earth, everyday language. Even words that seem unusual now ("caissons," or foundations, and "hod carrier," or a low-level laborer who brought supplies to tradesmen) were common in 1916. That accessible vocabulary points to ordinary, everyday people as his intended audience (A). The poet doesn't describe many women (only the office girls in line 52 and possibly the stenographers in line 48 and the scrubbers in line 61). However, that's not surprising; in 1916 men held most of the jobs. Nothing in the choice of language seems particularly aimed at either men or women, eliminating (B). The unrhymed free verse in this poem might make (C) seem like an attractive choice. However, the question asks about diction, not about poetic form, so (C) is incorrect.

7. **C** A simile compares two unlike things (here, inanimate steel girders and living ribs of bone), using "as" or "like." This particular simile reinforces the concept of the skyscraper having life. None of the other choices would apply to the quote in the question stem. An allusion, (A), is a brief reference to a significant person, place, or thing (such as a character in a Shakespearean play, or a place in a Greek myth). It depends on readers being familiar with the reference. A double entendre, (B), refers to a word or statement which can be interpreted in different ways. It is often used for humor or irony. Pathos, (D), is designed to trigger feelings of pity or sympathy in the reader.

8. **D** This is a tricky question that requires careful reading of the question stem. It says these four groups "have" characteristics in common—not "likely have" or "probably have." This stem isn't asking for inference or interpretation; it allows for only what the poem directly and specifically says. Since this is an EXCEPT/LEAST/NOT format question, cross out the EXCEPT and find the four answer choices that would be correct for the resulting standard format question. Choice (A) is correct: the construction workers enabled the skyscraper to exist, the office girls enable executives to send out their letters, the night cleaners enable workers to return the next day to an environment free of "human dust and spit, and machine grime" (lines 63–64), and the watchmen with their revolvers enable protection from intruders and from thieves who want the money in the steel safes. Only the members of the privileged class—the "corporation officers, lawyers, efficiency engineers" (lines 48–49)—get an office with their name on the door. In the poet's 1916 class society, no one from the other four groups would have that chance, so (B) is correct. Choice (C) is correct; the building has a soul in virtue of the "[men and women, boys and girls] . . . poured in and out all day" (lines 7–8) and the workers who built it (lines 30–32), while the scrubbers and watchmen who take over at night, after the "floors are emptied" (line 60), give the skyscraper its soul in the stars (lines 77–78). That leaves (D) as the correct EXCEPT answer. The narrator is neutral about the relationships between each of the four groups and the building. They may be proud of their association with it; they may not. From what the poem says, we don't know, and the question stem doesn't allow inferences.

9. **B** Again, careful reading of the question stem is essential. You're asked about the *significance* of lines 16–19 to the poem, not about what the words mean (C) or what the poet might be implying (D). Those two choices are both incorrect. Choice (A) is too narrow; it misses the connection between the life of people and the soul of the skyscraper that runs throughout the poem. Only (B) makes that connection.

Chapter 8 Summary

o   Don't worry about scansion (you know: iambic pentameter, dactyls, spondees, and the like). You probably won't see even one question on it.

o   Remember:
   •   Read the poem as prose.
   •   Focus on the main idea.
   •   When answering the questions, use POE and Consistency of Answers.

o   Be sure to read before and after highlighted sections.

o   Metaphysical poetry is excellent practice for the kind of poetry you'll see on the AP Exam. John Donne, Andrew Marvell, George Herbert, Thomas Carew, Abraham Cowley, and Richard Crashaw are all poets whose work provides excellent AP practice. Also, the poetry of Emily Dickinson and Robert Frost is rich in intricate grammatical structures.

o   On EXCEPT, NOT, and LEAST questions, cross out the negative word and eliminate any choice that fits the remaining question.

Chapter 9
The Idea Machine: Starting Your Essays with a High Score

> "
> Reading is my inhale, and writing is my exhale.
>
> —Glennon Doyle
> "

FROM IDEA TO EXECUTION

We're going to take you through our AP English writing process, one we've designed specifically for AP essays. The most stressful part of writing essays under time pressure is coming up with something to say quickly. In this chapter, we'll show you how to get the ideas that give you something to write about in the first place. We aren't going to teach you how to write; you've already spent years learning to write. However, AP essays are unlike anything you've had to write before, and you probably haven't spent years learning how to write them.

Approximately 90 percent of this chapter is about how to get an overall idea of your essay and create a great first paragraph. If you can get off to a good start, you're more than halfway to a great score.

THE APPROACH

Just as with the multiple-choice section, you want to have a common-sense, step-by-step approach to the essay section (and know how to use it). Here it is:

- Take a watch and note the time. Remember: 40 minutes per essay.
- Pick the essay (prose fiction analysis, poetry analysis, literary argument) you want to write first.
- Identify the key words in the essay prompt.
- Skim the passage.
- Work the passage, make notes, and identify quotations you will want to use.
- Use the Idea Machine (explained in this chapter) to plan your first paragraph.
- In your body paragraphs, support and develop the points you made in your first paragraph.
- Get a solid conclusion on the page. Your conclusion can be as important as your introduction, and it usually is.
- Repeat the process with the other essays.

Don't Write a Formal Outline

You don't have time to write an outline. Outlines are for organizing longer, more complex pieces of writing, like research papers, when you have the time to revise and plan. We know you've probably had outlining drummed into you by your teachers. But short essays, like the ones you'll write for the AP Exam, don't call for an outline. You don't even have time to rewrite. Our method shows you how to come up with a solid beginning from which you can build so that you can just write the rest of the essay without an outline.

The Idea Machine

We've developed a method of approaching AP essays that we call the "Idea Machine." Hey, don't get us wrong, the *real* idea machine is in your skull. The point here is to focus your brain, imagination, and analytical skills in a way that's productive for the AP Exam. This approach won't let you down. Use it, and your essays will shine.

The Idea Machine is a series of questions that direct your reading to the material needed to write an essay. Take these questions, apply their answers to the essay question, and in the end you'll find you've written the kind of essay the Readers want to see.

The Idea Machine

1. What is the meaning of the work?
   a. What is the literal, face-value meaning of the work?
   b. What feeling (or feelings) does the work evoke?
2. How does the author get that meaning across?
   a. What are the important images in the work and what do those images suggest?
   b. What specific words or short phrases produce the strongest feelings?
   c. What do the characters, setting, structure, or narrators tell you about the passage?

That may not look like much but, when we put all the pieces together in this chapter and the next, you'll see just how powerful of a tool we're giving you.

The Classic Essay Question

Whether you are working on a prose fiction analysis or poetry analysis passage, there is a classic essay question that you will be asked to address. Here it is in its most basic form:

> Read the following work carefully. Then, in a well-written essay, analyze the manner in which the author conveys ideas and meaning. Discuss the techniques the author uses to make this passage effective.

In your response you should do the following:

- Respond to the prompt with a thesis that presents a defensible interpretation.
- Select and use evidence to support your line of reasoning.
- Explain how the evidence supports your line of reasoning.
- Use appropriate grammar and punctuation in communicating your argument.

The classic essay question actually breaks down into three questions. The first two should look familiar because they're part of the Idea Machine.

1. What does the poem or passage mean?
2. How did the author get you to see that? Were elements like character, setting, structure, narration, and figurative language deployed? Which ones?
3. How do the answers to questions 1 and 2 direct your knowledge to adequately answer the question?

The first question is hidden but totally important. It's the foundation on which you build the rest of your essay. Your (high-scoring) essay should answer those three questions in that order. Question 2 is the one you'll be asked on the exam; the test-writers feel that question 1 is implied.

If the first question is "What does the passage or poem mean?" Well . . . what does that mean? What is *meaning*?

The Meaning of *Meaning*

For the AP essays, the meaning of a work of prose fiction or poetry is the most basic, flat, literal sense of what is said plus the emotions and passions behind that sense.

The passages and poems they ask you to write about on the AP English Literature and Composition Exam will present some event or situation in the same way a newspaper article presents an event or a situation. But AP essay passages will, of course, do more than that. They will make the event or situation "come alive" by bringing in human emotions and passions in such a way that those emotions and passions are as important as the facts.

Let's consider an example:

Think of how much will be lost by the Twitter version. Can the tweets really let us know Hamlet's suffering, his frantic (and occasionally crazed) attempts to figure out what is going on with his father and his uncle? Of course not, but those emotions are part of what the story means. They are the most important part of your essay.

Avoid Summary

You must absolutely avoid writing only a newspaper or social media version. Doing that amounts to a summary, something the AP Readers do not want. Discuss the way emotions are involved in the story and focus on the feelings the language produces, and you'll be discussing meaning in the right way. Always identify point of view, tone, and figurative language usage. Discussing these literary elements will ensure that you are moving beyond a summary.

Just Say No . . .

. . .to summaries! AP Readers want to see you analyze a literary work, not rehash what you read.

The Modified Classic Essay Question

Your AP Exam may well have the classic question on it almost word for word, but probably not. What you will likely see is a modified classic essay question. There are an endless number of modifications for the test-writers to throw at you. For example, the question might ask you to analyze "the narrator's attitude toward the nature of war," "the speaker's attitude toward society," or "the author's use of repetition."

Identify the Key Words in the Prompt

Of course, the specifics mentioned in the essay prompt are what you should pay close attention to when you read. Just as in the multiple-choice section, where looking at the questions can help you read the passages more actively, identifying precisely what the Readers want you to write about can help you focus on those aspects of the poem or prose fiction.

However, even if you're responding to a modified essay prompt, you should begin just as if you're answering the classic one. You want to talk about what meaning you found in the poem or passage, and then use that as a foundation to discuss the topic about which the question specifically asks.

Let's look at an example. (You don't need the actual passage to understand our discussion of the question here.)

> Read the passage carefully. Then, in a well-written essay, analyze how the author uses the interrelationship of humor, pity, and horror in the passage.

This seems like a simple enough question—until you try to answer it. How do you go about analyzing the interrelationship of humor, pity, and horror? Most students start out something like this:

> The story X by writer Z mixes humor pity and horror in an interesting way. It begins with a father meeting his son. The father seems like a funny guy because of things he does, but then we see that he is actually a person who arouses our pity because he goes too far, so far in fact, that the father becomes almost horrible.

The student who writes this response knows he's basically flailing. He's just trying to answer the question without looking foolish. If the student uses reasonable examples, writes with some organization and only a few grammatical errors, then the student will get a 3, a "limbo" score—not passing but not failing.

On the other hand, the student who understands that this question is a modified form of the classic question and knows how to use the Idea Machine will break it down.

What does the passage mean? What was I supposed to get from it? What did I get from it? Okay, I got that the passage was about a father and son and that the son feels his father is basically embarrassing. Yeah, that sounds about right. Now, let's see, how does the author get that across using humor, pity, and horror?

Notice how this student has taken the question, turned it into the classic question, and simply used the modification to focus on the point to be developed. The student began by describing the meaning of the story. ("The son feels his father is basically embarrassing" is the meaning. Remember that the meaning doesn't have to be complicated.) Then this student wondered, *How does the author get that across using humor, pity, and horror?* This student's opening is going to look something like this:

> In story X, writer Z shows us a son confronted by the embarrassing spectacle of his father. By shifting the son's perspective of his father from humor and pity, to horror, we see and feel the son's fluctuating, uncertain responses to his father's vulgarity and ignorance.

This student is writing about something, and it shows. She's on the way to a score of at least 4, and if the essay stays this clear and focused, it's going to earn a score of 6. Do you see how slight an alteration has been made between this response and the one that came before it? Yet there's a world of difference. The first student rephrased the question without really saying anything, and then began to work his way through the points, ticking them off . . . first humor, then pity, then horror. The second student began by answering the implied question in every essay: *What does this story mean?* Then she began to show how the author brought that meaning across.

The best part is that the second essay is easier to write than the first one. It's easier to write an essay about something than nothing. Writing a bogus essay is like trying to wind up a ball of string with nothing to wrap it around. The second essay is going to wrap itself neatly around the core of the story's meaning—the son's uncertain embarrassment at his father's behavior.

No Fear!

Sometimes the questions can be fairly intimidating, but don't let them throw you. Remember to use the Idea Machine. What does the passage mean? How does that meaning come across?

Once you've got that under your belt, you can think about how to focus on the points in a question about a poem. Let's look at an example:

> Read the poem carefully. Notice that the poem is divided into two stanzas and that the second stanza reapplies much of the first stanza's imagery. In a well-written essay, analyze how the author's use of language, including his use of repetition, reflects the content and tone of the poem.

You should look at the question and remember that it's just a modified version of the classic essay question. Ask yourself "What is the meaning?" and "How do I know it?" Then you can think about how the author uses imagery and figurative language to convey that meaning. In fact, this question almost organizes itself once you break it down. Your first paragraph should talk about what you get from the whole poem, and your subsequent paragraphs should discuss the language and meaning of each stanza. Your conclusion should look at the poem as an entire piece and reiterate your emphasis about why and how repetition is important in understanding the overall tone and theme of the poem.

A Great Start

The key to a great essay is a great start and the key to a great start is having an overall idea of what you're doing. We've shown you how to address the meaning (literal and emotional) of the poem right from the beginning, and that you must then address the "how" of the author's method. Taken together, these things will form your opening and the central idea around which you will write—the idea you will explain and support. If you're already a sharp, sensitive reader, following these instructions will lead you to high-scoring essays.

Sounds easy in principle. But are you ready? Let's go back to that tough, intimidating question we just looked at in the No Fear section, this time along with the poem that goes with it. We'll use our approach to come up with a good first paragraph for a high-scoring essay. Then we'll show you two powerful tools you can use to open up a passage and get the kinds of ideas that blow AP Readers away.

Dylan Thomas's "In My Craft or Sullen Art"

Read the poem carefully. Notice that the poem is divided into two stanzas and that the second stanza reapplies much of the first stanza's imagery. In a well-written essay, analyze how the author's use of language, including his use of repetition, reflects the content and tone of the poem.

In My Craft or Sullen Art

In my craft or sullen art
Exercised in the still night
When only the moon rages
Line And lovers lie abed
5   With all their griefs in their arms,
I labor by singing light
Not for ambition or bread
Or the strut and trade of charms
On the ivory stages
10   But for the common wages
Of their most secret heart.

Not for the proud man apart
From the raging moon I write
On these spindrift pages
15   Nor for the towering dead
With their nightingales and psalms
But for the lovers, their arms
Round the griefs of the ages,
Who pay no praise or wages
20   Nor heed my craft or art.

So, where do you begin? Well, before you begin to consider the repetition mentioned in the essay instructions, get the answers to the questions that let you write a classic essay. Use the Idea Machine.

- **What does the poem say, literally?** That shouldn't be too tough to answer, even if you don't know exactly what Dylan Thomas is trying to say. Put it in your own words. What does the poet say about his "craft or sullen art"? Take a moment to think about it and then read on.

You should have come up with something like this: "Dylan Thomas explains that he isn't writing for money or fame but for lovers who don't even care about his writing."

- **Okay, now what is the feel of the poem?** What emotions are conveyed? Is there an overall emotion? Again, think about it a moment before you read on.

It's a tougher question, isn't it? You probably went back to the poem to look at it again, thinking, "Just what emotion was I supposed to get? There's something there, but what?"

You might have picked up on a few aspects of the tone: pride, grief, loneliness, perhaps futility, and also perhaps the opposite of futility—a sense of total purpose. The poem has a truly complex emotional range. Don't let that scare you off; it only gives you more to write about.

- **What is the meaning of the poem for your AP essay?** Take your literal sense and your emotional sense, and combine them:

> Dylan Thomas's "In My Craft or Sullen Art" explores the pride, grief, loneliness, futility, and yet sense of total purpose that come from the author's struggle to write not for fame or for wealth but for "the lovers, their arms round the griefs of ages."

So far so good. But don't think we're finished. This sentence is just the answer to question 1 of the Idea Machine—what does the poem mean? If you're particularly astute, you may even notice that we haven't completely answered that question. We've only said what Thomas "explores." We haven't come out and taken a stand on exactly where Thomas's exploration has led him. Don't worry. You don't have to try to pin everything down all at once. If this essay were an assignment due at the end of the week, you'd want to write a rough draft that you could revise carefully later. Here on the AP Exam, you don't have the opportunity for careful revision. You don't have to write a perfect essay. The Readers don't expect you to, not even for a score of 6. Just stay with our method: what does the work mean, how does the author achieve his effects, and what does the question ask you to address?

The "Perfect" Essay
No one, not even the AP Readers, expects you to write the perfect essay. But what they DO want you to write is an essay that discusses the meaning of a literary work, how the author conveys that meaning, and how all of that ties into the question you are being asked.

Now you have the second part of our three-part approach to consider:

- **How does the author achieve his effects?** Perhaps in answering that question we can take more of a stand. How does Thomas bring his emotions into his sense of what writing means to him and (because the essay instructions demand we consider it) what does the repetition have to do with it?

How indeed? Thomas gets his message across in so compact a fashion that you may feel a little lost and overwhelmed. Remember, you're just trying to write a 40-minute essay on a poem you've never seen before. The Readers don't expect perfection or profound originality. They want to see you focus on saying *something*, and then say it as clearly as you can. In brief, they want to see you confidently develop your ideas as best you can.

Here's how we'd complete our opening statement and answer the question of how Thomas explores his sense of what, to him, it means to write:

> Dylan Thomas's "In My Craft or Sullen Art" explores the pride, grief, loneliness, futility, and yet sense of total purpose that come from the author's struggle to write not for fame or for wealth but for "the lovers, their arms round the griefs of ages." Thomas gives us an image of himself, laboring alone "by singing light" and contrasts this with an image of self-contained completeness, of lovers wrapped in each other's arms, oblivious to all the world and even to his poetry. By repeating these images, and key words like "moon," "rage," and "grief," he emphasizes the power of his emotions and the intensity of his need to define himself and the purpose of his art.

This opening gets our essay off to a great start. Of course, you might have had different ideas, and you undoubtedly would have phrased your ideas another way, even if you saw exactly what we saw in the poem. You might even have written two or three better sentences—although you wouldn't have had to in order to score well. This brings up our next point.

Have Confidence in Your Answer

Many other insights about Dylan Thomas's poem are waiting between the lines. It all depends on what you got from it. If you ask yourself, "How can I describe the subject of this poem in one word?" You will find that your answer, in this case, reflects the title of the poem. It is his writing. Then, ask yourself this question: "What is Dylan Thomas saying about the craft of writing?" The answer is the theme of the poem. If you look at the last few lines of the poem, you will discover the answer in those lines. Usually if you look at the title of the poem, the last few lines of the poem, and combine that with the one word that accurately describes the subject of the poem, you are on your way to accurately describing the theme of the poem. You want to make sure that you are on track with your interpretation because the Readers want to see that you have understood the point of the poem and can explain how this understanding helps you answer the essay question.

Use that literary vocabulary you've been building by studying the glossary. The Readers are paying attention to your craft of writing as you address the question. They want to see how the literary work you've been asked to write about acted on your imagination and how well you've managed to convey the impressions you've received.

Imagery and Words

Speaking of *imagination*, notice what we've done in the "how" part of our opening paragraph about the Dylan Thomas poem. We've discussed imagery and part of figurative language. We chose to mention the contrasting images of the author working alone and of the lovers in their self-enclosed togetherness. You might have chosen something else but the point to remember is this: *It's always a safe bet to talk about imagery.*

In writing (as opposed to cinema or theater or painting), an image is made of words. Is that obvious? Yes, it is. But just because it's obvious doesn't mean all students pay attention to that important fact. On the AP essays, your job is to discuss writing. Remember then that whenever you're discussing the imagery in a passage, you're discussing words. If a word sticks out as unusual or particularly vivid, think about it. Ask yourself, why did the author use *that* word? What effect does that word have? If you can think of something to say about the words an author has used to create an image and the specific effect those words have, by all means put it in your essay. You'll have the AP Readers eating out of your hand. One easy method of discussing imagery is to try to create a short film clip with your words based on what the poet has written.

Notice that in our sample opening, we zeroed in on the two most striking word choices in the poem: *rage* and *grief.* It's odd (and poetic) to say lovers have their arms around their griefs. And when was the last time you saw the moon raging? A lot of students run from unusual language like that. They think that the poet is just being a typical crazy artist who can't really be understood or that they'll misinterpret the phrase anyway and look dumb. But when you see unusual usages like that, consider them. Why that word? What does that word do to the feel of the piece? Thinking this way will jog ideas loose and result in material that makes for great AP essays. Notice also that both *rage* and *grief* have strong emotional content. Writing about the emotional content is the best way to let the Reader know you're really reading and not simply enacting some dry, mechanical exercise.

Opposition

If you've been following our discussion so far, you should see that you need to be able to pull ideas from the text you're working with so that you have ideas for your essay. Considering imagery and word choice is a good start, but there's one more concept we want you to think about as you read, something that should really help you find the ideas that you need to write a great essay.

How can you get to the heart of what you read on the AP English Literature and Composition Exam? How can you find something interesting and important to say about a passage quickly? What do you look for to see what makes a passage or a poem "tick"?

When in Doubt
The most important, most open-ended, most easily discussable aspect of a poem is almost always the imagery.

The answer is *opposition*.

Opposition vs. Conflict

Some people call opposition *conflict*, but we think that's too narrow a term. *Conflict* sounds like two people having a fight. Don't be crude. Be subtle. Opposition is everywhere in good writing, and the passages on the AP Exam will always be good sources. Seek it out as you read because opposition leads you to the important parts of a passage or poem.

Attune your reading to seeing opposition and you'll open up AP passages like cans of sardines. You'll have something around which to center your discussion of the way an author uses language, imagery, and tone to make their point. If you carefully read the question, you will notice that there is usually a comparison or contrast that it directs you to address. Sometimes it is subtle, but sometimes you are directed to focus your answer on a comparison or contrast noted within the passage or two passages.

So, What's Opposition?

Opposition occurs when any pair of elements contrast sharply. Another way to think about opposition is tension—think of the two opposing elements as if they were magnetized poles, attracting and repelling each other. Opposition provides a structure underneath the surface of the poem, which you will unlock by discovering the oppositional elements. Opposition might be as blatant as night and day. Or it might be less obvious: a character who's naïve and a character who's sophisticated. Opposition might be found in a story that begins with a scene in a parlor but ends with a scene around a campfire, which would be the opposition of indoors and outdoors. It would be easy to miss if you weren't looking for it, but it can often be found between the author's style and his subject. For example, a cerebral, intellectual style that's heavy on analysis in a story about a hog farmer would be opposition. Your essay should address why the author wrote that way and what effect it has on the story. Keep an eye out for any elements that are in contrast to each other as they'll often lead you to the heart of the story.

Let's look at that Dylan Thomas poem again. Notice what we went after in our opening paragraph: the image of the author working alone and the image of lovers in each other's arms. That's an opposition. Do you see how it's not exactly a conflict? It's a pairing of images whereby each becomes more striking and informative when placed against the other. Doesn't that pair of images seem central to the poem? Doesn't it seem there's something to talk about there? What it means exactly is open to interpretation, and that's exactly what you should do when you see elements opposed to each other: *interpret*. Don't worry about getting it right; there is no single right answer. The AP Reader will see that your searching intelligence has found the complexity of the material and is making sense of it. That's exactly what the Reader wants you to do. (And it's what very few students attempt to do.)

Opposition creates tension and mystery. What's the most mysterious line in "In My Craft or Sullen Art"? We think it's "And lovers lie abed/With all their griefs in their arms." That line alone has an opposition: if they're lovers, why do they have their griefs in their arms?

So your job is to figure out what Thomas means by that. The answer? Nothing simple, but something you can write about. Realize that you don't have to resolve opposition.

You don't have to interpret that line (or the poem) in a concrete way that makes absolute perfect sense. It's a poem, not a riddle.

Our opening paragraph mentioned a third opposition: Thomas's sense of futility and his sense of total purpose. The sense of futility in the poem comes from the statements that the lovers "pay no praise or wages," nor do they heed Thomas's "craft or art." Describing how Thomas gets across his deep sense of purpose is more difficult even though it is the stronger of the two impressions. In many ways the entire poem is about conveying the sense of purpose Thomas feels when writing poetry.

We found these things because we looked for the oppositions. Some oppositions are obvious. Like a tiger in a bus station, they catch your attention immediately and make you wonder what's going on. Good writers boldly toss together mismatched concepts, objects, and tones all the time. But good writers also work with quiet oppositions that aren't nearly so easy to spot. If you aren't paying attention, you'll feel what's going on without realizing where it's coming from. Many literary oppositions come from within one character. The character who wants two totally opposite things at the same time is a classic case of opposition, as is the character who badly wants something that he just isn't cut out for.

Another important opposition is *tone*. Some writers will write about the silliest thing possible in a deadly serious way. (This is generally done to make a situation funnier.) Still another opposition, one that is often handled with supreme delicacy and with seemingly infinite repercussions, is *time*. Writers will often let the past stand in opposition to the present. The story of a once proud family that has fallen on hard times is an example of a plot that uses the changes time brings to develop oppositions.

We could come up with hundreds of specific examples of oppositions in literature, but those examples won't do you any good if you haven't read the works. Our point here is to give you a tool with which to generate ideas for your AP essays.

You're probably still a little unclear as to how to apply this concept of oppositions to a short AP essay, but don't worry. The samples and examples in Chapter 10 will take you through several AP passages and point out how you might use oppositions to find ideas (while also boosting your essay scores into the 5s and 6s).

After the First Paragraph—Do an Essay Check

Looking back at our overall approach to the Essay section, you'll see that the second to last point is the recommendation to do an essay check. That sounds fancy, but all it means is that you should think briefly about the points you need to make in your essay.

The time to do this thinking is after you've written that first paragraph. The first paragraph comes from using the Idea Machine: discussing the meaning of the passage or poem (remember, the newspaper version plus emotion) and beginning to talk about how the author gets her point across. This method gives you a first paragraph that establishes the foundation on which the rest of your essay will be

Opposition in Your Essay
An AP essay won't get to all of these oppositions; it shouldn't try to. But you can be sure we'll mention that repetition plays a part.

One More Reminder About Our Essay Book
If you need more help on essays in a test setting, our book *How to Write Essays for Standardized Tests* contains advice and examples for best practices on an assortment of AP exams, plus ACT, and others!.

built. If it's hyperfocused, it will already set out the overall points you intend to cover but, even if it just gives you a general platform on which to build, you've got plenty, enough to put you miles ahead of the majority of other (flailing) students. The essay check is just a spot check, a place to pause, make sure you're on the right track, and haven't forgotten anything important. When you finish your first paragraph, stop and ask yourself the following questions:

- What points does my first paragraph indicate I'm going to cover?
- Do those points address the specifics the essay question calls for?
- In what order am I going to put my points?

When you've decided the order of your points, get back to writing. Your check shouldn't take more than a minute. The least important part of the check is deciding the order of your points. It's the closest thing to an outline you need to do, but don't overdo it. As long as you've paused to think about addressing the question, it makes sense to form a rough plan of how you'll proceed. But the idea is to make it easier for you to write, not to suffocate your writing. Be flexible. If it's convenient to change the order of your points as you write, change them. If you think of new things to say, say them!

Developing Your Essay

As you write, you'll notice things that you hadn't seen at first, things that will depart from your original ideas and take you in unexpected directions. Should you include these things? YES!

Remember...
It is impossible to write a tight, well-organized essay in 40 minutes—impossible. Style and flair aren't as important here as substance and the clarity of your ideas.

Many, many students are intimidated by the test. They think their writing has to be truly organized and tight and end up writing short, dry, little essays—essays that receive a score of 3. Go with the flow. As long as your ideas have some connection to the question that was asked, include them. Write a great first paragraph that sets you out in the right direction and then loosen up—you'll score high.

Once you've finished your first paragraph and your essay check, it's time to develop your essay. When it comes to development, each essay is unique. The best way to study development is through examples. The next chapter is devoted to sample essays; we'll show you how to put our method (and your ideas) into practice.

Chapter 9 Summary

o   If you can get off to a good start, you're more than halfway to a great score.

o   Use our approach:
  - Note the time. Remember, 40 minutes per essay.
  - Pick the essay (prose fiction, poetry analysis, literary argument) you want to write first.
  - Identify the key words in the essay prompt.
  - Skim the passage.
  - Work the passage, making notes and identifying quotations you will want to use.
  - Use the Idea Machine to plan your first paragraph.
  - In your body paragraphs, support and develop the points you made in your first paragraph.
  - Get a solid conclusion on the page.
  - Repeat the process with the other essays.

o   Don't write an outline.

o   Identify key words in the prompt.

o   Understand the question and how to turn the question into an *essay idea*.

- o Use the Idea Machine:
  - What is the meaning of the work? *Meaning* is literal meaning plus the emotions the work evokes.
  - How does the author get that meaning across?
    - o important images
    - o specific words or short phrases
    - o opposition

- o The Idea Machine is the tool that will help you apply your skills specifically to a 40-minute essay.

- o Any student who can write an adequate essay can write an AP essay that scores a 4 or higher.

- o Don't worry about being wrong. Have confidence in your interpretation.

- o Unusual language and imagery are great places to find essay ideas.

- o *Opposition* is created when any pair of elements in a story or poem contrasts sharply or subtly.

- o Look for elements that are in opposition. They'll lead you to the heart of the passage and give you material for the kinds of ideas that make AP Readers give out sixes.

- o Go with the flow. It is impossible to write a tight, well-organized essay in 40 minutes. Write a great first paragraph that sets you out in the right direction, and then loosen up. Don't digress, however, and start talking about irrelevant topics. Always stay focused on the text.

Chapter 10
Sample Poetry Analysis and Prose Fiction Analysis Essays

Here are two poems that rely a great deal on irony, similar to Robert Browning's "My Last Duchess," which you worked on back in Chapter 3. This time, the poems we are studying come with an essay question. Read the question and the poems and think about how you might write a response.

SAMPLE POETRY ANALYSIS ESSAY

William Blake's "The Chimney Sweeper" (Two poems)

Essay (Suggested Time—40 Minutes)

In the following poems by William Blake, the speaker, most likely a small child known as a chimney sweep, has been forced to work inside chimneys cleaning the interiors. Read the poems carefully. Then, in a well-written essay, compare and contrast the two poems and the ways that Blake uses poetic elements and techniques to express the plight of the chimney sweep.

The Chimney Sweeper

When my mother died I was very young,
And my father sold me while yet my tongue
Could scarcely cry " 'weep! 'weep! 'weep! 'weep!"*
So your chimneys I sweep and in soot I sleep.

Line
5   There's little Tom Dacre, who cried when his head
That curled like a lamb's back, was shaved, so I said,
"Hush, Tom! never mind it, for when your head's bare,
You know that the soot cannot spoil your white hair."

And so he was quiet, and that very night,
10 As Tom was a-sleeping he had such a sight!
That thousands of sweepers, Dick, Joe, Ned, and Jack,
Were all of them locked up in coffins of black;

And by came an Angel who had a bright key,
And he opened the coffins and set them all free;
15 Then down a green plain, leaping, laughing they run,
And wash in a river and shine in the Sun.

Then naked and white, all their bags left behind,
They rise upon clouds, and sport in the wind.
And the Angel told Tom, if he'd be a good boy,
20 He'd have God for his father and never want joy.

And so Tom awoke; and we rose in the dark
And got with our bags and our brushes to work.
Though the morning was cold, Tom was happy and warm;
So if all do their duty, they need not fear harm.

*   *The child's lisping attempt at the chimney sweep's
street cry, "Sweep! Sweep!"*

(1789)

The Chimney Sweeper

A little black thing among the snow,
Crying "'weep! 'weep!" in notes of woe!
"Where are thy father and mother? say?"
"They are both gone up to the church to pray.

Line
5   Because I was happy upon the heath,
And smil'd among the winter's snow,
They clothed me in the clothes of death,
And taught me to sing the notes of woe.

And because I am happy and dance and sing,
10 They think they have done me no injury,
And are gone to praise God and his Priest and King,
Who make up a heaven of our misery."
(1794)

Poetry Analysis Answers in General

Before we delve into these specific poems, we want to discuss some differences between prose fiction and poetry analysis. Poems are special cases because they deal in compressed language. Lyric poems (most of the poems on the AP English Literature and Composition Exam are lyric poems) often use a convention, simple on the surface but infinite in its varieties and depth. In this convention, the speaker of the poem (the "I") is addressing the reader directly, as prompted by a certain occasion or dramatic situation. If you pay attention to this lyric convention and its component parts, you may be able to understand a seemingly difficult poem more quickly. Not all poems on the AP Exam will exactly fit into this convention but most will. The two poems we've chosen to discuss here definitely do.

In the previous chapter, we introduced the Idea Machine—three questions to consider when looking at a work of literature. Do you remember them?

Go Online!
Check out us out on YouTube for test taking tips and techniques to help you ace your next exam at youtube.com/ ThePrincetonReview

> 1.   What does the poem or passage mean?
> 2.   How did the author get you to see that?
> 3.   How do the answers to questions 1 and 2 direct your knowledge to adequately answer the question?

The same three questions apply to the poetry analysis essay. Question 2, however, should be considered more like a drop-down kind of menu when you are writing about poetry.

Here are the three Idea Machine questions modified for the poetry analysis essay:

1. What's the literal meaning of the poem?
2. How did the author get you to see that?
   - What is suggested by the title?
   - Who is the speaker and who is the audience?
   - What is the dramatic situation that prompted the speaker to speak?
   - What problem is being explored in the poem, and does the poem find a solution?
   - What feelings do you get from the poem?
   - What is the overall effect of the poem?
3. How do the answers to the first two questions direct your knowledge to adequately answer the exam question?

You don't have to ask or answer all of the secondary questions under question 2, but the more answers you can find to these questions, the better your essay. Let's see how this method works by looking at these specific poems.

Discussion of "The Chimney Sweeper" by William Blake

Like many poems, these two could be the focus of a long discussion. A full class period could be spent analyzing these coupled poems as a group of interested students slowly circled them, discovered small details, and found ways to express their discoveries to each other. You don't have that time.

We won't be delving deeply into the many possible interpretations of these poems. The point here is to figure out what you could say about these poems in order to write an essay that answers the question. Let's use the poetry analysis essay Idea Machine— the simple, orderly process that you should apply to every AP English Literature essay.

First, tackle the question.

It is the classic AP essay question. That makes our lives a little easier. The Idea Machine will work perfectly here.

What's the literal meaning of the poem?

Here is some background that may prove helpful to your understanding. The speaker in both poems is a chimney sweep. In the late 18th and early 19th centuries, boys as young as six were indentured to masters as chimney sweeps by their families, who were too impoverished to keep the children at home. Young children were considered useful as chimney sweeps because they were small enough to get

Idea Machine in Action
On the following pages, we break down how to implement the Idea Machine strategy on the day of the exam.

up into the chimneys to clean them. But the dark, soot-encrusted chimneys were likely terrifying, and the sweeps were subject to a number of hazards, including cancer, broken bones, respiratory diseases, and even suffocation. It was common to see them on the streets of London, as coal-burning fireplaces were perhaps the most common way of heating homes and businesses. The plight of chimney sweeps was the subject of a report to British Parliament in 1817, more than 25 years after Blake's first poem was published. Ultimately, employment of young children in the chimney-sweep trade became illegal.

Both poems are from a larger project by William Blake, *The Songs of Innocence and of Experience*. The first poem is one of innocence; the second, one of experience.

If the AP exam writers were to use these poems or others that could benefit from historical background or allusions, the chances are that they wouldn't provide the historical or publication background as we just did. You will be provided with the years of publication (1789 and 1794, respectively), and a note that the poems were written in response to the poor conditions that caused young chimney sweeps to suffer. Most versions of the poem will carry a footnote to the first poem indicating that " 'weep! 'weep! 'weep!" is a child's version of the common chimney-sweep cry, "Sweep! Sweep!" But unless you've read about the plight of the chimney sweeps, the years, brief explanation, and footnote will provide very minimal explication of the historical background.

Fortunately, you don't need to know the background to understand these poems well enough to write a high-scoring essay on the AP exam. Recognizing the importance of the historical background helps, which is why many versions of the published poem include a brief note about it. But the AP exam writers will never choose a poem that relies on knowledge about historical context or allusions to historical events for its very sense.

Here's a quick summary of what you should have in mind after reading the first poem.

In the first three stanzas, a chimney sweeper speaks about how he came to be a sweep. He introduces a fellow chimney sweeper, Tom Dacre, and tells us a dream Tom had. The dream seems to comfort Tom about being a sweep. The poem ends with an injunction that chimney sweeps should do their duty, which will keep them from harm.

Let's look at the first poem in more detail. In its first stanza, the speaker tells us important information: his mother is dead and his father sold him while he, the speaker, was very young (lines 1–2), and that he is a chimney sweeper (line 4). As we saw in the footnote, the chimney sweeper's " 'weep!' 'weep!' 'weep!' 'weep!' "(line 3) resemble his cries of "sweep!"

In the next four stanzas, we receive important information about the chimney sweeper's environment, through the treatment and dream of Tom Dacre. Tom's hair is shaved (line 6), which he finds distressing; Tom cries, which reminds readers of the weeping in the first stanza. Told that a shaved head will at least protect his hair, Tom calms down, falls asleep, and has a dream which is both sinister and comforting. In it, "thousands of sweepers" (line 11) are "locked up in coffins of black" (line 12). In Tom Dacre's dream, the sweeps are released by an "Angel" with a "bright key" (line 13) who "set them all free" (line 14). They run, bathe in a river, and play in the sun (lines 15 and 16).

In the next stanza, they are not just free and playing but leaving the earth. They leave their bags behind (line 17) and rise on the clouds (line 18). Tom is told, in line 20, that "He'd have God for his father and never want joy."

In the last stanza, we return to earth and to the narrator addressing us directly. Tom wakes up, along with the other chimney sweeps (line 21) and prepares to go to work along with the other boys (line 22). In the last two lines, the narrator's voice shifts to a more omniscient tone, telling us that Tom, in contrast to his fear and tears in the second stanza, was "happy and warm" (line 23). Further, the narrator tells us "if all do their duty, they need not fear harm" (line 24). The line seems comforting. Yet the comfort is conditional; the sweeps must do their duty—work as a sweep without tears or complaint—to be without fear of being hurt.

Now let's look at the second poem. Here's a quick summary of what you should have in mind after reading the second poem. In the first stanza, an unnamed person overhears a chimney sweep crying "'weep!" Asked where his parents are, he says they have gone to church. The next two stanzas are the sweep talking: he seems angry that his parents have put him to work and becomes overtly condemnatory in the last stanza.

Now, let's look at the second poem in more detail. The narrator at first seems to be omniscient, talking about "A little black thing among the snow" (line 1) "crying 'weep! weep" (line 2). Because we are reading this poem in juxtaposition with the 1789 "The Chimney Sweeper" and because the title of this poem is also "The Chimney Sweeper," we might immediately think of the former poem's cry of the chimney sweeps. But, unlike the narrator of the first poem, this chimney sweep seems to have both parents, because when asked where his parents because are by an unnamed interlocutor (line 3), he replies that they've gone to church (line 4).

In the next stanza, the sweep speaks, addressing the audience directly. He says that his parents "clothed me in the clothes of death, / And taught me to sing the notes of woe" (lines 7–8). Although readers are not told what the clothes of death and notes of woe are, they can infer from the similarity of titles that they are the chimney sweep's black clothes and the street cry.

Yet in this poem, we are not given direct biographical detail, as we are in the first poem. The "father and mother" in line 3 are not only not dead, we are never told that they have "sold" their children, as line 2 of the first poem tells us. Then the speaker reiterates that his parents are currently in church, "to praise God and his Priest and King" (line 11).

Then there's an abrupt shift in tone in the last line. With "Who make up a heaven of our misery" (line 12), the speaker accuses the authority figures of church and state cited in the penultimate line of creating misery for the chimney sweeps.

In fact, the reader is to understand that perhaps those figures' ultimate realm of influence and authority, heaven, is created out of that pain.

The paragraphs preceding this one are a summary of the two poems. They are not an essay. In fact, you can use these paragraphs as a good example of what not to write on your AP essay. A literal reading is only a first step. Nothing is more mechanical or commonplace than a simple retelling of the passage. That kind of essay is going to score in the range of a 2 or a 3. If we apply the rest of the Idea Machine to this literal reading, we can move the score much higher. Let's continue with the Idea Machine. We're at question 2 of the Idea Machine: How did the author get you to see that?

- What is suggested by the title?

- Who is the speaker and who is the audience?

- What is the dramatic situation that prompted the speaker to speak?

- What problem is being explored in the poem, and does the poem have a solution?

- What feelings do you get from the poem?

- What is the overall effect of the poem?

What is suggested by the title? The title is simple on the surface. It's just three words, almost like the title of a painting in a museum. It indicates that the poem will be about a chimney sweeper. In the first poem, it lets the audience know that the "I" of the first stanza is a chimney sweeper. In the second poem, it provides a clue as to who the "little black thing among the snow" is and offers a clue about the "I" in the second stanza. Finally, the fact that the title is the same in both poems unifies them, and suggests that they are to be read in conjunction if readers don't already know.

Who is the speaker and who is the audience? The answer to this question is crucial for many poems. The primary speaker in both poems is a chimney sweep. He is telling the audience about his life as a chimney sweep, and what came before it. He is also discussing the plight of the chimney sweep with reference to spiritual and authority figures, such as the Angel and God (in the first poem) and God, Priest, and King (in the second poem). The chimney sweep in neither case appeals directly to the audience for sympathy but makes clear that the life can be a miserable one. The audience is the reader. The audience is also presumed to be sympathetic with the plight of the chimney sweeps, or at least to be susceptible to sympathy.

What is the dramatic situation that prompted the speaker to speak? If you can put the dramatic situation of these poems into your own words, you are off to a good start. While we know from our reading of literature that first-person narrators are not always trustworthy, in this case, they initially seem to be. There is nothing in a surface read of the poem to indicate otherwise. In the first poem, the speaker is talking about his own situation as a chimney sweep and his back story. Then, he discusses a boy presumably new to the trade, Tom Dacre, who is having his head shaved for the first time. The speaker comforts Tom about his hair. Tom's dream, narrated by the speaker, seems partly to be a comforting vision of heaven. The speaker then comes back to offer an adage: if the sweeps do their duty, they needn't fear any harm. In the second poem, the speaker seems also to be discussing his own life as a sweep, but his tone is dark and angry. His parents and other authority figures have seemingly all worked together to take him from the happiness of lines 5 and 9, believing they have not done him injury. But the last line, which directly indicates the sweeps suffer from their "misery," indirectly condemns parents and authority figures for using the sweeps' unhappiness to create "a heaven" from it.

What problem is being explored in these poems, and do the poems find a solution? It's clear that a social problem is being discussed in the poems. First, the chimney sweeps are deprived of parental comfort by being sold into a job in which they sweep chimneys (lines 2 and 4) and carry bags (lines 17 and 22), in the first poem. Second, it's a painful existence, in which they sleep in soot (line 4) and cry. In the second poem, they are deprived of happiness as well, and feel misery even more overtly.

The first poem seems initially to find a solution to the problem of their misery: they are presumably to find comfort in dreams of God as a father and doing their duty. Tom, after all, is "happy and warm" after the dream, despite the fact that it's cold outside. But can the reader fully trust this solution? There's disquieting coffin imagery in the third stanza of the first poem. If you follow the thread of metaphor, the later "clouds" they rise on may be heaven. They may be dead, then. So yes, their comfort might still be God, but they find comfort and release in death. Plus, of course, the coffins are black (line 12), a color associated with the sweeps' profession and its discomfort—and also frequently associated with death and mourning.

This might lead the reader to question whether the solution in the first poem—trust God as a father and do one's duty—is actually meant as a solution. Could it be ironic? After all, the last line says the sweeps "need not fear harm," but in the first stanza, the narrator has already suffered harm, in being sold and sleeping in soot.

If the conclusion of the first poem contains some irony, the reader might start to wonder if another problem is being addressed: religion and its role vis-à-vis the social problem. Is it really a comfort?

In the second poem, it clearly is not a comfort, at least to the narrator. The trappings of religion, such as the church, represent parental figures to the sweeps. But the actions of the parents, rather than exhibiting parental concern, endanger their children. His parents "clothed me in clothes of death/ And taught me to sing the notes of woe," the narrator tells us. Not only that, but they are oblivious, believing they have "done him no injury."

As the second poem comes to its final two lines, in fact, the narrator seems to move beyond the parents to higher authorities, the "God and his Priest and King" the parents praise. They, too, exhibit none of the care usually associated with these positions. In fact, the narrator says that these three entities—collectively referred to by the pronoun "who" in the final line—"make up a heaven of our misery." So God in the second poem definitely isn't the comforting father of the first poem. In fact, if the reader sees the pronoun "our" here as referring to the chimney sweeps, God and his Priest and King may have made up heaven as a comforting fiction for the chimney sweeps or may even be the *cause* of the sweeps' plight. So religion itself is part of the problem being explored.

In neither poem is there a specific solution to the problems explored.

What feelings do you get from the poem? You probably already noticed that the tool of "finding oppositions," which we discussed at great length in the preceding chapter, is coming into play in our discussion of this poem. There are several possible ways to interpret the first poem, for example. One could read it as a religious poem in which God and heaven are offered as a genuine comfort and refuge for Tom Dacre and the other chimney sweeps. Or one could see the ending as ironic—something Tom himself is expected to believe but that the reader is not expected to find persuasive. Or one could go further, especially when juxtaposed with the second poem, and believe that religion is created as a false comfort by church and other authorities.

Don't let the discovery of two (or more!) possible interpretations to any poem unnerve or confuse you. The AP Exam will feature complex poems full of these kinds of tensions. If they didn't, you'd have nothing to write about.

Readers of these poems sometimes feel that the first does offer a solution. Most think that the second poem is much darker. Some feel that the second poem is very cynical. Readers feel moved by the plight of the chimney sweepers, but some feel that the failure to offer a solution makes the poems unsatisfying.

What is the overall effect of the poem? Many readers have found great depth in these poems because they evoke such sympathy and because they can be so productively analyzed. The speaker in the first poem shows us his life and the life of Tom Dacre and offers a resolution of sorts. The speaker in the second poem shows us his life and offers a bleaker vision. Neither case offers a full resolution.

We came to all these points by thinking about the answers to the questions and by looking for oppositions. But we also had the time we needed, and we've had some practice at this kind of thing before. So . . .

Relax

Are you supposed to pick this all up in one or two readings? In between checking your watch to make sure you have time for the next two essays? Not likely. We just wanted to show you how much there is to unearth in a typical AP Exam passage or poem and how much our techniques can dig up for you. All you'd need to see about this poem on the actual test is that the speakers are in some kind of opposition—and that the narrator of the first one might be in opposition with Blake himself. If you saw that and looked for the ways Blake got that across, you'd find enough to write a great essay.

A Strong Beginning

You should be ready to finalize your opening. Here's an example.

> "The Chimney Sweeper" is a pair of poems written in the late eighteenth century about the plight of children forced to work as chimney sweeps. Although they seem to have profoundly different perspectives, the stylistic unity and similarities in figurative language indicate that William Blake blames social and religious authorities for the fate of the chimney sweeps in both.

Is this great writing? No. It won't win any prizes. But for the AP Exam, such writing is well on its way to a high score. Anything beyond this will impress your Reader. Let's take it apart for a moment, and then we'll finish the essay.

The beginning paragraph is a first pass at writing about meaning. We wanted to start with something more meaningful than "In 'The Chimney Sweeper' by William Blake. . . ." If you start that way, it's okay, and if the rest of your essay is any good, you'll score high. But the readers like to see something more than that. We opened with the idea that it's a pair of poems on a similar topic but that the narrator's perspectives are very divergent. Then, we link that to an opposition: the author's use of style and imagery, *not* what the narrators say, suggests a unity between the two poems, not a divergence. The Reader will be impressed that you forecast the main point so quickly.

Unfortunately, we ran out of steam before we could satisfy the overall goal of our beginning: to get at the meanings of the poems (literal and emotional) and explain how Blake gets the meanings across (we've barely started this process).

Keep Going

In the next section of our essay, we describe (not summarize!) what Blake's poem is, what it does, and how. This is a poem in which the overt statements of the narrator may not reflect what readers are expected to believe, nor what William Blake truly believes, nor what he thinks the reader might think he believes (did you get that?). There's a double meaning. On the AP English Literature and Composition Exam, any time you can show that a writer has created a double meaning, you have risen in the estimation of the Reader, who has likely been dealing with single meanings for most of the last hour of reading assignments. But we can't stop there; we have to explain both meanings. We chose to talk about the fact that the narrators express very different viewpoints about their lives. So initially these poems seem very different, right? But then we are going to segue to the idea that Blake wants the reader to see that the plights of the sweeps are the same in both.

How do we do this? Let's look at the first two paragraphs. You want to set up the first part of the argument, which is that the narrators differ. We also need to support these assertions with concrete examples from the text. That's our evidence.

While Readers don't have specific checklists to use, one aspect of your writing that every Reader will look for is fluid use of specific evidence to prove your point. Without evidence, your essay is an empty series of assertions. With evidence, you're building your case. Like this:

> Both narrators are chimney sweeps, but the tones contrast sharply. Though the first speaker has been cruelly "sold" into work very young, he offers comfort to a fellow sweep, Tom Dacre. He tells of Tom's dream: an "Angel" tells him "he'd have God for his father, and never want joy," implying at the end that all the chimney-sweeps can be comforted by a vision of heaven: "if all do their duty, they need not fear harm." The second speaker's tone is far more overtly unhappy. He condemns "God and his Priest and King" for causing the sweeps' plight—they "make up a heaven of our misery." His parents, who have "gone up to the church to pray," are responsible as well.

Okay. We've given evidence that there is contrast. But what about our friend double meaning? Time to introduce that idea. This is not a simple Case of the Two Contrasting Poems, as Nancy Drew might have called it. Let's introduce the opposition. And let's do it by pointing out the forms and shape of the poems, which tell us that the narrators' views aren't all there is. Then, we can talk about the literary methods that Blake uses to indicate to readers that something is going on beyond the surface of the poem. Let's talk literary methods and tricks! Let's talk imagery and metaphor! Again, let's use abundant examples from the text as evidence for the Reader that we know what we're talking about.

> On the surface, the narrators express quite different attitudes: one optimistic, one bitter. Yet the poems are unified by stylistic elements such as the identical title and the first stanzas, in which both use the "'weep! 'weep!" cry of the sweeps to remind the reader of a child's cry and evoke sympathy for the injustice being done. Through this unity, Blake shows that despite the stark contrast, the poems are a unit rather than two divergent works of art. The imagery of the two poems echoes as well, through Blake's use of white and black. Sweeps are linked with "soot" and "black coffins" in Poem 1, in vivid contrast to being "naked and white" later, in Tom's dream. The initial figure in Poem 2 mirrors this contrast: "a little black thing among the snow."

And Going

Then, we're going to pivot. Why does this imagery matter? Because it's the first indication we have that we are not to believe the narrator of the first poem. Let's hone in on that.

> These unified images make readers question the first narrator's optimism. The chimney sweeps in Poem 1 are, after all, "locked up in coffins of black" (chimneys are a metaphor for coffins: dark rectangles into which the boys' bodies are placed). While the freedom given them by the "Angel who had a bright key" evokes heaven (the boys "rise upon clouds" and go to a place where God is the father), it's also linked to death (coffins). This association is repeated and made explicit in Poem 2: the narrator is "clothed . . . in the clothes of death."

Is the product of our Idea Machine complete? Not quite. We haven't yet fully stated how Blake gets the idea across that the poems are unified, although we're well on the road. We're going to talk further about the shaping of the poem's meaning through irony, which we realize only from our analysis of the imagery above.

Here's the rest.

> This imagery shows that Blake intends the first poem's conclusion to be ironic. Despite the speaker's attempt to reassure, it's ultimately death the boys in Poem 1 are sold into. But Blake does not intend the ending of Poem 2 to be ironic. The speaker indicts religion, the state ("King"), and parents in the system that condemns him to a bleak life. The end—"our misery"—is abrupt: Blake intends readers to sympathize. Religion and duty are a false comfort in the first poem; in the second, religion and parents help nail the (figurative) coffin shut.

That's the end of our essay. It's not that long and much more could have been written. But that's it. That's all the time we had. So we wrote that and moved on. We checked our watch, and it said that we had used up 40 minutes. Is it the best piece of writing we've ever done? No. But will it earn a high score? Yes, high enough. Why?

First, as we said, the AP Readers are forgiving of some mistakes. The opening of the essay lets the Readers know that we understand some of the main aspects of the poem and are able to put this understanding into fairly clear sentences. Second, our essay continues to make good points. It talks about metaphor, irony, and the narrators' trustworthiness. We spread out well-chosen examples from most stanzas throughout each poem. We didn't digress for long, and we weren't overly repetitive. The Readers want to see your ideas. By making these insights clear and obvious to the Reader, you make it easy for the Reader to give you a better score.

Is this a well-organized essay? Not by the standards of the writing process. If you were writing for a take-home essay, this would be more like a free-writing, brainstorming session on the journey to a finished project. But by AP standards, this essay is pretty good. It begins with a clear direction, moves on to a consideration of oppositions, and finishes with specifically developed examples of style, imagery, and irony. For a first draft done in just 40 minutes top to bottom, the essay is admirable and will probably receive a 5.

SAMPLE ESSAY ON PROSE FICTION

Let's look at another sample. If you have time, try the question that follows and time yourself. At the very least, before you go to our sample essays (we've written two sample responses to this passage, one great and one fair), think about your first paragraph and try writing it in your head. But you really should practice writing a whole essay under time constraints.

Essay (Suggested Time—40 Minutes)

The following excerpt is from *Ultramarine* by Malcolm Lowry (published in 1933). Read the passage carefully. Then, in a well-written essay, analyze how Lowry uses literary elements and techniques such as imagery and interior monologue to paint a picture of Dana Hilliot, a young lad from a well-off family, as he ventures to sea as a sailor.

In your response you should do the following:

- Respond to the prompt with a thesis that presents a defensible interpretation.
- Select and use evidence to support your line of reasoning.
- Explain how the evidence supports your line of reasoning.
- Use appropriate grammar and punctuation in communicating your argument.

Puella mea[1] . . . No, not you, not even my supervisor would recognise me as I sit here upon the number six hatch drinking ship's coffee. Driven out and compelled to be chaste. The whole deep blue day is before me. The breakfast dishes must be washed up: the forecastle and the latrines must be cleaned and scrubbed—the alleyway too—the brasswork must be polished. For this is what sea life is like now—a domestic servant on a treadmill in hell! Labourers, navvies, scalers rather than sailors. The firemen[2] are the real boys, and I've heard it said there's not much they can't do that the seamen can. The sea! God, what it may suggest to you! Perhaps you think of a deep gray sailing ship lying over in the seas, with the hail hurling over her: or a bluenose skipper who chewed glass so that he could spit blood, who could sew a man up alive in a sack and throw him overboard, still groaning! Well, those were the ancient violences, the old heroic days of holystones; and they have gone you say. But the sea is none the less the sea. Man scatters even farther and farther the footsteps of exile. It is ever the path to some strange land, some magic land of faery, which has its extraordinary and unearthly reward for us after the storms of ocean. But it is not only the nature of our work which has changed, Janet. Instead of being called out on deck at all hours to shorten sail, we have to rig derricks, or to paint the smokestack: the only thing we have in common with Dauber, besides dungarees, is that we still "mix red lead in many a bouilli[3] tin." We batter the rusty scales off the deck with a carpenter's maul until the skin peels off our hands like the rust off the deck. . . . Ah well, but this life has compensations, the days of joy even when the work is most brutalising. At sea, at this time, when the forecastle doesn't need scrubbing, there is a drowsy calm there during the time we may spend between being roused from our bunks and turning out on deck. Someone throws himself on the floor, another munches a rasher; hear how Horsey's limbs crack in a last sleepy stretch! But when bells have gone on the bridge and we stand by the paintlocker, the blood streams red and cheerful in the fresh morning breeze, and I feel almost joyful with my chipping hammer and scraper. They will follow me like friends, throughout the endless day. Cleats are knocked out, booms, hatches, and tarpaulins pulled away by brisk hands, and we go down the ladder deep into the hold's night, clamber up along the boat's side, where plank ends bristle, then we sit down and turn to wildly! Hammers clap nimbly against the iron, the hold quivers, howls, crashes, the speed increases: our scrapers flash and become lightning in our hands. The rust spurts out from the side in a hail of sharp flakes, always right in front of our eyes, and we rave, but on on! Then all at once the pace slackens, and the avalanche of hewing becomes a firm, measured beat, of an even deliberate force, the arm swings like a rocking machine, and our fist loosens its grip on the slim haft—And so I sit, chipping, dreaming of you Janet, until the iron facing shows, or until eight bells go, or until the bosun comes and knocks us off. Oh, Janet, I do love you so. But let us have no nonsense about it.

---

[1] My girl (Latin)

[2] The men that tend the steam engines and boilers of the ship

[3] bullion

Discussion

Did you practice writing the essay on this passage? Did you time yourself? If so, great; if not, we hope you at least read the passage carefully and thought about how you would go about writing your first paragraph.

Oddly enough, writing about prose fiction can actually be more difficult than writing about poetry. Poetry often presents many difficulties to the reader caused by the density and complexity of poetic language. However, once interpreted, those same difficulties give you material to write about. Prose fiction presents the opposite problem. In general, assimilating the passage is pretty easy; the challenge is finding something worth saying about it. It is useful to remember that the literary devices you look for in poetry can also be pointed out in your essays on prose fiction.

As always, start out with the classic question and let the Idea Machine guide your thinking process. Of course, make sure that you allow the question to focus the development of your essay, and also note the time so that you don't go overboard and come up short on the last essay.

Below you'll find two responses to the passage. One is excellent, the other is mediocre. We'll discuss both responses after the samples are given. By the way, in these two essays we've taken out the annoying errors of diction and spelling that creep into every student's essay. We want you to read the essays for what they say and how they say it without distracting errors. The sentence construction reflects student writing, but in reality, both essays would have more language mistakes.

Sample Response to *Ultramarine*—Essay 1

In the passage, Malcolm Lowry effectively uses the resources of language to create an interior monologue (a mental speech) to dramatize the adventures a young English boy has aboard a ship, and shows the character of the boy, Dana Hilliot, as well. He uses vivid imagery and many details from the boy's life to show who Hilliot is and what he thinks, and captures the different rhythms of life aboard a ship.

First Hilliot thinks that no one, "not even my supervisor would recognise me. . . ." This shows that Hilliot thinks that he has changed and that life at sea has changed him. But he's happy, he likes the change, as he says, "The whole deep blue day is before me." But there are many conflicting feelings in Hilliot as he sits and drinks his coffee. For he quickly screams out, "this is what sea life is like now—a domestic servant on a treadmill in hell!" This shows the conflict that Hilliot undergoes. He doesn't know whether he thinks life at sea is great or a stinking hell. Lowry shows this by switching all the time between images that are pleasant, and images that are full of misery and despair and heartbreak. He really misses Janet and it shows. A sailor's life is lonely, and Lowry shows that. Lonely and boring sometimes, as hard as that may be to believe. But the boredom is broken up by danger and hardship. "We batter the rusty scales off the deck with a carpenter's maul until the skin peels off our hands like the rust off the deck . . ." is an example of the hardship. But immediately, the conflict shows up again. The very next sentence is, "Ah well, but this life has compensations, the days of joy even when the work is most brutalising."

Through it all though, Hilliot thinks of Janet. He begins thinking of her "Puella mea . . . ," which is Latin for "my girl" and ends saying "Oh, Janet, I do love you so." This tells us a great deal about Hilliot. He misses his girlfriend and is probably homesick for England too. These are normal reactions for the character of a young Englishman far from home, and by framing the story between these statements Lowry shows that the character of Dana Hilliot hasn't changed as much as he thinks it has. Hilliot is still a lonely young man with a great deal to learn.

Sample Response to *Ultramarine*—Essay 2

Who hasn't dreamed of throwing everything away and running off to sea? And yet very few people actually do run off to sea, probably because, at least in part, they realize (around the time they're packing all those wool sweaters into a duffle bag) that life at sea isn't just dropping anchor at exotic ports and gazing at the moon setting over the Indian Ocean. It's a hard, dangerous life. Better unpack the sweaters.

The passage shows the inner thoughts of one young man who actually did run off, and as he sits and thinks of the life he's leading and the life he's left behind, we get a picture of what a young sailor's life is really like. We get something else as well, a detailed portrait of a young, confused man, Dana Hilliot, and all the swirling emotions that he carries in his young heart. Hilliot is lonely, defiant, excited, bored, romantic, and cynical all at once.

The passage begins, "Puella mea . . ." Although that's Latin for "my girl," the translation isn't so important as the fact that it's Latin. Right from the beginning, Lowry shows us a fish out of water. Dana's educated, but how many of Dana's shipmates speak Latin? Probably none. Dana talks about how unrecognizable he's become. Maybe he really is unrecognizable to his old friends, but it's more likely that he can't recognize himself. He's gotten more than he bargained for, "this is what sea life is like now—a domestic servant on a treadmill in hell!" This is one of the recurring themes of the passage. Hard, dull work. Polishing brass. Chipping paint. Scrubbing and cleaning. It isn't a very romantic scenario. This theme tells us not just about sea life, but about Dana. He must have been pretty naïve to not know that a sailor works from daybreak into the night, and it's all manual labor.

Lowry gives us a picture of the wild, terrifying, intense life that Dana thought he was going to lead. He describes it to his girlfriend, to correct her and tell her the truth, but you can be sure that these were Dana's ideas of life at sea before he came to the ship. "Perhaps you think of a deep gray sailing ship lying over in the seas, with the hail hurling over her: or a bluenose skipper who chewed glass so that he could spit blood . . ." Well, Dana has learned that it isn't anything like that at all. His romantic dreams have been squashed, all except the sea. He still finds poetry in the sea. It is "ever the path to some strange land, some magic land of faery. . . ." This is the beauty that Dana really got on board for.

The passage then takes us even deeper into Dana's character. In the beginning, he talked about how horrible it was to be just a lackey, scrubbing decks. As he thinks deeper though, we see a real change in him. He loves the moments of calm, and is such a sensitive experiencer of the life around him that he even notes the way one of his fellows' joints crack, but the amazing thing is that he's learned to love the work. He describes it with relish, "I feel almost joyful with my chipping hammer and scraper. They will follow me like friends . . . The rust spurts out from the side in a hail of sharp flakes, always right in front of our eyes, and we rave, but on on!" The work, the hard relentless work, is the real adventure, and in those words "on on!" you can hear almost hear Dana's amazement at the fact that he can do it, he can keep going on.

In the end Dana's loneliness, cut off from his familiar life, returns him to being a moody "Romeo," dreaming of his girlfriend, imagining sweet-talking her. It wells up in him with the line, "Oh, Janet, I do love you so." But then comes the very last line of the passage, another abrupt change, "But let us have no nonsense about it." He's still a young person, pouring out his love to his girlfriend but then a second later he's pretending to be a tough guy, a sailor, who wants "no nonsense." By putting these lines, one after the other, Lowry shows Dana in the midst of growing up, and pretending to be more hardened than he is.

Discussion of Sample Responses 1 and 2

It shouldn't be too difficult to tell which is the better of the two responses. Essay 1 is clearly an average response from an intelligent student struggling to write a response about a passage he didn't get much from. Notice the mechanical repetition of the question and the mechanical, plodding way he works through the passage, not so much interpreting as it is summarizing. He did manage to address the question somewhat and did pull together a few simple insights into the passage. He would receive a score of 4. Not a terrible score by any means, but you can do better.

The biggest mistake the author of the first essay made was to choose to emphasize the life-at-sea aspect of the question. Unless an author is just setting the stage for what is to come, or planting some enormous symbol, almost every sentence in a novel or a story *is intended to reveal character*. This is especially true of the kind of accomplished writers you'll be dealing with on the AP Exam. When you read prose fiction on the AP Exam, always ask yourself what the sentences tell you about the people in the passage. In the Lowry passage, everything Dana thinks tells us something about Dana. The first student missed most of the psychological details of the passage and ended up floundering.

The author of the second essay worked with the Idea Machine. She asked herself about both the literal and emotional content of the passage. She kept an eye out for strong imagery and evidence of opposites. In doing so, she saw that the passage was filled with conflicting images. Dana loves Janet but then wants "no nonsense." Dana thinks the work is beneath him ("domestic servant"—Dana's the kind of kid who's used to having servants, not being one) and makes his shipboard life hell but, at the same time, he realizes that when he's lost in the physical frenzy of the labor, he finds the work exhilarating. The author of the second essay tried to put these oppositions together in a meaningful way. Most important, she knew to focus on character. By tying everything back to Dana's character she assured herself of a high score. In fact, the second essay would be scored a 6—the top score.

Also notice that the second essay does not begin with the typical restatement of the question. That doesn't mean that a Reader would look at the beginning of the second sample essay and think, "Oh my, what an original opening—this essay gets a high score." A nice opening isn't enough. You still have to write the essay. But, the Reader would think, "Hmm, this kid isn't writing like a robot . . . now if she can show me she understood the passage and communicate her understanding with anything like the flair of this opening, I'll give her a high score." In other words, yes, your opening can be a little stiff and dull (yes, you can paraphrase the question if you want to) if you write an otherwise good, insightful essay, but an original, interesting opening is better if you can write one without wasting a lot of time.

Essay Do's and Don'ts to Remember

After reviewing some sample essays, you probably have a good sense of what you need to accomplish to achieve a solid score. Some of this may seem basic and verge on the formulaic. Remember that your good ideas do need to be clear and well-organized. The following are tips for reviewing your own practice essays.

Your first paragraph should

- grab the reader (don't worry if you can't do this, but it helps)
- answer the question in the prompt
- preview the evidence you'll use to support your ideas

Your first paragraph should not

- go off on a tangent
- ignore the prompt
- merely restate the wording of the prompt

Your body paragraphs should

- have clear transitions and topic sentences
- provide evidence, in the form of quotations from the text, that supports your opinion
- explain how that evidence supports your point of view

Your body paragraphs should not

- rely on plot summary
- let quotation outweigh analysis
- ramble

Your conclusion should

- exist
- sum up the evidence for the jury
- contain any profound insights about the work that may have occurred to you while writing

Your conclusion should not

- suggest you didn't budget your time
- merely restate the introduction or prompt

Chapter 10 Summary

- o   Avoid summary.

- o   Get a feel for the passage.

- o   Notice imagery.

- o   Notice oppositions.

- o   Your essay doesn't have to be great, but you do have to show command of the English language. An AP essay that scores a 6 might not even be an "A" paper in English class. Of course not. It's a 40-minute essay on a story or poem you've never seen before.

- o   Show your verbal flair.

- o   It's okay to establish the foundation of your essay in two or three short opening paragraphs, if necessary.

- o   Your first paragraph should be free of error, but nobody writes an error-free paper. That doesn't mean be careless and sloppy. It means write as well as you can and don't worry about mistakes.

- o   If the question gives you the opportunity, write about character. The writing in AP passages almost always says something about character. This is especially true in the dialogue of a character, or in a first-person narration.

- o   A nice opening is icing on the cake.

- o   Make sure you leave yourself enough time to write a complete conclusion.

Chapter 11
Literary Argument

“

Art is a lie that makes us realize truth.

—Pablo Picasso

”

HOW DO YOU PREPARE FOR AN ESSAY ON *ANYTHING*?

The literary argument usually appears as the last of the three essays on the AP Exam. Unlike the prose fiction analysis or poetry analysis essays, the literary argument does not give you a text to work with; you must write an essay on a given theme using support drawn from your own reading.

Most people assume that the literary argument is the most difficult of the three essays, but this assumption is false. Even though the average score on the literary argument tends to be a little lower than on the other two essays, a close look at the data suggests that students who attempt the literary argument earn higher scores. Many students skip this essay altogether, so there are more scores of 0 here than on the prose fiction analysis and poetry analysis essays. On the other hand, more students earn scores of 5 and 6 on this essay than on the other two. The scores still tend to bunch up around the middle (the mean), but they spread out more across all the score ranges (a greater standard deviation). All the same, the literary argument is the most dreaded and anticipated portion of the AP Exam. It isn't worth any more than the other questions but, unlike the rest of the test, the literary argument question feels like the one you *have to* study for. At the same time, it's the question that most students feel like they *haven't* studied for, at least not enough.

We've shown you that you can and should study for the rest of the test. We *hope* we've shown you that knowing what you're doing on the Essay section is the way to shoot your scores through the roof. Now, what about the literary argument—how do you prepare for it?

The answer is simple. Use all the techniques we've already described for writing the prose fiction analysis and poetry analysis essays. Use the Idea Machine to direct your thoughts and answer the classic question as you go about answering the specifics of the question. The literary argument is no different from the other essays. There's just one more bit of preparation you need for the literary argument: three well-chosen works of literature that you know backward and forward.

WHAT THE TEST-WRITERS REALLY WANT FROM YOUR LITERARY ARGUMENT

You can, should, and *must* study a literary work for the literary argument. But what if the literary argument question asks for a theme that the work you've prepared doesn't address? Don't worry. The test-writers aren't trying to persecute you (although it does feel that way sometimes). Follow our instructions and you'll be prepared.

What the test-writers would really like to do is say, "Write an essay about any major literary work that you enjoyed. We just want to see how well you can write on a longer work that you've read and studied." Unfortunately, they can't ask you that directly because there would be no way to stop students from writing essays ahead of time (or having their dear Aunt Donna, the Pulitzer Prize–winning novelist, write an essay ahead of time) and memorizing them. The literary argument question is just a way of making sure that the student hasn't prepared the whole essay in advance.

However, the test writers don't want to ask literary argument questions that are too restrictive, either. They won't ask a question that points to just a handful of literary works, for example. They won't ask for an essay about "a character who may or may not be insane and who sees ghosts that may or may not be there." A few hundred students would get sixes by writing about Henry James's *The Turn of the Screw*. A few thousand would struggle to make this question make sense for *Hamlet* or *Macbeth*. The rest would just leave it blank.

The test writers go out of their way to make sure the literary argument question is truly open and provides an opportunity for a student who has read challenging literary works to write a good essay.

Let's look at the types of themes the literary argument question asks about. Remember, you can see real, previously asked essay questions at https://apcentral.collegeboard.org/courses/ap-english-literature-and-composition/exam.

Tasks of the Literary Argument

According to The College Board, the literary argument question assesses students' ability to do the following:

- Respond to the prompt with a thesis that presents a defensible interpretation.

- Provide evidence to support your line of reasoning.

- Explain how the evidence supports your line of reasoning.

- Use appropriate grammar and punctuation in communicating your argument.

As you can see, these tasks are things that you have been doing in class throughout the year, and can all be applied to thousands of literary works. At the same time, these tasks must be performed on command, and you cannot go ahead and write an essay ahead of time. The key to a great literary argument is having the right work for the theme, and knowing it cold.

So what works should you study?

Preparing for the Literary Argument

To be really ready for the literary argument, you should know at least three works very well. Two of them should be longer works that you've studied in class. We'll call these the *primary* works. The third work is a safeguard in case, for some reason, you can't apply your knowledge of the first works to the question at all, or in case you need to back up your points with another example. You have no idea what specific titles will be listed in that tally of potential works just beneath the Literary Argument question, so it's good to be well-versed in at least three important literary works. That way, you may see one of those three listed and it can be your primary work; then you can also discuss another important piece of literature. Trust us, the question stem may say that you need to choose only one work to discuss, but a Reader will be hugely impressed if you can adeptly discuss two or three pieces of literature. We'll provide you with a list of short *secondary* works that are useful for the AP Exam.

THE PRIMARY WORKS

Have two primary works that you know well. Your primary works should be fairly hefty. One of Shakespeare's plays or a thick, complex novel will do. The full-length works of the following authors are all good choices: Jane Austen, James Joyce, Joseph Conrad, Emily and Charlotte Brontë, Charles Dickens, Nathaniel Hawthorne, Herman Melville, Toni Morrison, Thomas Hardy, George Eliot, Fyodor Dostoevsky, and Thomas Mann. The object in choosing your primary works is to come up with two novels or plays that are so rich in incident and form that no matter what the literary argument question asks, you have something to say.

Choose Works You Already Know (and Love)

Just Say No . . . to Nonfiction

Remember: You must choose a work of fiction to write about in your literary argument.

You've already studied some literary works in school. Pick two and go over your notes. Read the books again or at least spend a few hours looking them over thoroughly. Pick your favorite work. If you fell in love with Shakespeare's *Hamlet*, great; use *Hamlet*. If you felt sleepy every time the word Shakespeare was mentioned but thought Dostoevsky's *Crime and Punishment* might change your life, then that's the work to use.

There are just a couple of exceptions to the favorite-work rule. Do not pick a short story, a work of nonfiction, or a poem. The literary argument questions, as a rule, say, "Choose a play or a novel: Do not choose a poem or short story." There have been very few exceptions to this rule, and the exception is that they'll allow complete epic poems. Now, if your favorite work of literature is really-honestly-no-I-loved-it Milton's *Paradise Lost* or Spenser's *The Faerie Queene* . . . well, okay, you could prepare those novel-length poems for the literary argument, but you'd still be better off with a novel. Short stories are wonderful reading material, but they are practically useless for the AP Exam; you're just not allowed to use them. They don't want students preparing to write literary arguments on short stories; they think it's too easy.

If you don't have a usable favorite work or are for some reason undecided about what to choose for your primary work, we highly recommend Shakespeare's plays, particularly *Hamlet*, *A Midsummer Night's Dream*, *King Lear*, *Othello,* and *The Tempest*. All of these plays are intricately plotted, contain elements of comedy and tragedy, and are incredibly rich in the kind of material about which literary arguments are written. The object in choosing your primary work is to find a work that can support any number of questions, and Shakespeare's works fit that bill better than any others of comparable length. As tough as Shakespeare's plays can be to read, they are considerably shorter than say, *Crime and Punishment* or *David Copperfield*. If you decide to go with Shakespeare, you could easily prepare to write about two plays in the time it takes to prepare to write about a longer novel. Just remember, we said we *recommend* Shakespeare. If you already know the work of another writer better, by all means prepare something else. But remember that we strongly recommend using a book you've already studied in class.

You'll be happy to know that in the past few years many contemporary books have appeared on the list of accepted sources for the literary argument. *There There* by Tommy Orange and *Little Fires Everywhere* by Celeste Ng are a couple of contemporary works that fall outside of the traditional primary works list but might be strong choices as one of your primary works.

Suggestions for Primary Works

Here are some other books we think make for good primary works. This list is not even close to complete, but it's a start. If you happen to know and love another long work inside and out, that's fine.

Emma by Jane Austen

Jane Eyre by Charlotte Brontë

Wuthering Heights by Emily Brontë

Don Quixote by Miguel Cervantes

White Noise by Don DeLillo

Bleak House by Charles Dickens

David Copperfield by Charles Dickens

Great Expectations by Charles Dickens

A Tale of Two Cities by Charles Dickens

Crime and Punishment by Fyodor Dostoevsky

Invisible Man by Ralph Ellison

The Sound and the Fury by William Faulkner

Tess of the D'Urbervilles by Thomas Hardy

The Scarlet Letter by Nathaniel Hawthorne

The Kite Runner by Khaled Hosseini

Their Eyes Were Watching God by Zora Neale Hurston

A Portrait of the Artist as a Young Man by James Joyce

Sons and Lovers by D. H. Lawrence

The Magic Mountain by Thomas Mann

One Hundred Years of Solitude by Gabriel García Márquez

Moby Dick by Herman Melville

Frankenstein by Mary Shelley

The Catcher in the Rye by J. D. Salinger

The Grapes of Wrath by John Steinbeck

Of Mice and Men by John Steinbeck

The Bonesetter's Daughter by Amy Tan

Anna Karenina by Leo Tolstoy

The Adventures of Huckleberry Finn by Mark Twain

Black Boy by Richard Wright

THE SECONDARY WORK

The secondary work is your just-in-case work and perhaps a bit more. The question just may not fit any aspect of your primary works. This is highly unlikely but, if this happens, you need to have something prepared. You don't want to be stuck trying to remember some book you haven't looked at since ninth grade. The other reason to prepare a secondary work is simply to have more options. If the question fits your secondary work perfectly, you'll want to use it. Prepare your secondary work well and in effect, you have three primary works. With well-chosen and well-prepared primary and secondary works, you would have to be extremely unlucky to find yourself faced with a literary argument question that did not fit any of the works.

Choose Something Different from Your Primary Works

Ideally, you want your secondary work to be as different as possible from your primary works. If you pick *Hamlet* as one of your primary works, you don't want to pick another Shakespearean tragedy starring a messed-up, confused, violent hero. In other words, don't pick *Macbeth*. You'd be much better off picking a comedy such as *A Midsummer Night's Dream*. Even better would be to pick a 20th-century comic novel like *Catch-22* by Joseph Heller or *A Confederacy of Dunces* by John Kennedy Toole. If you pick an extremely male-oriented work for one of your primary works, say *Invisible Man*, then Kate Chopin's *The Awakening* makes an excellent choice for a secondary work, as would Henry James's *The Turn of the Screw*, both of which feature female main characters.

Suggestions for Secondary Works

We've put together a list of secondary work books. These are all short novels, novellas, and plays that are acceptable to the AP Readers. Some works are not acceptable. Writing about *Family Guy*, episode 56, will result in a low score, as will writing about a Danielle Steele or Stephen King novel. Don't push it. You may think William Gibson's *Neuromancer* is a great book, but the AP committee probably won't be impressed and they'll lower your score.

The books on the following list were chosen according to the following guidelines: they're all recognized classics of which the AP Readers will highly approve. They're all short. Most important, they're all works that have been perfect fits with many literary argument questions.

We strongly recommend studying at least one of the works listed here. If you've read one of these works in class (and there's a good chance you have), by all means look it over again and prepare it for the AP Exam. An asterisk (*) means that the work is most highly recommended reading for the exam. Pick one of these and you won't go wrong.

Finally, if you really don't feel comfortable with any of the longer works that you've studied in class, are thinking of taking the AP Exam without having taken an AP course, or, well, slacked off in class—don't try to prepare a longer work for the AP Exam. Go straight to the list below and knock off two or three or four titles (remember, these are short works). You'll be prepared.

Novellas and Short Novels:

The Stranger by Albert Camus

The Awakening by Kate Chopin*

Heart of Darkness by Joseph Conrad*

Notes from the Underground by Fyodor Dostoevsky

The Old Man and the Sea by Ernest Hemingway

The Turn of the Screw by Henry James*

Death in Venice by Thomas Mann

Ballad of the Sad Café by Carson McCullers

Billy Budd by Herman Melville

A Sentimental Journey by Lawrence Sterne

The Death of Ivan Ilyich by Leo Tolstoy

Candide by Voltaire

Plays:

Who's Afraid of Virginia Woolf? by Edward Albee

Waiting for Godot by Samuel Beckett

A Man for All Seasons by Robert Bolt

The Cherry Orchard by Anton Chekhov

The Seagull by Anton Chekhov

Uncle Vanya by Anton Chekhov

Medea by Euripides*

A Doll's House by Henrik Ibsen*

Hedda Gabler by Henrik Ibsen*

The Crucible by Arthur Miller

Death of a Salesman by Arthur Miller

Emperor Jones by Eugene O'Neill

Hughie by Eugene O'Neill

Long Day's Journey Into Night by Eugene O'Neill

Antigone by Sophocles*

Oedipus Rex by Sophocles*

A Streetcar Named Desire by Tennessee Williams

The Glass Menagerie by Tennessee Williams

What Does "Prepare the Work" Mean?

We keep telling you to *prepare* your primary and secondary works. What does this mean? Two things:

1. Study the work as thoroughly as you can.
2. Write a first paragraph based on the classic question for each work you prepare.

Studying Your Primary and Secondary Works

Study the works you've chosen. Take notes. Record impressions. Map out different themes and examples of these themes within the work. Imagine important scenes as movies in your head. If you're reading this book early in the school year or in the summer before your AP English Lit course begins, you should consider prepping every work you read for class. This strategy will not only give you a broad array of works to select from on test day but will also improve your study habits. If you have a few months or a few weeks to prepare, then selecting two or three works you have studied will put you in a good place. If it's the week before the test, looking over the books to remind yourself of the plot lines and the names of the main characters might forestall those moments you lose when you're racking your brain, thinking, "Gatsby's girlfriend's name . . . Rose . . . Iris . . . Violet?"

How should you prepare the works?

- **Reread** your primary and secondary works within four weeks of the test. You want to have each one fresh in your mind.
- **Work from critical editions.** The books you should prepare for the AP Exam are the kinds of works that have been studied and restudied over the years. Although you can easily find your chosen texts in small, inexpensive reading editions, you should look for them in larger, critical editions that contain full introductions, notes, annotations, and sometimes appendices containing background material, biographical information, and samplings of past critical commentary. Whenever possible, use these fuller editions. Read as much of the supplementary material as you can stand. If you can put the work in a cultural context and discuss the political or sociological happenings of the time, the Reader's socks will undoubtedly be knocked off. No AP Reader is going to downgrade your essay because the points you make about the novel seem influenced by the opinions of other authors and critics. On the contrary, they'll think you're a genius. One student in a hundred actually bothers to read literary criticism about the book they have has prepared, but that's about the percentage of students who score a 6 on the literary argument. Coincidence?
- **Write your own study guide.** As much as some teachers might disparage store-bought or online study guides, they can be an invaluable supplement to your own study. (Note that we said "supplement." You still need to read the books.) Even better than a store-bought study guide, however, is one you've written yourself. You'll accomplish a lot of your review just by writing it. Moreover, once you're done, you'll have a study guide that highlights the aspects of a work you find most interesting—and those are the things you're most likely to write about on the exam.

Your custom study guide should be no longer than one page and should contain the following:

12 Is Key
The College Board suggests that AP English Lit teachers have their students read at least 12 works closely in class.

- **Plot**—You want to avoid plot summary in your literary argument, but it's still important to remember what happens—and *why*. Chapter by chapter or scene by scene, note what happens but focus on the major conflicts of the book. The details help you remember the specific chronology of the narrative; thinking about the larger conflicts puts the story into perspective.

- **Character**—Who's who? This list could be as simple as remembering how they spell their names or it can be as detailed as you want.

- **Themes**—What's the message or moral of the story? Avoid oversimplification.

- **Symbols**—Scarlet letters, green lights, white whales: what do they stand for and how do they help the author achieve their purpose?

- **Quotations**—"If you have tears, prepare to shed them now." (That's from *Julius Caesar*, in case you were wondering.) In the literary argument, it's important to provide support for your assertions, and even more important to avoid plot summary. Quoting your chosen work and explaining how the quote relates to the prompt demonstrates to the reader that you know and understand the work. Memorizing the quotes—and understanding what each means—allows you to write with more confidence.

A sample page of your self-made study guide might look like this:

The Seagull by Anton Chekhov

Act I—Lots of complaining (Masha's in mourning for her life, Treplev's mother Arkadina doesn't love him) as preparations are made for Treplev's play, starring Nina. The chain of unrequited lovers is introduced. Treplev loves Nina, Nina has a crush on Trigorin, Arkadina's acknowledged lover. Masha's mother Polina has the hots for Dorn, the local doctor. The play is experimental and a flop. Arkadina laughs at it, and Treplev's feelings are hurt. Trigorin takes an interest in Nina. Masha confesses to Dorn that she loves Treplev.

Act II—Midsummer squabbles on the estate—can Arkadina take the horses out or not. Nina thinks the great actress's demands are the most important thing. Treplev shoots a seagull and lays it at Nina's feet, threatening that one day he will *do the same to himself*. Nina dismisses his concerns, and Trigorin promptly begins seducing her. The dead seagull inspires Trigorin—a young girl lives by the lake like a seagull, but one day a man comes along and, for lack of anything better to do, destroys her.

Act III—Three big scenes: Masha tells Trigorin she's going to destroy her love for Treplev by marrying Medvedenko, the schoolmaster who pines for her. Arkadina changes Treplev's bandages (he's attempted suicide offstage between the acts). Arkadina fights with Trigorin, who wants to stay behind and complete his seduction of Nina, but Arkadina wants him out of there. As they're leaving together, Trigorin goes back for his walking stick. Nina goes to him; she's run away from home and heading to Moscow to become an actress. Trigorin gives her his address and asks her to come to him.

Act IV—Two years later. Masha has married Medvedenko, but she's still in love with Treplev and miserable. She's hoping Medvedenko's transfer will tear the love from her heart. Treplev brings Dorn up to date on Nina. She had a child by Trigorin, who managed to stay with Arkadina the whole time, and has returned to her. Meanwhile, Nina's acting career has been a disaster. Trigorin and Arkadina arrive. Trigorin is kind to Treplev's face, but behind his back, disparages his writing. After a quick game of lotto, the party relinquishes the study to Treplev. He struggles with his writing, then is surprised by Nina. He's been trying to see her. They reminisce about old times, and Nina compares herself to a seagull. She leaves as abruptly as she arrived. Treplev tears up his manuscripts and exits, just as Shamreyev shows Trigorin the stuffed seagull. A shot is heard offstage. Treplev has shot himself.

Characters

ARKADINA, an actress. 42 years old. Petty, vain, involved with writer Trigorin.

KONSTANTIN TREPLEV, Arkadina's son, an aspiring writer.

SORIN, Arkadina's brother and the owner of the estate where the play is set.

NINA, a young local girl and aspiring actress. Romantically involved with Treplev at the outset, later falls in love with Trigorin.

SHAMRAYEV, Sorin's estate manager.

POLINA, Shamrayev's wife. In love with Dorn.

MASHA, Shamrayev's daughter. In love with Treplev but will marry Medvedenko.

TRIGORIN, a writer. Spineless.

DORN, a doctor.

MEDVEDENKO, a schoolteacher. Obsessed with money.

Themes

Unrequited love and lots of it. Idealistic youth spoiled by the corruption of the real world. Struggle to create new art forms (Chekhov creating a new kind of drama in this play).

Symbols

The seagull: symbolic of youth. Trigorin sees it as emblematic of Nina and her innocence, which he will proceed to spoil. Treplev, who has shot a seagull, thinks it represents himself, and he shoots himself at the end of Act IV, just as he threatened when he laid the seagull at Nina's feet in Act II. Nina is a little confused about whether she's the seagull or not, as we see in her Act IV monologue.

Quotations

"I'm in mourning for my life; I'm depressed."—Masha, Act I. Opening lines of play, sets tone for what is to follow.

"I am a seagull; no, that's not it; I am an actress."—Nina, Act IV.

This study guide isn't perfect—it isn't very thorough—but it forces you to think about how the work is structured and how the author achieves his effects. While prepping this, you might note that each act begins with Masha, a minor character. In looking at criticism about the play, you might note that it was a failure when originally produced, possibly because Chekhov's effects are so subtle. Finally, after prepping the work in this way, you'll be certain about the names of the characters and what happens when, which will allow you to write with more clarity.

Prepare for the Literary Argument Ahead of Time

In addition to prepping the works, you should also write the first paragraph of a literary argument a couple of nights before the test. (Remember to use the Idea Machine: What does the work mean? What are the emotional contents of the work?) Writing the first paragraph shouldn't take you longer than 30 minutes, and when you consider how much time and stress it will save you on test day, surely you can see why it's a winning strategy.

While it's true that you have no idea what aspect of the work the prompt will ask you to address, we've supplied you with plenty of sample prompts with which to practice. Once you've seen a few, you'll be familiar with the kind of questions that appear on the exam and should see how altering one or two sentences in your sample introduction will probably save the day. And, even if you do end up writing an entirely new introduction on test day, you'll write with more confidence and skill if you've had some recent practice.

RECENT CHANGES

The literary argument prompt is a little intimidating, but since you've been studying all year for this test, you should have a pretty solid knowledge base regarding various themes in literature. Over the last few decades, this prompt has taken on various forms, and it was recently changed by The College Board from the "open prompt" to the "literary argument" prompt. Despite the name change, this prompt remains quite open, so you'll want to be sure that you have read an assortment of books, you have explored the themes, symbolism, and meanings of said books, and you can express your thoughts well. Because we can't see the test in advance, it's impossible to know just how simple or complex the prompt will be; therefore, it might help to consider some previous prompts so that you can prepare yourself with an arsenal of knowledge that will help you to answer appropriately and quickly.

In addition, the College Board has shared the wording that you will see in the Literary Argument question. The text in italics will vary by question, while the remainder of the prompt will be consistently used in all Literary Argument essay questions.

> *[Lead that introduces some concept or idea that students will be asked to apply to a text of their choosing.]*
>
> Either from your own reading or from the list below, choose a work of fiction in which *[some aspect of the lead is addressed]*. Then, in a well-written essay, analyze how *[that same aspect of the lead]* contributes to an interpretation of the work as a whole. Do not merely summarize the plot.

Chapter 11 Summary

o   When writing the literary argument, use all the techniques we've described for writing the prose fiction analysis and poetry analysis essays.

o   Don't worry about having to face an open question that doesn't apply to the works you've prepared. The test writers try to make the literary argument question broad enough so that you won't be lost—as long as you have *something* prepared.

o   Prepare two primary works and a secondary work.

o   If you've studied Shakespeare's work in class (and enjoyed it), we strongly recommend using a Shakespeare play as one of your primary works. His plays are chock-full of the material that literary arguments call for.

o   Choose works that you've already studied in class.

o   Our list of secondary works suggests novellas and plays that have proven useful on many AP literary arguments in the past.

o   Your secondary work should be as different as possible from your primary works. For example, if one of your primary works is a Shakespearean tragedy, pick a modern comic novella for your secondary work.

o   If possible, reread your primary and secondary works within four weeks of the test. Otherwise, at least skim the book and look over any class notes you have. Use critical editions if you can find them.

o   Write a sample first paragraph of the literary argument ahead of time. It's great practice for the real thing.

Part VI
Additional Practice Tests

Practice Test 2

The Exam

AP® English Literature and Composition Exam

At a Glance

Total Time
1 hour
Number of Questions
55
Percent of Total Grade
45%

DISCLAIMER: The official AP English Literature and Composition exam will be administered digitally. Instructions for the official exam may differ from this practice test.

Instructions

Section I has 55 multiple-choice questions and lasts 1 hour.

This section consists of selections from literary works and questions on their content, form, and style. After reading each passage or poem, select the best answer to each question.

You can go back and forth between questions in this section until time expires. The clock will turn red when 5 minutes remain—**the proctor will not give you any time updates or warnings**.

GO ON TO THE NEXT PAGE.

AP ENGLISH LITERATURE AND COMPOSITION

SECTION I

Questions 1 through 11 refer to the following. Read the following passage carefully before you choose your answers.

The passage, an excerpt from the novel Shirley *by Charlotte Brontë, published in 1849, discusses curates, members of the clergy in charge of parishes, in the nineteenth century.*

Par.

1   Of late years an abundant shower of curates has fallen upon the north of England: they lie very thick on the hills; every parish has one or more of them; they are young enough to be very active, and ought to be doing a great deal of good. But not of late years are we about to speak; we are going back to the beginning of this century: late years—present years are dusty, sunburnt, hot, arid; we will evade the noon, forget it in siesta, pass the midday in slumber, and dream of dawn.

2   If you think, from this prelude, that anything like a romance is preparing for you, reader, you never were more mistaken. Do you anticipate sentiment, and poetry, and reverie? Do you expect passion, and stimulus, and melodrama? Calm your expectations; reduce them to a lowly standard. Something real, cool, and solid lies before you; something unromantic as Monday morning, when all who have work wake with the consciousness that they must rise and betake themselves thereto. It is not positively affirmed that you shall not have a taste of the exciting, perhaps towards the middle and close of the meal, but it is resolved that the first dish set upon the table shall be one that a Catholic—ay, even an Anglo-Catholic—might eat on Good Friday in Passion Week: it shall be cold lentils and vinegar without oil; it shall be unleavened bread with bitter herbs, and no roast lamb.

3   Of late years, I say, an abundant shower of curates has fallen upon the north of England; but in eighteen-hundred-eleven-twelve that affluent rain had not descended.

    ….

4   The present successors of the apostles, disciples of Dr. Pusey and tools of the Propaganda, were at that time being hatched under cradle-blankets, or undergoing regeneration by nursery-baptism in wash-hand basins. You could not have guessed by looking at any one of them that the Italian-ironed double frills of its net-cap surrounded the brows of a preordained, specially-sanctified successor of St. Paul, St. Peter, or St. John; nor could you have foreseen in the folds of its long night-gown the white surplice in which it was hereafter cruelly to exercise the souls of its parishioners, and strangely to nonplus its old-fashioned vicar by flourishing aloft in a pulpit the shirt-like raiment which had never before waved higher than the reading-desk.

5   Yet even in those days of scarcity there were curates: the precious plant was rare, but it might be found. A certain favoured district in the West Riding of Yorkshire could boast three rods of Aaron blossoming within a circuit of twenty miles. You shall see them, reader. Step into this neat garden-house on the skirts of Whinbury, walk forward into the little parlour. There they are at dinner. Allow me to introduce them to you: Mr. Donne, curate of Whinbury; Mr. Malone, curate of Briarfield; Mr. Sweeting, curate of Nunnely. These are Mr. Donne's lodgings, being the habitation of one John Gale, a small clothier.

6   Mr. Donne has kindly invited his brethren to regale with him. You and I will join the party, see what is to be seen, and hear what is to be heard. At present, however, they are only eating; and while they eat we will talk aside.

7   These gentlemen are in the bloom of youth; they possess all the activity of that interesting age—an activity which their moping old vicars would fain turn into the channel of their pastoral duties, often expressing a wish to see it expended in a diligent superintendence of the schools, and in frequent visits to the sick of their respective parishes. But the youthful Levites feel this to be dull work; they prefer lavishing their energies on a course of proceeding which, though to other eyes it appear more heavy with *ennui*, more cursed with monotony, than the toil of the weaver at his loom, seems to yield them an unfailing supply of enjoyment and occupation.

8   I allude to a rushing backwards and forwards, amongst themselves, to and from their respective lodgings—not a round, but a triangle of visits.

GO ON TO THE NEXT PAGE.

1 ⬚ Mark for Review

"An abundant shower of curates" (paragraph 1) is an example of

- (A) satire
- (B) metaphor
- (C) oxymoron
- (D) irony

2 ⬚ Mark for Review

The lines "present years are dusty, sunburnt, hot, arid; we will evade the noon, forget it in siesta, pass the midday in slumber, and dream of dawn," (paragraph 1) most likely serve all of the following purposes EXCEPT

- (A) disengaging the reader from the present that opens the passage
- (B) exerting a hypnotic spell on the reader via parallelism
- (C) equating novel reading with sleep and dreaming
- (D) characterizing the past as arid and dusty

3 ⬚ Mark for Review

The tone of the description of the curates in paragraphs 1 and 2 is

- (A) realistic
- (B) admiring
- (C) arch
- (D) fearful

4 ⬚ Mark for Review

Which best describes the difference in the way the reader is addressed in paragraph 1 versus paragraph 4?

- (A) The reader is told the type of tale versus confidingly brought into a specific scene
- (B) The reader is promised an exotic romance versus given a prosaic scene
- (C) The reader is subtly placed on the side of the curates versus invited to laugh at them
- (D) The narrator is straightforward at first and ironic later

5 ⬚ Mark for Review

What does "lowly" most nearly mean in the context of paragraph 2: "Calm your expectations; reduce them to a lowly standard"?

- (A) Mean
- (B) Poor
- (C) Prosaic
- (D) Meek

GO ON TO THE NEXT PAGE.

6 ☐ Mark for Review

Which of the following best conveys the effect of the references to curates in the lines "successors of the apostles," "disciples of Dr. Pusey and tools of the Propaganda," "specially sanctified successor of St. Paul, St. Peter, or St. John" in the context of paragraph 4?

(A) They reinforce the earlier reference to Passion Week and Easter.

(B) The tone is admiring of the effort to keep religious beliefs alive in the current day.

(C) The phrases use parallelism and alliteration to convey the progression of religious life through history.

(D) The exalted comparisons mock curates in the current day.

7 ☐ Mark for Review

Which of the following statements best conveys the effect of the lines "nor could you have foreseen . . . the reading-desk" in paragraph 4?

(A) The imagery links "gowns" worn by christened babies and the "surplices" of curates

(B) The imagery expresses the cruelty of young curates

(C) The exaggerated diction makes religious life seem silly

(D) The ironic diction makes religious life seem cruel

8 ☐ Mark for Review

The narrator's perspective in this passage is

(A) disinterested journalist

(B) diffident investigator

(C) ironic chronicler

(D) sentimental storyteller

9 ☐ Mark for Review

The settings toward the end of the passage are described as a "neat garden-house," a "little parlour," and the "habitation of . . . a small clothier" (paragraph 5). What do these settings primarily convey?

(A) The middle-class, bourgeois existence of the curates

(B) A diminishment from the religious predecessors of the curates

(C) The stifling and confining propriety the curates must abide by

(D) The historical conditions of nineteenth-century England

10 ☐ Mark for Review

The word "affluent" in paragraph 3 most nearly means

(A) abundant

(B) wealthy

(C) liquid

(D) opulent

11 ☐ Mark for Review

What do the last two paragraphs indicate about the characters of the curates Mr. Donne, Mr. Malone, and Mr. Sweeting?

(A) They are virtually indistinguishable from each other.

(B) They are exuberant and boisterous.

(C) They are devoted to their duties.

(D) They are sociable with each other.

GO ON TO THE NEXT PAGE.

Questions 12 through 23 refer to the following. Read the following poem carefully before you choose your answers.

The poem below, "Planetarium" by Adrienne Rich, was first published in 1971.

Planetarium

Thinking of Caroline Herschel (1750–1848)
astronomer, sister of William; and others.

A woman in the shape of a monster
a monster in the shape of a woman
the skies are full of them

Line a woman   'in the snow
5   among the Clocks and instruments
or measuring the ground with poles'

in her 98 years to discover
8 comets

she whom the moon ruled
10 like us
levitating into the night sky
riding the polished lenses

Galaxies of women, there
doing penance for impetuousness
15 ribs chilled
in those spaces   of the mind

An eye,

         'virile, precise and absolutely certain'
         from the mad webs of Uranusborg

20   encountering the NOVA

every impulse of light exploding

from the core
as life flies out of us

         Tycho whispering at last
25   'Let me not seem to have lived in vain'

What we see, we see
and seeing is changing

the light that shrivels a mountain
and leaves a man alive

30 Heartbeat of the pulsar
heart sweating through my body

The radio impulse
pouring in from Taurus

35   I am bombarded yet   I stand

I have been standing all my life in the
direct path of a battery of signals
the most accurately transmitted most
untranslatable language in the universe
40 I am a galactic cloud so deep   so invo-
luted that a light wave could take 15
years to travel through me   And has
taken   I am an instrument in the shape
of a woman trying to translate pulsations
45 into images   for the relief of the body
and the reconstruction of the mind.

---

12   🔖 Mark for Review

What does the reverse parallelism of lines 1–2, "a woman in the shape of a monster/ a monster in the shape of a woman" most nearly convey?

Ⓐ That monsters and accomplished women like Caroline Herschel are viewed as similar

Ⓑ That explosions in astronomy can be monstrous

Ⓒ That women who go outside traditional occupations are monsters

Ⓓ That women in science were at one time viewed as monstrous

GO ON TO THE NEXT PAGE.

13 🔖 Mark for Review

What does "the skies are full of them" in line 3 convey in the context of the poem?

Ⓐ There are many more women in science waiting to be discovered.

Ⓑ There are many monstrous women.

Ⓒ The skies are full of witches.

Ⓓ The skies are full of stars.

14 🔖 Mark for Review

In line 13, "Galaxies of women, there", the word "there" most nearly seems to be everywhere EXCEPT

Ⓐ the night sky

Ⓑ a planetarium

Ⓒ the cosmos

Ⓓ Taurus

15 🔖 Mark for Review

The speaker likely says women are "doing penance" to highlight

Ⓐ the risks of scientific knowledge

Ⓑ the penalties for violating social constraints

Ⓒ women's traditional association with the home

Ⓓ the analogies between religious vocation and astronomy

16 🔖 Mark for Review

What metaphor is conveyed in the poem in lines 9–12, "she whom the moon ruled/ like us/ levitating into the night sky/ riding the polished lenses"?

Ⓐ That women are witches

Ⓑ That scientists are witches

Ⓒ That witches violate male power

Ⓓ That scientists court death and destruction

17 🔖 Mark for Review

What poetic device is used in lines 45–46 ("for the relief . . . and mind")?

Ⓐ Cacophony

Ⓑ Enjambment

Ⓒ Hyperbole

Ⓓ Alliteration

18 🔖 Mark for Review

The narrative "I" in the poem can best be described as

Ⓐ sorrowful that women astronomers were not appreciated at one time

Ⓑ angry that a women astronomer was not appreciated in her lifetime

Ⓒ eager to finish the analysis of the universe that Caroline Herschel started

Ⓓ receptive to knowledge about the universe and hoping to contribute

GO ON TO THE NEXT PAGE.

19 ☐ Mark for Review

The overall tone of the poem is

(A) anguished and militant

(B) peaceful and restrained

(C) satiric and demonic

(D) searching and analytical

20 ☐ Mark for Review

The first 10 stanzas are best understood as

(A) a tribute to Caroline Herschel and women like her

(B) a plea to appreciate early women in science

(C) a comparison of Caroline Herschel with Tycho Brahe

(D) a paean to the vision required to discover comets

21 ☐ Mark for Review

What does the unusual space in line 16, "in those spaces of the mind," convey in the context of the poem?

(A) Poems open new spaces in the mind.

(B) The poem is like a galaxy, with open spaces.

(C) It represents a pause for reading the poem aloud.

(D) The women in the night sky are expanding their minds.

22 ☐ Mark for Review

Lines 43–45, "I am an instrument in the shape/ of a woman trying to translate pulsations/ into images" most clearly mirror the sense of which earlier line in the poem?

(A) 6, "poles"

(B) 5, "instruments"

(C) 12, "lenses"

(D) 19, "Uranusborg"

23 ☐ Mark for Review

One of the effects of the last stanza's shift in focus is to

(A) extol the speaker's making of images

(B) lament that scientific data is more valued than images

(C) imply that people can be instruments for understanding the universe

(D) express fear about pulsations' effect on people

GO ON TO THE NEXT PAGE.

Questions 24 through 34 refer to the following. Read the following passage carefully before you choose your answers.

The selection is an excerpt from the novel Quicksand *by Nella Larsen, published in 1928.*

Par.

1   Helga Crane sat alone in her room, which at that hour, eight in the evening, was in soft gloom. Only a single reading lamp, dimmed by a great black and red shade, made a pool of light on the blue Chinese carpet, on the bright covers of the books which she had taken down from their long shelves, on the white pages of the opened one selected, on the shining brass bowl crowded with many-colored nasturtiums beside her on the low table, and on the oriental silk which covered the stool at her slim feet. It was a comfortable room, furnished with rare and intensely personal taste, flooded with Southern sun in the day, but shadowy just then with the drawn curtains and single shaded light. Large, too. So large that the spot where Helga sat was a small oasis in a desert of darkness. And eerily quiet. But that was what she liked after her taxing day's work, after the hard classes, in which she gave willingly and unsparingly of herself with no apparent return. She loved this tranquility, this quiet, following the fret and strain of the long hours spent among fellow members of a carelessly unkind and gossiping faculty, following the strenuous rigidity of conduct required in this huge educational community of which she was an insignificant part. This was her rest, this intentional isolation for a short while in the evening, this little time in her own attractive room with her own books. To the rapping of other teachers, bearing fresh scandals, or seeking information, or other more concrete favors, or merely talk, at that hour Helga Crane never opened her door.

2   An observer would have thought her well fitted to that framing of light and shade. A slight girl of twenty-two years, with narrow, sloping shoulders and delicate but well-turned arms and legs, she had, none the less, an air of radiant, careless health. In vivid green and gold negligee and glistening brocaded mules, deep sunk in the big high-backed chair, against whose dark tapestry her sharply cut face, with skin like yellow satin, was distinctly outlined, she was—to use a hackneyed word—attractive. Black, very broad brows over soft yet penetrating dark eyes, and a pretty mouth, whose sensitive and sensuous lips had a slight questioning petulance and a tiny dissatisfied droop, were the features on which the observer's attention would fasten; though her nose was good, her ears delicately chiseled, and her curly blue-black hair plentiful and always straying in a little wayward, delightful way. Just then it was tumbled, falling unrestrained about her face and on to her shoulders.

3   Helga Crane tried not to think of her work and the school as she sat there. Ever since her arrival in Naxos she had striven to keep these ends of the days from the intrusion of irritating thoughts and worries. Usually she was successful. But not this evening.

   ....

4   She was a failure here. She had, she conceded now, been silly, obstinate, to persist for so long. A failure. Therefore, no need, no use, to stay longer. Suddenly she longed for immediate departure. How good, she thought, to go now, tonight!—and frowned to remember how impossible that would be. "The dignitaries," she said, "are not in their offices, and there will be yards and yards of red tape to unwind, gigantic, impressive spools of it."

5   And there was James Vayle to be told, and much-needed money to be got. James, she decided, had better be told at once. She looked at the clock racing indifferently on. No, too late. It would have to be tomorrow.

   ....

6   To relinquish James Vayle would most certainly be social suicide, for the Vayles were people of consequence. The fact that they were a "first family" had been one of James's attractions for the obscure Helga. She had wanted social background, but—she had not imagined that it could be so stuffy.

7   She made a quick movement of impatience and stood up. As she did so, the room whirled about her in an impish, hateful way. Familiar objects seemed suddenly unhappily distant. Faintness closed about her like a vise. She swayed, her small, slender hands gripping the chair arms for support. In a moment the faintness receded, leaving in its wake a sharp resentment at the trick which her strained nerves had played upon her. And after a moment's rest she got hurriedly into bed, leaving her room disorderly for the first time.

8   Books and papers scattered about the floor, fragile stockings and underthings and the startling green and gold negligee dripping about on chairs and stool, met the encounter of the amazed eyes of the girl who came in the morning to awaken Helga Crane.

GO ON TO THE NEXT PAGE.

24 ⬚ Mark for Review

The tone of the beginning of the passage implies that Helga Crane is

(A) reflective

(B) sad

(C) lonely

(D) constricted

25 ⬚ Mark for Review

In paragraph 1, the words "the spot where Helga sat was a small oasis in a desert of darkness" is an example of what type of figurative language?

(A) Synecdoche

(B) Apostrophe

(C) Metaphor

(D) Simile

26 ⬚ Mark for Review

The narrator views Helga Crane as

(A) confused and unhappy

(B) isolated and temperamental

(C) snobbish and arrogant

(D) attractive and intelligent

27 ⬚ Mark for Review

In paragraph 1, "But that was what she liked . . . in which she gave willingly and unsparingly of herself with no apparent return," the word "unsparingly" most nearly means

(A) ruthlessly

(B) generously

(C) unmercifully

(D) indecisively

28 ⬚ Mark for Review

In relation to the first paragraph, the fourth paragraph represents a shift from

(A) realism to parody

(B) historical fiction to personal narrative

(C) an omniscient narrator's perspective to a character's thoughts

(D) an omniscient narrator to stream of consciousness

29 ⬚ Mark for Review

In paragraph 7, the statement "the room whirled about her in an impish, hateful way" uses which of the following to convey a sense of the room?

(A) Metaphor

(B) Metonym

(C) Onomatopoeia

(D) Personification

GO ON TO THE NEXT PAGE.

30 ☐ Mark for Review

The primary purpose of the passage is to

(A) establish the personality of Helga Crane

(B) examine the relationship of Helga Crane and James Vayle

(C) describe the social life of an educational institution

(D) present a pivotal moment for Helga Crane

31 ☐ Mark for Review

What does "yards and yards of red tape to unwind, gigantic, impressive spools of it" (paragraph 4) refer to?

(A) The bureaucratic offices of Naxos

(B) Evidence that the institution is impressive

(C) Breaking off her relationship to James Vayle

(D) The process of resigning from her work

32 ☐ Mark for Review

What is conveyed by the narrator saying that the clock was "racing indifferently on" (paragraph 5)?

(A) Helga Crane feels that time has gotten away from her.

(B) The outside world is indifferent to Helga Crane's decision.

(C) Helga Crane feels out of sync with time at Naxos.

(D) Helga Crane feels the world disapproves of her decision.

33 ☐ Mark for Review

The style of the passage as a whole can best be described as

(A) subjective and judgmental

(B) analytic and precise

(C) descriptive and figurative

(D) ironic and distanced

34 ☐ Mark for Review

In paragraph 8, the negligee "dripping about on chairs and stool" conveys all of the following EXCEPT

(A) it's falling from the chairs and stools

(B) Helga Crane has washed it

(C) it's made from a fluid material

(D) it's between several different places, like Helga Crane

GO ON TO THE NEXT PAGE.

Questions 35 through 45 refer to the following. Read the following poem carefully before you choose your answers.

The selection is an excerpt from the epic poem Paterson *by William Carlos Williams, published in five volumes from 1946 to 1958.*

Paterson lies in the valley under
the Passaic Falls
its spent waters forming the out-
Line line of his back. He
5   lies on his right side, head near the
thunder
of the waters filling his dreams!
Eternally asleep,
his dreams walk about the city
10   where he persists
incognito. Butterflies settle on his
stone ear.
Immortal he neither moves nor
rouses and is seldom
15   seen, though he breathes and the
subtleties of his
machinations
drawing their substance from the
noise of the pouring
20   river
animate a thousand automatons.
Who because they
neither know their sources nor
the sills of their
25   disappointments walk outside
their bodies aimlessly
for the most part,
locked and forgot in their desires
—unroused.

30   —Say it, no ideas but in things—
nothing but the blank faces of
the houses
and cylindrical trees
bent, forked by preconception
35   and accident—
split, furrowed, creased, mot-
tled, stained—
secret—into the body of the
light!

40   From above, higher than the
spires, higher
even than the office towers, from
oozy fields
abandoned to grey beds of dead
45   grass,
black sumac, withered weed-
stalks,
mud and thickets cluttered with
dead leaves—
50   the river comes pouring in above
the city
and crashes from the edge of the
gorge
in a recoil of spray and rainbow
55   mists—

(What common language to unravel?
. . . combed into straight lines
from that rafter of a rock's
60   lip.)

35 ☐ Mark for Review

What literary comparison is being used in lines 1–4, "Paterson
lies in the valley under / the Passaic Falls / its spent waters
forming the out-/ line of his back"?

(A) Zeugma

(B) Personification

(C) Pastoral

(D) Conceit

GO ON TO THE NEXT PAGE.

36 ☐ Mark for Review

What effect does the poet likely intend with the repetition of sounds in line 21, "animate a thousand automatons"?

(A) Underscore the multiplicity of the automatons that is the explicit subject of the lines

(B) Impart a musical and sing-song quality to the lines

(C) Portray the number of automatons as disquieting

(D) Emphasize the irony of inhuman creatures being animated

37 ☐ Mark for Review

What is being conveyed by "no ideas but in things," line 30?

(A) The individual elements of nature are more important than any idea.

(B) The automatons are more concerned with ideas than emotions.

(C) The only way to understand ideas is through things.

(D) Sleeping Paterson can't be woken up with ideas, but responds to things.

38 ☐ Mark for Review

In context, describing the "cylindrical trees" as "bent, forked by preconception / and accident" (lines 34-35) conveys which of the following?

(A) The heaviness of nature that would bend a tree mirrors the strength of the pouring river.

(B) All nature is cut in two ("forked"); one side is biology and one side is random events.

(C) Trees are formed by a combination of biology and random events.

(D) Trees are analogous to machines that have cylinders.

39 ☐ Mark for Review

In lines 40–50 ("From above . . . the river comes pouring in above"), what does the use of "even" most nearly convey in context?

(A) The river is more important than either religion (the "spires") or work ("office towers").

(B) Work ("office towers") is more important than religion ("spires").

(C) All natural elements contribute to the river.

(D) The river contributes to Paterson's abundance.

40 ☐ Mark for Review

The poem as a whole is best understood as

(A) a eulogy for a fading town

(B) an analysis of modern society

(C) a pledge of faith to a waterfall and a town

(D) a celebration of a waterfall and a town

41 ☐ Mark for Review

One effect of the shift in the speaker's focus in the third stanza is to

(A) imply that the river is mightier than Paterson

(B) introduce the river as distinct from Paterson

(C) argue that the river creates automatons

(D) emphasize the river's central position in the poem

GO ON TO THE NEXT PAGE.

42 ☐ Mark for Review

What best characterizes the relationship of the automatons and Paterson in lines 1–29 ("Paterson lies . . . unroused.")?

(A) Both their dreams walk around the city unseen

(B) Both are roused by the pouring, thundering river

(C) The automatons are being drained by industrialization and Paterson is being invigorated

(D) Paterson resides in his body, while the automatons walk around outside theirs

43 ☐ Mark for Review

The tone of lines 22–29 indicates that the speaker feels what about the automatons?

(A) Fear, as they are neither human nor natural

(B) Disinterest, as they are little more than statues

(C) Approval, as they are linked with the river's power

(D) Disdain, as they cannot connect with their disappointments

44 ☐ Mark for Review

Grammatically, the word "recoil" (line 54) is

(A) a verb

(B) an adverb

(C) a noun

(D) an adjective

45 ☐ Mark for Review

The unusual use of punctuation in lines 36–37 ("split, furrowed, creased, mot-/ tled,") and lines 56–57 ("What common language to un-/ ravel?") could be interpreted to suggest

(A) the speaker feels the world is fragmenting around the river and town, as the punctuation fragments language

(B) the speaker is emphasizing splitting and unraveling by making the words themselves split and unravel

(C) the words are moving to and fro as objects in a pouring river would move to and fro

(D) the speaker is conveying potential unexpected fragmentation in the city and the town

GO ON TO THE NEXT PAGE.

Questions 46 through 55 refer to the following. Read the following passage carefully before you choose your answers.

This passage is excerpted from Johnathan Swift's essay A Modest Proposal For Preventing the Children of Poor People From Being a Burthen to Their Parents or Country, and For Making Them Beneficial to the Publick, *published anonymously in 1729.*

Par.

1   It is a melancholy object to those, who walk through this great town, or travel in the country, when they see the streets, the roads, and cabbin-doors crowded with beggars of the female sex, followed by three, four, or six children, all in rags, and importuning every passenger for an alms. These mothers, instead of being able to work for their honest livelihood, are forced to employ all their time in stroling to beg sustenance for their helpless infants who, as they grow up, either turn thieves for want of work, or leave their dear native country, to fight for the Pretender in Spain, or sell themselves to the Barbadoes.

2   I think it is agreed by all parties, that this prodigious number of children . . . is in the present deplorable state of the kingdom, a very great additional grievance; and therefore whoever could find out a fair, cheap and easy method of making these children sound and useful members of the commonwealth, would deserve so well of the publick, as to have his statue set up for a preserver of the nation.

3   But my intention is very far from being confined to provide only for the children of professed beggars: it is of a much greater extent, and shall take in the whole number of infants at a certain age, who are born of parents in effect as little able to support them, as those who demand our charity in the streets.

      . . . .

4   The question therefore is, How this number shall be reared and provided for? which, as I have already said, under the present situation of affairs, is utterly impossible by all the methods hitherto proposed. For we can neither employ them in handicraft or agriculture; they neither build houses, (I mean in the country) nor cultivate land: they can very seldom pick up a livelihood by stealing till they arrive at six years old. . . .

5   I shall now therefore humbly propose my own thoughts, which I hope will not be liable to the least objection.

6   I have been assured by a very knowing American of my acquaintance in London, that a young healthy child well nursed, is, at a year old, a most delicious nourishing and wholesome food, whether stewed, roasted, baked, or boiled; and I make no doubt that it will equally serve in a fricasee, or a ragout.

7   I do therefore humbly offer it to publick consideration, that of the hundred and twenty thousand children, already computed, twenty thousand may be reserved for breed, whereof only one fourth part to be males; which is more than we allow to sheep, black cattle, or swine, and my reason is, that these children are seldom the fruits of marriage, a circumstance not much regarded by our savages, therefore, one male will be sufficient to serve four females. That the remaining hundred thousand may, at a year old, be offered in sale to the persons of quality and fortune, through the

kingdom, always advising the mother to let them suck plentifully in the last month, so as to render them plump, and fat for a good table. A child will make two dishes at an entertainment for friends, and when the family dines alone, the fore or hind quarter will make a reasonable dish, and seasoned with a little pepper or salt, will be very good boiled on the fourth day, especially in winter.

      . . . .

8   I grant this food will be somewhat dear, and therefore very proper for landlords, who, as they have already devoured most of the parents, seem to have the best title to the children.

46 ☐ Mark for Review

What does the "melancholy object" in paragraph 1 most likely refer to?

(A) Mothers and children begging

(B) The great numbers of poor people

(C) The roads, streets, and doors

(D) The problems poor people cause for wealthier people

47 ☐ Mark for Review

In relation to the first three paragraphs, the remainder of the passage serves primarily to

(A) provide reasons for overpopulation and poverty

(B) document data toward implementing the solution

(C) reassure readers of a solution to overpopulation and poverty

(D) propose a solution for overpopulation and poverty

GO ON TO THE NEXT PAGE.

48 ☐ Mark for Review

The narrator evidently believes someone should hit upon a "fair, cheap and easy method of making these children sound and useful members of the commonwealth" (paragraph 2). What does the narrator believe that method might be?

(A) Selling children to Barbadoes

(B) Training children as mercenary soldiers

(C) Teaching children about agriculture

(D) Eating children as food

49 ☐ Mark for Review

What is the narrator's tone throughout the passage?

(A) Patriotic and reverent

(B) Data-driven and scientific

(C) Reasonable and prudent

(D) Ridiculous and outlandish

50 ☐ Mark for Review

What is the narrator conveying in paragraph 8, in saying that the food is "very proper for landlords, who, as they have already devoured most of the parents, seem to have the best title to the children"?

(A) A foreshadowing that the parents might be next to be consumed

(B) A realistic look at how poorly the parents are treated by the landlords

(C) A satiric view of the avarice of landlords

(D) A comprehensive indictment of the landlords' greed

51 ☐ Mark for Review

In paragraph 4, "they can very seldom pick up a livelihood by stealing till they arrive at six years old," represents a shift from

(A) a dismissal of potential careers for the poor to a recommendation of the age at which working should begin

(B) a series of potential remedies for the commonwealth to an aside to readers contemptuous of the poor

(C) condescension toward poor children to contempt for poor children

(D) a discussion about why poor children can't be employed to a satiric acceptance that they may turn to stealing once they're six years old

52 ☐ Mark for Review

In "I grant this food will be somewhat dear," what does "dear" (paragraph 8) most nearly mean?

(A) Precious

(B) Expensive

(C) Heartfelt

(D) Affectionate

GO ON TO THE NEXT PAGE.

53 ☐ Mark for Review

Which of the following statements best conveys the effect of the sentences in paragraph 7 "I do therefore humbly. . . four females"?

Ⓐ The narrator is drawing an analogy between the children and livestock such as sheep and cattle in an attempt to make the proposal seem normal.

Ⓑ The diction employs mathematics to make the proposal seem as if it would make money.

Ⓒ The narrator points out that the children may be born outside marriage to make it seem as if the church would approve the proposal.

Ⓓ The argument portrays the poor as immoral.

54 ☐ Mark for Review

The passage as a whole is best understood as a

Ⓐ patriotic solution to a contemporary challenge

Ⓑ veiled plea for the poor to receive aid

Ⓒ satiric attack on proposals attempting to do good

Ⓓ political attack on the aristocracy

55 ☐ Mark for Review

What is the overall effect of "A child will make two dishes . . . especially in winter" in paragraph 7?

Ⓐ Clarifying just how horrifying the proposal is, by giving recipes for cooking the children

Ⓑ Underscoring how mundane solutions to poverty can seem, even if the effects are cruel

Ⓒ Equating the proposal to murder, by emphasizing what the children will undergo

Ⓓ Reassuring the aristocrats that the proposal will not be harmful

STOP
END OF SECTION I
IF YOU FINISH BEFORE TIME IS CALLED, YOU MAY CHECK YOUR WORK ON THIS SECTION.
DO NOT GO ON TO SECTION II UNTIL YOU ARE TOLD TO DO SO.

The Exam

AP® English Literature and Composition Exam

At a Glance

Total Time
2 hours
Number of Questions
3
Percent of Total Grade
55%

DISCLAIMER: The official AP English Literature and Composition exam will be administered digitally. Instructions for the official exam may differ from this practice test.

Instructions

Section II has 3 free-response questions and lasts 2 hours.

This section of the exam requires answers in essay form. Each essay will be judged on its clarity and effectiveness in dealing with the assigned topic and on the quality of the writing. In responding to Question 3, select a work of fiction that will be appropriate to the question. Use a work that you are familiar with either from your AP English Literature and Composition class or from other literature you have previously read.

You may pace yourself as you answer the questions in this section, or you may use these optional timing recommendations:

It is suggested that you spend an equal amount of time, approximately 40 minutes, on each question.

You may use scratch paper for notes and planning, but credit will only be given for responses entered in this application. Text you enter as an annotation will not be included as part of your answer. You can go back and forth between questions in this section until time expires. The clock will turn red when 5 minutes remain—**the proctor will not give you any time updates or warnings.**

GO ON TO THE NEXT PAGE.

AP ENGLISH LITERATURE AND COMPOSITION

SECTION II

In the following poem, "Eve Remembering," from *Five Poems* by Toni Morrison (2002), the speaker remembers and reflects upon her actions. Read the poem carefully. Then, in a well-written essay, analyze how Morrison uses poetic elements, techniques, and language to convey Eve's feelings about her canonical fall from grace.

Eve* Remembering

1

I tore from a limb fruit that had lost its green.
My hands were warmed by the heat of an apple
Fire red and humming.
Line I bit sweet power to the core.
5 How can I say what it was like?
The taste! The taste undid my eyes
And led me far from the gardens planted for a child
To wildernesses deeper than any master's call.

2

Now these cool hands guide what they once caressed;
10 Lips forget what they have kissed.
My eyes now pool their light
Better the summit to see.

3

I would do it all over again:
Be the harbor and set the sail,
15 Loose the breeze and harness the gale,
Cherish the harvest of what I have been.
Better the summit to scale.
Better the summit to be.
                                    —Toni Morrison

* In the Bible, Eve is the first woman; Adam is the first man. Eve eats an apple from the tree of knowledge, which God had forbidden them to eat. As a consequence, they fall out of favor with God and are banished from the Garden of Eden.

1   ☐ Mark for Review

In a well-written essay, analyze how Morrison uses poetic elements, techniques, and language to convey Eve's feelings about her canonical fall from grace.

In your response you should do the following:

- Respond to the prompt with a thesis that presents a defensible interpretation.
- Select and use evidence to support your line of reasoning.
- Explain how the evidence supports your line of reasoning
- Use appropriate grammar and punctuation in communicating your argument.

GO ON TO THE NEXT PAGE.

The following excerpt is from a short story entitled "An Anarchist" by Joseph Conrad, published in *A Set of Six* (1908). In this passage, the narrator is discussing a large company, its advertising, and its products. Read the passage carefully. Then, in a well-written essay, analyze how Conrad uses literary elements and techniques to portray the narrator's attitude toward the company and its activities.

Par.

1   That year I spent the best two months of the dry season on one of the estates—in fact, on the principal cattle estate—of a famous meat-extract manufacturing company.

2   B.O.S. Bos. You have seen the three magic letters on the advertisement pages of magazines and newspapers, in the windows of provision merchants, and on calendars for next year you receive by post in the month of November. They scatter pamphlets also, written in a sickly enthusiastic style and in several languages, giving statistics of slaughter and bloodshed enough to make a Turk turn faint. The "art" illustrating that "literature" represents in vivid and shining colours a large and enraged black bull stamping upon a yellow snake writhing in emerald-green grass, with a cobalt-blue sky for a background. It is atrocious and it is an allegory. The snake symbolizes disease, weakness—perhaps mere hunger, which last is the chronic disease of the majority of mankind. Of course everybody knows the B. O. S. Ltd., with its unrivalled products: Vinobos, Jellybos, and the latest unequalled perfection, Tribos, whose nourishment is offered to you not only highly concentrated, but already half digested. Such apparently is the love that Limited Company bears to its fellowmen—even as the love of the father and mother penguin for their hungry fledglings.

3   Of course the capital of a country must be productively employed. I have nothing to say against the company. But being myself animated by feelings of affection towards my fellow-men, I am saddened by the modern system of advertising. Whatever evidence it offers of enterprise, ingenuity, impudence, and resource in certain individuals, it proves to my mind the wide prevalence of that form of mental degradation which is called gullibility.

4   In various parts of the civilized and uncivilized world I have had to swallow B. O. S. with more or less benefit to myself, though without great pleasure. Prepared with hot water and abundantly peppered to bring out the taste, this extract is not really unpalatable. But I have never swallowed its advertisements. Perhaps they have not gone far enough. As far as I can remember they make no promise of everlasting youth to the users of B. O. S., nor yet have they claimed the power of raising the dead for their estimable products. Why this austere reserve, I wonder? But I don't think they would have had me even on these terms. Whatever form of mental degradation I may (being but human) be suffering from, it is not the popular form. I am not gullible.

....

5   The Maranon cattle estate of the B. O. S. Co., Ltd. . . . is also an island—an island as big as a small province, lying in the estuary of a great South American river. It is wild and not beautiful, but the grass growing on its low plains seems to possess exceptionally nourishing and flavouring qualities. It resounds with the lowing of innumerable herds—a deep and distressing sound under the open sky, rising like a monstrous protest of prisoners condemned to death. . . .

6   But the most interesting characteristic of this island (which seems like a sort of penal settlement for condemned cattle) consists in its being the only known habitat of an extremely rare and gorgeous butterfly. The species is even more rare than it is beautiful, which is not saying little. I have already alluded to my travels. I travelled at that time, but strictly for myself and with a moderation unknown in our days of round-the-world tickets. I even travelled with a purpose. As a matter of fact, I am—"Ha, ha, ha!—a desperate butterfly-slayer. Ha, ha, ha!"

7   This was the tone in which Mr. Harry Gee, the manager of the cattle station, alluded to my pursuits. He seemed to consider me the greatest absurdity in the world. On the other hand, the B. O. S. Co., Ltd., represented to him the acme of the nineteenth century's achievement.

8   . . . I don't see why, when we met at meals, he should have thumped me on the back, with loud, derisive inquiries: "How's the deadly sport to-day? Butterflies going strong? Ha, ha, ha!"

---

2   🔖 Mark for Review

In a well-written essay, analyze how Conrad uses literary elements and techniques to portray the narrator's attitude toward the company and its activities.

In your response you should do the following:

- Respond to the prompt with a thesis that presents a defensible interpretation.
- Select and use evidence to support your line of reasoning.
- Explain how the evidence supports your line of reasoning.
- Use appropriate grammar and punctuation in communicating your argument.

GO ON TO THE NEXT PAGE.

Many works of literature are concerned with loyalty. These concerns can take many forms. Characters may be struggling to decide who or what deserves their loyalty, and why. The objects of loyalty can be people, places, or concepts. A character's feelings of loyalty may change over time. The work may depict a test of loyalty, or changes in the object of a character's loyalty. Either from your own reading or from the list below, choose a work of fiction in which characters struggle with loyalty. Then, in a well-written essay, analyze how the treatment of loyalty contributes to an interpretation of the work as a whole. Do not merely summarize the plot.

A Doll's House
Age of Innocence
Anna Karenina
A Streetcar Named Desire
The Adventures of Huckleberry Finn
Angels in America
The Awakening
Breath, Eyes, Memory
The Bonesetter's Daughter
Cold Mountain
The Crucible
David Copperfield
Don Quixote
Father Comes Home from the Wars
The Goldfinch
The Handmaid's Tale
Henry IV, Part 2
Homegoing
The Iliad
King Lear
The Kite Runner
LaRose
The Lonely Londoners
Lord Jim
Macbeth
The Mambo Kings Play Songs of Love
Mansfield Park
Medea
Middlemarch
The Mill on the Floss
Of Mice and Men
The Oresteia
Paradise Lost
Persuasion
The Piano Lesson
The Scarlet Letter
Sense and Sensibility
Sula
The Sympathizer
Wuthering Heights

3 ☐ Mark for Review

In a well-written essay, analyze how the treatment of loyalty contributes to an interpretation of the work as a whole. Do not merely summarize the plot.

In your response you should do the following:

- Respond to the prompt with a thesis that presents a defensible interpretation.
- Provide evidence to support your line of reasoning.
- Explain how the evidence supports your line of reasoning.
- Use appropriate grammar and punctuation in communicating your argument.

STOP
END OF EXAM
IF YOU FINISH BEFORE TIME IS CALLED, YOU MAY CHECK YOUR WORK ON THIS SECTION.

Practice Test 2: Answers and Explanations

PRACTICE TEST 2 ANSWER KEY

1.	B	21.	D	41.	A
2.	D	22.	C	42.	D
3.	C	23.	C	43.	D
4.	A	24.	A	44.	C
5.	C	25.	C	45.	B
6.	D	26.	D	46.	A
7.	A	27.	B	47.	D
8.	C	28.	C	48.	D
9.	B	29.	D	49.	C
10.	A	30.	D	50.	C
11.	D	31.	D	51.	D
12.	A	32.	A	52.	B
13.	B	33.	C	53.	A
14.	D	34.	B	54.	C
15.	B	35.	B	55.	B
16.	A	36.	A		
17.	D	37.	C		
18.	D	38.	C		
19.	D	39.	B		
20.	A	40.	D		

PRACTICE TEST 2 EXPLANATIONS

SECTION I: MULTIPLE CHOICE

Questions 1–11

Charlotte Brontë (1816–1855) was a novelist. She initially published under the pseudonym Currer Bell; the initials were her own and the pseudonym was an attempt to disguise her identity, partly because women writers weren't generally accepted by the literary establishment at the time. This excerpt is from her novel *Shirley*, a regional novel about Yorkshire, labor unrest, and love in the early nineteenth century. Brontë was from a family of writers; her sisters Emily and Anne were both accomplished novelists as well.

1. **B** In context, "abundant shower of curates" means that curates are as abundant as raindrops in a rain shower. The correct answer is therefore (B), metaphor. Both (A) and (D), satire and irony, may tempt you slightly, as they are in the passage. But they aren't in the phrase, so cross them off. It's not (C), an oxymoron, because the phrase doesn't represent opposites. (It represents unlike things, but that's par for the course for metaphor, and they aren't opposites!)

2. **D** Remember that this is an EXCEPT/LEAST/NOT QUESTION. It's the *present* that is characterized as arid and dusty, so (D) is the correct answer choice.

3. **C** This is a classic question for Process of Elimination (POE). Is the description in paragraphs 1 and 2 realistic? The narrator tells you that the representations will be "real," but do you know they are? So much of the language is fanciful. Hmmm. Hold that thought, and don't choose this one right off the bat. Is it (B), admiring? The author states that they "ought to be doing a great deal of good," which holds the idea of their doing good in suspension rather than firmly stating that they do it—so it's not exactly admiring. Strike (B) out. Is it (C), arch? Arch means mischievous or saucy. That comment on doing good is somewhat arch. Keep this one. Are the paragraphs fearful, (D)? The tone definitely doesn't convey fear. Choice (C) it is.

4. **A** The narrator addresses the reader as an entity several times in this passage. Look carefully at the specific paragraphs. Choice (A) looks very good as an answer because the narrator tells the reader what to expect and then tells them they are about to see the characters. But always in this test, make sure you check the other answers briefly to make sure you aren't going astray. In (B), the reader is definitely *not* promised an exotic romance–quite the opposite. Choice (B) bites the dust immediately on those grounds. If a part of the answer is wrong, it *can't* be the correct response. In (C), you aren't really placed on the side of the curates, so out it goes. For (D), the narrator is arguably ironic in the beginning, so that's not a correct choice.

5. **C** Nicely enough, all the choices are potential meanings of *lowly* or closely aligned with it. So context is all; be sure to reread the lines surrounding the word. They imply that the narrator's tale will be *without* passion, stimulus, or melodrama; it will be, by contrast, *real, cool,* and *solid*. With that in mind, exercise your POE chops. Is it (A), mean? A definition that would work here is *miserly* or *stingy*. Is

that what our narrator is trying to convey in context? It doesn't seem that close (and it definitely isn't "mean" as in *cruel*). Is it poor, (B)? That seems even further away from the context. How about (C), prosaic? Some synonyms of prosaic are *commonplace*, *every day*, even *dull*. This seems to most match the context here so far. Is (D), meek, a contender? It's not as close as (C), certainly. Ah, the glories of utilizing POE, which lead you to (C) as the correct choice!

6. **D**   This can be a difficult passage to parse, especially given the fact that it isn't perfectly clear to contemporary readers what "Dr. Pusey and tools of the Propaganda" refer to! (Fun fact: he was a 19th-century theologian at England's Oxford University, engaged in religious controversies.) But it's good to know you don't have to know a thing about that to think through the phrases, right? Why? Just think about their effect on you as a reader vis-à-vis the paragraph because that's what the question is asking. Is it (A)? It could be. Hold that thought. Is it (B)? Well . . . people often admire religion. But is that the effect of these passages in context? Hold that thought, too. Is it (C)? Choice (C) seems very broad—beware of the overly general answer. Is it (D)? Ah, this seems like firmer ground than the others, because "disciples" and "successors" do refer directly to the curates, in context. And the passage is somewhat mocking. Choice (D) is closer than (A); in fact, it's the closest answer here, and so the correct answer choice.

7. **A**   What is going on here? The "gown" is a baby's christening gown, and it is linked via imagery with the surplices of curates (although the author ironically disavows this). Choice (A) is the correct answer. Were you tempted by (B)? Although the word "cruelly" is used, it's ironic (and it's not imagery, either), so that answer goes by the wayside. Neither (C) nor (D) is as close as (A).

8. **C**   How does the narrator come across to readers? This is a good one to utilize POE on as well. It doesn't appear likely that the narrator is (A), a disinterested journalist, if only because she tells us in paragraph 1 we will "dream of dawn." Journalists deal in facts, not dreams. (Yes, she tells us the story will be "real," but the dreams are in there, too.) Choice (B), a diffident investigator, is not the tone, either because nothing in particular is being investigated. Choice (C) appears to be closer than either of the first two, as she's chronicling two time periods, a present day and "eighteen-hundred-eleven-twelve," and the narrator's view of the curates is ironic. Is the narrator (D), a senti-mental storyteller? There's no sentiment; in fact, she tells you it won't be romantic in paragraph 2. Choice (C) it is.

9. **B**   Look carefully at context. These descriptions of the setting do convey a middle-class existence with "neat" and "parlour," so (A) looms as a possibility. Let's move on to (B), a diminishment from the reli-gious predecessors. Hmm, given that they are successors to St. Peter et al. (paragraph 4), diminishment is a distinct possibility. Mentally put (B) in the starting block. In (C), while "small" can be confining, "stifling" is too extreme, and we have no evidence that they are chafing under society's propriety. Yes, (D), the historical conditions, is a possibility, as parlors, clothiers, and garden houses likely existed. But it's not as close as (B). Choice (B) wins the prize!

10. **A**   While *affluent* in the present day is often used to describe wealthy people, a look at the highlighted paragraph will clue you in: that's not the case here, so (B) is not a correct answer choice. And while "affluent" does have a *meaning of river tributary*, context will tell you it's also not (C). Choice (D), opulent, is a synonym for *lush* and *wealthy*, so you can cross that off just like you did (B). Choice (A), abundant, is the correct answer.

11. **D**   While there is parallelism in the language that introduces Mr. Donne, Mr. Malone, and Mr. Sweeting, we don't have enough evidence to say whether (A) is true or not. To the wayside it falls. They are exuberant, but we don't know if that leads to boisterousness, so (B) falls, too. They are definitely *not* devoted by their duties; they'd rather be doing other things. Eliminate (C). The answer is (D), sociable with each other—they prefer "rushing backwards and forwards, amongst themselves, to and from their respective lodgings–not a round, but a triangle of visits" (paragraph 8).

Questions 12–23

An iconic feminist poet, Adrienne Rich was one of the best-known U.S. poets from the mid-20th century to her death in 2012. Rich was particularly known for her emphasis on representing women's voices and re-envisioning women's lives and choices. In many instances, she observed their power and agency vis-à-vis the patriarchal culture, dominant before the feminist movement began in the 1970s. This poem is about Caroline Herschel, an early astronomer who worked with her better-known brother William.

12. **A**   Be sure to always look at lines in context, reading the lines directly above and below. The closest answer here is (A), that the reverse parallelism in the lines suggests a similarity between monsters and accomplished women such as Caroline Herschel. Choice (C) might be tempting, but "traditional occupations" is too broad to be the answer—you know that the poem is talking about Caroline Herschel because of the epigraph, and while "others" are referred to, it's still not as close as (A). Choice (D) is also too broad. Choice (B) isn't relevant in context of the lines.

13. **B**   The line directly follows the two lines "A woman in the shape of a monster/ a monster in the shape of a woman," so the sense is closest to (B). If you see monstrous women as scientists, (A) is a possible interpretation of the lines, but it's not as close as (B). Although witches and monsters are often linked, (C) is more relevant later in the poem, and is not the answer here. Choice (D) isn't close in context.

14. **D**   This is an EXCEPT/LEAST/NOT question. "There" as a pronoun could refer to all of these except (D), Taurus. While Taurus is mentioned in the poem, it is not a reference for "there" in this context.

15. **B**   You can definitely use Process of Elimination (POE) on this. Is it the risks of scientific knowledge, (A)? But risks such as explosions come later in the poem. Penalties for violating social constraints, (B)? That's closer, as social constraints were against women achieving significant scientific knowledge in Caroline Herschel's lifetime. Choices (C) and (D) don't make sense in context. Choice (B) it is.

16. **A**   Let's see. The lines use "she" and "us" to say that these pronouns are ruled by the moon, rise (levitate) into the sky, and ride an object . . . just like, hey, witches ride broomsticks. "She" and very likely "us" are meant as women, so the metaphor operating is (A), women are witches. Could it be (B), scientists

are witches? But not all scientists are ruled by the moon—and linkage of women and the moon is a common literary association, so the metaphor breaks down there. There's nothing specifically about witches violating male power in these lines, so it can't be (C) in context. Choice (D) does not have contextual support in these lines either.

17. **D** The repetition of sounds close together, as "relief of the body/ and the reconstruction of the Mind" is (D), alliteration. It's none of the others. Review the glossary if this wasn't clear.

18. **D** The narrative "I" in this poem is receptive to knowledge about the universe and hoping to contribute, especially in the last stanza. Choice (D) is the correct choice. Choice (A), sorrowful, does not fit the overall tone of the poem when the narrative "I" speaks, and neither does (B), angry. She is more receptive than eager, (C). The "I" does seem to be at times analyzing a piece of the universe, but those points aren't as widespread as (D). Choice (D) it is.

19. **D** Use POE to cut your way through this. Is it anguished? Not really, so (A) is out. Peaceful doesn't describe the tone either, so (B) bites the dust. It certainly isn't (C). Choice (D) is the closest, conveying both the praise of Herschel and the contradictions of her.

20. **A** The poet is honoring Caroline Herschel and her achievements in the first 10 stanzas, so (A) is the closest answer. Choice (B) is too broad. In (C), although the text refers to "Tycho" in line 25, an AP test will never require you to have specific knowledge outside the poem. (Tycho Brahe was an early Danish astronomer, but you are free to slot that in as an irrelevant fun fact.) All you need to do is read the poem to figure out that (C) couldn't be the answer here because it doesn't fit all of the first 10 stanzas. Choice (D) does not fit the entire 10 stanzas' theme or tone.

21. **D** Be sure to read the lines immediately above and below and utilize POE throughout—it will be a big help here. In context, (A) and (B) are too broad. Choice (C) is irrelevant—poets don't put in spaces to guide oral readers. Choice (D) is the correct answer choice.

22. **C** Careful with this one. Look at what the lines are doing in the poem, not just at the words themselves. In other words, the answer isn't (B), instruments, just because the same words are used. In the phrase "I am an instrument," (line 43), an instrument is being actively used to understand and translate emanations from the sky. Does (A) do that? No, because it's a ground measurement. Choice (B) is something Herschel walked among, not actively used in the line. Choice (C) refers to instruments Herschel "rode." Ah, now we're getting somewhere; they were actively used to see the sky by something trying to decipher the universe. The speaker in "I am an instrument" is also trying to do that. (D), Uranusborg, is not relevant here. Choice (C) is the clearest answer choice.

23. **C** The narrative "I" moves to the foreground in this stanza. The speaker is trying to translate pulsations into images, but (A), extol, is not the tone here. Strike out (A). In (B), there is no sense that lament is the correct tone. Is it (C), implying that people can be instruments for understanding? That's the closest, as the speaker says "I am an instrument in the shape of a woman." In (D), fear doesn't fit the tone.

Questions 24–34

This passage is from *Quicksand* by Nella Larsen (1891–1964), published in 1928. It is a novel of the Harlem Renaissance and delves into themes of African American racial categorization, discrimination, and attendant social constraint.

24. **A** Many questions about tone on the exam require you to read and note vocabulary closely. The beginning of the passage carefully sets up several references to reflective light within a darkened environment; the reading lamp forms a "pool of light" and the brass bowl is "shining" although the room is in "soft gloom" and "dimmed" (paragraph 1). This gives a sense that the character Helga Crane is herself reflective within a dim environment, making the answer (A). There is no textual evidence that she is sad, (B). Don't be fooled by the description of her as "alone"; that is different from lonely, (C). While the passage later gives a sense that she is constricted in her environment, (D), the question clearly asks for the beginning of the passage, so that's not the correct answer here either.

25. **C** Metaphor, (C), is a comparison between two relatively unlike ideas in which one thing is likened to something else to convey a point. The room here is described as an oasis in a desert, but it's not actually a watering place, nor is Naxos the shifting sands of the Sahara. It's not (A), a synecdoche, which requires a part/whole relationship. Apostrophe, (B), occurs when a speaker addresses someone or something in a rhetorical manner, not expecting an answer. Is it a simile, (D)? It comes close, but a simile always uses *like* or *as* in making comparisons between the two things. Had the sentence read "was *like* a small oasis," this would have been the answer.

26. **D** Questions about the narrator's point of view rely on careful attention to vocabulary and tone. You are told in paragraph 2 that she has "delicate but well-turned arms and legs," and "an air of radiant, careless health," and her intelligence is conveyed by the books and environment, making (D) the answer. For the others, look at textual cues. Is she (A), confused and unhappy? She's not confused because she clearly believes she made a mistake and needs to leave. If part of the potential answer is wrong, it's all wrong. She's not isolated, either, because of James Vayle and the colleagues that could have been knocking on her door, so (B) isn't the correct answer. While the narrator tells us that Helga does care about the Vayles being a "first family" and that could be an indicator of snobbishness, you have no textual evidence of arrogance, so it's not (C).

27. **B** The word *unsparing* has two definitions: 1) not merciful (hard, ruthless) or 2) not frugal (liberal, generous). Look carefully at context to find answers like this. It's (B), generously, as it's allied with giving willingly. While (A), ruthlessly, and (C), unmercifully *could* be correct answers if you look solely at the vocabulary, context clearly rules those answers out in this instance. Indecisive, (D), doesn't make sense in the context.

28. **C** Look carefully at each section. It's definitely not (A), realism to parody, as there's no parody in the excerpt. Nor are either historical fiction or personal narrative (B) categories applicable to this excerpt. What you do have is (C), an omniscient narrator giving way to the character's thoughts and comments. Ding, ding! That's the correct answer. While (D) may seem tempting, the representations of Helga Crane's thoughts and comments don't add up to stream of consciousness, which is a flow of thoughts as the character thinks them.

29. **D** When an object is described in a way that has human attributes, the author is using which element of figurative language? Personification, (D), that's what! It isn't (A) because metaphor is a comparison between two unlike things, such as the room being an oasis. It isn't (B) because metonym is a word used to stand for something that it is associated with, such as "you owe allegiance to the crown" as a stand-in for owing allegiance to the king or queen. Choice (C) refers to words that imitate sounds, such as "buzz."

30. **D** The primary purpose in the passage is (D), to present a pivotal moment in which the character Helga Crane decides to leave where she is. Did (A) seem like a tempting choice? The passage does establish her personality, but it's much more a linkage between the setting and her personality: the primary action we see is her suddenly deciding she's a failure and she must leave. The passage spends a few lines each on (B) and (C), but neither of them are the primary purpose.

31. **D** The answer is (D), the process of resigning. How do you know? Immediately before these lines, she wants to depart but can't because the red tape needs to be unwound. Remember always to read a line above and below anything highlighted for a question. You can infer that she wants to resign from the institution she's teaching at, Naxos. Choice (A) is related to the red tape, but the location is where the process takes place rather than the process itself, so it's not a correct answer choice. In (B), her use of the word "impressive" to describe the bureaucracy of quitting is somewhat ironic. The phrase is not about James Vayle, so (C) is not the correct choice.

32. **A** Look closely at the text to choose this answer. Choice (A) is the correct choice, as Helga wants to talk to the "dignitaries" about leaving but then notices it's become too late. Both (C) and (D) possible answer choices but (C) is a bit too broad and in (D), "indifferently," isn't consistent with disapproval. And it's definitely not (B) because we know that at least James Vayle needs to be told—the entire world isn't indifferent to her.

33. **C** Choice (C) is the correct choice because the passage both describes and uses a great deal of figurative language. If you're not sure, run through the answer choices. It doesn't seem to be judgmental, so (A) is out. While it does analyze to some degree, "precise" isn't nearly as good a characterization of the style as (C), so it's not (B). It is not ironic, so (D) can be eliminated.

34. **B** While "dripping" could mean it's wet, from context you really don't know that Helga Crane has washed it—there is no evidence of what she did. The line does convey that it's all (A) and (C), and there is an implied linkage with (D). Choice (B) is the correct answer choice to this EXCEPT question.

Questions 35–45

This excerpt is from the poem *Paterson*, by William Carlos Williams (1883–1963). Williams was a modernist poet. He won the Pulitzer Prize in 1962. *Paterson* was written about a city in the region of his birth, northern New Jersey, where he also lived most of his life. It is a five-part epic published throughout the 1940s and 1950s. Williams was also a practicing physician and wrote essays and novels in addition to poetry.

35. **B** The lines use (B), personification, to identify the city Paterson with a man. Though parts of the poem are somewhat pastoral, (C), these lines are not, and pastoral is not a literary comparison but a genre. No other answer choice comes close.

36. **A** (B) is a partial answer, but it's not as close as (A). While the automatons may be disquieting, (C), the textual support for that is not in these lines, so (A) is also closer choice.

37. **C** The "things" seem to refer at least in part to nature, as exemplified by trees. But it also refers to houses, so (A) is shaky as a potential answer. Also, does the passage indicate that nature is more important than any idea? Not really. Eliminate (A). The automatons are not associated with this line, so strike out (B). Ah, things like houses and trees illuminate ideas, such as the immortality implied by the "body of the light" (lines 38–39), so (C) seems to do the trick. Choice (D) doesn't comport with the idea of the passage. The best answer is (C).

38. **C** POE away on these. Choice (A) seems a bit of a stretch. Is it (B)? Well, that is a potential reading. How about (C)? That seems much closer. Hold it. Choice (D) seems too much of a stretch as well. So if it's between (B) and (C), how do you choose? Can you be sure the speaker is talking about nature as a whole here? No, you can't because the poem is full of nature that isn't forked. Choice (C) is the better choice.

39. **B** Be sure to read the question and specific lines carefully. The answer is (B) because the river is higher *even* than the office towers—which allows us to infer that the office towers are the second-highest edifice in the town (so the church spires are lower). Metaphorically, work has trumped religion in the life of the city, as measured by the height of their respective buildings. It's very possible that other answers drew your eye. Choice (A) might be a good general answer, but it is not related to the use of "even," so it doesn't match the question. The same is true of (C) and (D).

40. **D** Although "dead" parts of nature are referred to several times, it's not a eulogy, so strike out (A). Analysis of society, (B), is too broad. Choice (C) doesn't represent the tone of the poem. The closest answer here is (D), a celebration of the waterfall and town.

41. **A**   The closest answer is (A). The river and falls have already been introduced as distinct from Paterson, so (B) isn't it. Choice (C) doesn't come close. Is it (D)? The shift actually indicates that the poem will move between Paterson and the river, not that the river will be central.

42. **D**   Close reading and Process of Elimination (POE) can help you with this one. Paterson's dreams "walk about the city" (line 9), but you have no textual evidence that the automatons dream. Strike out (A). Paterson "neither moves nor/ rouses" (lines 13–14) and the automatons are also "unroused" (line 29), so it can't be (B). Paterson and the automatons aren't antithetical to each other; they have commonalities, such as the unroused state. That knocks out (C) as a correct answer choice. Ah, (D), has strong textual support! Paterson has a back, a right side, and an ear (lines 4–12), so he's in a body (even if a fanciful one), while you are explicitly told that the automatons "walk outside/ their bodies" (lines 25–26). Choice (D) it is!

43. **D**   The closest answer is (D), as we are told "they don't know . . . their disappointments." Always look for textual support! While it might be natural to feel fear about automatons walking around, the tone is not fearful, so (A) is out. Were you prone to believe the automatons are little more than statues, as automatons are a type of robot? But the speaker devotes too many lines to them for (B), disinterest, to be a correct choice. The speaker also isn't approving, so (C) is out.

44. **C**   Recoil is often a verb. But the line uses it as a noun, so (C) is correct. If you fell for the trap (A), be sure to remember to always look at the lines—and you might want to review the grammar section.

45. **B**   Why are words hyphenated from line to line here? The sense of both lines is about splitting and unraveling, so (B) is the best choice. You have no evidence of (A); the hyphens representing fragmentation of city and town, nor of (C) or (D).

Questions 46–55

Jonathan Swift (1667–1745) was an Anglo-Irish writer of novels, tales, and essays. This excerpt is from *A Modest Proposal For preventing the Children of Poor People From being a Burthen to Their Parents or Country, and For making them Beneficial to the Publick*, an essay published in 1729. It was written in response to conditions of overpopulation and poverty in Ireland, and published anonymously.

46. **A**   If you look carefully at the passage, you'll see that the "melancholy object" are "beggars" "importuning every passenger for an alms." The correct response is therefore (A). Were you tempted by (B) or (C)? Both are close, but the high numbers in (B) only serve to heighten the effect of the "melancholy object," and the roadways in (C) are where it takes place. They are part of the scene but not the center of it. Wealthier people, (D), are not discussed in paragraph 1, so it can be eliminated.

47. **D**   What is the narrator doing in paragraphs 4 onward? Some reasons are provided, so (A) might be it. The narrator also documents data, so, hmmm, (B) could be the answer. Choice (C) is also potentially it, since our narrator definitely wants a solution. Ah, (D), proposing a solution for overpopulation and poverty is definitely it. Once you see this, you see that (A), (B), and (C) are less on the mark than (D).

48. **D** Although (A) and (B) are mentioned in the passage, these choices describe things that might be done with the children, not ways of making them useful members of society. In any case, they'd no longer be members of the society they grew up in. Strike both of them out. Choice (C) is mentioned in the passage as something that *cannot* be done. The author suggests, in paragraph 6, that children make "a most delicious nourishing and wholesome food." Choice (D), outlandish as it may seem, is the correct answer.

49. **C** Be careful with this question. Remember, tone is composed of many different features of writing. Go through your choices. Is it (A), patriotic and reverent? The author is thinking about the commonwealth, so set that aside for now. In (B), the narrator is certainly giving us data at one point, but it's not the overall tone. Eliminate (B). Is the narrator reasonable and prudent, (C)? Well, the *tone* is reasonable and prudent. This is the closest so far. (The solution may not be, but that's not what you're being asked.) He is discussing a common problem and earnestly attempting to solve it. Is the tone ridiculous and outlandish, (D)? Not really. Again, the solution may be but not the tone. Choice (C) is the correct answer.

50. **C** Is the answer (A)? Look at the tense; the parents have already been "devoured" (and it's a metaphor also, not literal eating!). Cross out (A). Is the narrator giving a realistic look, (B)? The narrator is also telling us with a straight face that eating children is "proper for landlords." Not realistic. Out it goes. Is it (C), a satiric view of the avarice of landlords? That's the closest, as the landlords are shown to have a propensity to devour the poor, despite the straightforward diction. It may be an indictment of landlord greed, (D), but it's not a comprehensive one, so (D) falls by the wayside. Choice (C) is the correct answer.

51. **D** Right before this paragraph, the narrator has been discussing how poor children can't be employed in agriculture or building. So (A) begins promisingly, as a dismissal of potential careers has happened. But the shift is *not* to a recommendation, so once you get to the end of (A), you should realize it won't do. Choice (B) should also be eliminated because what's going on is not a series of potential remedies. Choice (C) should go immediately because the shift isn't from condescension to contempt. Choice (D) begins promisingly as well . . . and also ends promisingly, as the highlighted portion indicates a satiric acceptance that the poor may turn to stealing, even though they can't do so until they turn six. Choice (D) it is! Remember, satire makes us aware of ridiculous expectations, such as talking about thievery as potential employment in the same way we would talk about agriculture or building.

52. **B** Several of these are in fact dictionary definitions of *dear*, so context, as ever in AP English, is all. The answer is (B), expensive. Were you tempted by (A), precious or (D), affectionate? Could there be some double meanings there, as the children may have been precious or affectionate before being eaten? Ah, but not to the landlords, who follow directly in context, so the answer is clearly (B). Choice (C) doesn't make sense in context.

53. **A** What's going on in the passage? Review it and wield your POE! Yes, there are definition analogies made between livestock and the children. Hold on to (A). Choice (B) initially seems correct, as the narrator is using mathematical figures left and right. But slam on the brakes when you get to "make money." That's not in the passage at all. Out goes (B). Choice (C) looks good at first, too, as the passage mentions children born outside wedlock. But the church doesn't enter it, so eliminate (C). Are the poor seen as immoral, (D)? Well, no marriage and the term "savages" are in there. But look at the question. Is that what is most conveyed? No, (A) is much closer to the effect of the sentences overall.

54. **C** Use POE to eliminate a lot of these. The ironic and satiric flashes should alert you to the fact that (A) can't really be correct, although it purports (on the surface) to be. It's not really sympathetic to the poor, either, so (B) is out. That leaves us with (C) and (D). There are some satiric jabs at the aristocracy, who are to blandly purchase children to eat, but it's not central enough to be the correct choice for a question like this. Choice (C) is it. Remember that satire is used to ridicule human folly. Yep, that's what's going on here.

55. **B** Let's POE away. Choice (A) does give recipes for cooking but is "horrifying" correct in context? It may seem tempting, but there's no blood or fear, as there is in horror. Let's hold that thought and move on to (B), emphasizing the mundanity of the solution. Yes, that seems possible—the recipes are very mundane. Let's keep (B) and move on to make sure the others aren't closer. Is it (C)? Nope, it's not that one. (Note that there's no reference to murder throughout.) It definitely isn't (D). The choice is (B).

SECTION II: FREE RESPONSE

Rubric—1 + 4 + 1 = 6 pts

A. Thesis (0–1 pts)
   o Responds to the prompt with a thesis that presents a defensible interpretation of the selected work.
B. Evidence and Commentary (0–4 pts)
   o Evidence: Provides specific evidence to support all claims in a line of reasoning.
   o Commentary: Consistently explains how the evidence supports a line of reasoning.
   o Explains how multiple literary elements or techniques in the poem contribute to its meaning.
C. Sophistication (0–1 pts)
   o Demonstrates sophistication of thought and/or develops a complex literary argument.

How to Score 6 points

Use The Idea Machine! The questions listed below will direct your reading to the material needed to write an essay.

The Idea Machine

1. What is the meaning of the work?
   a. What is the literal, face-value meaning of the work?
   b. What feeling (or feelings) does the work evoke?
2. How does the author get that meaning across?
   a. What are the important images in the work and what do those images suggest?
   b. What specific words or short phrases produce the strongest feelings?
   c. What do the characters, setting, structure, or narrators tell you about the passage?

Question 1—Poetry Analysis

- What is the meaning of the work?

  o Literal meaning: Eve, in the later years of her life, remembers her action in the Garden of Eden and doesn't regret it, feeling that her experiences outside the Garden have been worth cherishing

  o Feeling conveyed: Defiance, lack of regret, contentment in the decision she made and the life she has led

- How does the author get that meaning across?

  o Images and phrases to underline:

    ■ "My hands were warmed by the heat of an apple / Fire red and humming. / I bit sweet power to the core."

    ■ "led me far from the gardens planted for a child / To wildernesses deeper than any master's call."

    ■ "these cool hands guide what they once caressed; / Lips forget what they have kissed. / My eyes now pool their light"

    ■ ""Better the summit to scale. / Better the summit to be."

  o What do those phrases suggest?

    ■ Recasts the story of the moment Eve ate the apple as positive, happy, and understandable

    ■ Contrasts the Garden as juvenile and unfulfilling against the "deep wilderness" of experience and understanding; frames God as a "master" to be escaped

    ■ Imparts an impression of old age

    ■ Uses the mountain as a symbol of freedom and the fullness of life, showing her appreciation that her choice led to richness of experience

  o What do the characters, setting, structure, or narrators tell you about the passage?

    ■ Speaker: The speaker of the poem is biblical Eve.

    ■ Setting: The setting of the Garden is in opposition to the setting of the wilderness.

    ■ Structure: 3 stanzas. The first examines the past, the second focuses on the present moment, and the third explores an imagined reliving of her long life.

Sample first paragraph

Knowing or reading the biblical story of the Garden of Eden, one might expect the character of Eve to be full of regret for the action that resulted in being cast out by God. In Toni Morrison's "Eve Remembering," however, Eve is seen in her old age, full of self-worth, pride, and appreciation for the life and breadth of experience that resulted from her choice. Her retelling of the moment when she bit the apple, far from reading as an instance of sin or wrongdoing, concentrates on the sweet sensations of a positive and understandable action. She contrasts "the gardens planted for a child" against the "deep wilderness" of experience and understanding, making us see the Garden as, rather than a paradise, a pen to be escaped, with God as the "master" whose call she doesn't want or need to heed. In the final lines of the poem, Morrison uses the mountain summit as a symbol of the freedom and fullness of life Eve has achieved and imparts a sense of pride and happiness in her choices, contrasting sharply against what the Biblical story would lead us to expect and implying the value of making choices of our own.

Question 2—Prose Fiction Analysis

- What is the meaning of the work?
  - Literal meaning:
    - The narrator spent time on an estate of a meat-extract company, and spends a large portion of the passage complaining about advertising in general and that of B.O.S. in particular.
    - He doesn't like the gullibility that he feels the advertisements show in his fellow humans, and claims that *he* is not gullible.
    - The purpose of his stay there was to collect butterflies. He also complains about the manager of the cattle station and his rude and derisive attitude toward the narrator and his task.
  - Feelings conveyed: Annoyance, disgust, impatience, disapproval
- How does the author get that meaning across?
  - Images and phrases to underline:
    - "They scatter pamphlets also, written in a sickly enthusiastic style and in several languages, giving statistics of slaughter and bloodshed enough to make a Turk turn faint"
    - "The 'art' illustrating that 'literature' represents in vivid and shining colours a large and enraged black bull stamping upon a yellow snake writhing in emerald-green grass, with a cobalt-blue sky for a background. It is atrocious and it is an allegory."
    - "whose nourishment is offered to you not only highly concentrated, but already half digested. Such apparently is the love that Limited Company bears to its fellowmen—even as the love of the father and mother penguin for their hungry fledglings."
  - What do those phrases suggest?
    - Annoyance and incredulity toward the B.O.S. advertising campaign and those who are swayed by it; superiority about not being so gullible.
    - In general, impatience and disapproval with his fellow humans for being gullible and for valuing things the narrator has no time for and not valuing that which he finds valuable.
  - What do the characters, setting, structure, or narrators tell you about the passage?
    - Narrator: The speaker is disgusted with the company, and his feeling of superiority over its crude advertising contrasts with the station manager's certainty that the narrator is absurd and the company is the acme of achievement.
    - Setting: The distressing and disgusting nature of the Maranon estate meat-extract manufacturing operation is presented in opposition to the presence of the rare and beautiful butterflies.
    - Structure: The passage progresses from a description of how the narrator sees the estate to how he is seen while at the estate.

Sample first paragraph

Joseph Conrad really doesn't pull his punches in this excerpt from "An Anarchist": he uses sarcasm, harsh language, and a variety of disgusting imagery to let the reader know exactly how disillusioned he is with B.O.S. Co., Ltd. and its advertising and with his fellow humans in general. At the same time, he conveys his sense of superiority over those who "swallow" the advertising he feels is "atrocious," disgusting, and insulting, and over the station manager whose treatment of him he finds derisive. His brief mention of the "extremely rare and gorgeous butterfly" that is his actual reason for being in a location dominated by the meat-extract company he is so disgusted by serves as a contrast to the condemnatory nature of his diatribe: he does find beauty and value in the world, and is disappointed in the people around him for appreciating the wrong things and not valuing the only aspect of his environment that he finds worthwhile.

Question 3—Literary Argument

(This example uses Miguel de Cervantes's *Don Quixote*.)

- What is the meaning of the work?
  - o Literal meaning:
    - ■ After reading too many chivalry romance novels, Don Quixote decides to embark on an adventure of his own. His overactive imagination leads him, and his appointed squire, Sancho Panza, into battles with imaginary enemies. Don Quixote is mocked on his quest and claims defeat. Sancho encourages his master to keep believing in the life he has imagined.
- How does the author get that meaning across?
  - o Major themes in the work:
    - ■ The themes in the novel mimic the themes of traditional chivalry romance novels, such as romance, danger, and adventure. This is a reflection of Don Quixote's reading habits and the author's attempt to poke fun at these stories of chivalry.
  - o Theme related to the question: Loyalty
    - ■ Over the course of the novel, Sancho Panza remains loyal to Don Quixote, even though all of Don Quixote's friends refuse to entertain this creation of his imagination.
  - o Important scenes/imagery:
    - ■ When Don Quixote insists the windmills are giants, Sancho sees only windmills, but still he rushes to Don Quixote's side to ensure he is unharmed.
    - ■ After Sancho is fooled by the Duke and Duchess, he claims he would rather be happy as a laborer than miserable as a governor even though that means not having land as Don Quixote promised him.
    - ■ After Don Quixote returns home defeated, he gives up his belief in chivalry, but Sancho urges him not to lose faith.

Sample first paragraph

While reading the novel *Don Quixote* by Miguel Cervantes, it is challenging to understand why Sancho Panza remains loyal to Don Quixote until the very end. Don Quixote's reading habits result in a journey filled with physical and emotional pain on the part of the master and his appointed squire. Through imaginary battles and acts of humiliation, Sancho remains loyal to Don Quixote. Cervantes uses the relationship between these two characters to explore the relationship between loyalty and reason and what it means to believe. Though Sancho's original motivation may have been the prospect of land, he remains by his master's side long after the Duke and Duchess's act of humiliation.

HOW TO SCORE PRACTICE TEST 2

Section I: Multiple Choice

_____ × 1.2273 = _____
Number Correct   Weighted
(out of 55)   Section I Score
                              (Do not round)

Section II: Free Response

(See whether you can find a teacher or classmate to score your essays using the guidelines in Chapter 5.)

Question 1: _____ × 4.5833 = _____
              (out of 6)   (Do not round)

Question 2: _____ × 4.5833 = _____
              (out of 6)   (Do not round)

Question 3: _____ × 4.5833 = _____
              (out of 6)   (Do not round)

AP Score Conversion Chart English Literature and Composition

Composite Score Range	AP Score
107–150	5
90–106	4
73–89	3
56–72	2
0–55	1

Sum = _____
       Weighted Section II
       Score (Do not round)

Composite Score

_____ + _____ = _____
   Weighted   Weighted   Composite Score
Section I Score   Section II Score   (Round to nearest
                                         whole number)

Practice Test 3

AP® English Literature and Composition Exam

At a Glance

Total Time
1 hour
Number of Questions
55
Percent of Total Grade
45%

DISCLAIMER: The official AP English Literature and Composition exam will be administered digitally. Instructions for the official exam may differ from this practice test.

Instructions

Section I has 55 multiple-choice questions and lasts 1 hour.

This section consists of selections from literary works and questions on their content, form, and style. After reading each passage or poem, select the best answer to each question.

You can go back and forth between questions in this section until time expires. The clock will turn red when 5 minutes remain—**the proctor will not give you any time updates or warnings**.

GO ON TO THE NEXT PAGE.

AP ENGLISH LITERATURE AND COMPOSITION

SECTION I

Questions 1 through 12 refer to the following. Read the following passage carefully before you choose your answers.

The passage is an excerpt from The Awakening *by Kate Chopin, published in 1899.*

Par.

1   A green and yellow parrot, which hung in a cage outside the door, kept repeating over and over:

2   *"Allez vous-en! Allez vous-en! Sapristi!* That's all right!"

3   He could speak a little Spanish, and also a language which nobody understood, unless it was the mockingbird that hung on the other side of the door, whistling his fluty notes out upon the breeze with maddening persistence.

4   Mr. Pontellier, unable to read his newspaper with any degree of comfort, arose with an expression and an exclamation of disgust.

5   He walked down the gallery and across the narrow "bridges" which connected the Lebrun cottages one with the other. He had been seated before the door of the main house. The parrot and the mockingbird were the property of Madame Lebrun, and they had the right to make all the noise they wished. Mr. Pontellier had the privilege of quitting their society when they ceased to be entertaining.

6   He stopped before the door of his own cottage, which was the fourth one from the main building and next to the last. Seating himself in a wicker rocker which was there, he once more applied himself to the task of reading the newspaper. The day was Sunday; the paper was a day old. The Sunday papers had not yet reached Grand Isle. He was already acquainted with the market reports, and he glanced restlessly over the editorials and bits of news which he had not had time to read before quitting New Orleans the day before.

7   Mr. Pontellier wore eye-glasses. He was a man of forty, of medium height and rather slender build; he stooped a little. His hair was brown and straight, parted on one side. His beard was neatly and closely trimmed.

8   Once in a while he withdrew his glance from the newspaper and looked about him. There was more noise than ever over at the house. The main building was called "the house," to distinguish it from the cottages. The chattering and whistling birds were still at it. Two young girls, the Farival twins, were playing a duet from "Zampa" upon the piano. Madame Lebrun was bustling in and out, giving orders in a high key to a yard-boy whenever she got inside the house, and directions in an equally high voice to a dining-room servant whenever she got outside. She was a fresh, pretty woman, clad always in white with elbow sleeves. Her starched skirts crinkled as she came and went. Farther down, before one of the cottages, a lady in black was walking demurely up and down, telling her beads. A good many persons of the *pension* had gone over to the *Chênière Caminada* in Beaudelet's lugger to hear mass. Some young people were out under the wateroaks playing croquet. Mr.

Pontellier's two children were there—sturdy little fellows of four and five. A quadroon nurse followed them about with a faraway, meditative air.

9   Mr. Pontellier finally lit a cigar and began to smoke, letting the paper drag idly from his hand. He fixed his gaze upon a white sunshade that was advancing at snail's pace from the beach. He could see it plainly between the gaunt trunks of the wateroaks and across the stretch of yellow camomile. The gulf looked far away, melting hazily into the blue of the horizon. The sunshade continued to approach slowly. Beneath its pink-lined shelter were his wife, Mrs. Pontellier, and young Robert Lebrun. When they reached the cottage, the two seated themselves with some appearance of fatigue upon the upper step of the porch, facing each other, each leaning against a supporting post.

10   "What folly! to bathe at such an hour in such heat!" exclaimed Mr. Pontellier. He himself had taken a plunge at daylight. That was why the morning seemed long to him.

11   "You are burnt beyond recognition," he added, looking at his wife as one looks at a valuable piece of personal property which has suffered some damage. She held up her hands, strong, shapely hands, and surveyed them critically, drawing up her fawn sleeves above the wrists. Looking at them reminded her of her rings, which she had given to her husband before leaving for the beach. She silently reached out to him, and he, understanding, took the rings from his vest pocket and dropped them into her open palm. She slipped them upon her fingers; then clasping her knees, she looked across at Robert and began to laugh. The rings sparkled upon her fingers. He sent back an answering smile.

12   "What is it?" asked Pontellier, looking lazily and amused from one to the other. It was some utter nonsense; some adventure out there in the water, and they both tried to relate it at once. It did not seem half so amusing when told. They realized this, and so did Mr. Pontellier. He yawned and stretched himself. Then he got up, saying he had half a mind to go over to Klein's hotel and play a game of billiards.

13   "Come go along, Lebrun," he proposed to Robert. But Robert admitted quite frankly that he preferred to stay where he was and talk to Mrs. Pontellier.

14   "Well, send him about his business when he bores you, Edna," instructed her husband as he prepared to leave.

15   "Here, take the umbrella," she exclaimed, holding it out to him. He accepted the sunshade, and lifting it over his head descended the steps and walked away.

16   "Coming back to dinner?" his wife called after him. He halted a moment and shrugged his shoulders. He felt in his vest pocket; there was a ten-dollar bill there. He did

not know; perhaps he would return for the early dinner and perhaps he would not. It all depended upon the company which he found over at Klein's and the size of "the game." He did not say this, but she understood it, and laughed, nodding good-by to him.

17 Both children wanted to follow their father when they saw him starting out. He kissed them and promised to bring them back bonbons and peanuts.

————

1 🔖 Mark for Review

The tone of the beginning of the passage is

(A) cacophonous

(B) whimsical

(C) brooding

(D) satirical

2 🔖 Mark for Review

Paragraph 4 establishes Mr. Pontellier as

(A) fastidious and officious

(B) intolerant and judgmental

(C) restless and volatile

(D) surreptitious and untrustworthy

3 🔖 Mark for Review

The parrot's chatter made at the beginning of the passage helps to establish

(A) the unpleasantness of the setting

(B) Mr. Pontellier's restlessness and discomfort

(C) the tension between Mr. Pontellier and Robert

(D) a sense of unease between man and nature

4 🔖 Mark for Review

In the sentence "He was already acquainted with the market reports . . . he had not had time to read before quitting New Orleans the day before" (paragraph 6) the word "quitting" means

(A) finishing

(B) leaving

(C) giving up

(D) dismissing

5 🔖 Mark for Review

Mr. Pontellier's attitude toward his companions on Grand Isle could be characterized as

(A) aloof

(B) curious

(C) mistrustful

(D) warm

GO ON TO THE NEXT PAGE.

6 ☐ Mark for Review

In the sentence "Mr. Pontellier's two children were there— sturdy little fellows of four and five" in paragraph 8, the word "sturdy" helps to establish

(A) Mr. Pontellier's self-satisfaction with his children

(B) the children's ability to withstand Mr. Pontellier's neglect

(C) parallels between the children and their mother

(D) suspicion that Mr. Pontellier is not the children's biological father

7 ☐ Mark for Review

In paragraphs 9 and 10, which word complements our understanding of Mr. Pontellier's personality?

(A) Smoke

(B) Idly

(C) Gaunt

(D) Folly

8 ☐ Mark for Review

Paragraphs 9 and 10 reveal

(A) Mr. Pontellier's thinly veiled dislike of Robert

(B) Mr. Pontellier's envy of late risers

(C) Mr. Pontellier's concern for his wife's health

(D) Mr. Pontellier's self-righteous contempt toward his wife

9 ☐ Mark for Review

In the line "You are burnt beyond recognition" in paragraph 11, Mr. Pontellier uses which literary device to provoke a reaction from his wife?

(A) Hyperbole

(B) Onomatopoeia

(C) Assonance

(D) Understatement

10 ☐ Mark for Review

Paragraph 11 serves to introduce

(A) Mrs. Pontellier's unattractive appearance

(B) an indication that the relationship between Mr. and Mrs. Pontellier is strained

(C) a suggestion that Robert is uncomfortable around Mr. Pontellier

(D) Mrs. Pontellier's dominant position in the marriage

GO ON TO THE NEXT PAGE.

11 ☐ Mark for Review

The description of the interactions between Mrs. Pontellier and Robert conveys a tone of

- Ⓐ unapologetic intimacy

- Ⓑ passionate longing

- Ⓒ polite tolerance

- Ⓓ underlying antagonism

12 ☐ Mark for Review

Paragraphs 13 and 14 serve to further clarify

- Ⓐ Mr. Pontellier's indifference toward his marriage

- Ⓑ Mr. Pontellier's disdain for his children

- Ⓒ Mr. Pontellier's fear of Robert's influence over his wife

- Ⓓ Mr. Pontellier's loathing of idle chit-chat

GO ON TO THE NEXT PAGE.

Questions 13 through 23 refer to the following. Read the following poem carefully before you choose your answers.

This poem, "Old Year and New Ditties—No. 3" by Christina Rossetti, was published in Goblin Market and Other Poems *in 1862.*

Old Year and New Ditties—No. 3

Passing away, saith the World, passing away:
Chances, beauty and youth sapped day by day:
Thy life never continueth in one stay.
Line Is the eye waxen dim, is the dark hair changing to gray
5 That hath won neither laurel nor bay?
I shall clothe myself in Spring and bud in May:
Thou, root stricken, shalt not rebuild thy decay
On my bosom for aye.
Then I answered: Yea.

10 Passing away, saith my Soul, passing away:
With its burden of fear and hope, or labor and play;
Hearken what the past doth witness and say:
Rust in thy gold, a moth is in thine array,
A canker is in thy bud, thy leaf must decay.
15 At midnight, at cockcrow, at morning, one certain day
Lo the bridegroom shall come and shall not delay:
Watch thou and pray.
Then I answered: Yea.

Passing away, saith my God, passing away:
20 Winter passeth after the long delay:
New grapes on the vine, new figs on the tender spray,
Turtle calleth turtle in Heaven's May.
Tho' I tarry, wait for Me, trust Me, watch and pray.
Arise, come away, night is past and lo it is day,
25 My love, My sister, My spouse, thou shalt hear Me say.
Then I answered: Yea.

---

13   🔖 Mark for Review

How many speakers does the poem directly present?

(A) One

(B) Three

(C) Four

(D) Five

---

14   🔖 Mark for Review

"Laurel" and "bay" (line 5) are allusions to

(A) flowers highly prized for their rarity which bloom briefly and beautifully and then die

(B) leaves traditionally woven into wreaths to honor poets

(C) traditional symbols for Homer and Ovid, respectively

(D) traditional symbols for true faith and pious conduct, respectively

---

15   🔖 Mark for Review

Which of the following lines contains an image NOT echoed closely elsewhere in the poem?

(A) Line 6

(B) Line 7

(C) Line 13

(D) Line 14

GO ON TO THE NEXT PAGE.

16 ☐ Mark for Review

Which of the following choices best characterizes the speaker's attitude in each of the poem's three stanzas, respectively?

(A) Realization of death's inevitability; fear of physical decay; passive acceptance of what cannot be escaped

(B) Realization that death will come before one's ambitions have been achieved; dismay over the visible signs of physical decay; supplication for the healing powers of divine intervention

(C) Sorrow and mild surprise at the arrival of early death; deepening awareness of death's certainty; hopefulness for a place in the afterlife

(D) Acknowledgment of death's inevitability; understanding of the need to prepare oneself; happiness at the prospect of union with the divine

17 ☐ Mark for Review

In the context of the poem, "a moth is in thine array" (line 13) is intended to imply that the

(A) narrator's body is being consumed by cancer, or a cancer-like disease

(B) narrator's soul contains a destructive element which, unless the narrator takes some action, will render it unworthy of the afterlife

(C) narrator's soul is corrupted with sin that only death can purge

(D) narrator's soul is getting ready for decay

18 ☐ Mark for Review

Lines 15 and 16 ("At midnight . . . shall not delay:") suggest that

(A) the principal narrator's final hour will come, despite the small uncertainty of knowing exactly what hour that will be

(B) the bridegroom mentioned in line 16 will arrive at three distinct times

(C) the hour when a deadly illness first infects the principal narrator cannot be avoided

(D) a mysterious and evil stranger will arrive at some time between midnight and morning

19 ☐ Mark for Review

In the third stanza, "winter" can be taken to represent

(A) long disease

(B) earthly life

(C) the coldness of the grave

(D) aging and loss of vigor

GO ON TO THE NEXT PAGE.

20 ☐ Mark for Review

Which of the following statements most accurately characterizes the relationship of the imagery in the third stanza to that of the first and second stanzas?

(A) The third stanza weaves together the wedding-day imagery of the second stanza and the springtime imagery of the first stanza, thereby reconciling those earlier stanzas' differing views.

(B) Through its imagery, the third stanza further develops the themes which were advanced by the first stanza and then questioned by the second stanza.

(C) The third stanza echoes much of the first two stanzas' imagery, but recasts that imagery so that what earlier had been likened to decay is instead characterized as renewal.

(D) By echoing the imagery of the earlier stanzas, the third stanza reaffirms and repeats the views advanced by those stanzas.

21 ☐ Mark for Review

Line 16 ("Lo the bridegroom shall come and shall not delay:") provides an example of

(A) apostrophe

(B) enjambment

(C) personification

(D) mixed metaphor

22 ☐ Mark for Review

In context, the word "spray" (line 21) most nearly means

(A) tree

(B) blanket

(C) a small branch

(D) a liquid mist

23 ☐ Mark for Review

The grammatical subject of the sentence that begins at line 24 ("Arise, come away") is

(A) "Arise"

(B) "night is past and lo it is day"

(C) "My love, My sister, My spouse"

(D) "thou"

GO ON TO THE NEXT PAGE.

Questions 24 through 36 refer to the following. Read the following passage carefully before you choose your answers.

The selection is an excerpt from the novel Barchester Towers *by Anthony Trollope (the second book in the* Chronicles of Barsetshire *series), published in 1857.*

Par.

1   It is not my intention to breathe a word against Mrs Proudie, but still I cannot think that with all her virtues she adds much to her husband's happiness. The truth is that in matters domestic she rules supreme over her titular lord, and rules with a rod of iron. Nor is this all. Things domestic Dr Proudie might have abandoned to her, if not voluntarily, yet willingly. But Mrs Proudie is not satisfied with such home dominion, and stretches her power over all his movements, and will not even abstain from things spiritual. In fact, the bishop is henpecked.

2   The archdeacon's wife, in her happy home at Plumstead, knows how to assume the full privileges of her rank, and express her own mind in becoming tone and place. But Mrs Grantly's sway, if sway she has, is easy and beneficent. She never shames her husband; before the world she is a pattern of obedience; her voice is never loud, nor her looks sharp; doubtless she values power, and has not unsuccessfully striven to acquire it; but she knows what should be the limits of a woman's rule.

3   Not so Mrs Proudie. This lady is habitually authoritative to all, but to her poor husband she is despotic. Successful as has been his career in the eyes of the world, it would seem that in the eyes of his wife he is never right. All hope of defending himself has long passed from him; indeed, he rarely even attempts self-justification; and is aware that submission produces the nearest approach to peace which his own house can ever attain.

4   One other marked peculiarity in the character of the bishop's wife must be mentioned. Though not averse to the society and manners of the world, she is in her own way a religious woman; and the form in which this tendency shows itself is by a strict observance of Sabbatarian rule. Dissipation and low dresses during the week are, under her control, atoned for by three services, an evening sermon read by herself, and a perfect abstinence from any cheering employment on the Sunday. Unfortunately for those under her roof to whom the dissipation and low dresses are not extended, her servants namely and her husband, the compensating strictness of the Sabbath includes all. Woe betide the recreant housemaid who is found to have been listening to the honey of a sweetheart in the Regent's park, instead of the soul-stirring discourse of Mr Slope. Not only is she sent adrift, but she is so sent with a character, which leaves her little hope of a decent place. Woe betide the six-foot hero who escorts Mrs Proudie to her pew in red plush breeches, if he slips away to the neighbouring beer-shop, instead of falling in the back seat appropriated to his use. Mrs Proudie has the eyes of Argus for such offenders. Occasional drunkenness in the week may be overlooked, for six feet on low wages are hardly to be procured if the morals are always kept at a high pitch, but not even for grandeur or economy will Mrs Proudie forgive a desecration of the Sabbath.

---

24   ☐ Mark for Review

Which of the following descriptions is an example of the narrator's use of irony?

Ⓐ "It is not my intention to breathe a word against Mrs Proudie" (paragraph 1)

Ⓑ "the bishop is henpecked" (paragraph 1)

Ⓒ "doubtless she values power, and has not unsuccessfully striven to acquire it" (paragraph 2)

Ⓓ "it would seem in the eyes of his wife he is never right" (paragraph 3)

---

25   ☐ Mark for Review

Mrs. Proudie's authoritarian character is shown most pointedly in the phrase

Ⓐ "not satisfied with such home dominion" (paragraph 1)

Ⓑ "knows how to assume the full privileges of her rank" (paragraph 2)

Ⓒ "submission produces the nearest approach to peace" (paragraph 3)

Ⓓ "the soul-stirring discourse of Mr Slope" (paragraph 4)

GO ON TO THE NEXT PAGE.

26 ▢ Mark for Review

The use of the word "titular" in the sentence "The truth is that in matters domestic she rules supreme over her titular lord, and rules with a rod of iron" in paragraph 1 is an example of

Ⓐ hyperbole

Ⓑ metonym

Ⓒ onomatopoeia

Ⓓ irony

27 ▢ Mark for Review

In the context of the passage, the phrase "if not voluntarily, yet willingly" (paragraph 1) is used to show Dr. Proudie's attitude toward

Ⓐ the duties that the clergy are expected to assume

Ⓑ entering the institution of marriage

Ⓒ granting his wife some power

Ⓓ the hiring of domestic help

28 ▢ Mark for Review

The description of Mrs. Grantly serves to

Ⓐ provide another example of the power of the aristocracy

Ⓑ imply specific faults of Mrs. Proudie

Ⓒ suggest a rivalry between her and Mrs. Proudie

Ⓓ assert why women should be seen and not heard

29 ▢ Mark for Review

The narrator's attitude toward Mrs. Proudie can best be described as one of

Ⓐ pity

Ⓑ objectivity

Ⓒ emotional judgment

Ⓓ sardonic condemnation

30 ▢ Mark for Review

Which of the following best describes Dr. Proudie's relationship to his wife?

Ⓐ Morally devoted

Ⓑ Completely servile

Ⓒ Awkwardly tender

Ⓓ Thoroughly uxorious

31 ▢ Mark for Review

The author attributes Dr. Proudie's attitude and behavior most clearly to

Ⓐ ambition

Ⓑ pride

Ⓒ pacifism

Ⓓ spirituality

GO ON TO THE NEXT PAGE.

32 ▢ Mark for Review

In the context of paragraph 4, the word "character" in the sentence "Not only is she sent adrift, but she is so sent with a character, which leaves her little hope of a decent place" is best interpreted as meaning

(A) dubious personage

(B) reference

(C) antagonist

(D) conscience

33 ▢ Mark for Review

What is the effect of the repetition of the phrase "Woe betide . . ." in the final paragraph?

(A) It retards the tempo of the prose.

(B) It satirizes the fate of the servants.

(C) It highlights the drama of the situation.

(D) It changes the point of view of the narrator.

34 ▢ Mark for Review

In context, the adjective "recreant" in the sentence "Woe betide the recreant housemaid . . . listening to the honey of a sweetheart in the Regent's park, instead of the soul-stirring discourse of Mr Slope" (paragraph 4) is best interpreted as meaning

(A) unfaithful and disloyal

(B) engaging in a pastime

(C) refreshing

(D) craven and cowardly

35 ▢ Mark for Review

Which of the following best describes the effect of the last paragraph?

(A) It suggests a cause of Mrs. Proudie's moral transformation.

(B) It introduces Mr. Slope as an observer of Mrs. Proudie's actions.

(C) It counters speculations about Mrs. Proudie's character.

(D) It illustrates how Mrs. Proudie's religious beliefs reflect her character.

36 ▢ Mark for Review

The style of the passage as a whole can best be described as

(A) humorless and pedantic

(B) effusive and subjective

(C) descriptive and metaphorical

(D) witty and analytical

GO ON TO THE NEXT PAGE.

Questions 37 through 46 refer to the following. Read the following poem carefully before you choose your answers.

The following poem is called "In Excelsis." It was written by the poet Amy Lowell and published in 1922.

In Excelsis

You—you—
Your shadow is sunlight on a plate of silver;
Your footsteps, the seeding-place of lilies;
Your hands moving, a chime of bells across a windless air.
Line
5   The movement of your hands is the long, golden running of
      light from a rising sun;
   It is the hopping of birds upon a garden-path.

As the perfume of jonquils, you come forth in the morning.
Young horses are not more sudden than your thoughts,
10   Your words are bees about a pear-tree,
   Your fancies are the gold-and-black striped wasps buzzing
      among red apples.
   I drink your lips,
   I eat the whiteness of your hands and feet.
15   My mouth is open,
   As a new jar I am empty and open.
   Like white water are you who fill the cup of my mouth,
   Like a brook of water thronged with lilies.

You are frozen as the clouds,
20   You are far and sweet as the high clouds.
   I dare to reach to you,
   I dare to touch the rim of your brightness.
   I leap beyond the winds,
   I cry and shout,
25   For my throat is keen as is a sword
   Sharpened on a hone of ivory.
   My throat sings the joy of my eyes,
   The rushing gladness of my love.

How has the rainbow fallen upon my heart?
30   How have I snared the seas to lie in my fingers
   And caught the sky to be a cover for my head? How have you
      come to dwell with me,
   Compassing me with the four circles of your mystic
      lightness,
35   So that I say "Glory! Glory!" and bow before you
   As to a shrine?

Do I tease myself that morning is morning and a day after?
Do I think the air is a condescension,
The earth a politeness,
40   Heaven a boon deserving thanks?
   So you—air—earth—heaven—
   I do not thank you,
   I take you,
   I live.
45   And those things which I say in consequence
   Are rubies mortised in a gate of stone.

---

37 ☐ Mark for Review

The phrase "I drink your lips,/I eat the whiteness of your hands and feet" (lines 13–14) serves to

(A) describe the antagonistic interactions of the speaker and her subject

(B) point out the beauty of the poem's subject

(C) make clear that the speaker's relationship to her subject is more physically based than it is emotionally significant

(D) underscore the speaker's delight in the physical characteristics of her lover

38 ☐ Mark for Review

Which of the following best conveys the meaning in context of "How have I snared the seas to lie in my fingers/And caught the sky to be a cover for my head?" (lines 30–31)?

(A) The speaker is impressed with the physical feats she can perform now that her relationship has blossomed.

(B) The speaker cannot believe her good fortune at being in such a wonderful relationship.

(C) The sea and sky, representing the relationship, are protecting the speaker from harm.

(D) The speaker feels amazement at how beautiful the world around her looks because of the new perspective granted by her relationship with her lover.

GO ON TO THE NEXT PAGE.

39 ☐ Mark for Review

The use of repetition and punctuation in the first line of the poem could be interpreted to suggest

(A) the speaker's amazement at the existence of her subject

(B) the difficulty that the speaker has communicating with the poem's subject, even though they are in love

(C) the speaker's inability to make her sentiments clear

(D) the speaker's thoughts are being interrupted by everyday life or other concerns

40 ☐ Mark for Review

The speaker compares her beloved to all of the following EXCEPT

(A) the clouds

(B) bees buzzing among fruit

(C) heaven, the earth, and the air

(D) the perfume of flowers

41 ☐ Mark for Review

The third stanza of the poem principally suggests that

(A) the speaker of the poem is fragile, like a jar made out of pottery or glass

(B) the speaker is ready and waiting to receive the experiences and emotions that her relationship and/or her lover provides for her

(C) the speaker loves the flowers of which her lover reminds her

(D) the poem's speaker is similar to many of nature's treasures, such as the lilies in the brook

42 ☐ Mark for Review

Which word is a metaphor for the poem itself?

(A) Sun

(B) Perfume

(C) Morning

(D) Rubies

43 ☐ Mark for Review

Which stanza most suggests the religious level of devotion felt by the poem's speaker?

(A) 2

(B) 3

(C) 4

(D) 5

44 ☐ Mark for Review

"As the perfume of jonquils, you come forth in the morning" (line 8) is an example of

(A) personification

(B) metaphor

(C) simile

(D) metaphysical conceit

GO ON TO THE NEXT PAGE.

45 🔖 Mark for Review

The poem's final stanza suggests which of the following?

Ⓐ The speaker is thankful for the gift of heaven.

Ⓑ The speaker sees the elements of the earth in her lover.

Ⓒ The speaker's lover is similar to the morning.

Ⓓ The speaker values her lover more than rubies.

46 🔖 Mark for Review

The poem states or implies which of the following?

Ⓐ The speaker's lover is far away from her.

Ⓑ The speaker shows reverence for the natural world.

Ⓒ The speaker fears losing her lover to someone else.

Ⓓ The speaker believes that heaven is necessary to her well-being.

GO ON TO THE NEXT PAGE.

Questions 47 through 55 refer to the following. Read the following poem carefully before you choose your answers.

The poem "February" comes from the book Morning in the Burned House *and was published in 1995 by Margaret Atwood.*

February

Winter. Time to eat fat
and watch hockey. In the pewter mornings, the cat,
a black fur sausage with yellow
Line Houdini eyes, jumps up on the bed and tries
5   to get onto my head. It's his
way of telling whether or not I'm dead.
If I'm not, he wants to be scratched; if I am
He'll think of something. He settles
on my chest, breathing his breath
10   of burped-up meat and musty sofas,
purring like a washboard. Some other tomcat,
not yet a capon, has been spraying our front door,
declaring war. It's all about sex and territory,
which are what will finish us off
15   in the long run. Some cat owners around here
should snip a few testicles. If we wise
hominids were sensible, we'd do that too,
or eat our young, like sharks.
But it's love that does us in. Over and over
20   again, He shoots, he scores! and famine
crouches in the bedsheets, ambushing the pulsing
eiderdown, and the windchill factor hits
thirty below, and pollution pours
out of our chimneys to keep us warm.
25   February, month of despair,
with a skewered heart in the centre.
I think dire thoughts, and lust for French fries
with a splash of vinegar.
Cat, enough of your greedy whining
30   and your small pink bumhole.
Off my face! You're the life principle,
more or less, so get going
on a little optimism around here.
Get rid of death. Celebrate increase. Make it be spring.

---

47 ☐ Mark for Review

In the last line of the poem, the word "increase" is referring to

Ⓐ escalation

Ⓑ strength

Ⓒ intensification

Ⓓ growth

48 ☐ Mark for Review

The reference to "sharks" (line 18) is an example of

Ⓐ metonymy

Ⓑ apostrophe

Ⓒ personification

Ⓓ a simile

49 ☐ Mark for Review

In line 4, the word "Houdini" serves the purpose of

Ⓐ revealing the magic found in having pets

Ⓑ elaborating on the cat's animosity towards the interloper

Ⓒ emphasizing the striking appearance of the cat's eyes

Ⓓ accentuating the cat's mystical qualities

GO ON TO THE NEXT PAGE.

50 ☐ Mark for Review

Lines 25–26 most directly suggest that

(A) the narrator dreads February because of Valentine's Day

(B) the narrator finds the dead of winter to be a trying time

(C) paradoxically, life can sometimes emerge from death

(D) there is a natural cyclical pattern of renewal that the narrator has forgotten

51 ☐ Mark for Review

Overall, the speaker's attitude toward the subject of the poem is one of

(A) pessimism and impatience

(B) devotion and fear

(C) love and anger

(D) reverence and awe

52 ☐ Mark for Review

In lines 2–11, the relationship between the speaker and her cat is most directly implied to be

(A) a miserable coexistence

(B) one-sided on the narrator's part

(C) a necessary evil

(D) marked by begrudging affection

53 ☐ Mark for Review

In lines 27–28, the speaker

(A) reveals her struggles through thoughts of food

(B) loses herself in the experience of her meal

(C) is driven solely by her lust for food

(D) is unsure if she should indulge her craving

54 ☐ Mark for Review

Grammatically, the word "off" (line 31) functions as a

(A) noun

(B) adjective

(C) direct object

(D) verb

55 ☐ Mark for Review

Which of the following best describes the use of rhetorical devices in the poem?

(A) The author uses them to imply that the speaker is questioning the morality of pet ownership.

(B) The author uses them to emphasize how overwhelmed the speaker is.

(C) The author uses them to introduce new aspects of her characterization of her cat.

(D) The author uses them to convey the speaker's awe of the natural world.

STOP
END OF SECTION I

**IF YOU FINISH BEFORE TIME IS CALLED, YOU MAY CHECK YOUR WORK ON THIS SECTION.
DO NOT GO ON TO SECTION II UNTIL YOU ARE TOLD TO DO SO.**

AP® English Literature and Composition Exam

SECTION II: Free-Response Questions

At a Glance

Total Time
2 hours
Number of Questions
3
Percent of Total Grade
55%

Instructions

Section II has 3 free-response questions and lasts 2 hours.

This section of the exam requires answers in essay form. Each essay will be judged on its clarity and effectiveness in dealing with the assigned topic and on the quality of the writing. In responding to Question 3, select a work of fiction that will be appropriate to the question. Use a work that you are familiar with either from your AP English Literature and Composition class or from other literature you have previously read.

You may pace yourself as you answer the questions in this section, or you may use these optional timing recommendations:

It is suggested that you spend an equal amount of time, approximately 40 minutes, on each question.

You may use scratch paper for notes and planning, but credit will only be given for responses entered in this application. Text you enter as an annotation will not be included as part of your answer. You can go back and forth between questions in this section until time expires. The clock will turn red when 5 minutes remain—**the proctor will not give you any time updates or warnings.**

GO ON TO THE NEXT PAGE.

AP ENGLISH LITERATURE AND COMPOSITION

SECTION II

In the following poems, "To an infant" by Samuel Taylor Coleridge (1912) and "Infant Sorrow" by William Blake (1794), the speakers explore infancy. Read the poems carefully. Then, in a well-written essay, analyze how the authors use poetic elements and techniques such as imagery to reveal their attitudes toward infancy.

1 ☐ Mark for Review

In a well-written essay, analyze how the authors use poetic elements and techniques such as imagery to reveal their attitudes toward infancy.

In your response you should do the following:

- Respond to the prompt with a thesis that presents a defensible interpretation.
- Select and use evidence to support your line of reasoning.
- Explain how the evidence supports your line of reasoning.
- Use appropriate grammar and punctuation in communicating your argument.

To an Infant

Ah cease thy tears and sobs, my little life!
I did but snatch away the unclasped knife:
Some safer toy will soon arrest thine eye,
Line And to quick laughter change this peevish cry!
5 Poor stumbler on the rocky coast of woe,
Tutored by pain each source of pain to know!
Alike the foodful fruit and scorching fire
Awake thy eager grasp and young desire:
Alike the good, the ill offend thy sight,
10 And rouse the stormy sense of shrill affright!
Untaught, yet wise! mid all thy brief alarms
Thou closely clingest to thy mother's arms,
Nestling thy little face in that fond breast
Whose anxious heavings lull thee to thy rest!
15 Man's breathing miniature! thou mak'st me sigh—
A babe thou art—and such a thing am I!

To anger rapid and as soon appeased,
For trifles mourning and by trifles pleased;
Break friendship's mirror with a tetchy blow,
20 Yet snatch what coals of fire on pleasure's altar glow!
Oh thou that rearest with celestial aim
The future seraph in my mortal frame,
Thrice holy Faith! whatever thorns I meet
As on I totter with unpractised feet,
25 Still let me stretch my arms and cling to thee,
Meek nurse of souls through their long infancy!

Infant Sorrow

My mother groaned, my father wept;
Into the dangerous world I leapt,
Helpless, naked, piping loud,
Like a fiend hid in a cloud.
Line
5 Struggling in my father's hands,
Striving against my swaddling bands,
Bound and weary, I thought best
To sulk upon my mother's breast.

GO ON TO THE NEXT PAGE.

The following excerpt is from Tommy Orange's novel *There There* (2018). **Read the** passage carefully. Then, in a well written essay, analyze how the narrator uses literary elements and techniques to portray the **characters'** relationship to their environment.

Par.

1   Getting us to cities was supposed to be the final, necessary step in our assimilation, absorption, erasure, completion of a five-hundred-year-old genocidal campaign. But the city made us new, and we made it ours. We didn't get lost amidst the sprawl of tall buildings, the stream of anonymous masses, the ceaseless din of traffic. We found each other, started up Indian Centers, brought out our families and powwows, our dances, our songs, our beadwork. We bought and rented homes, slept on the streets, under freeways, we went to school, joined the armed forces, populated Indian bars in the Fruitvale in Oakland, and in the Mission in San Francisco. We lived in boxcar villages in Richmond. We made art and we made babies and we made way for our people to go back and forth between reservation and city. We did not move to cities to die. The sidewalks and streets, the concrete absorbed our heaviness. The glass, metal, rubber and wires, the speed, the hurtling masses—the city took us in. We were not Urban Indians then. This was part of the Indian Relocation Act, which was part of the Indian Termination Policy, which was and is exactly what it sounds like. Make them look and act like us. Become us. And so disappear. But it wasn't just like that. Plenty of us came by choice, to start over, to make money, or just for a new experience. Some of us came to cities to escape the reservation. We stayed after fighting in the second world war. After Vietnam too. We stayed because the city sounds like a war, and you can't leave a war once you've been, you can only keep it at bay—which is easier when you can see and hear it near you, that fast metal, that constant firing around you, cars up and down the streets and freeways like bullets. The quiet of the reservation, the side-of-the-highway towns, rural communities, that kind of silence just makes the sound of your brain on fire that much more pronounced.

2   Plenty of us are urban now. If not because we live in cities than because we live on the internet. Inside the high rise of multiple browser windows. They used to call us sidewalk Indians. Called us citified, superficial, inauthentic, cultureless refugees, apples. An apple is red on the outside and white on the inside. But what we are is what our ancestors did. How they survived. We are the memories we don't remember, that live in us, that we feel, that make us sing and dance and pray the way we do, feelings from memories that flare and bloom unexpectedly in our lives like blood through a blanket from a wound made by a bullet fired by a man shooting us in the back for our hair, for our heads, for a bounty, or just to get rid of us.

3   When they first came for us with their bullets, we didn't stop moving even though the bullets moved twice as fast as the sound of our screams, and even when their heat and speed broke our skin, shattered our bones, skulls, pierced our hearts, we kept on, even when we saw the bullets send our bodies flailing through the air like flags, like the many flags and buildings that went up in place of everything we knew this land to be before. The bullets were premonitions, ghosts from dreams of a hard fast future. The bullets moved on after moving through us, became the promise of what was to come, the speed and the killing, the hard fast lines of borders and buildings. They took everything and ground it down to dust as fine as gunpowder, they fired their guns into the air in victory and the strays flew out into the nothingness of histories written wrong and meant to be forgotten. Stray bullets and consequences are landing on our unsuspecting bodies even now.

---

2   🔖 Mark for Review

In a well written essay, analyze how the narrator uses literary elements and techniques to portray the characters' relationship to their environment.

In your response you should do the following:

- Respond to the prompt with a thesis that presents a defensible interpretation.
- Select and use evidence to support your line of reasoning.
- Explain how the evidence supports your line of reasoning.
- Use appropriate grammar and punctuation in communicating your argument.

GO ON TO THE NEXT PAGE.

In his satirical essay "Thoughts on Various Subjects, Moral and Diverting" (1706), Jonathan Swift wrote: "When a true genius appears in the world, you may know him by this sign, that the dunces are all in confederacy against him." Either from your own reading or from the list below, choose a work of fiction in which the main character finds himself in conflict with the social or moral values of his environment. Then, in a well-written essay, analyze how that tension contributes to an interpretation of the work as a whole. Do not merely summarize the plot."

The Age of Innocence
Americanah
The Bell Jar
The Bonesetter's Daughter
Breath, Eyes, Memory
Brighton Beach Memoirs
Ceremony
Cold Mountain
Death of a Salesman
Exit West
Great Expectations
Gulliver's Travels
Home
Homegoing
The Hummingbird's Daughter
Kindred
The Kite Runner
Lonely Londoners
The Mambo Kings Play Songs of Love
Mansfield Park
The Mill on the Floss
Mrs. Dalloway
My Ántonia
The Namesake
Native Son
Paradise Lost
The Piano Lesson
The Poisonwood Bible
Pudd'nhead Wilson
Pygmalion
Quicksand
The Return of the Native
The Scarlet Letter
Song of Solomon
Sons and Other Flammable Objects
The Sound and the Fury
The Tempest
Their Eyes Were Watching God
Where the Dead Sit Talking
Wuthering Heights

3 ☐ Mark for Review

In a well-written essay, analyze how the tension of a character in conflict with the social or moral values of his environment contributes to an interpretation of the work as a whole. Do not merely summarize the plot.

In your response you should do the following:

- Respond to the prompt with a thesis that presents a defensible interpretation.
- Provide evidence to support your line of reasoning.
- Explain how the evidence supports your line of reasoning.
- Use appropriate grammar and punctuation in communicating your argument.

STOP
END OF EXAM
IF YOU FINISH BEFORE TIME IS CALLED, YOU MAY CHECK YOUR WORK ON THIS SECTION.

Practice Test 3:
Answers and
Explanations

PRACTICE TEST 3 ANSWER KEY

1.	A	21.	C	41.	B
2.	B	22.	C	42.	D
3.	B	23.	D	43.	D
4.	B	24.	A	44.	C
5.	A	25.	C	45.	C
6.	A	26.	D	46.	D
7.	B	27.	C	47.	D
8.	D	28.	B	48.	D
9.	A	29.	D	49.	C
10.	B	30.	B	50.	B
11.	A	31.	C	51.	A
12.	A	32.	B	52.	D
13.	C	33.	C	53.	A
14.	B	34.	A	54.	D
15.	C	35.	C	55.	D
16.	D	36.	D		
17.	D	37.	D		
18.	A	38.	B		
19.	B	39.	A		
20.	C	40.	B		

PRACTICE TEST 3 EXPLANATIONS

SECTION I: MULTIPLE CHOICE

Questions 1–12

This passage is from *The Awakening* by Kate Chopin, published in 1899. It is considered an early feminist novel and delves into the themes of gender roles and social constraint.

1. **A** Like many questions on the exam, this question is essentially a sophisticated vocabulary question. The key to understanding it is to note the unpleasant noises made by the birds at the outset. There is no sense of the playfulness of whimsy, (B), and though it isn't a lighthearted start, it is too lively and raucous to be brooding, (C). There is no humor intended to be satirical, (D). It's all about the noise; (A) is correct.

2. **B** Although the passage is written in third person, there is a clear sense of Mr. Pontellier's distaste for his environment. He doesn't know what he wants, but it's not this. We do see an "exclamation of disgust" in the text, which might suggest volatility, (C). Though he may share some of the pettiness of the truly officious, (A), we do not see him as being particularly tidy, organized, or neat, nor do we see any signs of a fiery temper, so you can eliminate (C). Choice (D) can also be eliminated because he is transparent almost to a fault. Phrases like "expression and exclamation of disgust," along with the tendency for people to "cease to be entertaining," show his judgmental and intolerant nature.

3. **B** Though Mr. Pontellier does not seem particularly happy or comfortable in his environment, we have no reason to believe that this retreat at Grand Isle is anything but pleasant, so eliminate (A). At this point, we haven't been introduced to Robert or Mrs. Pontellier, which means (C) can be eliminated. And while there is initial annoyance at the various birds mentioned, this is not a consistent nature motif that goes beyond the beginning of the passage. Therefore, eliminate (D). The passage does depict Mr. Pontellier as being restless, unsatisfied, and out of place throughout, as exemplified by such words as "maddening," "restlessly," and referring to his "disgust" at his lack of "any degree of comfort." Choice (B) is the correct answer.

4. **B** The writers of the exam love to include words with many viable definitions and then ask the reader to choose the best one. This can be tricky if the word is used in an unconventional or dated manner as it is here. It is up to the reader to decipher the definition based on the context. In this situation, Mr. Pontellier is speaking about his time in New Orleans prior to arriving at Grand Isle. Choice (B) is the best option because it makes sense that he did not have time to read the paper prior to leaving the day before.

5. **A** Mr. Pontellier appears completely devoid of any meaningful connection to humanity. He doesn't hate people, but he doesn't seem to like anyone, either. He shows no signs of curiosity, (B), or warmth, (D), toward others, and his ambivalence toward his wife's friendship with Robert does not connote mistrust, (C). Indeed, people often "cease to be entertaining" to him, and he easily walks away from them when they become tiresome, making (A) the best answer.

6. **A** Though Mr. Pontellier doesn't seem to care much for humanity, he apparently takes pride in having robust children. We may hope that the children have the necessary thick skin to tolerate their father, but we do not know whether he is neglectful, so get rid of (B). We receive surprisingly little physical description of Mrs. Pontellier, so (C) is likely incorrect. Although Mr. Pontellier is portrayed as being of "medium height" and "slender build," we have no evidence that the children are not his, nor does he express any suspicion of this, so eliminate (D). To call his children "sturdy" is downright effusive coming from Mr. Pontellier, but it is the only possible answer. Choice (A) is correct.

7. **B** If you are stumped by the wording or intent of this question, you might be able to use your sense of diction to figure out the answer. One of these words is not like the others. Choice (A), smoke, implies something noxious or implies the presence of fire—neither of which is evident in Pontellier's depiction. Choice (C), gaunt, may describe his appearance somewhat but not his personality. Pontellier's use of "folly" gives us the impression that he wouldn't know a good time if it bit him, so eliminate (D). Choice (B) is correct.

8. **D** If you are familiar with this work already, you may be inclined to think (A) is correct. But in this passage, there is no evidence of any animosity on Mr. Pontellier's behalf toward Robert, so (A) is not true. He mocks the two adults for committing the "folly [of bathing] at such an hour in this heat." Eliminate (B). Mr. Pontellier's scolding of his wife and his judgment of her looks as "property that had suffered some damage" shows a complete lack of concern for his wife's health, so eliminate (C). This statement does, however, clearly illustrate contempt, and furthermore, his pride in having gone swimming at dawn shows how much he likes himself and congratulates himself for his choices—in other words, his self-righteousness. Therefore, (D) is the answer.

9. **A** Again, we have a literary term identification question. Onomatopoeia, (B), is a literary device in which a word imitates the sound it makes, like "crack" or "boom." Assonance, (C), uses vowel-sound repetition to create internal rhyme. Understatement, (D), occurs when a speaker uses less intensity or enthusiasm to express something than the occasion or feeling warrants. Mr. Pontellier's charged and scolding statements toward his wife are, essentially, the opposite of this. Hyperbole, (A), is exaggeration for effect, and, since Mr. Pontellier recognizes his wife and Robert, one can assume that they are not literally "burnt beyond recognition."

10. **B** The description of Mrs. Pontellier's "strong, shapely hands" does not make her sound unattractive, eliminating (A). There is no suggestion that Robert is uncomfortable around Mr. Pontellier, (C). In fact, Robert seems oblivious to him, focusing only on Mrs. Pontellier. The characterization of Mrs. Pontellier as a "piece of personal property" in her husband's eyes does not support the idea that she is the dominant one in their relationship, so (D) is incorrect. A strained relationship (B) is supported throughout the selection: in Mr. Pontellier's criticism and way of looking at his wife, in her trip to the beach with Robert and in her exchange of laughter with him.

11. **A** Once again, if you have read the novel, you could get into trouble here. Later on in *The Awakening*, there is quite a bit of passion, conflict, and secrecy, but none of this is evident in the opening chapter, eliminating (B) and (D). While the interactions between Mrs. Pontellier and Robert relegate Mr. Pontellier to awkward "third wheel" status, the slowness of their stroll from the water, the way they sit facing each other, and the "answering smile" she gives Robert all indicate a closeness that eliminates (C), leaving (A) as the answer.

12. **A** Though Mr. Pontellier seems to criticize nearly everyone and everything, he does not extend this attitude toward his children, so (B) cannot be true. On the contrary, though Mr. Pontellier does not allow his children to follow him to Klein's, he does "kiss them and promise to bring them back bonbons and peanuts." If Pontellier is concerned about his wife's friendship with Robert, he certainly doesn't show it. Instead, he encourages his wife to spend time with him until "he bores you." Therefore, (C) is incorrect, as he doesn't fear Robert. While loathing small talk might be in line with his character, there is no evidence that Mr. Pontellier does so in paragraphs 13 and 14. Eliminate (D). When his wife asks him whether he'll be returning for dinner, his response is very indicative of his character and thus his attitude toward his marriage: he shrugs. This means that (A) is the answer.

Questions 13–23

The passage is by Christina Rossetti (1830–1894) and was written when she was in her early thirties. The poem's spiritual, death-haunted theme is typical of Rossetti, who was beset with ill health her entire, and relatively long, life.

The Rossettis, Christina and her brothers, William Michael and Dante Gabriel, were at the center of an influential mid-19th-century arts movement called the Pre-Raphaelite Brotherhood. Pre-Raphaelite painting and writing were concerned with medieval themes, romance (often tinged with self-destruction or death), nature, nostalgia, vivid imagery, and color.

Christina's brother Dante (arguably the leader of the Pre-Raphaelite movement) is guilty of one of the truly cheese-ball acts of narcissism in literary history. When Dante Gabriel Rossetti's wife died, the painter-poet buried the manuscripts of several of his poems in the casket with her. Ah, love. Seven years later he decided maybe it wasn't such a good idea and had the mess dug up so he could get his poems back. The last laugh, however, is on Dante, whose reputation is waning. His sister Christina, however, has acquired a growing respect from the literary world after many years spent in her brother's shadow.

The poem on the test (like almost everything Christina Rossetti wrote) is a meditation on the transience of life and the inevitability of death. When, in the third stanza, God promises to come for the poet when her hour arrives, the poem becomes an avowal of faith.

Although the bulk of the poem's meaning is accessible to most readers, the questions asked on the test lay several traps for the unwary. When reading and interpreting poetry, be on guard against making assumptions that can't be justified. Several questions have incorrect choices that suggest the principal narrator is on her deathbed. You should not reason that the poem's intense contemplation of death indicates the speaker is gravely ill or about to die; those are unwarranted assumptions. Do not assume or infer anything that is not very close to what is actually written in the passage. (And this goes for reading sections on any standardized test!)

Another difficulty you face when answering the questions on the Rossetti passage is that the questions ask about some of the poem's subtler points. There are several questions, for example, about the important shift in the recurrent nature imagery in the poem's final stanza. Complications also rise from the presence of multiple speakers in the poem.

This long-standing tradition of conversing with the spiritual forces of the cosmos may seem a hopelessly old-fashioned device, but poets up to the present day continue to create interesting and important works using this convention. The Rossetti poem, however, not only has the speaker in dialogue with the metaphysical world, but also takes matters a degree further in the second stanza by having the Soul speak with the voice of the past. Following the line "Hearken what the past doth witness and say:" the Soul presents what the past has to say about human mortality. You needed to understand that in this stanza the past is *not* being directly presented as a speaker. In fact, the past is probably not even being quoted; the Soul is interpreting the past for the benefit of the principal narrator. This is a tangled piece of rhetorical construction and causes most students some problems.

Overall, the passage, taken together with its questions, is at the difficult end of the spectrum of work you will see on the AP English Literature and Composition Exam.

13. **C** As noted in the passage description, this is a tough question. Most students choose (D), five. But the past is not a speaker. The past is being interpreted for the principal narrator by the Soul. Another choice that sophisticated readers sometimes pick is (A), one. The reasoning behind choosing (A) is usually that only the poet is speaking; the Soul, World, and God represent elements and ideas within the poet. In this reading, the poem is a kind of internal monologue in which the poet sorts out her feelings about death and the afterlife. This interpretation is absolutely plausible. (Rossetti certainly did not intend for you to think she had actually held a conversation with the World or with God.) The problem is that it is an *interpretation*. The question asks, "How many speakers does the poem directly present?" The emphasis is on what the poem presents, not what the poem might suggest. The question is not asking for an interpretation but simply for what the poem presents. It presents four speakers, so (C) is the correct answer.

14. **B** This is one of the relatively rare knowledge questions on the test. You either know it or you don't. Eighty to ninety percent of the test is about your ability to understand the material you read, both the details and the larger picture. But there are some facts that the test-writers feel they can expect you know. They expect you to know the basic terminology of literary criticism and form (for example: simile, metaphor, couplet), and they occasionally ask about those literary historical references a well-read individual should recognize. This question is an example of the latter.

In ancient Greek and Roman society, a garland of laurel and bay leaves was awarded in recognition of triumph in sports, war, or poetry. The original "gold medal" of the Olympics was a laurel wreath, as is that wreath you always see framing Julius Caesar's bald pate. The reason the answer specifically mentions poets is that laurel (bay is a variety of laurel) was the symbolic flower of Apollo, patron God of poetry. Even today, when people are honored as the national poet, their title is *poet laureate*. Speaking of honors, graduation from college with a bachelor's degree will mean that you have earned your bacca*laureate*, a term derived from the medieval university tradition of crowning graduates with laurel.

15. **C** The incorrect answers all make use of imagery that draws on living things, especially plants, and of the changing seasons. In line 13, the image of "Rust in thy gold" is the one image of the poem that draws neither on the seasons nor on living things.

16. **D** The key to answering this question correctly is Process of Elimination (POE). Be methodical by checking each of the answer choices' explanation with the first stanza. This should help you get rid of (C), since a surprise does not seem to be found in the stanza. Choice (A)'s explanation of the second stanza doesn't fit, so you can eliminate it right there. Choice, (D), with its expression of happiness, fits the third stanza better than (B), in which "supplication for divine intervention" doesn't adequately convey the idea that the speaker in the stanza is actually God.

17. **D** The question shouldn't have given you too much trouble. Basically, you were asked what "a moth in thine array" is meant to signify metaphorically. The image is yet one more description of the natural aging process. The incorrect choices offer various misreadings, either seeing illness where none is present or spiritual anxieties that neither the line in question, nor the poem as a whole, is concerned with.

18. **A** Understanding the lines in question is not as much about the lines themselves as it is about letting them make sense in the overall context of the poem. If you understood the bulk of the poem, then this question shouldn't have been difficult. If the poem itself gave you trouble, this question might have as well. The incorrect choices offer various misreadings and overinterpretations. Don't get too bogged down. Try Process of Elimination, and if you're still stuck, take a guess and move on.

19. **B** Always return to the passage. The third stanza presents a dramatic reversal in the poem's meaning and direction by refiguring imagery from the previous stanzas with an antithetical meaning. In the first two stanzas, Spring and the imagery of spring are used to represent youth, energy, and life. You might easily think, then, that Winter, as Spring's opposite, represents aging and loss of vigor, (D), or perhaps the coldness of the grave, (C), that is, death itself. But the question asks for the meaning of Winter in the *third* stanza. In this stanza God says that now "Winter passeth after the long delay." What follows are images of spring now clearly tied to death and the afterlife. Spring in the final stanza is a metaphor for the joy of reunion with God. In the final stanza, God offers death as a joyous, spring-like occasion. It is earthly life, separate from the Maker, which is the long Winter (B).

20. **C** As with all questions with longer answers, you must read carefully and eliminate when an answer is partially correct. "Partially correct" is what we call "half wrong," and as you know, "half wrong = all wrong." Otherwise, the reasoning behind this question is fully covered in the explanation to question 19.

21. **C** This is another terminology question. If it gave you any trouble, refer to our glossary of literary terms for the AP English Literature and Composition Exam. Also, remember to use Process of Elimination to get rid of those answers you are sure are wrong and guess with what is left. No blanks!

22. **C** This is essentially a vocabulary question, but chances are you were unfamiliar with the passage's usage of the word "spray." Figure out the meaning from the context. None of the incorrect answer choices makes sense in context except possibly (A), and we hope that between (A) and (C), you chose (C).

23. **D** You are certain to see a question (or two or three) like this one on your test. If you got this question wrong, brush up on your skills with our section on grammar for the AP English Literature and Composition Exam (pages 95–96). As outlined in that section, the best way to figure out the construction of the kind of sentence the test-writers like to ask about is to rewrite the sentence (in your mind—you shouldn't need to actually write it down) into a more natural form. The sentences are never straightforward "subject, verb, direct-object, indirect object" sentences like "Jack threw the ball to me." The sentence that begins on line 24, "Arise, come away, night is past and lo it is day,/ My love, My sister, My spouse, thou shalt hear Me say," should be rewritten:

"Thou shalt hear me say, 'Arise, come away, night is past and lo it is day,

   My love, My sister, My spouse.'"

Notice we've put quotation marks around what God reports he will say. This is how the sentence would normally be punctuated. If you rewrite it in this manner, you should be able to see that "Thou" is the subject, so (D) is your answer.

Questions 24–36

This passage is from Anthony Trollope's novel *Barchester Towers*, the second of his Barsetshire novels. It was written in 1857 and, unlike many Victorian novels, was more concerned with the topics of the day than the recent past. However, like the Victorian prose you are apt to see on the test, the sentences can be somewhat convoluted, with multiple negations and other forms of twisted syntax. Tone isn't always easy to discern. Close reading is essential.

24. **A** The narrator states, "It is not my intention to breathe a word against Mrs Proudie," but then spends several paragraphs doing just that. Choice (B) is a colloquialism derived from figurative language describing a domineering wife. Because domineering is precisely what Mrs. Proudie is said to be, there is no irony here. Choice (C) is the juxtaposition of Mrs. Grantly, the archdeacon's wife, but there isn't enough said about her to know if this is ironic or not. Choice (D) might be construed as hyperbole, but it certainly is not the opposite of the author's intended meaning.

25. **C** Although (C) describes Dr. Proudie, it does so in the context of how Mrs. Proudie's despotic behavior has cowed him. While tempting, (A) refers much more closely to Mrs. Proudie's ambitions and how they extend beyond the normal sphere of the wife of a bishop. Choice (B) refers to Mrs. Grantly, not Mrs. Proudie. Choice (D) refers to something Mrs. Proudie expects those under her roof to submit to, but it is not as pointed an example of her authoritarian nature as (C) is.

26. **D**   Dr. Proudie is, in name, or title ("titular"), the lord of Mrs. Proudie but, as the passage explains in great depth, it is Mrs. Proudie, in actuality, who lords over her husband. The situation is the opposite of what it is in name and that is a stellar example of irony (D). Hyperbole is exaggeration, which does not apply here, so eliminate (A). Choice (B) does the same thing, but with a fancier word. Choice (C) might appeal to a student who knows that onomatopoeia has something to do with how words sound, and "titular" does sound funny—but it's not a noun or verb, so it can't really sound like the noise made by the thing it describes.

27. **C**   The phrase states that in domestic matters, he would not have offered the power to his wife but was happy to cede it. Choices (B) and (D) are based on careless reading of the phrases "domestic" or the vague memory that the passage was about his marriage. Choice (A) takes deceptive language from elsewhere in the passage.

28. **B**   In the context of the passage, which is devoted to describing Mrs. Proudie's character, the example of Mrs. Grantly, the archdeacon's wife, is used to describe Mrs. Proudie by contrast. Mrs. Grantly's virtues are laid out, and the transition into the subsequent paragraph, "Not so Mrs Proudie," makes the author's intention clear. Choice (A) is a trap answer designed to snare the careless reader who sees the words "the full privileges of her rank," which actually pertain to her role as a clergyman's wife. Choice (C) is probably the most evil of all trap answers, one designed to catch the rare student who may have read this novel or its sequels—in particular, *Framley Parsonage*, in which the rivalry of Mrs. Grantly and Mrs. Proudie is given substantial attention. It certainly is not the author's intention to suggest a rivalry, although he may have intended to foreshadow it. Choice (D) has some merit. From the description of Mrs. Grantly, it certainly seems as if the author favors women who exert their power domestically and privately. The passage states, "before the world she is a pattern of obedience; her voice is never loud . . . she knows what should be the limits of a woman's rule." Nevertheless, the language in the answer choice, "assert why women should be seen and not heard," suggests that the author provides evidence for a position stronger than the one he actually takes.

29. **D**   Choice (A), pity, is best used to describe how the author feels toward Dr. Proudie, "her poor husband." Although the narrator may feign an appearance of objectivity, his opening comments make it clear that what he presents is his subjective opinion, so eliminate (B). Given that, (C), emotional judgment, might be tempting, but his language is strong enough to justify (D), sardonic condemnation. He is certainly mocking Mrs. Proudie, and his judgment of her does condemn her behavior.

30. **B**   We do not get a sense of Dr. Proudie's devotion to his wife or of his moral compass, no matter what we might want to infer from knowing his profession, so (A) is out. Choice (B) is supported by the text of the third paragraph. Choices (C) and (D) suggest a happy and loving marriage, not the picture painted by this paragraph.

31. **C**   He is described as "aware that submission produces the nearest approach to peace which his own house can ever attain." Choice (A) refers most nearly to a quality best attributed to Mrs. Proudie. Choice (B) is not supported by the text. Choice (D) is a trap answer for those who read quickly and saw that the passage was about the clergy and religious matters.

32.　**B**　Even if you weren't familiar with the Victorian use of "character" as shorthand for "character refer-ence," you could derive the meaning from the context of the passage—the maid has been dismissed and because of this "character," she is unable to find decent employment. Choices (A), (C), and (D) all prey on a reader's familiarity with the dictionary definitions of the word, as opposed to the contextual meaning.

33.　**C**　The repetition of the phrase "Woe betide" accentuates the seriousness of the servants' situation. It nei-ther slows down the prose, as in (A), nor satirizes or mocks the servants' fate, as in (B). The phrase is consistent with the narrator's attitude throughout the rest of the passage, so (D) is incorrect.

34.　**A**　The maid in question has been unfaithful to her duty. As is par for the course on a single phrase or word question, the primary dictionary definition, (D), is offered as an answer choice, as is a word it kind of sounds like, (B). The other choices have no merit whatsoever.

35.　**C**　The point of the paragraph is to illustrate Mrs. Proudie's hypocrisy. The paragraph does so by showing how strict she is in applying the rules to others when it comes to this single point of religious belief, although she is given to "[d]issipation and low dresses" the rest of the time. Choice (A) might be tempting because of the religious aspect, but in no place does this paragraph suggest a transformation for the domineering Mrs. Proudie. Choice (B) also has its merits, as this paragraph is where Mr. Slope is intro-duced, but no mention is made of him observing Mrs. Proudie (quite the contrary, one is expected to observe Mr. Slope). For similar reasons, the mention of religion, (D), might be attractive but as men-tioned above, it doesn't counter speculation about her despotic reign.

36.　**D**　The author analyzes Mrs. Proudie in an amusing way, mocking her cleverly by first pointing out her flaws in contrast to a social equivalent, and then by exposing her hypocrisy. Most of the other answers fall into the half-right, half-wrong category, and using Process of Elimination will save the day here. Choice (A) is wrong on both counts—the passage is neither humorless nor pedantic. Although the passage is certainly subjective, it is hardly emotional, so as long as you know the definition of effusive, you can eliminate (B). Choice (C) starts out stronger; the passage is certainly descriptive. Alas, a few metaphors do not a metaphorical passage make. If you chose (C) or even kept it on your first pass through the answer choices, don't kick yourself. Close answer choices are one of the ways a question can be made more challenging.

Questions 37–46

This poem was written in 1922 by Amy Lowell, one of the leading female poets of her day, who was known for her frank and emotion-filled depictions of relationships and sensual love, and for being at the forefront of imagism, a literary movement of the early 20th century.

Amy Lowell has sparked recent critical interest because of her interesting use of language and sensual themes. The title ("In Excelsis") refers to the Latin exclamation of praise that is a part of the Catholic Mass. In this poem, the rejoicing is due to the speaker's lover, whom she talks about throughout. A challenging part of this poem is keeping track of what Lowell is referring to with each of her many uses of figurative language, particularly simile and metaphor. If you've done that successfully, you probably won't have too much trouble with most of the questions. Using Process of Elimination carefully will definitely help you spot the small differences between answer choices that are often key to picking the correct one.

37. **D** The interactions cannot be described as antagonistic, so eliminate (A). The other choices look temping because they all have to do with the physicality of the speaker's lover, who is the subject of the poem. However, you can't justify the idea that the relationship is more physical than emotional—that's too much reading into the lines. Eliminate (C). Choices (B) and (D) are similar, but the lines go beyond pointing out the beauty and, with their action verbs ("eat" and "drink"), imply that the speaker is having some interaction or feeling about the physicality of the person she's talking about. That makes (D) the better answer, but this is definitely a tough one!

38. **B** The meaning of the given phrase is actually fairly straightforward, so the key is to not read too much into it. Choice (A) is a bit too literal an interpretation. Choice (D) is certainly a possible interpretation, but it strays a bit far from the words themselves—it might be appropriate to write in an essay, but not in a multiple-choice question. Choice (C), with its interest in the physical world (the sea and sky) is a bit too literal again, just like (A).

39. **A** The speaker repeats "you" with a dash like that almost as if she can't believe that her lover even exists, and this fits tonally as well as in terms of the content with the rest of the poem. (Remember to keep your answers consistent!) No difficulty, (B), or inability, (C), is expressed anywhere else, and while the use of the dashes might suggest (D), there's no evidence for that in the poem either.

40. **B** This question requires a bit of close reading. Choices (A) and (D) were probably fairly easy for you to spot (and, therefore, to eliminate, since we're looking for the thing that is NOT supported by the passage here!). However, eliminating (C) requires an understanding of the last stanza, in which the comparison made is less obvious: The speaker draws that comparison to say that her lover is as necessary to her as those other things which one takes for granted. Choice (B), by the way, is a comparison drawn in the poem, but it's a comparison to the lover's "fancies," or ideas, not to a lover's personal characteristics, so it is the odd one out.

41. **B** The speaker is comparing herself to a jar that will be filled, which fits with the language of (B). The same comparison is mentioned in (A), but that choice gets the point of the comparison wrong. Choice (C) is not supported by the passage. Choice (D) looks good, except that it's the subject of the poem, not the speaker, who is referred to with those comparisons. Make sure you read the answer choices as carefully as you do the poem!

42. **D** All of the choices are metaphors used in the poem, but (A), (B), and (C) are all about either the speaker's lover or her relationship. Choice (D) gets at the thrust of that last stanza: it's the "things which [she] say[s]" that are compared to rubies—and the poem itself is what she's saying.

43. **D** The use of the word "shrine," at which the speaker will kneel, is your major clue here (stanza 5). The other stanzas suggest devotion, certainly, but other than the title and maybe some coded references to Jesus imagery (which the test won't expect you to pick up on), there's nothing else here that's religious.

44. **C** This question relies on your knowledge of the terms in the glossary, so study them if you had trouble. Since this is a comparison using the word "as," it is a simile, not any of the other terms listed. Choice (D), a metaphysical conceit, would be associated with John Donne and his era, and because this poem was written in the 20th century, it definitely doesn't apply.

45. **C** Choice (A) is untrue: the speaker is actually using heaven as an example of something she takes for granted, rather than something she is thankful for. Rule out (A). Similarly, you can rule out (B) and (D), which recycle words like "earth" and "rubies" from the last stanza but do not match the theme. Choice (C) is correct in that neither the morning nor her lover is something that the author feels the need to thank the universe for: they're both simply things she needs to survive. The correct answer is (C).

46. **D** Consistency of Answers (see Chapter 4) should help you identify (D) as correct, especially at this point when you've done so many questions in this passage. Choice (B) looks tempting, but it mixes up parts of the passage: it's her lover that the speaker is reverential toward, not nature. Choice (A) might also look good, but it refers to a figurative, not literal, idea expressed in the poem. Her lover isn't really as far away as the high clouds. In fact, we don't know that the lover is actually any place in particular at all. Therefore, (D) is the answer.

Questions 47–55

This is a poem by Margaret Atwood, an award-winning Canadian poet, novelist, teacher, and environmentalist. She is wildly prolific and known in present times most famously for her book *The Handmaid's Tale*, which was made into a popular television show. This poem, "February," was published in her poetry collection *Morning in the Burned House* (1995). It is an exploration of sexual repression and the cold of winter months through the use of an annoying, needy, cat and the promise of Spring.

47. **D** Based on the context of the last line of the poem, "increase" will be the opposite of "death" and result in something like "spring." Choice (D), growth, is the correct answer.

48. **D** Metonymy, (A), is a thing or concept that is not called by its own name, but by the name of something intimately associated with that thing or concept. Apostrophe, (B), is a literary device in which a speaker addresses a person or object in a rhetorical manner, not expecting an answer. In this case, the narrator was not addressing the sharks directly. Had the sharks been referred to as "doing" something human, then personification, (C), would be correct. As it is, "sharks" are used to refer to their practice of eating their young in a hyperbolic suggestion that humans also try it, an example of a simile. The correct answer is (D).

49. **C** "Houdini eyes" is a reference to Harry Houdini, an early 20th century magician known for his sensational escape acts. (A) and (D) are both traps related to Houdini's "magic," but the phrase is simply a descriptor for the cat's appearance, or (C). Eliminate (B), as the description does not reference any "animosity" on the part of the cat. The correct answer is (C).

50. **B** The lines in question here, "February, month of despair, with a skewered heart in the centre," show the narrator's winter struggle punctuated by Valentine's Day. While (A) is tempting, it goes beyond the scope of the text. Choice (B) is an appropriate match, but (A), (C), and (D) go beyond the scope of the text. The correct answer is (B).

51. **A** Whether the subject is February, dead of winter, or the kitty cat that the speaker addresses, the speaker pretty clearly demonstrates "pessimism and impatience." Some examples: interpreting the cat's motives to be as base as "telling whether or not [the narrator is] dead," directing the cat to "get going on a little optimism," or the claim the narrator "think[s] dire thoughts." Eliminate (B), (C), and (D) for being too positive. The correct answer is (A).

52. **D** In lines 2–11, the narrator details how the cat "jumps up on the bed," "wants to be scratched," and "settles on [the narrator's] chest." While the narrator does include complaints about the cat, she ultimately allows all of the cat's attempts to be close to her, which matches (D). Eliminate (A) for miserable, (B) for one-sided, and (C) for evil. The correct answer is (D).

53. **A** In lines 27–28, the narrator's "dire thoughts" are much more significant than her food cravings are. To claim that she "loses herself" or is "driven solely" by food goes beyond the scope of the text, so eliminate (B) and (C). Similarly, there is no indication of how the narrator feels about the food, so eliminate (D). The correct answer is (A).

54. **D** While "off" usually functions as an adjective, adverb, or preposition, in this case, it takes the place of the verb in the implicit command for the cat to "[get] off my face!" Therefore, (D) is correct.

55. **D** Choice (B) is close to being correct, but "overwhelmed" is a little too strong to be adequately supported by the poem. The other answer choices are all based on various misreadings: Choice (A) makes too much of the poem's religious references, (C) may be true of some of the rhetorical devices but not all of them. The correct answer is (D).

SECTION II: FREE RESPONSE

Rubric—1 + 4 + 1 = 6 pts

A. Thesis (0–1 pts)
  o Responds to the prompt with a thesis that presents a defensible interpretation of the selected work.
B. Evidence and Commentary (0–4 pts)
  o Evidence: Provides specific evidence to support all claims in a line of reasoning.
  o Commentary: Consistently explains how the evidence supports a line of reasoning.
  o Explains how multiple literary elements or techniques in the poem contribute to its meaning.
C. Sophistication (0–1 pts)
  o Demonstrates sophistication of thought and/or develops a complex literary argument.

How to Score 6 points

Use The Idea Machine! The questions listed below will direct your reading to the material needed to write an essay.

The Idea Machine

1. What is the meaning of the work?
   a. What is the literal, face-value meaning of the work?
   b. What feeling (or feelings) does the work evoke?
2. How does the author get that meaning across?
   a. What are the important images in the work and what do those images suggest?
   b. What specific words or short phrases produce the strongest feelings?
   c. What do the characters, setting, structure, or narrators tell you about the passage?

Question 1—Poetry Analysis

- What is the meaning of the work?
  - Literal meaning:
    - "To an Infant": The speaker relates to the infant and wishes for a parent figure
    - "Infant Sorrow": Upon entering the dangerous world, the infant feels intense emotions.
  - Feelings conveyed:
    - "To an Infant": overcome with emotions, delight, desire, helplessness
    - "Infant Sorrow": anxiety, overwhelm, exhaustion

- How does the author get that meaning across?
  - Images and phrases to underline:
    - "To an Infant":
      - "Ah cease thy tears and sobs, my little life"
      - "As I totter on with unpracticed feet"
    - "Infant Sorrow":
      - "Into the dangerous world I leapt, / Helpless, naked, piping loud"
      - "Struggling in my father's hands, / Striving against my swaddling bands"
  - What do those phrases suggest?
    - "To an Infant": a parallel between the speaker and the infant
    - "Infant Sorrow": an emphasis on the harsh reality of being born
  - What do the characters, setting, structure, or narrators tell you about the passage?
    - Speaker:
      - "To an Infant": The speaker is relating to the infant
      - "Infant Sorrow": The speaker is an infant
    - Setting:
      - "To an Infant": The speaker only describes watching the infant; it is as if the setting of this event falls away and there is only the infant acting as a newborn would.
      - "Infant Sorrow": The world as it is seen for the first time and how startling it can be
    - Structure:
      - "To an Infant": Three stanzas. The first ends with a comparison between the infant and the speaker, the next stanza details their similarities, and the third stanza illustrates the longing the speaker feels to receive the same treatment as the infant.
      - "Infant Sorrow": Two stanzas. The first describes the shocking event of the infant's birth; the second describes the child's reaction to the world.

Sample first paragraph

Both Samuel Taylor Coleridge's "To An Infant" and William Blake's "Infant Sorrow" are, at the heart of them, poems about babies. Blake's poem is forceful in tone: its few lines describe the birth of the speaker as an intense experience, showing the speaker leaping "Into the dangerous world . . . / Helpless, naked, piping loud." The baby is shown to struggle and strive before becoming tired and "sulking upon my mother's breast." While pithy, it provides a powerful image of the difficult experience of meeting the world for the first time. Coleridge's poem, on the other hand, starts with a delighted tone, as the speaker observes a baby doing the weird things babies do—but then evolves into self-reflection. Saying "A babe thou art—and such a thing am I," the speaker reflects on the ways he is like a baby, and then expresses the desire for a parent figure as a religious plea: "Still let me stretch my arms and cling to thee, / Meek nurse of souls through their long infancy!" Whereas Blake is most concerned with the emotions and experience of the baby, Coleridge finds philosophical satisfaction in turning observations of the baby into religious allegory.

Question 2—Prose Fiction Analysis

- What is the meaning of the work?
  - Literal meaning:
    - We (Native Americans) were sent to the cities to assimilate, but instead we preserved our culture. We also came for other reasons.
    - We've been insulted for being inauthentic and cultureless, but we preserve in ourselves even the memories we don't remember.
    - The colonizers came and killed us and took the land and made it unrecognizable to us: the bullets they killed us with were premonitions of the modern reality.
  - Feelings conveyed: perseverance, defiance, pain
- How does the author get that meaning across?
  - Images and phrases to underline:
    - "our assimilation, absorption, erasure, completion of a five-hundred-year-old genocidal campaign"
    - "We didn't get lost amidst the sprawl of tall buildings, the stream of anonymous masses, the ceaseless din of traffic"
    - "The glass, metal, rubber and wires, the speed, the hurtling masses"
    - "This was part of the Indian Relocation Act, which was part of the Indian Termination Policy, which was and is exactly what it sounds like."
    - "We did not move to cities to die."
    - "even when we saw the bullets send our bodies flailing through the air like . . . the many flags and buildings that went up in place of everything we knew this land to be before"
  - What do those phrases suggest?
    - Acknowledgment of brutal truths; descriptions of the overwhelming aspects of cities
    - A comparison of traumatic generational memory to the bullets with which Native Americans were shot when scalping was still practiced
    - The bullet motif recurs, connecting the violence done against Native Americans to the concurrent cultural erasure
  - What do the characters, setting, structure, or narrators tell you about the passage?
    - Narrator: Narrator refers to their community as a unit: "we" and "us."
    - Setting: The industrial and cold description of the city is in opposition with the liveliness of Indian Centers.
    - Structure: Begins with the trauma inflicted on Native Americans by relocating them to cities, progresses to illustrate the larger trauma of colonialism, and explores how the past does not stay in the past, but rather is forever.

Sample first paragraph

Seeing an environment through the eyes of a group of people forced into it is necessarily a different take than that of those who chose it. Tommy Orange speaks for Native Americans in *There There*, and presents a picture of a people who are aware of the brutality they were subjected to, who persevered, and who preserved what they could of their culture even through multiple eras of violence. Whereas most of the description in the passage is of Native Americans in the modern era being relocated to cities (a physical setting), a constant motif runs through the passage alluding to the bullets that were "fired by a man shooting us in the back for our hair, for our heads, for a bounty, or just to get rid of us," an allusion to the earlier practice of scalping that is a potent symbol of the many kinds of violence done against Native Americans in the U.S. (the deeper cultural setting). The author uses this powerful imagery and some brutal truths to show us the pain, perseverance, and defiance of a people who continue to refuse to leave their culture behind.

Question 3—Literary Argument

(This example uses Mohsin Hamid's *Exit West*.)

- What is the meaning of the work?
  - Literal meaning:
    - The novel explores all of the aspects of life that are affected by migration. It uses the doors to represent emigration: what it means to leave everything and everyone you know for a future you cannot yet imagine.
- How does the author get that meaning across?
  - Major themes in the work:
    - What it means to be free, human connection, love, opportunity
  - Theme related to the question: Morality
    - As the novel progresses, Saeed finds himself drifting apart from Nadia. Saeed once admired Nadia's independence but grows to resent it in response to their changing environment. Saeed's morals are different from Nadia's and he judges her for it, which in part leads to their separation.
  - Important scenes/imagery:
    - Saeed resents Nadia for wearing her robe because she does not wear it for the reasons he feels she should. Saeed feels the robe represents a respect for religion and culture; Nadia wears it to maintain her independence by keeping others at a distance.
    - Once Nadia and Saeed travel through the door, their relationship changes forever. Saeed no longer talks to Nadia the way he once did because his beliefs and how he sees the world are tied to his morals. Because Nadia does not share his beliefs, he keeps this part of himself from her.

Sample first paragraph

Mohsin Hamid's *Exit West* tells the story of two characters falling in and then out of love. As the environment around Saeed and Nadia changes, so does their relationship to each other. In their home country, Saeed and Nadia are made closer by their differences. Saeed admires Nadia's independence while she admires how he sees their world. As the two immigrate through the doors, altering their environment in a search for freedom and safety, they alter their relationship forever. Now, in an unfamiliar place, their difference of morals creates a growing divide between them. Saeed finds himself resenting Nadia's rejection of his morals, seeing it as a rejection of their home.

HOW TO SCORE PRACTICE TEST 3

Section I: Multiple Choice

_____ × 1.2273 = _____
Number Correct   Weighted
(out of 55)   Section I Score
                        (Do not round)

Section II: Free Response

(See whether you can find a teacher or classmate to score your essays using the guidelines in Chapter 5.)

Note: this score conversion chart should only be used as an estimate.

Question 1:   _____ × 4.5833 = _____
                 (out of 6)   (Do not round)

Question 2:   _____ × 4.5833 = _____
                 (out of 6)   (Do not round)

Question 3:   _____ × 4.5833 = _____
                 (out of 6)   (Do not round)

AP Score Conversion Chart English Literature and Composition

Composite Score Range	AP Score
107–150	5
90–106	4
73–89	3
56–72	2
0–55	1

Sum = _____
          Weighted Section II
          Score (Do not round)

Composite Score

_____ + _____ = _____
Weighted   Weighted   Composite Score
Section I Score Section II Score (Round to nearest
                                whole number)

NOTES

NOTES

NOTES

NOTES